THE SEARCH

A Student Workbook Based on
The Search for Significance

ROBERT S. MᶜGEE
& IAN FLIPPIN

LifeWay Press®
Nashville, Tennessee

Contents

PART 1 LIVELIHOODS AND THE POVERTY CONTEXT

PART 2 UNDERSTANDING THE SITUATIONS AND STRATEGIES OF POOR PEOPLE

PART 3 THE POLICY IMPLICATIONS OF URBAN LIVELIHOODS ANALYSIS

PART 4 URBAN POVERTY REDUCTION: LESSONS FROM EXPERIENCE

PART 5 CONCLUSIONS

List of Tables, Figures and Boxes

TABLES

FIGURES

Boxes

List of Acronyms and Abbreviations

ABO	area-based organization
ASA	Association for Social Advancement
BDS	business development services
CAP	community action plan
CBO	community-based organization
CDS	Community Development Society
CGAP	Consultative Group to Assist the Poorest
CIDA	Canadian International Development Agency
CSD	Commission for Sustainable Development
CSO	civil society organization
DFID	Department for International Development
GRO	grass-roots organization
GDP	gross domestic product
GNP	gross national product
GoI	Government of India
GoJ	Government of Jamaica
IDD	International Development Department
IEHS	infrastructure and environmental health services
IIED	International Institute for Environment and Development
JUPP	Jamaica Urban Poverty Project
KRC	Kingston Restoration Company
MAPP	municipal action planning process
MPCO	multi-purpose community organization
MSP	multi-stakeholder partnership
NGO	non-governmental organization
NHC	neighbourhood committee
OECD	Organization for Economic Cooperation and Development
PANA	participatory appraisal and needs assessment
PL	poverty line
PMC	programme monitoring committee
PPA	participatory poverty assessment
PPP	public–private partnership
PROSPECT	Programme of Support for Poverty Elimination and Community Transformation
PSC	project steering committee
PUSH	Peri-urban self-help
RDC	Residents' Development Committee
ROSCA	rotating savings and credit association
SAP	structural adjustment programme
SDC	Swiss Agency for Development and Cooperation

SDT	Slum Development Team
SEWA	Self-Employed Women's Association
Sida	Swedish International Development Cooperation Agency
SIP	Slum Improvement Project
SPARC	Society for the Promotion of Area Resource Centres
TB	Tuberculosis
UBS	Urban Basic Services
UCD	Urban Community Development Department
UNCHS	United Nations Centre for Human Settlements (Habitat)
UNDP	United Nations Development Programme
UNESCO	United Nations Educational, Scientific and Cultural Organization
UNICEF	United Nations International Children's Emergency Fund
USAID	United States Agency for International Development
ZDC	Zone Development Committee

About the Authors

Mansoor Ali is a project/programme manager at the Water, Engineering and Development Centre (WEDC), Loughborough University, specializing in urban infrastructure and services for the poor. He has worked mainly in the urban waste subsector and has researched and published extensively on the linkages between urban waste, poverty and livelihoods. He has also initiated a number of activities in knowledge management at WEDC, including electronic discussions, preparation of CD-Roms and synthesis notes.

Philip Amis is a senior lecturer in the International Development Department, School of Public Policy at the University of Birmingham. His main research interests and consultancy experience are in urban poverty and development in sub-Saharan Africa and South Asia. He was team leader of an Impact Assessment Study of the Department for International Development's (DFID) Slum Improvement Projects in India in 1996–1997.

Jo Beall is a reader in the Development Studies Institute at the London School of Economics, where she directs the Development Management Programme. Her research areas include urban poverty, governance and social development, as well as gender and social policy. She has conducted extensive research in Southern Africa and South Asia and has advised a range of national and international development agencies, including United Nations (UN) agencies, the World Bank and DFID.

Alison Brown is a senior lecturer (part-time) in the Department of City and Regional Planning at Cardiff University and a planning consultant, with a specialism in international planning practice. She is a chartered town planner and spent ten years in the Middle East working as an adviser to the governments of Oman and Qatar, and on a World Bank-funded study of Amman Municipality in Jordan. Since joining Cardiff she has undertaken short-term DFID-funded projects in Zimbabwe and Lesotho.

Nick Devas is a senior lecturer in the International Development Department, School of Public Policy at the University of Birmingham, specializing in public finance, local government finance, decentralization, urban governance and management. He has worked in local government in the United Kingdom (UK), and has been involved in consultancy, research and training in, among other countries, Indonesia, China, Cambodia, Kenya, South Africa, Lesotho, Botswana, Hungary and Romania.

Emma Grant works as a researcher and consultant on urban environment and health issues among low-income populations, with a particular focus on Latin America. Her current research is on social capital and violence, and their links to health and governance. She is based at the Faculty of the Built Environment, South Bank University, London, where she is also studying for a PhD.

John Grierson has 26 years' experience of private sector development, enterprise development, employment creation, training and project management in Africa, Asia and Eastern Europe. He has worked for a wide range of international and national agencies and non-governmental organizations (NGOs) on policy formulation, programme and project design and backstopping, training and evaluation. He is currently a consultant attached to Entec AG (Switzerland) and FTP International (Helsinki), and has also researched and published on enterprise development and training for self-employment.

Malcolm Harper worked for nine years in a medium-sized household hardware manufacturing business in England. He then taught in Nairobi, from 1970 to 1974, before becoming Professor of Enterprise Development in Cranfield School of Management. Since 1995 he has worked independently, mainly in India. He has published some 20 books and numerous articles on various aspects of self-employment, enterprise development and microfinance, and his research and consultancy work in Africa, Latin America and the Caribbean, the Middle East, Asia and the UK has been supported by a wide range of national, international and non-governmental development agencies.

Trudy Harpham is Professor of Urban Development and Policy at South Bank University, London. Originally a geographer, she is a specialist in urban health in developing countries and has written the main textbooks on this subject. She regularly advises DFID, the World Health Organization (WHO), the Swiss Development Agency for Cooperation (SDC), the United Nations Centre for Human Settlements (UNCHS) (Habitat), the World Bank and the US National Academy of Science. She is currently undertaking research on social capital and health in developing countries and on child poverty and health. She also manages a PhD programme on urban development and health at South Bank University.

Darren Hedley has worked with CARE International in Zambia for seven years, as programme manager for PUSH II and PROSPECT in Zambia, and more recently as programme director of Urban INSAKA, a regional research, training and consultancy unit. With a background in community development, resource management and international policy, his previous work experience includes community development and environmental health work in Sri Lanka, Costa Rica, Russia, and with a Native Canadian NGO. He is currently pursuing a PhD at the School for Policy Studies, University of Bristol, UK, focusing on inter-sectoral policy networks for urban water and sanitation in Africa.

Sue Jones is an urban planner and social anthropologist who has been involved in a range of projects during the last 15 years. Initially working on a World Bank-funded Urban Development Project in Jordan, she has subsequently been involved in other urban poverty and community-based action, including inputs to DFID poverty responses in India, Kenya, Botswana and Jamaica at various stages of design, implementation and evaluation. Having worked in private practice, local and national government and for NGOs, she is particularly concerned about the linkages between policy and practice and institutional change to support poverty action. She now works freelance and has set up a consortium, *workingtogether ltd*, with local consultants from around the world.

Tony Lloyd-Jones is a senior lecturer and researcher in urban design and development at the University of Westminster, and urban policy and physical planning adviser to DFID. With a background as a practising community architect and planner, he has conducted urban development-related research in Asia, Africa and Latin America. He is currently responsible for coordinating DFID's urban livelihoods approach and for the UK government's international and European Union (EU) liaison on UN human settlements and Habitat Agenda policy-related matters.

Susan Loughhead was the social development adviser in DFID's Urban Poverty Group in Delhi between 1998 and 2000. Since then, she has worked with DFID India on the India Urban Strategy and with DFID's Urban Group in London to produce the *Urban Target Strategy Paper*. She is currently an urban policy adviser for DFID in London, supporting implementation of the *Urban Target Strategy Paper* and also works with the NGO Crime Concern involved in urban regeneration in the UK.

Sheilah Meikle is a senior lecturer in the Development Planning Unit, University College London, where she is the director of the Masters programme in social development policy, planning and practice. She has extensive international experience.

Geoffrey Payne is a consultant specializing in urban housing, local land development, land tenure and project design issues. Recent and current assignments focus on public–private partnerships (PPPs) in land for housing and innovative approaches to secure tenure for the urban poor, together with the development of multistakeholder urban projects in Lesotho, Cuba and elsewhere. He is joint editor of the *Urban Projects Manual* (Liverpool University Press, 2nd edition, 2000), editor of *Common Ground: Public/Private Partnership in Land for Housing* (IT Publications, 1999), and author of *Urban Land Tenure and Property Rights in Developing Countries: A Review* (Overseas Development Administration/IT Publications, 1997).

Sue Phillips is an anthropologist and urban planner who has worked on urban poverty programmes in South Asia, the Middle East and the UK. Her experience ranges from project design to implementation support, impact assessments and evaluations. She worked as DFID's social development adviser in its urban poverty office in India from 1993 to 1996, where she was instrumental in refocusing a long-established programme away from infrastructure delivery to poverty reduction. Her main areas of interest are poverty reduction, livelihoods and participation. She is a director of Social Development Direct, a network of independent social development consultants.

Carole Rakodi was at the Department of City and Regional Planning, Cardiff University, from 1978 to 2001, after working for seven years in Zambia on urban planning and housing. While at Cardiff she published extensively on urban land, housing, upgrading of informal settlements, planning, participation, poverty and household strategies and related matters, and carried out research in a number of countries, including Zimbabwe, Ghana and India. She is editor of *The Urban Challenge in Africa: Growth and Management of its Largest Cities* (United Nations University Press, 1997). She worked for DFID on the Kenyan urban poverty programme in 1996 and 1997, and in early 2002 took up a post as Professor of International Urban Development in the International Development Department, School of Public Policy at the University of Birmingham.

Stuart Rutherford is a practitioner of microfinance, currently as the founding chairman of *Safe*Save, an organization that offers ultra-flexible financial services to slum dwellers in Dhaka. He also writes and teaches on microfinance, his best known work being *The Poor and Their Money*, which deals with how poor people manage their financial affairs. Born in London and trained as an architect, he has spent most of his adult life abroad, in Latin America, Africa and Asia. He is now based in Japan.

David Sanderson trained as an architect before taking a Masters degree in development practices. He has worked on a range of disaster and development-related programmes throughout the world, and has written and contributed to several publications on the themes of urbanization, risk and livelihoods. He is currently Technical and Policy Adviser at CARE International UK.

David Satterthwaite is director of the Human Settlements Programme at the International Institute for Environment and Development (IIED), London, and editor of the journal *Environment and Urbanization*. A development planner by training, with a doctorate in social policy, he has been part of IIED's research programme on human settlements since 1978, working mainly on poverty reduction and environmental problems in cities. He has advised international agencies and the UK and Swedish governments' aid programmes. Recent publications include, as co-author, *Environmental Problems in an Urbanizing World* (Earthscan, 2001), as editor, *The Earthscan Reader on Sustainable Cities* (Earthscan, 1999) and as editor and principal author, *An Urbanizing World: Global Report on Human Settlements 1996* (Oxford University Press, 1996).

Cecilia Tacoli is a senior research associate at IIED, London. She is a sociologist and development geographer who has, since joining IIED in 1996, been responsible for a research project on rural–urban interactions, livelihood strategies and socio-economic change, which involves collaborative research in Africa, Asia and Latin America. She has also advised international and donor agencies. Her previous professional experience includes working for UNICEF in Sierra Leone, as a trainer on gender and community development for international NGOs, and as resident sociologist in Mali for a rural water supply project funded by the Italian government.

Foreword

In 2000 DFID published a series of papers setting out the government's strategy for addressing the development targets of the international community, now enshrined in the United Nations Millennium Declaration. These papers included a strategy for *Meeting the Challenge of Poverty in Urban Areas.* As the world becomes progressively more urbanized, the most visible impact is in the poorer developing countries, where urban poverty is growing rapidly. Meeting the target of halving the proportion of those suffering from abject poverty between 1990 and 2015 requires this challenge to be addressed. Urban development, if managed properly, can make a significant contribution to improving the livelihoods of poor people, both those living in cities and those in the rural hinterlands. If mismanaged, urbanization will severely limit the achievement of equitable human development.

In 1998, I wrote the foreword to the DFID publication, *Sustainable Rural Livelihoods – What Contribution Can We Make?* I am pleased to have this opportunity to commend this latest compendium of thinking by a range of development researchers and practitioners. The work was commissioned by DFID to discuss the application of the sustainable livelihoods perspective to the urban context.

As the title of this book indicates, the livelihoods approach is intended to contribute to development policy and practice so that it is poverty-focused, and starts from the perspective of the people who are themselves living in poverty. On this basis, it can help ensure that measures to reduce poverty and improve the lives and livelihoods of poor people, whether urban or rural, provide the maximum benefit. It is to be hoped that this book will make a significant contribution to improving the lives, and expanding the livelihood opportunities, of the inhabitants of the cities and towns of the developing world, the populations of which are set to grow by 2 billion additional urban dwellers over the next 30 years.

Clare Short
Secretary of State for International Development
United Kingdom

Preface: The Sustainable Livelihoods Approach and the Department for International Development

Rapid urbanization is likely to increase the proportion of the global population living in cities from around a half to more than two-thirds in the next 20 years. As a consequence, the problems of people living in extreme poverty in urban areas will be of growing importance in the development agenda. In recognition of this trend, the Department for International Development (DFID) has recently produced its first urban strategy, *Meeting the Challenge of Poverty in Urban Areas* (DFID, 2001a). This is one of a series (see Box P.1) designed to inform the process of achieving internationally agreed poverty reduction and other development targets and the United Kingdom (UK) government's commitment to these as set out in the 1997 White Paper on international development 'Eliminating World Poverty: A Challenge for the 21st Century' (DFID, 1997).[1]

Box P.1 *DFID's Strategies for Achieving the International Development Targets*

Halving world poverty by 2015: economic growth, equity and security
Realizing human rights for poor people
Making government work for poor people
Meeting the challenge of poverty in urban areas
Better health for poor people
Achieving sustainability: poverty elimination and the environment
Poverty elimination and the empowerment of women
Addressing the water crisis – healthier and more productive lives for poor people

---

DFID's urban strategy draws specific attention to the dynamic nature of poverty in the urban areas of developing countries, noting the many factors that affect the movement of people into and out of poverty. It suggests how the livelihoods of poor people can be better understood, and how policies can be more effective in helping people to build on their assets and gain access to services and livelihood opportunities. A more recent White Paper on international development, 'Eliminating World Poverty: Making Globalisation Work for the Poor' (DFID, 2001b) adds a further policy dimension to DFID's international development strategy. It provides an analysis of globalization in the context of population increases and demographic changes and sets out a policy framework for better managing the globalization process to support the livelihoods of poor people.

The White Papers on international development and DFID's strategy papers endorse the 'Sustainable Livelihoods' approach as a means of analysing development problems and informing the design of policies and programmes intended to meet the overarching goal of poverty reduction. Until recently, this approach has been developed largely in a rural development context.

The sustainable livelihoods concept surfaced in the Brundtland Report (*Our Common Future*) of the World Commission on Environment and Development in 1987. Since then, the terminology of sustainable livelihoods has been widely adopted. In the context of the UN Commission for Sustainable Development (UNCSD), it is still often presented mainly in terms of the impact of human livelihoods on the environment.

However, in the rural livelihoods work of the late 1980s and early 1990s, while environmental sustainability retained central importance, there was a strong and developing poverty focus. Inherent in this conception of livelihoods is the notion that the relative poverty or economic well-being of poor people should be understood from the point of view of the people themselves. From this perspective, poverty has many dimensions and the condition of poverty or well-being for most people and households changes over time. It cannot be represented adequately solely by income-related poverty lines or simple measures of consumption. Instead, it requires a holistic and participatory appraisal of the range of livelihood activities that people draw upon, and of the strategies they employ. Of particular importance are the assets available to the poor in implementing their livelihood strategies and overcoming their vulnerability to conditions outside their control. The emphasis is on building on their 'wealth' rather than on their poverty.

This people-centred view provides a balance to the global and more strategic perspective normally offered by a sustainable development policy approach. It provides a structured conceptual and programme framework for sustainable human development. It is particularly appropriate for achieving poverty reduction in the local development context, in relation to policies designed to enable better access for poor people to land, shelter, markets and sources of income, to information and education, and to health and other essential services.

This concept of sustainable livelihoods has been developed and put into practice by a number of development agencies in recent years. They include CARE International (see Chapter 16) and Oxfam, as well as the Canadian International Development Agency (CIDA), the Swedish International Development Cooperation Agency (Sida), the World Bank and the United Nations Development Programme (UNDP). Each of the agencies has developed the livelihoods idea with a different emphasis, although all share the same basic concerns. CARE places a particular stress on livelihoods at the household level, for example, and is concerned with 'secure' rather than 'sustainable' livelihoods. (Chapter 1 explores definitions of sustainability in relation to livelihoods in further depth.) Oxfam emphasizes the right to a sustainable livelihood, while UNDP places a greater priority on the impact of technology and intervenes at the level of 'adaptive strategies'. DFID's emphasis is on support to assets and improved access to them by the poor. It is making use of a sustainable livelihoods approach in its broader policy dialogue and in gaining an improved understanding of the impact of governance and human rights issues on the livelihoods of the poor.

The development of DFID's sustainable livelihoods approach, developed jointly with a number of other partners, has been led by the Rural Livelihoods and Environment Division (formerly Natural Resources Division) and is currently being led by the Sustainable Livelihoods Support Office.[2] The adoption of the sustainable livelihoods terminology and approach, and the change in the name of the department itself, reflects the new focus on the concerns of poverty reduction, as set out in the international development White Paper (DFID, 1997). The same White Paper identified sustainable livelihoods as an approach to achieving poverty elimination (rather than simply a goal in its own right).

Within DFID, a sustainable livelihoods approach is seen as a way of thinking about the objectives, scope and priorities for development, as a framework for analysis and design, and as a basis for evaluating interventions with respect to their effectiveness in achieving poverty reduction. Conceptually and practically, it is a merger of evolving thought and development practice aimed at poverty reduction.

The sustainable livelihoods approach is thus seen as complementary to more traditional approaches to development. In particular, it provides a holistic and cross-sectoral approach to problem definition and analysis, and the evaluation of programmes and policies. However, unlike the integrated area-based planning approaches that were in vogue in both rural and urban development in the 1970s, the sustainable livelihoods approach encompasses a sectoral approach to the design of programmes. A holistic analysis can allow for multiple 'entry points' in terms of particular sectoral interventions, and the outcomes that are desired may be either single or multidimensional.

This book sets out to address the question of whether a livelihoods approach is equally appropriate for the urban context and whether it can provide an effective framework for addressing the issue of urban poverty and its elimination. In answering this question, the various authors contributing to this book present a range of views. Although some of the contributors express a degree of scepticism or adopt a critical view of the development of the livelihoods approach to date, it is fair to say that the volume as a whole represents a positive endorsement of the value of a livelihoods perspective in the urban context. It is also an important contribution to the conceptual work that needs to be done to adapt livelihoods ideas to the particularities of urban poverty and development.

This volume was commissioned by DFID's Infrastructure and Urban Development Department (IUDD) to help provide an urban dimension to the livelihoods approach. Its aim is not to produce an urban livelihoods policy for DFID, but to contribute to the wider debate about the usefulness and application of such an approach. Contributions have been commissioned from UK-based researchers undertaking relevant research under DFID auspices and from practitioners involved in some urban projects supported by the department. In all projects referred to, local colleagues played a key role in the research, project design or implementation and their contribution to the findings and experiences commented on in this book is acknowledged. The intention is to provide a source-book summarizing the existing state of knowledge on livelihoods in an urban context and to reflect critically on conceptual issues raised by the approach in this context. Because of the very broad and inclusive range of its subject matter, it can also serve as a more general sourcebook for urban development-related issues.

Within the framework of a livelihoods perspective, it provides an up-to-date, analytical review of most of the issues facing development practitioners in the 'urban century'.[3]

The format for the publication parallels that of the 1998 DFID publication, *Sustainable Rural Livelihoods – What Contribution Can We Make?* (Carney, 1998), which serves a similar function as a livelihoods sourcebook for the rural context and *Sustainable Livelihoods: Lessons from Early Experience* (Ashley and Carney, 1999). However, while *Urban Livelihoods: A People-Centred Approach to Reducing Poverty* may be seen as a 'sister' publication to the DFID rural livelihoods work, our aim in this work is not to perpetuate or reinforce the existing rural–urban dichotomy. As several of the contributors to this volume point out, urban and rural livelihoods are closely related in many different ways. It is more appropriate to consider urban and rural areas as part of a continuum and not in isolation from one another. Certainly, in the context of rural–urban relationships, the livelihoods approach has much to offer.

Tony Lloyd-Jones
December 2001

NOTES

1 The seven international development targets for the year 2015 are based on development goals agreed at the series of UN global conferences held during the 1990s. These were adopted by the OECD in its development strategy, *Shaping the Twenty First Century* (1996). They have since been agreed by the international community as a whole and largely absorbed within the Millennium Development Goals set out in the UN Millennium Declaration. This includes an extended list of 18 targets, including an 'urban' target: 'By 2020, to have achieved a significant improvement in the lives of at least 100 million slum dwellers' – pertinent to the aims of this publication
2 www.livelihoods.org
3 Work on methodological approaches to analysing poverty and livelihoods was also commissioned. This has been published

REFERENCES

Ashley, C and Carney, D (1999) *Sustainable Livelihoods: Lessons from Early Experience*, DFID, London
Carney, D (ed) (1998) *Sustainable Rural Livelihoods – What Contribution Can We Make?* DFID, London
DFID (1997) *Eliminating World Poverty: A Challenge for the 21st Century*, White Paper on international development, The Stationery Office, London
DFID (2001a) *Meeting the Challenge of Poverty in Urban Areas,* strategies for achieving the international development targets, DFID, London
DFID (2001b) *Eliminating World Poverty: Making Globalisation Work for the Poor*, White Paper on international development, The Stationery Office, London
OECD (Organization for Economic Cooperation and Development) (1996) *Shaping the Twenty First Century: The Contribution of Development Cooperation*, Development Assistance Committee, OECD, Paris

Dedication

This volume is dedicated to Cedric Pugh who kindly read the manuscript in draft form but did not live to see it published

Acknowledgements

Each of the draft chapters of this volume was read by at least one member of staff of the Department for International Development, based either in London or in one of the Development Divisions overseas. Their comments are gratefully acknowledged, although they and their employer bear no responsibility for the information and views included in this volume, which are those of the authors alone. The contribution of Roger Few, who undertook part of the editing work, and the assistance of Anne Thomson and Alison Brown who read the entire manuscript and made contributions to its improvement and to the concluding chapter, are warmly acknowledged. Finally, thanks to Laura Dobbs for assistance with the diagrams.

The research and project experience drawn on in this volume involved the collaboration of many people. For convenience, a limited number of contributors based in the UK were invited to reflect on the findings and outcomes of a range of projects, all of which involved colleagues based elsewhere in the world. Without these collaborative efforts, the findings and experiences would have been less rich and much less convincing. It is impossible to name all those whose work has been drawn on, but their contribution has been indispensable.

Introduction

Carole Rakodi

A number of researchers and development agencies have been developing a livelihoods approach as a way to improve understanding of the situation and actions of poor people; as a guide to thinking about the objectives, scope and priorities for development; as a framework for designing policies and practical interventions; and as a basis for evaluating interventions with respect to their effectiveness in achieving poverty reduction. It is an approach that aims to put people and the households in which they live at the centre of the development process, starting with their capabilities and assets, rather than with their problems. However, the situation of poor households is determined not just by their own resources but by the economic, social and political context in which they live: global and local economic forces, social and cultural change, policy and government action. Thus a focus on poor people and their households has to be situated within a wider context.

Much of the work that has been undertaken to date (analysis of the strategies of peasant households, the development of an analytical framework, the evaluation of early experience and provision of guidance to policy-makers) deals with the rural dimension. This book examines the findings of recent research on urban poverty, the applicability of the livelihoods conceptual framework to urban areas, the scope and outcomes of some recent urban poverty reduction projects, and the possible implications of adopting a livelihoods approach to analysis, policy formulation and project design and implementation. It adopts an urban focus, but it is acknowledged that it is inappropriate to consider 'rural' or 'urban' areas in isolation, and so the relationships and links between rural and urban areas and people are emphasized. In addition, there are no specific chapters or sections on certain factors and issues, such as the environment, health or gender. Instead, these are considered important to all aspects of the discussion and will be discussed in an integrated way throughout.

The book is divided into five parts. In Part 1, conceptual and definitional issues are discussed, and then the broader context for the discussion of urban issues is described. In Chapter 1, the concept of a household livelihood strategy is introduced and situated within the broader context of a livelihood framework. The various concepts used in the book are introduced and, following a preliminary discussion, definitions that are adopted by the contributors are given. Urban households, rich or poor, earn their living, interact with other people, seek shelter and services, and try to influence politicians in an environment that is the product of wider economic, social and political forces. The key national economic and urban trends are analysed in Chapter 2, the inappropriateness of considering 'urban' areas in isolation is stressed, and attention is drawn to the need to consider rural–urban relationships and links.

In Part 2, our current understanding of the situation of poor urban people and their households is summarized, drawing on recent research throughout the developing world. In Chapter 3, Sheilah Meikle identifies significant characteristics and trends in the urban context and explores their implications for the situation and livelihood strategies of poor people and households. The chapter considers the economic context, primarily as it impacts on employment and the occupations of the poor; the political context, especially in terms of the representation of the poor in decision-making; the physical and environmental context, with particular reference to the living conditions and health of poor people; the stock of capital assets in urban areas which are potentially available to poor people and the factors that govern access to those assets. David Satterthwaite and Cecilia Tacoli explore the ways in which rural and urban residence influence the incidence and nature of poverty and deprivation. With particular emphasis on urban people and households, the chapter first explores differences in urban and rural contexts of relevance to poverty, recognizing that, because of the characteristics of production patterns, rural–urban links and the diversity of conditions in both rural and urban areas, the validity of the distinction is limited. Second, it considers areas of commonality between rural and urban areas in terms of livelihood frameworks, with particular attention to locations that are the interface between rural and urban areas. In the final chapter in this part, Jo Beall analyses the interplay between resources and access, starting at a household level. She focuses first on how people compose their livelihoods, with reference to work and social relations in households and communities of which they are part. Second, she examines the linkages between households and communities and the wider social, economic and political processes operating in and on the city.

The aim of Part 3 is to analyse the policy implications of what we know about urban livelihoods: the situations and strategies of poor people. First, types of policy which need to be considered are identified, with a view to making a preliminary identification of alternative policy goals: changing the context, increasing the stocks of assets, increasing opportunities for and relieving constraints on accessing or using assets. A number of policy issues are then identified which are taken up by various contributors. Philip Amis attempts to identify the transmission mechanisms between economic growth in cities and towns and poverty reduction in order to identify potential roles for the public sector, particularly local government, in ensuring both that economic activities flourish and that poor residents are able to take advantage of the opportunities created by them. Stuart Rutherford, Malcolm Harper and John Grierson then identify and discuss appropriate ways in which individuals, households and their livelihoods can be supported. The development of financial, human and physical capital, they argue, is likely to require accessible financial and business development services, as well as education and training.

Sue Phillips explores the implications for policy and practice of what we know about social capital in the lives and strategies of poor residents. Drawing particularly on the experience in DFID-funded slum improvement projects in India, she considers appropriate kinds of support to social networks, people's organizations, and so on, given what we know about social and power relations, social heterogeneity, the transience of urban populations and processes of social change.

A series of chapters then deal with aspects of the physical environment, while reflecting on the economic, social and political relationships that are critical to living conditions. First, Geoffrey Payne explores the policy implications for land tenure and shelter of what we know about the roles of land and housing in the livelihood strategies of urban households: their important implications for security, the role they play in providing shelter and a location for economic activity, and their potential as assets. Trudy Harpham and Emma Grant consider the implications of a livelihoods approach for urban health (environmental health and health services) and identify the policy implications, especially with respect to improving environmental health. Mansoor Ali then explores the implications of this discussion for the provision of infrastructure and environmental health services. Alison Brown and Tony Lloyd-Jones consider the implications of what we know about urban livelihoods for spatial planning and planning for access, transport and infrastructure at the city and local levels. Nick Devas then analyses the implications for the governance and management of policies designed to support the livelihoods of the poor, with reference to politics and decision-making at city and local levels and to some specific urban management issues, especially resource allocation.

The aim of Part 4 is to assess some lessons of project implementation. This draws both on the experience of projects supported by DFID and on comparative research on the outcomes of a number of poverty-reduction projects. The longest standing and largest scale DFID support has been to projects in a number of Indian cities. Susan Loughhead and Carole Rakodi review the evolution of these projects, exploring how the approaches adopted in earlier projects have changed as the understanding of poverty has improved. Two smaller-scale and more recent initiatives are then described. Sue Jones outlines the development of the Jamaica Urban Poverty Project (JUPP), emphasizing the arrangements for decision-making and implementation as much as the content or outcomes of the project. David Sanderson and Darren Hedley describe how CARE International UK's projects in Lusaka, Zambia, have evolved, as understanding of the situation and the needs of poor households in informal settlements has grown, leading, in the most recent project, to the adoption of a specific livelihoods approach to selecting project activities. Lastly, David Satterthwaite reports findings from a recent review of experiences with urban poverty-reduction projects in which NGOs have played a major role.

In Part 5, the final part of the book, two sets of conclusions are drawn. First, drawing on the experience of both the projects discussed in Part 4 and others, Sue Jones reflects critically on the implications for project and programme design of a livelihoods approach. She reviews some of the issues that emerge from recent experience and suggests ways in which participatory, process-oriented projects to reduce poverty at the city and community levels might be designed. Lastly, Carole Rakodi summarizes the main areas of agreement on urban poverty reduction; reflects critically on the conceptual issues raised by the adoption of a livelihoods framework for analysing urban poverty; reviews key policy implications; and identifies issues where further research is needed.

Part 1
Livelihoods and the Poverty Context

The two chapters in Part 1 provide a starting point for the remainder of the book. First, the recent origins of a livelihoods approach to analysis, policy identification and project planning are discussed and its component concepts reviewed. Second, some of the main characteristics of urban areas are identified to provide a context for the more specific chapters that follow.

Chapter 1

A Livelihoods Approach –
Conceptual Issues and Definitions

Carole Rakodi

INTRODUCTION

The increased attention being paid to livelihoods in both research and policy follows from a wide recognition that few rural or urban households, especially poor households in middle- and low-income countries, rely on a single income-generating activity (farming or wage employment) to support themselves. Drawing on Chambers and Conway (1992), a livelihood is defined as comprising '. . . the capabilities, assets (including both material and social resources) and activities required for a means of living' (Carney, 1998, p4). Coupled to this definition, and based on the recognition of the importance of the natural resource base to rural livelihoods and the vulnerability that so frequently characterizes the position of poor rural households:

> *A livelihood is sustainable when it can cope with and recover from stresses and shocks and maintain or enhance its capabilities and assets both now and in the future, while not undermining the natural resource base* (Carney, 1998, p4).

Drawing on a decade or more of research on peasant agriculture, including the responses of peasant farmers to external shocks and trends, policy change and particular interventions, the concept of livelihoods goes beyond notions of 'poverty' and embodies a number of important additional elements. Research on urban poverty in the 1990s, stimulated by the adverse impact of recession and stabilization and structural adjustment policies on many urban groups, and seeking to develop a more appropriate conceptualization of urban poverty than that traditionally used, drew on this rural work. Many of the concepts were found to be appropriate and were adopted and adapted in work on urban poverty. Others have proved more problematic.

In this chapter, the key concepts will be introduced to provide a starting point for the discussion in the remainder of the book. Before introducing the concept of a household livelihood strategy and the elements of a livelihoods framework, poverty, deprivation and well-being are discussed. A livelihoods approach to development draws on a conceptual framework which may be used as a basis for analysing, understanding and managing the complexity of livelihoods, enabling complementarities and trade-offs between alternative supporting activities to be assessed and providing a basis for identifying policy objectives and interventions (Carney, 1998). Current users of such a framework are in broad agreement on its key components, although precise conceptualization varies and emphases differ. Because the initiative for this publication came from DFID (and also for convenience) our starting point will be the framework currently being used in the DFID approach, but it will be subject to critical appraisal and the frameworks being used by other organizations and researchers will be referred to where appropriate. The emphasis on sustainable livelihoods in particular needs careful consideration in an urban context and so the final section of this chapter will review some conceptual and definitional issues raised by the question of sustainability.

Contributors to this volume use many of the concepts introduced here, as well as a livelihoods framework, as their starting point. Some focus on one or more concepts or components of the framework, others consider it as a whole. Following their critical analysis of the applicability of a livelihoods framework for analysis and policy in the urban context, the final chapter will reflect on the key issues arising out of the analysis and identify how our conceptualization might be further improved as a basis for research, policy and action.

POVERTY, DEPRIVATION AND WELL-BEING[1]

Households or individuals are considered poor when the resources they command are insufficient to enable them to consume sufficient goods and services to achieve a reasonable minimum level of welfare. The value of goods and services consumed, whether purchased, gifts or self-produced, is expressed in monetary terms, enabling the definition of a poverty line (PL). This may refer to either absolute or relative poverty: the former is based on the cost of a basic food basket, with (the poverty line) or without (the food poverty line) other necessities, for a particular country or subnational area at a particular date; the latter refers to consumption equal to a proportion of total or average consumption. Conventional PLs are widely used because it is generally accepted that 'inadequate command over commodities is the most important dimension of poverty, and a key determinant of other aspects of welfare, such as health, longevity and self-esteem' (Lipton and Ravallion, 1995, p2553). Moreover, they provide indicators suitable for making comparisons in time and space. Many refinements have been developed, but methodological problems still abound. In addition, there are a variety of conceptual problems.

Consumption is generally considered to provide a better (more appropriate and more accurately measured) indicator than income. Adjustments for variations in the cost of living, the value of home production or goods/benefits received in kind, and for inflation can now be built into estimates of household consumption. The extent to which these methodological refinements improve the accuracy of poverty estimates depends on the quality of the data: it is difficult to estimate consumption in economies which are only partly monetized, in which households consume their own production, where household and business accounts are not separated and unsold goods consumed within the household, and in which many of the business activities of women and children are underreported. Also the income from illegal activities is not reported and expenditure on items such as alcohol is reported unreliably.

Furthermore:

- Levels of access to publicly supplied goods and common pool resources are important components of welfare, vary between households, but may or may not be included in estimates of consumption (see also Maxwell, 1999).
- Minimum consumption requirements are typically based on the food expenditure necessary to attain some recommended food energy intake, but there is little reliable evidence on the energy requirements of different groups of people.
- The definition of 'non-food necessities' varies between countries, subnational areas, sociocultural groups, households and individuals.
- Poverty-line analysis has neglected the dynamics of poverty and has failed to distinguish between transient and persistent poverty, and between different household trajectories: impoverishment, stability or improved well-being.[2] However, the methods used do not allow for unequal distribution of consumption between household members, scale economies, changing household composition, problems in identifying 'households' and their 'heads', or the flow of resources between coresident households and other family members.

A further problem with PL analysis is that indicators based on household consumption do not capture all dimensions of poverty, especially from the viewpoint of poor people themselves. Research on the perceptions and definitions of poverty used by the poor shows, first, that poverty is not defined solely in terms of low incomes, but uses broader concepts of deprivation and insecurity; and second, that any attempt to place monetary values on these aspects of personal, household and social deprivation involves so many arbitrary assumptions that it is likely to be meaningless.

Deprivation occurs when people are unable to reach a certain level of functioning or capability. Chambers (1989), for example, includes physical weakness, isolation, vulnerability and powerlessness in addition to lack of income and assets. Baulch (1996) identifies a pyramid, starting from income poverty as the most measurable, to access to common pool resources, state-provided commodities, assets, dignity and autonomy. Difficulties arise, first, in reaching a common understanding of 'deprivation' (let alone equivalent terms in other languages) (Moore et al, 1998), and, second, in measuring non-monetary components of poverty and weighting them against monetary components (Maxwell, 1999).

Defining a household as poor in terms of consumption may not capture all deprived households and individuals. First, although income poverty is generally important in poor people's own perceptions of ill-being, other aspects of material poverty and ill-being which arise from social relationships are also important and may offset stable or increasing incomes (Moore et al, 1998). Therefore national

household sample surveys may not identify women, for example, as a disproportionately poor group, but if deprivation includes social subordination, reduced
life chances and excessive workloads, all or specific categories of poor women are
undoubtedly deprived (Booth et al, 1998).

The concept of deprivation therefore adds further dimensions to income
poverty which are highly relevant to the situation of poor people. Commonly
used indicators of deprivation were initially derived from analyses of the
characteristics of poor individuals and households based on household sample
surveys, and this may be one appropriate way of deriving such indicators.
However, definitions of who is considered poor in terms of income and consumption were framed and these indicators initially selected by the non-poor and
outsiders. The categorizations may not coincide with the perceptions of the poor
themselves, with respect to either who is considered poor, or how their poverty
and dependence is understood. In addition, the approach casts the poor as passive
victims. The concepts discussed below seek to address some of the main shortcomings of a money-metric understanding of poverty and externally defined
indicators of deprivation. In addition, they move beyond outcomes – states of
poverty, deprivation or well-being – to processes of impoverishment, increased
welfare, exclusion or inclusion.

HOUSEHOLD STRATEGIES

For some time now, work on rural poverty has revolved around the belief that
households aim at secure livelihoods. Households, it is suggested, have access to
a portfolio of assets, both tangible (stores of cash and food, and resources such
as land, physical investment or skills) and intangible (claims on others and the
government, and access rights, for example, to services). They make decisions
about how the portfolio is used: for example, for earning, by disposal, to fulfil
kinship obligations and responsibilities, to develop mutual support networks, or
by changes to diet. The strategy open to a household depends both on the portfolio held and on the household's capability to find and make use of livelihood
opportunities. The latter, in turn, depends in part on the household's composition
(Chambers, 1989; Chambers and Conway, 1992). The strategies adopted aim: to
cope with and recover from stress and shocks, by stinting, hoarding, protecting,
depleting or diversifying the portfolio; to maintain or enhance capability and
assets; and to provide sustainable livelihood opportunities for the next generation. Faced with shock, stress or risk, households devise coping strategies to
protect their social reproduction and enable recovery. These may be ineffective
if, in the long term, consumption declines and/or assets are lost permanently, or
if successive calls on particular strategies deplete the natural, social or financial
resources on which households or communities call. Poverty is thus characterized
not only by a lack of assets and inability to accumulate a portfolio of them, but
also by lack of choice with respect to alternative coping strategies. The poorest
and most vulnerable households are forced to adopt strategies which enable them
to survive but not to improve their welfare.

As in rural areas, so in urban areas: households seek to mobilize resources
and opportunities and to combine these into a livelihood strategy which is a mix

of labour market involvement; savings; borrowing and investment; productive and reproductive activities; income, labour and asset pooling; and social networking (Grown and Sebstad, 1989). Both material and human resources are available. Households and individuals adjust the mix according to their own circumstances (age, life-cycle stage, educational level, tasks) and the changing context in which they live. Economic activities form the basis of a household strategy, but to them, and overlapping with them, may be added migration movements, maintenance of ties with rural areas, urban food production, decisions about access to services such as education and housing, and participation in social networks.

Few households in poor countries are able to support themselves on the basis of a single business activity (farming or non-farm) or full-time wage employment. Given limited capital and skills, a poor person's scope for developing an enterprise with ample profit margins is limited and, in any case, the risk of relying on a single business is too great. Farm incomes or wages, moreover, have often fallen further and further behind the minimum required to support a family as recession and structural adjustment policies have bitten.

The 'livelihoods' concept is a realistic recognition of the multiple activities in which households engage to ensure their survival and improve their well-being, as will be explored further below (see also Ellis, 1998). Since it rests on the two further concepts of 'household' and 'strategy', however, some initial caveats relating to these terms need to be noted.

A household is commonly defined as 'a person or co-resident group of people who contribute to and/or benefit from a joint economy in either cash or domestic labour' – that is, a group of people who live and eat together. Many urban families do indeed fit this definition, are comprised of single people or nuclear families, with or without additional 'permanent' resident relatives, and identification of the 'household head' is unproblematic. However, many do not and, even for those that do, household income poverty analysis tends to skate over many of the complexities, treating households as black boxes and as self-evident and easily defined stable units. Households change over time, as they evolve through a life-cycle, as their members age and their status changes in culturally prescribed ways, and as decisions are made about the movement of their members. Household composition is both a determinant of the capabilities, choices and strategies available to a household, and may be an outcome of strategic decisions about fertility or where members of the family reside. The notion of a cohesive, mutually supportive and enduring household also has strong ideological and religious underpinnings which may be rather a long way from reality.

The concept of 'strategy' has the advantage of restoring agency to poor people, rather than regarding them merely as passive victims. However, some analysts cast doubt on the extent to which poor households have sufficient control over their assets and environment to be able to pursue goal-oriented behaviour, suggesting that most can merely react opportunistically to changing circumstances within or outside the household to try to defend themselves against further impoverishment, keep themselves on an even keel or engage in more risky but potentially more profitable economic activities that, if successful, lead to increased prosperity.

Moreover, some analysts have taken issue with the term 'household strategy' because of its implication that 'households' make decisions and that these decisions are based on an explicit process of setting objectives and planning their achievement. People, of course, make decisions, not the analytical construct termed a household, while the term strategy should be used as shorthand for a series of choices constrained to a greater or lesser extent by macroeconomic circumstances, social context, cultural and ideological expectations and access to resources (Wolf, 1990). While decisions about household matters may be made jointly and on an equal basis by household members, the distribution of power within the household is generally more complex, with men normally having more say than women or children:

> [N]egotiation within different sorts of household cannot be under-
> stood in isolation from the ways in which both men and women
> are engaged in other arenas and networks of relationships (Hart,
> 1997).

Decisions about the allocation of the personal resources of household members (labour time earnings) are influenced by their relative bargaining power, their motives and the expectations of wider social groups, especially kinship networks. The notion of a 'household strategy' conceals individualistic behaviour, inequalities, conflict and impermanence. It is clear that, first, many common assumptions about households should not be taken at face value, and second, that analysis and action should not concentrate on households to the exclusion of individuals and wider social groups, from 'communities' to global organizations.

A Livelihoods Framework

Recognition that households construct their livelihoods both on the basis of the assets which are available to them and within a broader socio-economic and physical context underlie recent attempts to devise a schematic model of the factors that need to be taken into account in analysis and policy. This, as outlined in the Preface, has been central to the development of thinking within DFID. However, other organizations have been involved in a parallel thought process and some of their ideas will also be mentioned here.

The main components of a livelihoods framework have been captured diagramatically in Figure 1.1. Inevitably, any diagram, or indeed any framework, is an oversimplification of a complex reality and should be treated merely as a guide or lens through which to view the world. Its value lies in its ability to capture key components and their interrelationships as a starting point for identifying critical analytical questions and potential leverage points where intervention might be appropriate – not in whether it portrays the whole of reality, everywhere and at all times, but whether it provides insightful analysis and appropriate action. The arrows portray dynamic and complex relationships and influences, not direct causality.[3]

Carney (1998) suggests that the framework is a tool that can serve the following purposes:

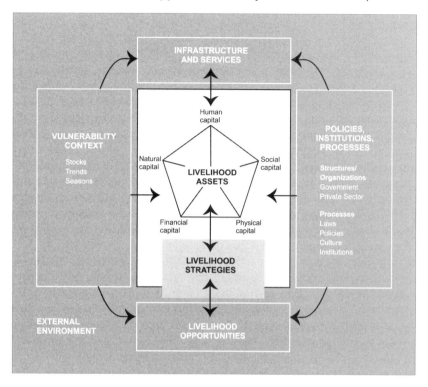

Figure 1.1 *Livelihoods framework*

Source: Developed from DFID Sustainable Livelihoods Guidance Sheets, Section 2.1 by Tony Lloyd-Jones

- To define the scope of and provide the analytical basis for livelihoods analysis, by identifying the main factors affecting livelihoods and the relationships between them.
- To help those concerned with supporting the livelihoods of poor people to understand and manage their complexity.
- To become a shared point of reference for all concerned with supporting livelihoods, enabling the complementarity of contributions and the trade-offs between outcomes to be assessed.
- To provide a basis for identifying appropriate objectives and interventions to support livelihoods.

At the centre of the framework are the assets on which households or individuals draw to build their livelihoods. These will be introduced here, but are considered in greater depth in later chapters. They are influenced by the context, which refers to the sources of insecurity to which poor people and their assets are vulnerable. Access to and use of assets is influenced by policies, organizations and relationships between individuals and organizations. The strategies which individuals and households adopt produce outcomes, which are defined in terms of greater or less well-being.

Assets[4]

Livelihoods approaches propose that thinking in terms of strengths or assets is vital as an antidote to the view of poor people as 'passive' or 'deprived'. Central to the approach is the need to recognize that those who are poor may not have cash or other savings, but that they do have other material or non-material assets – their health, their labour, their knowledge and skills, their friends and family, and the natural resources around them. Livelihoods approaches require a realistic understanding of these assets in order to identify what opportunities they may offer, or where constraints may lie. Proponents argue that it is more conceptually appropriate, empirically sound and of more practical use to start with an analysis of strengths as opposed to an analysis of needs. However, it has also been suggested that there is a danger that this emphasis may restrict policy and actions to households that have some assets on which they can build and neglect the poorest and the destitute, who may be effectively assetless.

At household, community and societal levels, the assets available are said to constitute a stock of capital: '. . . stuff that augments incomes but is not totally consumed in use' (Narayan and Pritchett, 1999, p871). This capital can be stored, accumulated, exchanged or depleted and put to work to generate a flow of income or other benefits. Social units need, it is suggested, to call on stocks of all types of capital (human, social, political, physical, financial and natural), although their ability to do so varies and there are trade-offs between the different types, which are briefly defined in Box 1.1. (Note that this list is neither the only way of categorizing assets nor is it exhaustive.)

Both the quantity and quality of labour resources available to households are subsumed under human capital (or capabilities). Both are important to the fulfilment of productive and reproductive tasks. The ability of households to manage their labour assets to take advantage of opportunities for economic activity is constrained, first by the levels of education and skills and the health status of household members, and second by the demands of household maintenance. Households may respond to economic stress by resorting to low-return subsistence or survival activities, increasing participation rates or increasing returns to labour by increasing its productivity. Lack of human capital in the form of skills and education affects the ability to secure a livelihood more directly in urban labour markets than in rural areas.

Social capital is defined as 'the rules, norms, obligations, reciprocity and trust embedded in social relations, social structures, and society's institutional arrangements, which enable its members to achieve their individual and community objectives' (Narayan, 1997, p50). For social interaction to be termed 'capital', it must be persistent, giving rise to stocks (for example, of trust or knowledge) on which people can draw, even if the social interaction itself is not permanent (Collier, 1998). Levels of social capital and the ability to call on the social networks involved vary in space and time. They may break down because of repeated shocks (such as drought), economic crisis or physical insecurity (such as violence and crime) (Moser, 1996; Booth et al, 1998). Social networks are not all supportive of the poor or effective as social capital and are generally thought to be less robust in urban areas because of the mobility and heterogeneity of their populations. Closely linked to social capital is political capital, based on access

---

Box 1.1 *HOUSEHOLD LIVELIHOOD ASSETS*

Human capital
The labour resources available to households, which have both quantitative and qualitative dimensions. The former refer to the number of household members and time available to engage in income-earning activities. Qualitative aspects refer to the levels of education and skills and the health status of household members.

Social and political capital
The social resources (networks, membership of groups, relationships of trust and reciprocity, access to wider institutions of society) on which people draw in pursuit of livelihoods.

Physical capital
Physical or produced capital is the basic infrastructure (transport, shelter, water, energy, communications) and the production equipment and means which enable people to pursue their livelihoods.

Financial capital
The financial resources available to people (including savings, credit, remittances and pensions) which provide them with different livelihood options.

Natural capital
The natural resource stocks from which resource flows useful to livelihoods are derived, including land, water and other environmental resources, especially common pool resources.

Source: Carney, 1998, p7

---

to the political process and decision-making, and best seen as 'a gatekeeper asset, permitting or preventing the accumulation of other assets' (Booth et al, 1998, p79).

Physical capital includes productive and household assets, including tools, equipment, housing and household goods, as well as stocks (such as jewellery). The ability to invest in production equipment may directly generate income and enhance labour productivity. Shelter is similarly multifunctional, potentially providing income from rent as well as a location for home-based enterprise. Infrastructure, sometimes categorized separately as it represents predominantly public rather than private investment and a collective rather than individual resource (see Figure 1.1), is important both for household maintenance and for livelihoods. Important for health and social interaction, and thus contributing to human and social capital, it also enables people to access, and directly supports, income-generating activities.

Urban economies are highly monetized and so access to a monetary income is essential for survival. Moreover, both the ability of households to weather stresses and shocks and their livelihood options are influenced by their ability to accumulate or access stocks of financial capital to smooth consumption, cushion shocks and invest in productive assets, including the health and skills of house-hold members, business enterprises and housing. The lack of financial services suitable for poor urban households constrains their ability to save and obtain credit.

Direct access to and the use of natural capital is, in some respects, less significant to the urban poor. Although land and security of tenure are major issues, there is some doubt about whether urban land can best be conceptualized as 'natural capital'. However, urban residents are indirectly (and sometimes directly) dependent on natural resources, as these are the basis for supplies of food, energy and water to cities.

Carney (1998) presents the different types of assets in the shape of a pentagon (Figure 1.2). It is suggested that access by households or groups to each type of asset can be plotted subjectively along the axes to provide a starting point for thinking about how and in what combination assets translate into livelihoods.

The livelihoods framework suggests that there is a close link between the overall asset status of an individual, household or group, the resources on which it can draw in the face of hardship and its level of security. Moreover, the assets available influence the scope for it to improve its well-being, both directly by increasing its security and indirectly by increasing people's ability to influence the policies and organizations which govern access to assets and define livelihood options. Bebbington (1999) reinforces this broad view of assets by making two distinctions. The first is between assets as providing a means of seeking a living and assets as giving meaning to a person's world, in turn influencing livelihood decisions. The second is between assets as resources that people use to build a livelihood and assets as sources of capability to act, engage and change the world. Analysis of portfolios of assets may occur for individuals or households, although Carney (1998), perhaps with villages in mind, suggests that it is most likely to be conducted for social groups:

> *As a rule of thumb, when plotting asset status, the further a group lies from the central intersection of the pentagon the more robust its members are likely to be. Generally speaking it is the overall area of a pentagon (the shape created when asset status is plotted on each axis) that is important, rather than the absolute magnitude of access to any particular type of capital'* (Carney, 1998, p8).

A variety of options are available to poor households for the management of their assets, such as (Rakodi, 1999):

- investment in securing more of an asset, as a way of ensuring long-term security, a hedge against uncertainty and a means of generating more, or more diversified, flows of income or production;
- substitution of one asset for another;
- disposal, to compensate for a consumption shortfall or to release funds for investment; or
- sacrifice of the ability to access and utilize an asset in future, because of short-term shocks or stresses.

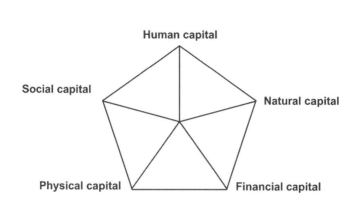

Different shaped pentagons – changes in access to assets

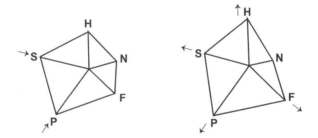

The pentagon on the left shows reasonable, but declining, access to physical capital and limited access to natural capital Social capital is also falling. Perhaps the people whose livelihood assets are represented live in an urban area but do not have the skills or finance to invest in infrastructure maintenance. The decline of social capital also constrains their ability to form shared work groups. The pentagon on the right shows the situation after support that has extended access to financial capital (perhaps through group-based microfinance schemes that help build social capital) as well as providing skills and training (human capital). Together these enable the people to maintain and extend their physical capital. Access to natural capital remains unchanged.

Figure 1.2 *The asset pentagon*

Source: DFID Sustainable Livelihoods Guidance Sheets, Section 2.3

For individual households or groups of households in settlements or regions, the strategies which they are able, or choose, to adopt vary over time and according to circumstances. Thus households, communities or regions may experience different pathways of chronic or transient poverty, impoverishment or improved well-being (Rakodi, 1999).

The next step in analysis, therefore, is to capture the dynamics of changing access to assets, exploring trends for different assets and different wealth or social groups, analysing their causes and identifying trajectories. Such an analysis may reveal the combination and sequencing of assets and livelihood strategies which result in the impoverishment of some households and groups, but the increased security and improved well-being of others (Carney, 1998).

Vulnerability

The assets which poor people possess or have access to, the livelihoods they desire and the strategies they adopt are influenced by the context within which they live. This is conceptualized as having two broad dimensions: factors that influence their vulnerability, and policies, institutions and processes. Vulnerability refers to:

> . . . the insecurity of the well-being of individuals, households or communities in the face of a changing environment. Environmental changes threatening welfare can be ecological, economic, social or political . . . With these changes often come increasing risk and uncertainty and declining self-respect. Because people move into and out of poverty, the concept of vulnerability better captures processes of change than more static measures of poverty (Moser, 1996, p2; see also Moser, 1998).

Key features of poverty are a high degree of exposure and susceptibility to the risk of crises, stress and shocks, and little capacity to recover quickly from them. To understand the sources of vulnerability, Carney (1998) suggests that it is necessary to analyse trends (resource stocks, demographic change, available technologies, political representation and economic trends), shocks (the climate and actual or potential conflicts) and culture (as an explanatory factor in understanding how people manage their assets and the livelihood choices they make). It is also possible to distinguish between:

- long-term trends, such as demographic trends or changes in the natural resource base;
- recurring seasonal changes, such as prices or employment opportunities; and
- short-term shocks, such as illness, natural disaster or conflict.

This classification neglects infectious and parasitic diseases, and chemical and physical hazards. The large concentrations of population, industry and road traffic which occur in cities mean that, when poorly managed, threats to health from disease and hazards are severe (Satterthwaite, 1997; see Chapters 4 and 12).

Analysing vulnerability involves identifying not only the threats to individuals and households and their assets, but also their resilience – their ability to mobilize assets to exploit opportunities and resist or recover from the negative effects of the changing environment. The ability of households to avoid or reduce vulnerability, and to increase economic productivity depends, as suggested above, on their initial assets and on their ability to transform those assets into income, food or other basic necessities, by intensifying existing, developing new, or diversifying their strategies (Moser, 1996; 1998).

CARE addresses the issue of vulnerability by distinguishing between promotion, protection and provisioning, in different combinations aimed at increased livelihood security. Protection implies helping to prevent a decline in security, by preventing erosion of productive assets or assisting in their recovery. Provisioning refers to the direct provision of assistance to maintain nutritional levels and save lives, generally in situations of emergency (for communities or households). Its aim is to achieve a transition from provision to protection, and then to promotion (Carney et al, 1999). It recognizes that provisioning is short term and deals only with symptoms, that protection tackles the immediate causes of impoverishment and that only promotion addresses underlying or basic causes of insecurity and vulnerability in order to build up households' asset base, to increase the range of options open to them, and to improve their resilience in the long term (Drinkwater and Rusinow, 1999).

In work for the World Bank's Social Protection Unit, Siegel and Alwang (1999) distinguish between *ex ante* and *ex post* household risk-management strategies, the choice of which is influenced by the nature of the risk (a threat to an individual household such as illness or to a group – for example, flooding), the size and type of the group a household can call on for assistance and types of strategy open to a household. Households may take precautions to reduce the probability of a risky event (for example, immunizing their children) or mitigate its impact (perhaps by investing in savings or social capital), or may react to an event, if these precautions are insufficient, by various coping strategies, such as selling an asset, working longer hours or obtaining assistance from within their social networks or, if available, from a state protection programme.

Policies, Institutions and Processes

The institutions (structures or organizations) referred to in the livelihoods framework (Figure 1.1) are both public (for example, political, legislative, governmental) and private (for example, commercial, civil, NGOs). Processes are what influence or transform how organizations and individuals interact and may be formal or informal. They include policies, laws, social norms, rules of the game and incentives. They embody power and gender relations and have a significant impact on the access of the poor to all types of assets and on the effective value of those assets. They influence entitlements and also constrain access, whether intentionally or unintentionally. In conjunction with people's asset status, they help to define what livelihood strategies or activities are available and attractive. In addition, markets and legal restrictions influence the extent to which one asset can be converted into another, the scope for which influences people's ability to manage their portfolio to withstand shocks and stresses and take advantage of opportunities (Carney, 1998; Scoones, 1998). Although economic, social and political relationships create poverty and wealth, they are not set in stone.

Depending on the assets and capabilities people have at their disposal, especially social and political capital, the relationships that secure access and the mechanisms through which resources are reproduced, changed and distributed can be renegotiated (Bebbington, 1999).

The policies, organizations, institutions and processes that are relevant to livelihood strategies operate at all levels, from the household to the international arena. Economic and labour market conditions and policies, programmes of support for livelihood activities, community development, tenure and shelter policies, healthcare and environmental sanitation programmes, spatial planning, access and infrastructure policies and arrangements for governance are the key policies and structures in an urban context and will be explored in the third part of the book.

Initially given more emphasis by non-governmental organizations (NGOs) such as CARE and Oxfam are rights: the right to a secure livelihood (CARE) or access to secure paid employment with labour rights and improved working conditions (Oxfam) (Carney et al, 1999). Currently, DFID is exploring the links between human rights and development, placing an emphasis on building the accountability of public sector organizations through enhancing poor people's access to information and participation in decision-making, and strengthening the claims of the most vulnerable to the social, political and economic resources that all should enjoy.

Livelihood Opportunities and Outcomes

Non-agricultural economic activities concentrate in cities to realize economies of agglomeration. The labour market opportunities associated with diverse mixes of manufacturing and service enterprises are, of course, what explain the enormous attraction of cities for in-migrants. The interaction between these livelihood opportunities and household assets influences both the strategies they adopt and their outcomes. If the outcomes of the livelihood strategies adopted by poor people are to be positive, they should improve incomes, increase well-being, reduce vulnerability, improve food security and make more sustainable use of natural resources. Inequalities of power and conflicts of interest are somewhat downplayed in this view and will emerge in later discussions of the urban context.

SUSTAINABILITY

Sustainability is considered by DFID to be the 'core concept' of the livelihoods framework when applied to rural areas, without which development effort is wasted. In this context, sustainability is used to mean not only continuing poverty reduction, but also environmental, social and institutional sustainability. The approach therefore starts with people but, it is asserted, 'does not compromise on the environment' (Carney, 1998, p4), which is mainstreamed within the framework. However, sustainability is a problematic concept and so far in this introduction its use has been studiously avoided.

To most people, *environmental* or *ecological sustainability* (keeping natural capital intact) is the central element of sustainability. In rural areas, problems may arise if short-term survival rather than the sustainable management of natural capital is prioritized by people living in absolute poverty or those trying to produce more, perhaps resulting in environmental degradation. Nevertheless, it is possible to conceive of alternative livelihood strategies that do not degrade the natural resource base and that might be supported by policy.

Urban centres, however, consume natural resources (water, land, energy, raw materials), irrevocably change the natural resource base and generate large volumes of waste. It is possible to envisage less wasteful resource use, for example, by:

- increasing densities, to reduce the energy consumed in transport;
- conserving non-renewable resources;
- increasing the use of renewable resources;
- devising waste-management systems which ensure that wastes do not overtax the capacity of local or global sinks to absorb or dilute them; and
- the conversion of open-ended waste-disposal systems to closed loops by reuse and recycling.

However, this makes urban centres less environmentally damaging rather than sustainable in the sense used above and is not the central concern of this book.

Second, the concept of *social sustainability* is also problematic, as it may so easily come to mean 'acceptable within the status quo' when social change (redistribution of wealth and power) is what is needed to achieve lasting poverty reduction. In DFID's view it is achieved when social exclusion is minimized and social equity maximized (see also de Haan, 1999).

Administrative sustainability means ensuring that an organization, the tasks for which it is responsible or the services it provides, continues to function over the long term and may subsume financial sustainability. Organizational sustainability might be expected to have a positive relationship with economic growth. However, the relationship between environmental sustainability and economic growth is much more problematic, since economic growth generally implies increased resource consumption and waste generation, while not guaranteeing decreased poverty and increased equity. Using the concept of *economic sustainability* (achieving and maintaining a base-line level of economic welfare) does not address these problematic trade-offs explicitly.

The most commonly accepted definition of sustainable development is 'meeting the needs of the present without compromising the ability of future generations to meet their own needs'. In the urban context, *development* has been elaborated as meaning to meet:

- economic needs, including access to an adequate livelihood, and economic security when unable to secure a livelihood;
- social, cultural, environmental and health needs, including shelter, basic social and environmental services, a living environment protected from environmental hazards; and
- political needs, including freedom to participate in politics and decision-making.

Sustainability may be interpreted as implying doing this in ways which ensure a high quality environment for urban dwellers, minimize the transfer of environmental costs to people and ecosystems around the city, and meet consumption needs without undermining environmental capital (Satterthwaite, 1997).

Sustainable is also applied specifically to livelihoods in the DFID framework. Thus:

> *A livelihood is sustainable when it can cope with and recover from stresses and shocks, maintain or enhance its capabilities and assets, while not undermining the natural resource base* (Scoones, 1998, p5).

This definition embodies resilience, the ability to cope, adapt and improve well-being, and also avoiding depletion of stocks of natural resources to a level which results in a permanent decline in the rate at which the natural resource base yields useful products or services for livelihoods. It is acknowledged that conflicts will occur and trade-offs will have to be made between these different elements of sustainability, although questions about sustainability for whom, and by what criteria, are not addressed.

In practice, it is helpful to separate the two basic elements in this usage. The ability to recover from shocks and stresses and maintain or enhance assets is more appropriately termed *security*. While in rural areas the cushions against shocks may well be natural assets, this is much less likely in urban areas where people are more dependent on cash incomes, unless they are able to access land and housing with secure tenure or rural natural resources. Some urban livelihoods may depend on natural resources, but the great majority do not draw directly on natural capital. The wider environmental impact of urban economic activities, such as manufacturing, transport or construction, is beyond the control of individuals or households and is not dealt with in this volume.

Because of the definitional difficulties discussed in this section, alternative terms will be used where possible: social inclusion, acceptability to disadvantaged social groups, continued and improved organizational functioning, and lasting or continued poverty reduction. That economic, financial, institutional and social sustainability are not discussed explicitly does not mean that lasting improvements to organizational capacity and people's well-being are considered unimportant. Environmental sustainability can be defined as 'minimizing or halting the transfer of costs from city-based production, consumption or waste generation to other people or ecosystems, both now and in the future' (Satterthwaite, 1999, p9). Here, concern will focus on livelihood security (which does not preclude attention to environmental implications but does not place them centre stage).

CONCLUSION

The adoption of a livelihoods approach has a number of implications for policy and action. DFID states these as normative principles (Carney et al, 1999):

- It is a *people-centred approach* which views the world from the point of view of the individuals, households and social groups who are pursuing livelihood strategies in volatile and insecure conditions and with limited assets. It implies that:

  > *sustainable poverty elimination will be achieved only if external support focuses on what matters to people, understands the differences between groups of people and works with them in a way that is congruent with their current livelihood strategies, social environment and ability to adapt* (Carney et al, 1999, p8).

- It must therefore be *responsive and participatory* – poor people themselves must be key actors in identifying and addressing livelihood priorities. Outsiders need processes that enable them to listen and respond to the poor.
- Because it is responsive, because people, households and groups do not see the world in a sectoral way, and because analysis demonstrates the interdependent nature of factors affecting livelihoods, it needs to adopt a *holistic* perspective.
- This does not remove the necessity for an understanding of macroeconomic conditions, and of markets for land, labour, products and finance, nor does it downplay the role of government and therefore the significance of governance and delivery arrangements. The approach therefore needs to be *multi-level*, ensuring both that microlevel activity informs the development of policy and an enabling environment, and that macrolevel structures and processes support people to build on their own strengths (Carney et al, 1999).
- Policy-making and implementation therefore implies a continued process of negotiation, as meanings and objectives are defined and redefined, linkages and trade-offs analysed, options and choices identified, and decisions reached. In this context, agreement and action can be achieved only by *partnership* between local institutions, involving both the public and private sectors.

Operationalizing a livelihoods approach implies:

- direct support to assets, by providing poor people with better access to the assets and resources that act as a foundation for their livelihoods and may also be valued for other reasons; and
- support to the more effective functioning of the organizations, policies and processes that influence access to assets and the livelihood strategies open to poor people.

This may involve three types of activity:

- Enabling actions that support policies and improve the context for poverty reduction.
- Inclusive actions that are broad-based and improve opportunities and services generally, addressing issues of equity and barriers to the participation of poor people.
- Focused actions that are targeted directly at the needs of poor people.

Inevitably, there will be conflicts and trade-offs between the principles outlined above – one of the issues considered by contributors to the remainder of the book.

NOTES

1 This section draws on earlier work (Rakodi, 1991, 1995, 1999) and also Guhan and Harriss, 1992; Lipton and Ravallion, 1995; Hanmer et al, 1997
2 Attempts to address this gap in recent years include Grootaert et al (1997), Baulch and Hoddinott (eds) (2000) and Sahn and Stifel (2000)
3 There may be deficiencies in the diagram and scope for improving its content and design. However, contributors deliberately focus on discussing the concepts, relationships and processes portrayed and not on a critical analysis of the diagram itself
4 This section draws on Scoones, 1998; Carney, 1998 and Rakodi, 1999

REFERENCES

Ashley, C and Carney, D (1999) *Sustainable Livelihoods: Lessons from Early Experience*, DFID, London

Baulch, R (1996) 'Neglected trade-offs in poverty measurement', *IDS Bulletin*, vol 27, pp36–43

Baulch, B and Hoddinott, J (eds) (2000) *Economic Mobility and Poverty Dynamics in Developing Countries*, Frank Cass, London

Bebbington, A (1999) 'Capitals and capabilities: a framework for analyzing peasant viability, rural livelihoods and poverty', *World Development*, vol 27, no 12, pp2021–2044

Booth, D, Holland, J, Hentschel, J, Lanjouw, P and Herbert, A (1998) *Participation and Combined Methods in African Poverty Assessment: Renewing the Agenda*, Department for International Development, Social Development Division, African Division, London

Carney, D (1998) 'Implementing the sustainable rural livelihoods approach', in Carney, D (ed) *Sustainable Rural Livelihoods: What Contribution Can We Make?* Department for International Development, London, pp3–23

Carney, D, Drinkwater, M, Rusinow, T, Neefjes, K, Wanmali, S and Singh, N (1999) *Livelihoods Approaches Compared*, Department for International Development, London

Chambers, R (1989) 'Vulnerability, coping and policy', *IDS Bulletin*, vol 20, no 2, pp1–7

Chambers, R and Conway, G (1992) *Sustainable Rural Livelihoods: Practical Concepts for the 21st Century*, University of Sussex, Institute for Development Studies, DP 296, Brighton

Collier, P (1998) *Social Capital and Poverty*, Social Capital Initiative WP 4, World Bank, Washington, DC

de Haan, A (1999) *Social Exclusion: Towards an Holistic Understanding of Deprivation*, Department for International Development, Social Development Department Dissemination Note No 2, London

Drinkwater, M and Rusinow, T (1999) 'Application of CARE's livelihoods approach', paper presented to the Department for International Development, Natural Resource Advisers Conference

Ellis, F (1998) 'Household strategies and rural livelihood diversification', *Journal of Development Studies*, vol 35, no 1, pp1–38

Grootaert, C, Kanbur, R and Oh, G-T (1997) 'The dynamics of welfare gains and losses: an African case study', *Journal of Development Studies*, vol 33, no 5, pp635–657

Grown, C A and Sebstad, J (1989) 'Introduction: toward a wider perspective on women's employment', *World Development*, vol 17, no 7, pp937–952

Guhan, S and Harriss, B (1992) 'Introduction', in Harriss, B, Guhan, S and Cassen, R H (eds) *Poverty in India: Research and Policy*, Oxford University Press, Bombay, pp1–24

Hanmer, L, Pyatt, G and White, H (1997) *Poverty in Sub-Saharan Africa: What Can We Learn from the World Bank's Poverty Assessments?*, Institute for Social Studies, The Hague

Hart, G (1997) 'From 'rotten wives' to 'good mothers': household models and the limits of economism', *IDS Bulletin*, vol 28, no 3, pp14–25

Lipton, M and Ravallion, M (1995) 'Poverty and policy', in Behrman, J and Srinavasan, T N (eds) *Handbook of Development Economics*, vol 3, Elsevier Science, Amsterdam, pp2251–2637

Maxwell, S (1999) 'The meaning and measurement of poverty', *ODI Poverty Briefing 3*, February

Moore, M, Chondhary, M and Singh, N (1998) *How Can We Know What they Want? Understanding Local Perceptions of Poverty and Ill-being in Asia,* University of Sussex, Institute for Development Studies, WP 80, Brighton

Moser, C O N (1996) *Confronting Crisis: A Comparative Study of Household Responses to Poverty and Vulnerability in Four Poor Urban Communities*, World Bank, Environmentally Sustainable Development Studies and Monographs Series No 8, Washington, DC

Moser, C O N (1998) 'The asset vulnerability framework: reassessing urban poverty reduction strategies', *World Development*, vol 26, no1, pp1–19

Narayan, D (1997) *Voices of the Poor: Poverty and Social Capital in Tanzania*, World Bank Environmentally Sustainable Development Studies and Monograph Series No 20, Washington, DC

Narayan, D and Pritchett, L (1999) 'Cents and sociability: household income and social capital in rural Tanzania, *Economic Development and Cultural Change*, vol 47, no 4, pp871–897

Nunan, F and Satterthwaite, D (1999) *The Urban Environment*, Urban Governance, Partnership and Poverty, Theme Paper 6, International Development Department, School of Public Policy, University of Birmingham, Birmingham

Rakodi, C (1991) 'Women's work or household strategies?' *Environment and Urbanisation*, vol 3, no 2, pp39–45

Rakodi, C (1995) 'Poverty lines or household strategies? A review of conceptual issues in the study of urban poverty', *Habitat International*, vol 19, no 4, pp407–426

Rakodi, C (1999) 'A capital assets framework for analysing household livelihood strategies', *Development Policy Review*, vol 17, no 3, pp315–342

Sahn, D E and Stifel, D C (2000) 'Poverty comparisons over time and across countries in Africa', *World Development*, vol 28, no 12, pp2123–2155

Satterthwaite, D (1997) 'Sustainable cities or cities that contribute to sustainable development?' *Urban Studies*, vol 34, no 10, pp1667–1691

Satterthwaite, D (1999) 'The key issues and the works included', in Satterthwaite, D (ed) *The Earthscan Reader in Sustainable Cities*, Earthscan, London, pp3–21

Scoones, I (1998) *Sustainable Rural Livelihoods: A Framework for Analysis*, University of Sussex, Institute for Development Studies, WP 72, Brighton

Siegel, P B and Alwang, J (1999) *An Asset-based Approach to Social Risk Management: A Conceptual Framework*, World Bank, Human Development Network, Social Protection Unit, SP DP 9926.1, Washington, DC

Wolf, D L (1990) 'Daughters, decisions and domination: an empirical and conceptual critique of household strategies', *Development and Change*, vol 21, pp43–74

Chapter 2

Economic Development, Urbanization and Poverty

Carole Rakodi

The concern of this book is with livelihoods in urban areas. To set the scene briefly, recent urbanization trends will be described in this chapter and some background information on poverty and inequality in urban areas will be presented. However, urban centres cannot be considered in isolation: economic growth and poverty in towns and cities is closely linked both to national economic performance and national development policies. Before examining the urban situation, therefore, broad trends in development are sketched, drawing attention to the relationships between economic growth, inequality and poverty reduction.

ECONOMIC DEVELOPMENT: GROWTH, INEQUALITY AND POVERTY REDUCTION

Between 1975 and 1995 real per capita gross national product (GNP) in developing countries increased at an average annual rate of 2.3 per cent. However, this average conceals slow and even negative growth in many countries in the 1980s, as well as geographical differences: extremely rapid growth (7.3 per cent per annum) in East Asia, but a decline of –0.9 per cent per annum over the two decades in sub-Saharan Africa (UNDP, 1999, p183).

Globalization and liberalization have resulted in expanding exports and phenomenal growth of capital flows, but there are great disparities in experience across countries and regions:

> *The top fifth of the world's people in the richest countries have enjoyed 82% of the expanding export trade [between the 1970s and 1997] and 68% of foreign direct investment – the bottom fifth, barely more than 1%* (UNDP, 1999, p31).

Some developing countries have made major advances, as trade in manufacturing, services and 'knowledge goods' has grown, but others have missed out entirely, reinforcing economic stagnation and low human development.

Conventional economic theory predicts that trade liberalization will increase productivity and wages, especially for tradable goods, thus expanding jobs and opportunities for poor people. Some countries, especially in East and Southeast Asia, have been able to take advantage of global opportunities to achieve economic growth and reduce poverty. Globalization, however, is bringing not only economic growth and reduced poverty, but also economic decline, increased inequality and impoverishment. In Latin America, inequality worsened in the 1980s, following two decades of improvement – the poorest 10 per cent suffered a 15 per cent drop in their share of income, wiping out the improvements in distribution before the crisis (UNDP, 1999, p39). However, trends in inequality vary between countries. In some – for example, Ecuador, 1970–1990, Malaysia, 1967–1989, India, 1970–1979 and Costa Rica, 1970–1989 – average incomes of the poor grew ahead of per capita GNP, whereas in Brazil and Kenya the reverse was true (UNDP, 1999). Income inequalities have grown markedly in recent years in China, Indonesia, Thailand and other East and Southeast Asian countries that had achieved high growth in earlier decades, while at the same time improving income distribution and reducing poverty. Despite reductions in the proportion of poor people in many Latin American countries, they still, in the mid-1990s, have higher levels of poverty than expected for their average per capita incomes. Recent research shows that this can be explained by the high level of inequality, linked to high levels of inequality in income-generating assets, especially human capital (Attanasio and Székely, 1999).

In addition to recent increases in inequality in many countries, jobs and incomes have become more precarious. In Latin America, for example, labour market 'flexibility' has increased. By 1996, the share of workers with no or more flexible contracts had increased to 30 per cent in Chile, 36 per cent in Argentina, 39 per cent in Colombia and 41 per cent in Peru. Informal employment had expanded to 58 per cent, and 85 out of every 100 new jobs were informal (UNDP, 1999, p37; see also UNCHS, 1996). In addition, real wages and informal sector earnings fell in many countries in the 1980s (Gilbert, 1994). Although there was a modest recovery in the 1990s, wages did not reach pre-crisis levels and insufficient jobs were generated to keep pace with labour force growth (Watt, 2000).

Some parts of the developing world have enjoyed levels of growth that are high enough to reduce poverty in recent decades. The most recent World Bank estimates show that both the share of population and the number of people living on less than a dollar a day declined substantially in the mid-1990s, after increasing in the early 1990s, although the numbers rose again in the aftermath of the financial crisis of the late 1990s[1] (see Table 2.1). The declines in numbers were due almost entirely to reduced poverty in East Asia, especially in China, although progress was partly reversed by the crisis and stalled in China. In South Asia, despite economic growth, the proportion of people living in poverty declined only very slightly during the 1990s, and the absolute numbers of poor people continued to increase. In Latin America and Africa, the share of poor people did not change and numbers increased, while in the countries of the former Soviet bloc, both the share and the numbers increased. The incidence of poverty is greatest in

Table 2.1 *Income poverty by region, selected years 1987–1998*

| | Share of population living on less than US$1 a day per cent | | | | |
	1987	1990	1993	1996	1998 (preliminary)
East Asia and Pacific	26.6	27.6	25.2	14.9	15.3
excluding China	23.9	18.5	15.9	10.0	11.3
Europe and Central Asia	0.2	1.6	4.0	5.1	5.1
Latin America and the Caribbean	15.3	16.8	15.3	15.6	15.6
Middle East and North Africa	4.3	2.4	1.9	1.8	1.9
South Asia	44.9	44.0	42.4	42.3	40.0
Sub-Saharan Africa	46.6	47.7	49.7	48.5	46.3
Total	28.3	29.0	28.1	24.5	24.0
excluding China	28.5	28.1	27.7	27.0	26.2

Source: World Bank (2001) *Attacking Poverty. World Development Report 2000/2001 summary,* World Bank, Washington, DC, p9

sub-Saharan Africa (46.3 per cent) and South Asia (40 per cent) (World Bank, 1999, 2001). Between 1995 and 1997 only 21 developing countries (12 in Asia) met or exceeded the 3 per cent per annum per capita increase in growth needed to reduce poverty (World Bank, 2000, p25).

These figures conceal many differences between and within countries. For example, in Africa as a whole, growth picked up in the 1990s, but stalled again following the financial crisis, which resulted in lower commodity prices and slower world trade growth. Some countries that implemented structural adjustment policies experienced declines in income poverty, such as Côte d'Ivoire, Ghana, Mauritania and Uganda, but others, such as Nigeria and Zimbabwe, experienced sharp increases, as did the many countries engulfed in conflict and those affected by adverse weather conditions (World Bank, 1999).

Measures of health and education provide another perspective on development and living standards. What is important here is that many low-income countries with slow economic growth have managed an improvement in the indicators of well-being (life expectancy, infant mortality, primary school enrolment, adult literacy, gender disparities). Some of these gains have been eroded by prolonged economic crisis (UNCHS, 1996, Chapter 3). On average, the life expectancy of people in developing countries rose from 55 years in 1970 to 65 years in 1997, but 33 countries have seen life expectancy decline since 1990 (World Bank, 1999, p15). For example, there has been a decline in life expectancy in a number of African countries, including Zimbabwe, Uganda, Rwanda and Zambia since 1980, which has been exacerbated by HIV/AIDS. Infant mortality rates continued to decline in the 1990s in all regions except Eastern Europe and Central Asia, but rose in some countries, including Kenya and Zimbabwe. Primary school enrolment increased overall between 1970 and the 1990s, but sub-Saharan Africa has experienced no improvement since the early 1980s and 16 countries suffered a decline in net enrolment in the early 1990s, while less than half of eligible children were enrolled in nine countries, all except one in Africa.

Moreover, two-thirds of the children not attending school were girls. The incidence of adult illiteracy fell in developing countries from around 45 per cent in 1980 to 30 per cent in 1995, but almost all this decrease is due to progress in East Asia. The number of illiterate adults grew in South Asia and sub-Saharan Africa and two-thirds of them are women (World Bank, 1999, p20–24). Even in some countries that have experienced periods of rapid economic growth and have reached middle-income levels, satisfactory levels of well-being and service provision have not been achieved. In addition, a number of other indicators are still very unsatisfactory – nearly three-fifths of the population of developing countries lack basic sanitation, a third have no access to clean water, a quarter lack adequate housing, a fifth of children have insufficient nutritious food and a similar proportion do not complete five years of school. Before examining the patterns of growth, inequality and poverty in urban areas, urbanization trends will be reviewed very briefly.

URBANIZATION

The world's urban population is set to rise by almost 1.5 billion people in the next 20 years. In developing countries, the share of the population living in urban areas is likely to rise from half today to about two-thirds by 2025. Already in 1997, 74 per cent of the population of Latin America and the Caribbean, 67 per cent in low- and middle-income countries in Europe and Central Asia, and 58 per cent in the Middle East and North Africa lived in urban areas, but sub-Saharan Africa (with 32 per cent), East Asia and the Pacific (with 33 per cent) and South Asia (with 27 per cent) are yet to begin the urban transition (World Bank, 2000, p47).

The number of cities has increased dramatically and will continue to increase: in 1970 there were 163 cities with populations of 1 million or more; today there are about 350. Although most attention tends to be given to the largest cities, in 1995 only 15 per cent of the world's urban population lived in mega-cities (population 5 million or more), while 21 per cent lived in large cities, and 64 per cent in small and medium cities (those with populations of less than 1 million). Between 1970 and 1990, although in absolute numbers mega-cities accounted for a very large share of urban population growth, their populations were growing the slowest of all the city-size categories, while small cities (those with a population of less than half a million) grew most rapidly (World Bank, 2000).

The global figures given above must be handled with considerable care. First, definitions of 'urban' vary between countries, and a change of definition by one or two of the most populous countries – for example, India or China (see Box 2.1) – would make a big difference to the proportion of the world's population that is considered to be urban. Second, in many countries, especially in Africa, economic crises and periods of conflict have resulted in a lack of reliable and up-to-date censuses, and many urban population figures are in fact extrapolations (Rakodi, 1997). Third, the administrative boundaries used for estimates of urban population do not necessarily coincide with the built-up area of towns and cities.

Administrative boundaries often lag behind population growth, or functional cities are divided between more than one administrative area. In some places, urban administrative boundaries are drawn loosely, including large rural areas within them. Fourth, urban growth is comprised of natural increase, net in-migration and extensions of administrative boundaries. The latter result in sudden large increases in the population of an urban centre which distorts both past growth rates and, in turn, population projections.

BOX 2.1 *CHINA'S URBAN POPULATION*

In China in 1990, just over a quarter of the population was categorized as urban (302 million, compared with 130 million in 1978). Of the increase since 1978, 35 per cent was due to net in-migration, 25 per cent to natural increase and 40 per cent to changes in the urban administrative system. If an alternative definition of urban areas had been applied in 1990, over half of the national population would have been categorized as urban. The proportion urban is exaggerated by the inclusion of rural populations within urban boundaries, but this is counter-acted by the failure to count large numbers of mobile/temporary residents as urban (Kirby, 1994).

However approximate our current and future estimates of the number of people living in urban centres, 'the speed of urbanization and the enormous numbers involved make it one of the major development challenges of the 21st century' (World Bank, 2000, p47).

URBAN CENTRES: ECONOMIC GROWTH, INEQUALITY AND POVERTY

Cities as Engines of Economic Growth?

There is a clear association between economic growth and urbanization. However, this correlation masks complex cause-and-effect relationships. In industrial countries, economic growth and structural transformation accompanied urbanization. The association between urbanization and rising per capita income has held in Europe, Latin America and more recently much of Asia. The East Asian experience with sustained economic growth and successful rural development suggests that the pattern might be repeated: South Korea transformed itself from a society that was 80 per cent rural and in which agriculture contributed 37 per cent of GDP to one that is 80 per cent urban and the share of agriculture under 6 per cent in 20 years (World Bank, 2000, pp47–48). Elsewhere, particularly in Africa, the link between economic growth and urbanization has not been evident. Only 9 per cent of Africa's labour force is employed in industry compared with 18 per cent in Asia, which has seen comparable rates of urbanization (World Bank, 2000, p130).

The removal of restrictions on migration, conflicts and the absence of rural development push people to urban areas which, in the absence of economic growth and industrialization, lack the resources to accommodate them productively. Some analysts have identified an 'urban bias' in policy and resource allocation arising from the political power of urban populations. This is said to have prevented the adoption of pro-agriculture and pro-rural policies, hindering development and encouraging over-rapid rural–urban migration. Many of the policy reforms associated with structural adjustment were designed to eliminate perceived urban biases in policy and resource allocation. As a result, any remaining urban bias in wages and policies has now virtually disappeared.

Economic growth is always accompanied by urbanization because goods and services are often produced most efficiently in densely populated areas that provide access to a pool of skilled labour, a network of complementary firms which act as suppliers and a critical mass of customers. For this reason, as countries develop, cities account for an ever-increasing share of national income. Urban areas generate 55 per cent of GNP in low-income, 73 per cent in middle-income and 85 per cent in high-income countries (World Bank, 2000, p126). The growth sectors of national economies (manufacturing and services) are usually concentrated in cities where they benefit from higher levels of efficiency related to proximity and ample markets for inputs, outputs and labour, and where ideas and knowledge are generated and diffused.

Productivity is highest in large cities (1 million plus), although there may be diseconomies of congestion in the largest, eventually leading to decentralization and dispersal. However, firms that do not derive sufficient benefits to justify high land and labour costs prefer smaller cities which may have specialized economies and/or provide access to markets in their regional hinterlands.

In addition to urbanization resulting from the structural transformation of a national economy, cities, because of their locational attractions for high productivity economic activities, may also contribute significantly to economic growth. To realize this potential, they must provide efficient and attractive places to do business. The most important features of cities in this respect are the availability of basic infrastructure and services, land markets which enable firms and households to make efficient decisions about where to locate, and a healthy and knowledgeable labour force. In practice, poor governance, inappropriate policies and the economic difficulties faced by many countries in the 1980s and 1990s have reduced their efficiency as locations for enterprises. In particular, inappropriate regulatory policies and a lack of investment in infrastructure and services increase the operating costs of organizations, including businesses in both the formal and informal sectors and government itself.

The discussion above has concentrated on the relationship between economic growth and level of urbanization. However, the latter is likely to reflect not only the level of per capita gross domestic product (GDP) and the nature of a country's economy, but the definition of urban that is used, the nature of agriculture, physical factors such as the size and topography of the country, political and cultural factors, and government policies. These influences on urbanization are not discussed further in this volume.

Inequality and Poverty in Cities

Supporters of the 'urban bias' hypothesis since the 1970s have used the higher average wages and incomes which typify urban areas to support their case. However, this use of averages has always been oversimplified and has concealed gross inequalities in incomes and well-being within urban areas. Although cities are associated with economic growth, not all residents benefit. The implementation of wage freezes and other labour policies, public sector retrenchment, the abolition of controls and subsidies on food and other prices, and reduced public sector spending during structural adjustment, as was intended, hit urban areas particularly hard. Within cities, while many middle-income people were affected, often the costs of adjustment fell disproportionately on the urban poor, at least in the short term, threatening the security of their livelihoods, reducing their incomes and resulting in deteriorating access to basic services (Gilbert, 1994; Ruel et al, 1999). There is evidence, moreover, that the financial crisis of the late 1990s had a particularly adverse effect on urban residents – for example, the proportion of South Korea's urban population that was poor increased from 8.6 per cent in 1997 to 14.8 per cent in December, 1998 (World Bank, 1999, p9):

> *The urban poor were faced with a price-income squeeze, as the effects of unemployment and downward pressure on wages were compounded by the marketisation of public goods. The majority of new recruits to the labour market were left with underemployment in the informal sector as the only option left open to them .... [This sector is] generally characterised by small-scale, household-based, insecure, legally unrecognised, and untaxed work* (Watt, 2000, p103).

As numbers seeking income-generating opportunities in the informal sector have increased, incomes have fallen. The sector has become overcrowded, at the same time as purchasing power has decreased as a result of falling real wages and job shedding in the formal sector. Not only was the informal sector unable to absorb everyone who needed work, as shown by rising levels of open unemployment, it absorbs some people more easily than others (Gilbert, 1994). Even where jobs are generated as a result of economic growth or globalization, the poor may not benefit because of their limited human capital. Women may have greater opportunities in cities than in rural areas, but more commonly are disadvantaged relative to men and have been particularly vulnerable to downward pressures on incomes. In addition, the increasing importance of the informal sector has eroded the tax base, leading to a growing reliance on taxes on consumption and trade which are often regressive (Watt, 2000).

Ranis et al (2000) summarize empirical studies that demonstrate the link between additional years of education and increased earnings. In addition, educational and skill levels are positively related to the rate of technological change in industry; thus investment in education and health are also important to economic growth. They show how health, primary and secondary education and good nutrition raise the productivity of workers; secondary education, including vocational education, facilitates the acquisition of skills and managerial capacity; and tertiary education supports the development of basic science and the selection and adaptation of technology. In addition, as education becomes more widely accessible, low-income people are better able to seek out economic opportunities, so there are positive effects on their well-being from both increased incomes and reduced fertility (Ranis et al, 2000).

Inequality is generally greater in urban areas. This can be illustrated with reference both to incomes and quality of life. The Gini coefficient is a recognized way of indicating income inequality: it illustrates how far an income distribution is away from perfect equality; thus higher values mean greater inequality. It is generally, although not always, higher in urban areas. For example, in the Philippines, the Gini coefficient is 0.43 in urban and 0.38 in rural areas (Balisacan, 1993, p538). In Madagascar, in the capital it is 0.48, compared with 0.40 in rural areas (World Bank, 1996a). In Tanzania, the ratio of the per capita expenditure of households in the richest quintile to those in the poorest was 6.35:1 in urban and 5.25:1 in rural areas in the mid-1990s (World Bank, 1996b).

On average, indicators show that people are better off in urban areas, but poor urban dwellers are likely to be subject to higher levels of air pollution, crime and violence than better off residents, and health conditions may be worse for the urban poor than for the rural poor. Among the municipalities which make up Greater São Paulo, for example, the infant mortality rate varied by a factor of three, with the highest rate being 60 per 1000 live births in 1992 (UNCHS, 1996, p107). In Bangladesh, the infant mortality rate in 1981 was 112.2 per 1000 in rural areas, 99.4 per 1000 for the urban non-slum population and 152–180 per 1000 for the slum population (Khundker et al, 1994, p23). A review of infant and child mortality data from 20 demographic and health surveys found that rates in rural areas were generally higher than in urban areas without piped water, and these in turn were higher than in urban areas with piped water. Overall, poor urban children had a 57 per cent greater under-five mortality risk than wealthier urban children, but a 17 per cent lower risk than rural children. However, in some countries, the mortality risk of the urban poor exceeded that of the rural poor (Bicego and Ahmad, 1996). Figures from Côte d'Ivoire, Ghana, Jamaica and Peru in the late 1980s show that the proportion of rich urban people (the richest 20 per cent) seeking treatment when ill was between 1.3 and 1.6 times the proportion of poor urban people with access to healthcare (World Bank, 1999, p18).

The locus of poverty is shifting to urban areas, partly because of the effects of recession and adjustment, partly because of the in-migration of the rural poor, and partly because of the increased share of the urban population in the total. Drawing on research work undertaken by the International Food Policy Research Institute, some available data are given in Table 2.2, for eight low- and middle-income countries, accounting for two-thirds of the developing world's people (Haddad et al, 1999). In a majority of the countries the absolute number of poor people living in urban areas and urban areas' share of overall poverty increased during the period (generally the mid-1980s to mid-1990s) for which data was available. In India, for example, '. . . the number of poor rural individuals was flattening out in the 1970s, with the numbers of urban poor catching up over the 1980s and 90s, as reflected by an increasing share of the poor living in urban areas' (Haddad et al, 1999, p1897). Sahn and Stifel's (2000) analysis of 11 African countries using an index of household assets (see Chapter 1) also showed

Table 2.2 *Changes in urban and rural poverty over time*

Country	Survey year	Urban poverty incidence	Rural poverty incidence	Percentage of poor in urban areas	Number of urban poor (000s)
Bangladesh	1983–1984	50.8	60.4	11.5	6737
Bangladesh	1991–1992	45.2	63.0	11.8	7781
Colombia	1978	12.1	38.4	35.8	2052
Colombia	1992	8.0	31.2	37.4	1825
Nigeria	1985–1986	31.7	49.5	22.1	8092
Nigeria	1992–1993	30.4	36.4	31.0	10,234
Indonesia	1990	10.3	23.1	16.4	5760
Indonesia	1993	5.2	16.5	14.7	3637
India	1977–1978	40.5	50.6	19.3	64,335
India	1993–1994	30.5	36.7	23.3	75,932
China	1988	6.7	32.7	6.8	20,281
China	1995	8.0	28.6	10.8	29,298
Pakistan	1984–1985	38.2	49.3	24.8	11,522
Pakistan	1991	28.0	36.9	26.2	10,635
Ghana	1987–1988	27.3	41.9	23.7	1132
Ghana	1992–1993	26.5	33.9	28.6	1348

Source: Haddad et al, 1999, pp1894–1895

reductions in the proportion of urban households below a real poverty line, except in Kenya, 1993–1998, Madagascar, 1992–1997, Uganda, 1988–1995 and Zimbabwe, 1988–1994. However, in the early 1990s, both increases and decreases in poverty incidence were relatively small, indicating a general picture of stagnation.

However, reliable data are not widely available. In particular, relatively few countries have trend data from at least two successive surveys, which are also disaggregated for urban and rural areas. The incidence of urban poverty varies enormously and the figures available are often unreliable because they do not allow (accurately) for the higher cost of living in cities, are not adjusted for changes in the cost of living over time, do not use comparable poverty lines between surveys and countries, may use different definitions of urban over time or between countries, and generally refer to urban and rural administrative areas rather than built-up areas or labour market areas. These problems illustrate some of the difficulties faced by analyses of income poverty and suggest that other indicators of deprivation are likely to be more useful in assessing the welfare of urban residents.

Other indicators may or may not bear out findings on the incidence of and trends in urban income poverty. For example, Haddad et al (1999) examine undernutrition, using figures for underweight children in 14 countries. Their findings are similar: although prevalence is greater in rural areas:

> . . . for 12 out of the 16 country spells [that is, the intervals between
> surveys] the absolute number of underweight children in urban
> areas is increasing and at a faster rate than the numbers in rural
> areas. For 10 of the 16 country spells both the absolute number of
> underweight children in urban areas and the share of underweight
> children in urban areas are increasing (Haddad et al, 1999, p1897).

RURAL–URBAN LINKS

The discussions of urbanization and urban inequality and poverty above treat urban areas as distinct. In practice, they should not be dealt with in isolation. Nor should characteristics or activities be attributed to 'cities' or 'towns' when these apply to actors (politicians, enterprises, households, individuals) who may operate in both urban and rural areas. Tacoli (1998) suggests that there are two types of rural–urban linkages: flows of people or goods and sectoral interactions. Flows of people are complex – they are multidirectional and of differing duration and variable composition. Sectoral interactions refer to 'rural' sectors in urban areas – for example, urban agriculture – and 'urban' sectors in rural areas – non-farm activities such as manufacturing or the production of building materials.

In principle, urban and rural areas can enjoy mutually beneficial links and promote economic growth in towns and cities. Improved urban management does not imply neglecting rural development. Cities benefit when agricultural productivity increases. Growing rural economies provide markets for urban services and manufactured goods, including equipment, agrochemicals and consumer goods. A boom in commercial agriculture boosts demand for marketing, transportation, construction and finance. In Africa, every US$1 of additional output in the agricultural sector generates an extra US$1.50 of output in the non-farm sector, much of which may be located in urban areas. In Asia that figure is US$1.80 (World Bank, 2000, p128). Rural areas also benefit from the growth of cities which provide markets for agricultural products and for rural non-farm output, and from increased productivity resulting from technology transfers, services, education and training.

It should be recognized that rural–urban links may also have negative consequences. For example, increased agricultural production to satisfy urban demand may deplete environmental capital, urban expansion may compete for rural resources, such as land and water, and urban growth is likely to generate increased waste and pollution. Care must be taken, moreover, not to equate urban and rural areas with all urban and rural residents. In rural areas, access to land, capital and labour determine the extent to which farmers can benefit from urban markets – smaller farmers may not be able to do so and there may be other barriers to accessing markets, including physical remoteness or social and gender obstacles. In urban areas, as noted above, poor people often lack the human and social assets that are needed to access secure and well-paid jobs and lucrative business opportunities. Increased interaction between urban and rural areas, therefore, may increase inequality and the vulnerability of those groups with the least assets, rather than benefiting them.

Policy interventions may be needed to tackle bottlenecks that deter positive interaction between urban and rural areas and the constraints that prevent poor people in urban, rural and peri-urban areas taking advantage of livelihood opportunities arising out of that interaction.

Finally, categorizing households and individuals as 'urban' or 'rural' may be artificial. Many straddle both sectors, as individuals or by links with other household and family members via trade, flows in kind, remittances or maintaining multilocal households. In both urban and rural areas, significant proportions of households rely on a combination of agricultural and non-agricultural income sources. In addition, as noted above, urban boundaries are often drawn for administrative convenience. Many households live in peri-urban areas outside the urban boundary but derive their livelihoods from work within it, while people living inside the urban boundary engage in activities such as farming, fishing, collecting wood or trading which take them to the surrounding rural areas.

The issues discussed in this section are taken up and discussed in more detail in Chapter 4.

NOTE

1   The numbers are estimated from those countries in each region for which at least one survey was available during the period 1985–1998. For the 1998 estimates the poverty line used is US$1.08 per day in 1993 purchasing power parity terms, which corresponds to the median of the ten lowest poverty lines in low-income countries. Many aspects of this method have been questioned, but the controversies will not be discussed here

REFERENCES

Attanasio, O and Székely, M (1999) *An Asset-based Approach to the Analysis of Poverty in Latin America*, Inter-American Development Bank, Office of the Chief Economist, WP#R-376

Balisacan, A M (1993) 'Agricultural growth, landlessness, off-farm employment and rural poverty in the Philippines', *Economic Development and Cultural Change*, vol 41, no 3, pp533–562

Baulch, R (1996) 'Neglected trade-offs in poverty measurement', *IDS Bulletin*, vol 27, pp36–43

Bicego, G and Ahmad, O (1996) *Infant and Child Mortality*, Macro International Inc, Demographic and Health Surveys, Comparative Studies No 20, Calverton, MD

Bruce, L (1989) 'Homes divided', *World Development*, vol 17, no 7, pp979–991

Gilbert, A (1994) 'Third world cities: poverty, employment, gender roles and the environment during a time of restructuring', *Urban Studies*, vol 31, no 4/5, pp605–633

Haddad, L, Ruel, M T and Garrett, J L (1999) 'Are urban poverty and undernutrition growing? Some newly assembled evidence', *World Development*, vol 27, no 11, pp1891–1904

Hanmer, L, Pyatt, G and White, H (1997) *Poverty in Sub-Saharan Africa: What Can We Learn from the World Bank's Poverty Assessments?*, Institute for Social Studies, The Hague

Khundker, N, Mahmud, W, Sen, B and Ahmed, M U (1994) 'Urban poverty in Bangladesh', *Asian Development Review*, vol 12, no1, pp90–116

Kirkby, R (1994) 'Dilemmas of urbanisation: review and prospects', in Dwyer, D (ed) *China: The Next Decades*, Longman, Harlow, pp128–55

Narayan, D (1997) *Voices of the Poor: Poverty and Social Capital in Tanzania*, World Bank Environmentally Sustainable Development Studies and Monograph Series No 20, Washington, DC

Ninan, K N (2000) *Economic Reforms in India: Impact on the Poor and Poverty*, Institute of Development Studies WP 102, Brighton

Rakodi, C (1997) 'Introduction', in Rakodi, C (ed) *The Urban Challenge in Africa: Growth and Management of its Large Cities*, United Nations University Press, Tokyo, pp1–13

Ranis, G, Stewart, F and Ramirez, A (2000) 'Economic growth and human development' *World Development*, vol 28, no 2, pp197–219

Ruel, M T, Haddad, L and Garrett, L (1999) 'Some urban facts of life: implications for research and policy', *World Development*, vol 27, no 11, pp1917–1938

Sahn, D E and Stifel, D C (2000) 'Poverty comparisons over time and across countries in Africa', *World Development*, vol 28, no 12, pp2123–2155

Tacoli, C (1998) 'Rural–urban linkages and sustainable rural livelihoods', in Carney, D (ed) *Sustainable Rural Livelihoods: What Contribution Can We Make?*, Overseas Development Institute for Department for International Development, London, pp67–79

UNCHS (1996) *An Urbanizing World: Global Report on Human Settlements, 1996*, Oxford University Press, New York

UNDP (1999) *Human Development Report 1999*, Oxford University Press, New York

Watt, P (2000) *Social Investment and Economic Growth: A Strategy to Eradicate Poverty*, Oxfam, Oxford

World Bank (1996a) *Madagascar Poverty Assessment*, World Bank, Washington, DC

World Bank (1996b) *Tanzania: The Challenge of Reforms: Growth, Incomes and Welfare*, World Bank, Washington, DC

World Bank (1999) *Poverty Trends and Voices of the Poor*, World Bank, Washington, DC

World Bank (2000) *Entering the 21st Century: World Development Report 1999/2000*, Oxford University Press, New York

World Bank (2001) *Attacking Poverty. Overview, World Development Report 2000/ 2001*, World Bank, Washington, DC

Part 2

Understanding the Situations and Strategies of Poor People

The contributors to Part 2 attempt to synthesize what we know about urban poverty and the livelihood strategies of poor people, drawing on a range of previous research undertaken by themselves and others.

Chapter 3

The Urban Context and Poor People

Sheilah Meikle

INTRODUCTION

The livelihoods of the poor are determined predominantly by the context in which they live and the constraints and opportunities this location presents. This is because context – economic, environmental, social and political – largely determines the assets accessible to people, how they can use these, and thus their ability to obtain secure livelihoods. Furthermore, the short- and long-term livelihood aims of poor men and women are products of the context of which they are part, as they are in large part a response to the opportunities and constraints available.

It is context that makes an urban livelihood distinctive. Both urban and rural contexts are dynamic and multifaceted, but the urban is more complex. Urban areas provide a greater number and variety of services. In urban areas cash transactions are more common; poor urban people are more dependent on cash incomes and often they lack access to the common property resources, such as water and fuel, that are available in rural areas. They exist in inferior residential and working environments and, because of the fragmented and diverse social environment of urban areas, are less likely to have support from social networks. As in rural areas, the quality of life of poor men and women is influenced by what local governments do or do not do. The relationships between the poor, local governments and other actors in the political context are critical to their well-being.

The influences of context on household livelihoods and livelihoods in turn on their context are mediated by policies, institutional or organizational structures and a variety of processes, which are themselves products of the context. Such policies, institutions and processes are not restricted to the local level but operate at all levels – international, national and local – as well as across the public and private (commercial and civil) sectors.

The variable contexts, together with the policies, institutions and processes that they incorporate, determine the vulnerability of households. Not only do they influence the long-term stresses and short-term shocks that affect household livelihoods, but they also have a strong influence on how poor households can respond to such impacts. Every component of an area's context can incorporate elements that potentially contribute to increased vulnerability. Although the main sources of vulnerability may vary from place to place, as discussed later in this chapter and in Table 3.1, certain elements are common to urban areas throughout the developing world:

- the informal legal status of poor men and women;
- poor living environments; and
- poor urban men and women's dependence on a cash economy for basic goods and services.

Thus the seeds of vulnerability are present in urban areas. If households are to have more secure livelihoods and be less vulnerable, there is, as discussed in detail in Part 3, a need for urban contexts to be transformed.

The purpose of this chapter is to identify significant characteristics of the urban context and their implications for poor people and households, including the ways in which they determine the assets and entitlements available to poor people and the extent of their vulnerability. Finally, a range of possible policy interventions is identified.

THE URBAN CONTEXT AND POOR PEOPLE

Most urban areas, despite distinctive individual attributes, share similar economic, environmental, social and political characteristics. These have implications for how poor men and women live and frequently mean that the livelihood strategies of the urban poor have to be different from those of their rural counterparts. Aspects of the economic, environmental, social and political context in which poor people live are identified below.

The Economic Context

Urban areas can be engines of economic growth (Harris, 1992; UNCHS, 1996; and see Chapter 2). They are the locations for complex networks of activities essential to basic human functions of living and working, and operate by drawing on the skills and labour of their populations (Mattingly, 1995). The actual and perceived economic opportunities available in urban areas mean that they attract migrants from rural areas or less developed urban areas in search of work and a chance to improve their lives. The job opportunities available for the urban poor, whether migrants or city grown, depend on their skills. While migrants tend to be younger, more adventurous and more entrepreneurial than those who remain in their home areas (Harris, 1992; Drakakis-Smith, 1995), the assets of some can be no more than malnourished children and a variety of diseases.

Despite a generally more buoyant economy in urban, compared with rural areas, there are often high levels of unemployment and underemployment. Many urban poor people survive through undertaking a variety of activities which mainly take place in the informal sector. Even when they are fully employed, they produce little towards their social well-being. The most vulnerable, and the least secure or skilled, engage in a variety of marginal, often illegal or semi-legal activities, such as begging, waste picking or prostitution.

Not all those working in the informal sector are poor, nor do all those working in the formal sector avoid poverty. In many countries, such as Tanzania, upper- and middle- as well as lower-level government employees can be poor or on the borderline of poverty. In most cases their monthly salaries provide for only a very small proportion, perhaps only a few days' worth, of their monthly needs. They therefore commonly undertake a variety of additional jobs and activities, mostly in the informal sector, to supplement their incomes. Informal activities generally provide the poor with low cash incomes and insecure conditions. Some exceptions who have large incomes as a result of informal activities include loan sharks, pimps and traders in drugs.

As indicated above, the urban economy depends on cash. Goods such as water, food and housing have to be bought in the market whereas in rural locations access to these resources, for many rural households, may not involve cash purchases. This means that the urban poor need higher cash incomes than most rural households in order to survive (Wratten, 1995; Satterthwaite, 1997).

The urban economy does not function in isolation. It is affected by national and international policies (Douglass, 1998), as Pryke explains:

> *The 'liberalisation of the global economy' has become the dominant force shaping urbanisation in developing countries. City governments have little choice but to operate along the lines laid down by the dominant rhythm of neo liberalism* (Pryke, 1999, p229).

Such global forces frequently have mixed impacts on poor households and in particular on the condition of women (Katepa-Kalala, 1997; Beall and Kanji, 1999; Moser, 1998). Previously, under policies of modernization, formal employment increased as a result of growth in manufacturing industry and an ever expanding public sector. However, since the 1980s, policies such as structural adjustment have affected employment in many areas. Losses of formal manufacturing jobs in some countries and sectors, as well as 'down-sizing' of the public sector, have resulted in large numbers losing their jobs. Some have become the 'new poor' and others are now on the borderline of poverty. Such men and women look for jobs in other areas, such as the part-time service sector or the informal sector (Potter and Lloyd-Evans, 1998; UNCHS, 1996).

Nigeria and Cuba provide good examples of the growing importance of urban agriculture as a strategy for the urban poor to cope with the household insecurity and malnutrition that have resulted from negative global economic impacts. In Nigeria, the poor themselves, in response to their greatly reduced purchasing power, arising from higher prices and reduced incomes following economic structural adjustment, undertake urban agriculture on any 'spare' piece of urban land (Ezedinma and Chukuezi, 1999). Cuba demonstrates how government intervention can greatly improve the livelihoods of the poor. Here urban agriculture is formalized by a government programme of self-provision gardens.

These are provided either on private land or on state land which the gardeners can use at no cost. It is estimated that Havana has over 26,000 self-provision gardens (Moskow, 1999).

The Environmental Context

Poor urban men and women live in environmental conditions that are vastly inferior to the urban middle classes who are located in areas served by basic services such as piped water and sanitation systems. Poor households are forced, because of their low incomes, to make a trade-off between the quality and location of where they live. In order to live in a preferred location with access to livelihood-generating assets at prices they can afford, they are obliged to live in cheap, high density, environmentally poor locations. This means that they are commonly concentrated on polluted land and/or physically dangerous sites which are close to industrial facilities, toxic waste, solid-waste dumps, contaminated watercourses, railway lines and roads, or on hillsides and river plains which are susceptible to landslides and flooding. As a result they suffer from diseases, such as typhoid, diarrhoeal diseases, cholera, malaria and intestinal worms, which are associated with contaminated water and food, poor drainage and solid-waste collection, proximity to toxic and hazardous wastes and exposure to air and noise pollution.

The poor physical and environmental context which is the lot of the poor is the result not only of rapid urbanization and industrialization and limited resources, but critically of a lack of political will of urban and national governments and individuals to invest in much needed infrastructure. In her work on India's politics of sanitation, Chaplin (1999) argues that this lack of political commitment is because:

> ... the middle class has been able to monopolise what basic urban services, such as sanitation, the state has provided. The consequence has been a lack of interest in sanitary reform and the exclusion of large sections of Indian society from access to these basic urban services (Chaplin, 1999, p145).

She develops her argument further by explaining that this is because the middle classes now feel safe because they are protected by modern medicine and civil engineering from the health risks associated with proximity to slum areas. As a result, they, unlike the middle classes of 19th century Britain, do not pressurize the public sector for improved sanitation services for urban areas as a whole. At the same time, in most urban areas, the poor lack the power to influence water and sanitation policy.

Whatever the reason for the appalling environmental conditions in which poor people live, the situation is far from satisfactory when their health is endangered and they are also obliged to devote time which could otherwise be used for productive income-generating work to obtaining daily supplies of potable water or fuel. Such activities may absorb the energies of several family members (Douglass, 1998).

The Social Context

Cities are more culturally diverse and are likely to be less safe and more socially fragmented than rural areas, many of which are more homogeneous and socially stable. Urban neighbourhoods contain a diversity of households which are often fluid in their structure. This social diversity is likely to create tensions and the need for different survival strategies from those practised in rural areas (Wratten, 1995; Rakodi, 1993; Moser, 1996). However, a key asset for both the urban and the rural poor is social capital, which:

> ... refers to features of social organisation, such as trust, norms, and networks that can improve the efficiency of society by facilitating co-ordinating actions. Further, like other forms of capital, social capital is productive, making possible the achievement of certain ends that would not be attainable in its absence. For example, a group whose members manifest trustworthiness and place extensive trust in one another will be able to accomplish much more than a comparable group lacking trustworthiness and trust (Coleman, cited in Putnam, 1995, p167).

As well as local social relations, social capital may also include the wider networks of social relations between poor and non-poor, including systems of patronage – systems which are not always benign, as, for example, with the Chinese Triads and the Russian Mafia.

Strong linkages based on kinship or other ties exist between urban and rural households which may rely on each other for support in response to crises or shocks, when social capital often transcends the city to include wider rural–urban linkages (Tacoli, 1998).

It is widely acknowledged, not only by development professionals but by the poor themselves, that social capital is a valuable and critical resource which contributes to their well-being, especially during times of crisis and socio-economic change (Moser, 1996; Dersham and Gzirishvili, 1998; Douglass, 1998). There is evidence that the existence of informal social networks significantly decreases the likelihood of poor men and women perceiving their household's food, economic or housing conditions as vulnerable (Moser, 1996; Dersham and Gzirishvili, 1998).

It is difficult to identify the general characteristics of social capital in urban areas, as the concept is rooted in relationships between specific individuals and groups, and therefore is tied to specific locations. However, the various theoretical interpretations of urban poverty have clear implications for social capital. One ongoing debate is concerned with whether the urban poor suffer from conditions of social disintegration and community breakdown or whether they rely on strong networks of solidarity between groups and individuals.

Today, urban poverty is still characterized in these dual terms. On the one hand are ideas of urban blight, linking poverty to family break-up, drug use, crime and social disintegration (which would be expected to undermine the social capital of the poor), an idea often linked to studies of the 'inner city' in developed/Northern countries (Wratten, 1995). As explained by Moser (1998, p4):

*Community and inter-household mechanisms of trust and collabor-
ation can be weakened by greater social and economic heterogeneity. This contrasts with the 'moral economy' of rural areas,
where the right to make claims on others, and the obligation to
transfer a good or service is embedded in the social and moral
fabric of communities.*

On the other hand are those writers who point to the existence of strong community and household networks and the importance of 'social capital' as an asset
for the urban poor (Douglass, 1998; Dersham and Gzirishvili, 1998). The reason,
it is suggested, that some families in some contexts have been able to improve the
conditions of their lives has been traced to individual, household, social and
community networks of mutual support. While poor communities may have
internal solidarity they may be excluded from wider social networks. Simply by
living in informal settlements, communities may be excluded from neighbourhood opportunities and access to the services they need.

The Political Context

The urban poor are linked into structures of governance through their dependence on or exclusion from the delivery of infrastructure and services by urban
institutions, as well as through the impact of meso- and macrolevel policies (Beall
and Kanji, 1999; Katepa-Kalala, 1997). As explained in a recent editorial,
municipal authorities have a significant impact on the livelihoods of the poor:

*Urban poverty is much influenced by what city municipal govern-
ments do – or do not do; also by what they can or cannot do. This
is often forgotten – as discussions of poverty and the best means to
reduce poverty tend to concentrate on the role of national government and international agencies. One reason why the role of local
government has been given so little attention has been the tendency
to view (and measure) poverty only in terms of inadequate income
or consumption. As an understanding of poverty widens – for
instance to include poor quality and/or insecure housing, inadequate services and lack of civil and political rights – so does the
greater current or potential role of local government to contribute
to poverty reduction (IIED, 2000, p3).*

The same editorial highlights four matters of commonality and contrast in regard
to how 12 cities do or could address the needs of the poor. Two relate to constraints on the power of municipalities which limit how they can act. First, most
have very limited power, resources and capacity to raise revenues and many have
to refer decisions about local level investments to higher level authorities. Second,
complex political economies influence who secures land for housing, infrastructure and housing. The third relates to how municipalities, through undertaking
inappropriate anti-poverty policies and practices, can harm low-income groups
living in their jurisdiction. Finally, there is a wide range of political structures in
urban areas, some of which are more accountable and responsive to the needs of

urban poor groups than others. The linkages between the poor and city institutions are therefore problematic.

A number of analysts have highlighted the weaknesses of specific local governments which are unable or, because of a lack of political pressure, fail to address the needs of the poor and in some cases actively exclude and discriminate against them. Bangalore, as shown by Benjamin (2000), provides an example of such a 'divided' city where public policy treats the poor inequitably, resulting in disparities between the rich and the poor.

In the light of the inability of the state to deliver, there has been a shift in state–community relationships, with a renewed interest in decentralization, democracy and citizen participation (Banuri, 1998). This is linked both to democracy for its own sake and to state attempts to devolve responsibility to the poor to pay for their own infrastructure and services. 'Further . . . the rise of the NGO movement in many countries has provided substitutes for government action' (Banuri, 1998, p2). Such civil society organizations can have a critical role in urban areas in strengthening democracy, helping to secure inclusive development strategies and directly reducing poverty. It should not be assumed, however, that all civil society organizations play a positive role in urban poverty reduction; some may have a neutral or even a negative impact (Mitlin, 1999; Douglass, 1998; Beall, 1997).

Whether the poor are actively involved in systems of city governance depends on their legal status, which can be ambiguous. For example, as discussed earlier, the high cost of shelter in cities means that poor households are frequently forced to occupy marginal land illegally. As a result, they lack tenure rights and may be excluded from the right to register and vote. Migrant workers also generally lack formal registration or rights, even where they spend long periods residing in cities. In China, for example, where migrant workers are estimated to represent 20 per cent of the population of many cities, they lack all formal rights to public services and are excluded from governance decisions. While the tenure status of many poor urban residents throughout the world has precluded their involvement in urban governance, the situation is better in some places than others. Changes in ethos and policy approaches have meant that some previously excluded groups now have a voice in the decision-making process. Two countries where this is the case are the Philippines and Brazil. In the former 'squatters', or informal occupants, are increasingly integrated into systems of political decision-making, as in the *barangay* system in the Philippines (Meikle and Walker, 1999), while in Pôrto Alegre in Brazil the poor are included in the innovative participatory budgeting process which is taking place in that city (Abers, 1998).

THE URBAN CONTEXT AND ASSETS

Entitlements or rights to access assets which households can then manage and thus transform into an income, food or other basic necessities to secure a livelihood are determined by contextual factors. An understanding of this relationship is essential if interventions are to reduce successfully the vulnerability and strengthen the livelihoods of poor men and women. The urban setting results in a different emphasis for each type of livelihood asset identified by Carney (1998). Thus, for example, natural capital is generally of less significance in an urban setting and financial capital is more significant. Moreover, if there is to be a complete understanding of the significance of each type of asset, it is necessary to distinguish between assets that are significant because they are relatively available – and thus figure largely in the asset portfolios of poor households (for example, common property resources such as rivers or dump sites) – and assets that are significant because they are ascribed particular importance or value by men and women pursuing livelihood strategies and who may therefore make an extra effort to invest in them or seek them out (perhaps credit, education or information, for example).

Many of the specific assets that could be expected to fall under the headings of 'physical capital' or 'economic and social infrastructure' (for example, sewerage, schools, transport infrastructure, banking systems) are not owned by the men and women who use them as livelihood assets. This highlights the fact that the existence of assets alone is not sufficient to promote livelihoods – what is key is their accessibility. This is determined by the entitlements that men and women are able to command, which largely relate to contextual factors (the institutional structures and processes that determine people's legal, social and economic rights).[1] This distinction occasionally leads to confusion about what constitutes an asset and what is a contextual factor determining access to an asset. For example, the existence of schools is irrelevant to people who are unable to use them due to economic or legal factors.

Capabilities, such as health, knowledge and skills, are assets in the most direct form – 'human capital' attributes owned by the individual to whom they apply. However, the ability to build them up depends on access to social and economic infrastructure, which in turn depends on physical distance from, basic information about, rights of access to and the ability to meet the costs of the services concerned. Again *access* is the key. The services and facilities themselves belong individually or collectively to or are provided by others.

Chambers' (1997) distinction between tangible and intangible assets helps to clarify this by distinguishing between material assets that households may own or control and factors which enable them to access resources as assets in themselves. Some examples of assets and their links with urban contextual factors are given in Box 3.1.

THE URBAN CONTEXT, VULNERABILITY AND TRANSFORMATION

Vulnerability, as explained in Chapter 1, refers to the susceptibility of individuals, households or communities to sudden shocks or longer-term stresses imposed by changing economic, environmental, social or political contexts. Analysing the nature of vulnerability involves analysing not only the responses to external shocks or threats to household welfare, but also the resilience of households in terms of their ability to recover from any negative impacts and the speed of that recovery (Moser, 1998; Carney, 1998). Because assets act as a buffer against vulnerability, resilience is closely linked to access to and control over assets. Thus a family employing diversified livelihood strategies and with a number of workers is less vulnerable to, and will recover more quickly from, a household member losing a job than a household with only one breadwinner.

It is now generally accepted that understanding the vulnerability of the poor and the ways that they cope with it is essential for well-informed policy and action (Carney, 1998; Moser, 1996, 1998; Dersham and Gzirishvili, 1998; Watkins, 1995). There is ample evidence to show that many past interventions have contributed to increasing the vulnerability of already vulnerable livelihoods. Internationally conceived and nationally implemented structural adjustment programmes (SAPs), which had adverse impacts on the poor in the pursuit of macroeconomic objectives and locally determined and executed evictions of informal communities, are examples.

SAPs have increased the vulnerability of many poor urban households, through the loss of secure public sector employment, the removal of state subsidies on basic goods and services, and the effects of free market policies on employment. Whether or not these processes have adversely affected the poor depends on how successful state welfare and employment systems were in reaching the poor in the first place. In India, for example, there is evidence that only a small proportion of the funds devoted to poverty reduction programmes ever reaches the poor – meaning that reforms have had more of an effect on the middle classes than on the poor (Harris et al, 1993). However, because the loss of public subsidies may affect the conditions of the poor, more socially sensitive approaches to structural adjustment have been introduced since the late 1980s in an attempt to diminish the impact of subsidy reductions on the poor. This is to be achieved by targeting instead of completely removing public subsidies and transfers, an approach that has been successful in some countries (Mehrotra and Jolly, 1997).

The eviction of informal communities, as explained by Audefroy (1994), can have wider ranging livelihood impacts than just the loss of housing. In the course of being moved to other locations, evicted households may also lose access to key markets or livelihood resources, and the disruption of whole communities poses significant threats to social networks and capital.

This chapter has shown that the existing context of urban areas, which incorporates 'the structures (organizations, from layers of government through to the private sector in all its guises) and processes (policies, laws, rules of the game and incentives) which define people's livelihood options' (Carney, 1998, p8), means that poor men and women are susceptible to a wide range of stresses and shocks. The specific nature of these and the assets available to cope with them vary from location to location. However, it is clear that lack of legal status, a poor living environment and dependence on the cash economy for basic goods and services are at the root of, and contribute to, the insecurity of the livelihoods of the urban poor. It makes sense therefore to focus transforming activities on:

- Ensuring that the poor have recognized and acknowledged rights to assets and the opportunity to access assets, including the right to participate in the governance of the communities in which they live.
- The establishment of healthy living environments, with appropriate infrastructure and services.

• Facilitating access to the support mechanisms (financial and social) and education and training which protect poor residents from the worst excesses of the market and enable them to participate fully in the local economy.

Box 3.1 Assets Commonly Used by the Urban Poor

Financial

Savings	Income derived from the sale of their labour, pensions and remittances from outside the household supply cash flows. When there is a surplus, some of this flow may be saved as financial capital or converted into some other asset, such as jewellery, which can be sold or pawned at a later date (Chambers, 1997; UNCHS, 1996). Mechanisms to facilitate saving can help in dealing with stresses and shocks and building up financial assets.
Access to credit	Affordable credit is important for enterprise development, purchasing shelter or funding some forms of infrastructure. It is also helpful in day-to-day financial management. Until the establishment of the Grameen Bank and other such formal micro-credit institutions, the poor tended only to have access to small community/cooperative credit funds (ROSCAs). The *Gamiaya*, which is found in Egypt, where each household contributes a standard amount each week and has access to all or part of the fund in times of need, is an example. Such funds were not often intended for funding enterprises or purchasing shelter.

Human

Labour	The capacity to work is the main capital of the urban poor.
Health	As the sale of labour is important in the context of urban economies, health is vital in determining the quality of the labour of the poor.
Education and other skills	Likewise, accessibility to education and training provides the opportunity for poor men and women to improve the value of their human capital.

Natural

Natural capital is less significant in cities. Nevertheless the widespread practice of urban agriculture (Rakodi, 1993) means that for some urban residents, land is an important asset. As urban agriculture is often practised on marginal or illegally occupied land, it is frequently vulnerable to environmental contamination or the threat of eviction. In addition, while natural resources and/or common property resources (such as rivers or forests) are generally less significant assets for poor urban residents, some natural resources are used in urban settings. Rivers in particular may be used as a source of water for washing and even drinking, and for livelihood activities, such as fishing or poultry rearing (DFID, 1998). In addition, the health impacts of the environment have an indirect impact on human capital – clean, safe local environments may therefore be considered an asset.

Physical

Housing | Housing is often one of the most important assets for the urban poor as it is used for both productive (renting rooms, using the space as a workshop area) and reproductive purposes in addition to shelter (Moser, 1998).

Livestock | Livestock is generally less important in cities. Nevertheless, many urban residents undertake livestock rearing for the pot or for sale. Even downtown residents may rear small animals such as chickens or rabbits in crowded living spaces (Rakodi, 1997).

Economic and social infrastructure | Access to education and health facilities provides the opportunity for poor households to improve their own 'human capital' and is often the justification for much rural–urban migration.

Production equipment | Equipment, such as machinery, utensils for preparing cooked food for sale and motorized or non-motorized vehicles, is vital to many household enterprises.

Social

Social support mechanisms | The network of support and reciprocity that may exist within and between households and within communities and on which people can call may provide poor households with access to, for example, loans, child care, food and accommodation (Moser, 1998; Dersham and Gzirishvili, 1998).

Information | A key aspect of social networks is access to information about opportunities and problems – one important area is information about casual labour markets and other opportunities.

Source: Developed from Meikle et al, 1999

The positive policy approaches of some local authorities show that such transformations are possible through innovative governance of urban areas. This implies governance which encourages the partnership and participation of all, including the poor, who themselves, through participating in the decision-making process associated with identifying their priorities and the ways in which these can be addressed, are empowered to influence their own conditions. Table 3.1 summarizes some of the vulnerabilities that are common among the urban poor and provides examples of active transforming interventions that might improve the situation.

Table 3.1 *Vulnerabilities common among the urban poor and transforming actions*

	Vulnerabilities	Examples of active gendered transforming interventions
Legal status		
Informal or casual wage employment	Those in wage employment generally lack labour rights. They are therefore susceptible to sudden unemployment and the dangers accruing to unprotected working conditions (long hours, poor pay, insanitary or unsafe conditions) (Potter and Lloyd-Evans, 1998)	• Establish appropriate employment and health and safety regulations (care must be taken not to drive activities underground)
Shelter and land	Urban residents living on illegally occupied land or in informal low-cost rental housing lack legal tenure rights. As such they experience poor housing quality and face the threat of summary eviction. Linked to housing rights, those residents undertaking urban agriculture may also lack legal tenure and risk losing their access to land and crops	• Remove legislation that prevents women inheriting and owning land and property • Regularization of tenure • Identify and target the needs of the poorest
Political rights	Informal residents lacking legal registration may be disenfranchised and excluded from political decision-making and, in addition, may suffer from police harassment and extensive bureaucratic bullying (Wratten, 1995)	• Enfranchise excluded groups • Strengthen CBOs and NGOs • Improve dialogue between communities and local government by establishing participatory inclusive decision-making processes
Services and infrastructure	Lack of legal status may also limit the access of informal residents to basic social services (health and education), or financial services (for example, bank loans).[1] In addition, the prevalence of illegal connections to infrastructure (such as electricity and water) mean that many informal residents are vulnerable to the sudden withdrawal of key services, and may also be fined or punished for illegal use of these services	• Through participatory processes identify and focus on the priorities of the poor • Through partnership with CBOs and NGOs develop accessible and sustainable infrastructure systems

The local environment

Physical environment	Poor living environments often endanger the lives and health of the urban poor, especially where they are forced to live and work in marginal areas because of a lack of cheap alternatives. This creates further vulnerability, as ill health undermines one of the chief assets of the urban poor – their labour (Satterthwaite, 1997)	• Increase the availability of safe and affordable land for the poor • Establish and enforce appropriate environmental regulations
Social environment	The social context in cities may be characterized by crime, fragmentation and other social problems which reduce the ability of households to support one another (Wratten, 1995). Whole communities, because they are living in illegal settlements, may be excluded from access to services. Within communities some men and women may be excluded from livelihood opportunities due to differences such as culture/ethnicity which result in their exclusion from social networks (Beall and Kanji, 1999)	• Where appropriate, legalize informal settlements to ensure access of the poor to livelihood opportunities • Ensure access of the poor to assets by adopting pro-poor processes and access • Strengthen support mechanisms, for example, by supporting CBOs • Design interventions to be inclusive
Dependence on the cash economy	'Free' goods and services, such as common land, water and fuel, are rare in cities. Most of the basic living needs of urban residents must be paid for in cash – making the urban poor particularly vulnerable to market vagaries such as inflation and the removal of government subsidies (Moser 1998). In addition dependence on the cash economy frequently means that poor households are vulnerable to debt (especially where they cannot rely on informal social networks for loans). Borrowing, normally at usurious rates, may lead to long-term indebtedness, with disastrous results such as bonded child labour	• Provide and/or support low cost credit and financial services • Assist communities to improve their livelihoods through establishment of innovative funding support mechanisms for microenterprises • Ensure economic change is managed to minimize the impact on the poor • Provide safety nets • Where appropriate, target the needs of the poorest.

Source: Developed from Meikle et al, 1999

[1] For example, Harris et al (1993, p60) in their study of the labour market in Cuttack, India, cite the case of SUME public microcredit scheme which, though aimed at the poor, was inaccessible to most slum dwellers. Loans were dependent on possession of a ration card. However, these were unavailable to slum dwellers who were unauthorized occupiers of land

NOTE

1   Entitlements are defined as a 'bundle of commodities over which a person can establish command' (Dreze and Sen cited in Meikle and Walker, 1998). Furthermore, entitlements may include access to social services, such as education and health, and earnings from labour (Meikle and Walker, 1998)

REFERENCES

Abers, R (1998) 'Learning democratic practice: distributing government resources through popular participation in Pôrto Alegre, Brazil', Douglass, M and Friedman, J (eds) *Cities for Citizens: Planning and the Rise of Civil Society in a Global Age*, John Wiley & Sons, Chichester, pp39–45

Audefroy, J (1994) 'Eviction trends world-wide – and the role of local authorities in implementing the right to housing', *Environment and Urbanization*, vol 6, no 1, pp8–24

Banuri, T (1998) 'Operationalizing the Sustainable Livelihoods Approach. The Civil Society Alternative', UNDP, New York

Beall, J (1997) 'Assessing and responding to urban poverty: lessons from Pakistan', *IDS Bulletin*, vol 28, no 2, pp58–67

Beall, J and Kanji, N (1999) *Households, Livelihoods and Urban Poverty*, Urban Governance, Partnership and Poverty WP 3, International Development Department, School of Public Policy, University of Birmingham, Birmingham

Benjamin, S (2000) 'Governance, economic settings and poverty in Bangalore', *Environment and Urbanization,* vol 2, no 1, pp35–56

Carney, D (1998) 'Implementing the sustainable livelihoods approach', in Carney, D (ed) *Sustainable Rural Livelihoods: What Contribution Can We Make?*, DFID, London, pp3–23

Chambers, R (1997) *Whose Reality Counts: Putting the Last First,* Intermediate Technology Publications, London

Chaplin, S E (1999) 'Cities, sewers and poverty: India's politics of sanitation, *Environment and Urbanisation,* vol 11, no 1, pp145–158

DFID (1998) *Guidance Manual on Water Supply and Sanitation Programmes*, HMSO, London

Dersham, L and Gzirishvili, D (1998) 'Informal social support networks and household vulnerability: empirical findings from Georgia', *World Development,* vol 26, no 10, pp1827–1838

Douglass, M (1998) 'World city formation on the Asia Pacific Rim: poverty, "everyday" forms of civil society and environmental management' in Douglass, M and Friedman, J (eds) *Cities for Citizens: Planning and the Rise of Civil Society in a Global Age*, John Wiley, Chichester, pp107–137

Drakakis-Smith, D (1995) 'Third world cities: sustainable urban development', *Urban Studies*, vol 32, no 4/5, pp659–677

Ezendima, C and Chukuezi, C (1999) 'A comparative analysis of urban agriculture enterprises in Lagos and Port Harcourt, Nigeria', *Environment and Urbanization,* vol 11, no 2, pp135–144

Harris, N (ed) (1992) *Cities in the 1990s: The Challenge for Developing Countries*, UCL Press, London

Harris, N, Rosser, C and Kumar, S (1993) 'India: slum improvements programme: slum dwellers and the Cuttack labour market', Overseas Development Administration, Contract Reference CNTR 92/1095A, London

International Institute for Environment and Urbanisation (IIED) (2000) 'Editor's Introduction: towards more pro-poor local governments in urban areas', *Environment and Urbanization*, vol 11, no 2, pp3–11

Katepa-Kalala, P (1997) *Sustainable Livelihood Approaches in Operation: A Gender Perspective*, UN Development Programme, New York

Mattingly, M (1995) *Urban Management in Less Developed Countries*, Working Paper No 72, Development Planning Unit, University College London

Mehrotra, S and Jolly, R (1997) *Development with a Human Face: Experiences in Social Achievement and Economic Growth*, Clarendon Press, Oxford

Meikle, S and Walker, J (1998) 'English and Chinese Glossary of Key Social Development Concepts and Terms', a paper prepared for DFID, Development Planning Unit, University College London, London

Meikle, S and Walker, J (1999) 'Resettlement policy and practice in China and the Philippines' ESCOR research scheme number R6802, DFID, London

Meikle, S, Ramasut, T and Walker, J (1999) *Sustainable Urban Livelihoods: Concepts and Implications for Policy,* Research paper for DFID, Cnt No 954482, Development Planning Unit, University College London, London

Mitlin, D (1999) *Civil Society and Urban Poverty,* Urban Governance, Partnership and Poverty WP 5, International Development Department, School of Public Policy, University of Birmingham, Birmingham

Moser, C (1996) *Confronting Crisis: A Comparative Study of Household Responses To Poverty and Vulnerability in Four Urban Communities*, ESD, World Bank, Washington, DC

Moser, C (1998) 'The asset vulnerability framework: reassessing urban poverty reduction strategies' *World Development,* vol 26, no 1, pp1–19

Moskow, A (1999) 'Havana's self-provision gardens', *Environment and Urbanization,* vol 11, no 2, pp127–133

Potter, R and Lloyd-Evans, S (1998) *The City in the Developing World*, Longman, Harlow

Pryke, M (1999) 'City rhythms: neo-liberalism and the developing world', in Allen, J et al (eds) *Unsettling Cities: Movement/Settlement,* Routledge, New York and London, pp229–270

Putnam, R (1995) *Making Democracy Work: Civic Traditions in Modern Italy*, Princeton University Press, Princeton

Rakodi, C (1993) 'Planning for whom?' in Devas, N and Rakodi, C (eds) *Managing Fast Growing Cities: New Approaches to Urban Planning and Management in the Developing World*, Longman, Harlow, pp207–235

Rakodi, C (1997) 'Poverty lines or household strategies? A review of conceptual issues in the study of urban poverty', *Habitat International,* vol 19, no 4, pp407–426

Satterthwaite, D (1997) 'Urban poverty: reconsidering its scale and nature' *IDS Bulletin,* vol 28, no 2, pp9–23

Tacoli, C (1998) 'Rural – urban linkages and sustainable rural livelihoods' in Carney, D (ed) *Sustainable Rural Livelihoods*, DFID, London, pp67-92

UNCHS (1996) *An Urbanising World: Global Report on Human Settlements*, Oxford University Press, New York

Watkins, K (1995) 'Poverty and livelihoods' in *Oxfam Poverty Report*, Oxfam, Oxford

Wratten, E (1995) 'Conceptualising urban poverty' *Environment and Urbanization*, vol 7, no 1, pp11–36

Chapter 4

Seeking an Understanding of Poverty that Recognizes Rural–Urban Differences and Rural–Urban Linkages

David Satterthwaite and Cecilia Tacoli

INTRODUCTION

Recent conceptualizations of livelihoods have proposed frameworks that seek to reflect the diversity and complexity of ways in which different groups make a living. They also highlight how policies must build on the existing strengths of people's livelihood strategies in order to expand their options and choices (Bebbington, 1999; Carney, 1998; Scoones, 1998). These frameworks have been developed from a rural perspective, and while they are sufficiently broad to incorporate non-natural resource-based livelihood strategies – for example, income diversification and rural–urban linkages (Ellis, 1998; Tacoli, 1998), as well as some variations in the nature of the vulnerability context – their usefulness in urban contexts still has to be tested. In particular, it is the frameworks' ability to account for the specific characteristics of the livelihood strategies of the poorer or more vulnerable urban groups and to recognize the non-livelihood related aspects of deprivation in urban areas that needs to be explored. With this in mind, this chapter discusses commonalities and differences between rural poverty and urban poverty, and their implications for policy interventions. The underlying argument is that, while the often neglected sectoral and spatial linkages and interdependencies between urban centres and countryside are often critical both for local economic development and for the livelihood strategies of poor (and non-poor) groups, there are also crucial differences in the urban and rural vulnerability contexts which require careful understanding and consideration.

Developing a livelihoods framework for urban areas is also complicated by diversity in urban contexts, not only between different urban centres but also between different locations within urban centres (especially larger ones). For instance, in any major city there are many differences between the various housing submarkets used by low-income groups in terms of the quality of housing, the quality and availability of basic infrastructure and services, the level of insecurity (including the risk of eviction), the nature of social capital and the accessibility of different income-generation opportunities. So, to understand poverty and the best means to address it, we need to understand how local contexts influence poverty and what changes in local contexts can reduce it. The differences between rural and urban areas is one useful way to emphasize important differences in local contexts, but the diversity among different urban areas (and different rural areas) and the many linkages between rural and urban areas make the dividing lines between rural and urban contexts imprecise.

The chapter first stresses the importance of agriculture for the economy of many urban centres, and the extent to which many urban and rural dwellers rely on access to a variety of urban and rural assets for their livelihoods. It then highlights the differences in rural and urban contexts of relevance to poverty reduction, while recognizing the limitations of the distinction. It then relates differences and commonalities between rural and urban areas to livelihoods frameworks, with a particular interest in locations that are the interface between rural and urban areas, and considers how governments and international agencies can respond more effectively to rural–urban differences and rural–urban linkages.

THE IMPORTANCE OF AGRICULTURE FOR THE ECONOMY OF MANY URBAN AREAS

Reviews of urban change within nations or subnational regions often highlight how many of the fastest growing urban centres are within areas with the most rapid increase in the value of agricultural production (Hardoy and Satterthwaite (eds) 1986; Blitzer et al, 1988; UNCHS, 1996; Afsar, 2000). Many successful cities that now have large industrial, commercial and service economies initially developed on the basis of prosperous agriculture nearby. An analysis of urban change in Bangladesh during the 1980s found that many of the most rapidly growing urban centres were serving areas with rapidly growing rural economies (Afsar, 2000). In the Upper Valley of Rio Negro in Argentina, economic growth and urbanization were driven by the growing of fruit and high-value vegetables and the many forward and backward linkages generated by the growing, harvesting, collecting, storing and processing of these (Manzanal and Vapnarsky, 1986).

Important factors influencing the extent to which agriculture supports prosperous local urban centres include the value per hectare of the crops (the higher the value, the more local urban development); the potential for local value added activities (and the scale of forward and backward multiplier linkages); and the land-owning structure (the greatest stimulus to local urban development generally being if there are a large number of prosperous, relatively small farms growing high-value crops).

Other factors also need to be taken into account. These include the market or institutional arrangements for supplying farmers with inputs (and capital) and for collecting, processing and marketing their outputs. For example, small farmers around Paraguay's capital Asunción are unable to benefit from their proximity to urban markets as lack of access to credit and low incomes prevents them from investing in high-value cash crops or intensifying their production (Zoomers and Kleinpenning, 1996). Commercial crops almost always demand greater outlays on inputs and even on additional labour than traditional subsistence crops and so are beyond the possibilities of low-income farmers. In many countries, markets tend to be dominated by large local merchants who control access to transport and marketplaces and, in many instances, to capital, credit and information, thereby diminishing the incomes of cultivators and often steering much of the value of agricultural production out of the locality (Tacoli, 1998).

There is little evidence of governments recognizing the potential for prosperous agriculture to support urban development. Many booming agricultural towns and cities have been starved of the funds needed to support their economic expansion and to serve the needs of their rapidly growing populations. In some instances, agricultural policies have prevented or discouraged rural producers from diversifying production and trapped them in low-profit crops with few forward and backward linkages, as in many Asian nations where the national policy aimed to ensure that rice production could feed urban populations. Comprehensive rural–urban development frameworks and regional spatial planning in the 1970s and 1980s generally concentrated on trying to expand industrial production in smaller urban centres and often failed to identify and support the potential comparative advantage of each locality. However, this failure to support prosperous agriculture that could in turn underpin urban development is also related to political constraints – for instance, inequitable land-owning structures, limited possibilities for farmers to move to higher value crops and pricing, and marketing structures that keep down rural incomes. While many of these reflect constraints at the national level, the growing internationalization of trade and production is an increasingly important dimension which affects local economies through the rise of international agro-industry and the resulting marginalization of small farmers (Bryceson et al, 2000).

HOUSEHOLD LIVELIHOOD STRATEGIES ALONG THE RURAL–URBAN CONTINUUM

Many rural and urban residents rely on a combination of both rural- and urban-based assets or income sources, and access to these is often essential for the survival strategies of poorer households as well as for the accumulation strategies of better-off groups. For example, urban demand (and markets) can be critical for rural producers, while at the same time many urban enterprises rely on rural consumers. Small and intermediate urban centres are often linked to the surrounding rural settlements by complex two-way interactions which include trade, employment and the provision of services such as hospitals and secondary education (Kamete, 1998). People may move between rural and urban areas following employment opportunities, often on a temporary basis – for example, in Colombia coffee farms provide seasonal work for low-income urban residents who combine it with informal sector activities in the cities during the rest of the year (Hataya, 1992). It is now widely acknowledged that access to non-agricultural employment is increasingly important for rural populations and that in many cases diversification of income sources is an effective survival strategy for vulnerable groups with limited access to assets (Ellis, 1998). Some studies have shown that it is generally farmers with very small holdings who have the greatest reliance on off-farm income.

For rural populations, migration is an important way to increase or diversify income and/or to ensure access to assets. In many cases, movement is temporary and seasonal and complements farm employment. In other instances, one or several members of the household migrate for longer periods of time but maintain strong links with relatives in their home areas. These two-way linkages may include sending remittances from urban to rural areas, but also sending food from rural to urban areas. In addition, investing in property such as housing, land or cattle in the home area is often an important element of a migrant's livelihood strategy, and relatives and kin are those most likely to take care of these assets in the migrant's absence (Afsar, 1999; Krüger, 1998; Smit, 1998). Rural-based relatives may also perform the crucial role of bringing up the children of migrants for whom workloads and living conditions in urban centres can make child care problematic, while urban-based relatives often provide critical support to new migrants. However, linkages between migrants and non-migrants are not always strong, especially where migrants have limited or no access to rural assets such as natural capital, especially land (because of their gender, income, ethnicity, or religious and/or political affiliation), and as a result have little reason to maintain links or invest in their home areas. Nevertheless, there is ample evidence to show that in many circumstances multispatial households are able to secure access to a range of assets encompassing both rural and urban locations, which in turn can provide safety-nets or opportunities for cross-sectoral investment.

Strong rural–urban links at household level mean that increased poverty in rural areas often impacts negatively on urban areas and vice versa. It is assumed that falling crop prices or declining rural production mean a sharp rise only in rural poverty, but these also mean a falling demand for the goods and services provided by many urban enterprises to rural enterprises or households. An increase in urban poverty also implies that there are fewer job opportunities in urban areas for rural dwellers, reduced remittance flows from urban to rural areas, less urban demand for rural products and possibly more urban to rural migration, which could increase dependency burdens in rural areas.

Policies which affect the viability and effectiveness of livelihoods that straddle the rural–urban divide can be divided into at least two broad categories. On the one hand, national and local level policies tend to neglect the importance of migrants' remittances and investment in their home areas. For example, non-residents may not benefit from services, housing loans and relief measures for loss of property in rural areas, even if they consider these as home and their investment benefits the whole settlement. On the other hand, macrolevel economic reform often does not take into account the fact that policies rarely affect only one sector of the economy. Moreover, global liberalization of trade and production is at the root of significant changes in patterns of agricultural production, industrialization and internal and international labour migration. These changes bring new sets of constraints but also potential opportunities and are reflected in the increasing complexity of livelihood strategies which are tending in many places to include a wider range of spatially separated assets and a growing diversity in the form, direction and composition of population movements. The key issue for governance is to ensure that the asset bases of both urban and rural dwellers are protected, and that they are able to influence the setting of policies and the allocation of public resources.

RECOGNIZING THE DIFFERENCES BETWEEN RURAL AND URBAN CONTEXTS

While appreciating the multiple connections between many rural and urban areas, we also need to recognize the differences between them. One of the most important, in regard to poverty, is the difference in the level of income needed to avoid poverty. The methods used by most governments and international agencies to define the income level needed to avoid poverty do not recognize just how expensive essential non-food items are for many poorer groups in many cities.

Many works on poverty assume that the income level needed to avoid poverty is the same in rural and urban areas. Many governments explicitly or implicitly assume this to be the case as they set a single income-based or consumption poverty line to cover both rural and urban households. The World Development Report 2000/2001 also makes this assumption, as it estimates the scale of poverty globally based on a US$1 a day poverty line (World Bank, 2000). National or international income poverty lines are generally based on estimates of the cost of an 'adequate' diet with some minor additional amount added for non-food expenditures (for instance, a 15–30 per cent upward adjustment from the cost of a food basket based on what is considered to constitute an adequate diet).

However, studies of the expenditures of low-income urban households show that many face particularly high costs for non-food items, typically on water from vendors, sanitation from pay-as-you-use facilities, healthcare and medicines (especially where there are no government or non-profit services), housing rent or the cost of land and self-build, schools (especially where government provision is poor) and public transport (especially where peripheral/distant locations are chosen because the land is cheaper and/or households have more chance of developing their own homes without fear of eviction). Of course, considerable care is needed in drawing on this evidence because it usually shows not the income needed to avoid poverty but the high cost of inadequate provision. A low-income family that is paying 20 per cent of its income to rent a tiny room with no piped water supply and no sanitation facility and another 10 per cent on water purchased from a vendor (but at prices that are too high to allow the purchase of sufficient to meet its household needs), is not avoiding deprivation by spending 30 per cent of its income on these necessities. It might need to spend the equivalent of 60 per cent or more of its income to get adequate quality accommodation with adequate provision for water and sanitation. The link between the extent of deprivation faced by low-income households and the quality of government is obvious, since with efficient infrastructure and service provision the income needed to avoid poverty is much reduced. Where there is competent, effective government, poorer urban groups will benefit from better infrastructure and services because of the economies of scale and proximity that urban areas provide. But where urban governments are ineffective and unrepresentative, urban living conditions for poorer groups may be as bad or worse than rural conditions.

One of the great unknowns is how much the level of income needed by a household to avoid poverty varies from place to place. Many (or most?) urban households need a higher cash income than many (or most?) rural households for:

- *Public transport* for getting to and from work and essential services; various studies of urban poor communities show public transport costs representing a significant part of total household expenditure, especially for poorer groups living on city peripheries because only here could they find land sites on which to build housing.
- *Schools*, where school fees and associated costs, including getting to and from school, are higher than in rural areas. Even if schools are free, there may be other costs, such as the cost of uniforms or examination fees, which make it expensive for poor urban households to keep their children at school (see, for example, Kanji, 1995).
- *Housing* for rent or, if living in a self-built house, because access to a land site for the house and building materials is more expensive. Many tenant households spend more than a third of their income on rent. Households who rent rooms or who live in illegal settlements may also be paying particularly high prices for water and other services.
- *Access to water,* and in some instances to sanitation and rubbish collection. For many urban households, the payments made to water vendors represent a major item of household expenditure – often 10 per cent and sometimes 20 per cent of household income – with particular case studies showing even higher proportions (see, for instance, Cairncross, 1990). Many urban households also have to pay for rubbish collection and for access to latrines. There is a growing literature showing the extent to which large sections of the population in many cities have no sanitation facility at all in their home, and public or communal provision is so poor or so expensive that they resort to defecation outside, or what is termed in the Philippines as 'wrap and throw' (this literature is summarized in Hardoy et al, 2001).
- *Food*, as food is more expensive, especially for urban households who have no possibility of growing any food and/or raising livestock.
- *Healthcare*, if this is more expensive in urban areas or no public or NGO provision is available and private services have to be purchased. A study in a 'slum' area in Khulna, Bangladesh, highlighted the very large economic burden caused by poor health associated with poor quality housing, and how the economic cost in terms of income lost from days off work and from medical expenses was greater than the cost of improving the infrastructure to eliminate the health problems (Pryer, 1993).

- *Child care*, where all adult household members have to find income-earning opportunities and child care is needed but there are no low-cost or no-cost solutions, although often this difficulty is solved through reciprocity at community level or leaving older siblings in charge.
- *Payments* to community-based organizations (CBOs), or for bribes to police, or fines when arrested for illegal street vending.

One reason for the underestimation of the income needed for non-food items when setting a poverty line may be the inappropriate transfers of experience from high-income countries. Methodologies for setting income-based poverty lines which link the income to the cost of food were often developed in countries where healthcare and education were free and available to all, where virtually all housing had provision for water, sanitation and drainage, and where there were separate social programmes to allow people below the poverty line access to shelter. In such situations, it is more valid to link poverty lines with the cost of food, since access to adequate quality housing, healthcare and education are either free or guaranteed through other measures.

There may also be many rural contexts where households face particularly high costs. Income-based poverty lines may also need to be adjusted regionally if they are to reflect the income level that is needed to avoid poverty. Much rural deprivation may also be linked more to the unavailability of services than to the lack of income. There are also many aspects of deprivation in both rural and urban areas that are not linked to income levels, including limited or no right to make demands within the political system or to get a fair response, and discrimination in (among other things) labour markets and access to services and justice. Higher incomes do not necessarily guarantee access to basic services, including good quality education, healthcare, emergency services and protection from crime and violence.

There are also important differences between most rural and most urban areas in:

- The mix of assets that best serves poor households in reducing their vulnerability to shocks and stresses – for instance, the economic role of housing as a production base is important for many low-income urban households (see, for instance, Kellett and Tipple, 2000). Housing also provides a location within reach of income-earning opportunities or an income-generating asset in the form of rooms that can be rented out.
- The constraints on low-income households' ability to acquire the kinds of assets that reduce their vulnerability to economic (or health) stresses and shocks.
- The environmental health risks that low-income households face. Large populations, highly concentrated in urban areas with a lack of provision for water, sanitation, drainage and with high risks of accidental fires, produce some of the world's most life-threatening settlements (Cairncross et al, 1990; WHO, 1992).
- The factors that explain the exclusion of low-income households from the infrastructure and services that are essential for health and development. For many rural dwellers, the problem is their physical distance from schools,

health centres, emergency services, courts, banks, politicians and institutions to enforce the rule of law, and the inconvenience and high cost of transport. For large sections of the urban population, it is not distance but exclusion for economic, social or political reasons. A squatter household living 200 metres from a hospital, secondary school or bank, or 50 metres from a water mains or sewer can be as effectively excluded from these as a rural dweller living 20 miles away from such a facility (although the squatter household may have the advantage of being able to tap illegally into a water main). *Proximity does not imply access.*

- The extent and nature of the influence of 'good' or 'bad' governance on poverty. Amis (1999) suggests that one of the most important aspects of a pro-poor urban policy is to stop urban governments inhibiting or destroying the livelihoods and homes of poorer groups. One characteristic of urban areas is the multiplicity of laws, norms, rules and regulations on land use, enterprises, buildings and products. Many of these deem illegal most of the ways in which urban poor groups find and build their homes and develop their livelihoods (Hardoy and Satterthwaite, 1989). As a result, bureaucratic rules and regulations, and formal and informal institutional structures generally have more influence in urban areas on access to employment, land and basic services. They also have a larger potential impact on poorer groups if misapplied, for example, large-scale evictions, harassment of hawkers, access to resources through exploitative patron–client relationships, and contravention of civil and political rights or corruption.

These and many other key differences between rural and urban contexts are not recognized in much of the literature on poverty. For instance, they are hardly discussed at all in the World Development Report 2000/2001 which focuses on poverty (World Bank, 2000).

THE IMPRECISION IN RURAL–URBAN DISTINCTIONS

Having stressed how much rural and urban contexts differ, and how much this affects the nature of poverty and the best means of addressing it, we have to recognize how fuzzy the lines are between rural and urban, not only because of the rural–urban flows and interdependencies noted earlier but also because of imprecise distinctions. Three examples of this are: the imprecision in urban definitions; the number of urban dwellers who work in agriculture; and the similarities in poorer groups' exposure to environmental hazards in rural and urban settings.

The criteria used by governments to define urban populations are not very successful at separating settlements with urban characteristics from those with non-urban characteristics. If the two most important urban characteristics are taken to be a concentration of non-agricultural production (and, by implication, an economically active population that makes a living from secondary or tertiary activities) and a sufficiently large, high-density concentration of people to warrant different kinds of infrastructure and service provision than more scattered and lower density rural settlement patterns, then urban definitions generally do not succeed in separating these. Most discussions of rural–urban differences seem oblivious of the lack of precision in such definitions. Virtually all ignore the fact that the large differences in the ways that governments define urban areas compromise the validity of international comparisons of rural–urban gaps. For instance, it is not comparing like with like if we compare the level of urbanization (the percentage of population in urban centres) of a nation which defines urban centres as all settlements with 20,000 or more inhabitants, with another that defines urban centres as all settlements with more than 1000 inhabitants.

The importance of agriculture for the livelihoods of urban dwellers is difficult to gauge because of the lack of data. Most data on urban occupational structures come from censuses and it is often difficult to get census data on particular cities or these are only published many years after the census was taken. Statistics on urban occupational structures are also unlikely to include most of those who engage in urban agriculture, especially those working part time or outside their work hours, or not registered as working in agriculture. Employment surveys or census forms often require that each person is registered as working in one occupation (Smit et al, 1996).

Although there are significant differences between rural and urban areas in the environmental health context, there are also important commonalities, perhaps most especially in the environmental hazards faced by many low-income groups in urban and rural areas. For instance:

- No water supply fully protected from contamination (especially from faecal matter).
- Difficult access to sufficient water (although for many rural dwellers, this is because of distance, while for many urban dwellers it is more likely to be because of long queues at standpipes and irregular supplies).
- Inadequate provision for latrines.
- High levels of overcrowding within homes made of flammable materials and with high risks of accidental fires linked to the use of open fires, kerosene stoves or lights, or candles.
- High levels of indoor air pollution linked to the use of smoky fuels and open fires, or smoky stoves.

DIFFERENCES AND COMMONALITIES IN LIVELIHOODS FRAMEWORKS

The differences between (most) rural and (most) urban contexts and the extent to which local contexts influence the scale and nature of poverty (and the most effective means of reducing it) caution against any attempt to develop a single 'sustainable livelihoods framework' of relevance to both rural and urban areas. It is worth remembering that the sustainable livelihoods framework developed by Chambers and Conway, on which much of the new thinking about poverty draws, was developed in large part to emphasize the diversity of local contexts (see Chambers and Conway, 1992). Chambers' and Conway's work explicitly focused on rural areas to challenge inaccurate assumptions about rural poverty. It was developed primarily to widen an understanding of the needs of those who obtain their living from agriculture and livestock, and its stress on sustainability was in part because of the dependence of most poor rural dwellers on natural capital, so soils, forests and freshwater systems need to be exploited in a sustainable manner (and poor dwellers' access to them also sustained). This cautions against assuming that the framework developed for rural livelihoods can be transferred to urban contexts where a much smaller proportion of poor groups depend for their livelihoods on access to natural capital. In regard to much urban poverty, there are also limits on what external agencies can do to improve livelihoods for the poor, as agencies have limited powers to change the structural constraints on people's ability to develop better remunerated livelihoods. However, in contrast to most rural areas, there are more possibilities of reducing other aspects of deprivation (including access to justice, law and order, and basic affordable services). A concentration on 'livelihoods', moreover, can miss other key aspects of deprivation, including those that are particularly relevant for many urban households.

Another reason for caution is the extent to which attempts to generalize about sustainable livelihoods frameworks (so they have validity for both rural and urban areas) fail to draw on urban analysis. For instance, there is a rich and varied urban literature stretching back several decades which highlights such sustainable livelihoods issues as: the diversity of livelihood sources for poorer groups (including the importance of self-production for many); the many kinds of shocks or stresses from which they are at risk; the importance of assets for reducing vulnerability (and the role of social relations in this); and the importance of better governance (and of more accountable and democratic government) for giving poor groups more protection (for instance, of their civil and political rights) and more influence on policy and resource allocations. A recent paper that compared the sustainable livelihoods approaches of different agencies claimed that one important characteristic of this framework was that it helped to bridge the gap between macropolicies and microrealities, and to guard against anti-poverty endeavours being conceived and implemented from the national level (Carney et al, 2000). It also suggested that little attention had been given to the manner in which (or where) people live and the resources (assets) used for pursuing livelihoods. While this commentary may be valid for work in rural areas, it has less validity for urban areas, as can be seen in the large and well-established literature on both these themes.

However, the sustainable livelihoods framework has certain key concepts that are valuable for a better understanding of urban poverty (and how to reduce it) if considered within an understanding of each urban area's local context. The stress on more participatory models of engagement between 'the poor' and external agencies and the stress on supporting capabilities (and improving health and education) obviously has universal validity. The importance for most poor households of a stronger asset base both for higher incomes and for reducing vulnerability to shocks and stresses is valid for both rural and urban areas, although the assets that are most useful for poorer groups will vary from context to context. Similarly, the need for an understanding of the causes of vulnerability and the measures to reduce it has universal validity, although the measures that most effectively reduce vulnerability will generally differ (both between rural and urban areas and within different urban areas and different rural areas). Good governance will be important for rural and urban areas, although differences exist in the ways in which policies, institutions and governance influence poverty. As noted earlier, many urban poor groups are particularly vulnerable to 'bad' governance.

COMBINING AN UNDERSTANDING OF RURAL–URBAN CONNECTIONS AND DISTINCTIONS

Thus, we need to evolve an understanding of poverty that:

- encompasses both rural and urban populations and the interconnections between them;
- acknowledges that where people live and work and other aspects of their local context influence the scale and nature of deprivation; and
- recognizes that there are typical urban and rural characteristics that cause or influence poverty, although care is needed in making generalizations because of great diversity between different urban and rural locations.

Table 4.1 illustrates this. It emphasizes some of the most 'rural' characteristics in the column on the left and some of the most 'urban' characteristics in the column on the right. But these should be regarded as two ends of a continuum, with most urban and rural areas falling somewhere between these extremes. Earlier sections highlighted the importance of non-farm income sources for many rural households (including remittances from family members working in urban areas) and the importance of agriculture and/or of rural links for many urban households. For all the other contrasts between rural and urban highlighted in Table 4.1, there are many exceptions. It is also useful to see in the middle of the continuum between extreme rural characteristics and extreme urban characteristics a rural–urban interface in which there are complex mixes of characteristics. For instance, many of the areas around prosperous cities or on corridors linking cities have a multiplicity of non-farm enterprises and a considerable proportion of the economically active population that commutes daily to the city or finds work seasonally or temporarily in urban areas. Many rural areas also have tourist industries that have fundamentally changed employment structures and income sources.

THE RURAL–URBAN INTERFACE AROUND CITIES[1]

Cities generally transform large rural areas around them – for instance, as a result of growing demand for:

- Land for non-agricultural uses (including housing and industries that seek to avoid environmental regulations or need large sites).

Table 4.1 *The rural–urban continuum*

Rural	Urban
Livelihoods drawn from crop cultivation, livestock, forestry or fishing (that is, the key for a livelihood is access to natural capital)	Livelihoods drawn from non-agricultural labour markets, making/selling goods or services
Access to land for housing and building materials not generally a problem	Access to land for housing very difficult; housing and land markets highly commercialized
More distant from government as regulator and provider of services	Vulnerable to 'bad' governance at the local level because of reliance on publicly provided services and restrictive regulation.
Access to infrastructure and services limited (largely because of remoteness, low population density and limited capacity to pay)	Access to infrastructure and services difficult for low-income groups because of high prices, illegal nature of their homes (for many) and poor governance
Less opportunities for earning cash, more for self-provisioning. Greater reliance on favourable weather conditions	Greater reliance on cash for access to food, water, sanitation, garbage disposal, transport to work
Access to natural capital as the key asset and basis for livelihoods	Greater reliance on the house as an economic resource (space for production, access to income-earning opportunities; asset and income-earner for owners, including de facto owners)
But also	
Urban characteristics in rural locations (for example, prosperous tourist areas, mining areas, areas with high-value crops and many local multiplier links, rural areas with diverse non-agricultural production and strong links to cities)	Rural characteristics in urban locations (for example, urban agriculture, 'village' enclaves, access to land for housing through non-monetary traditional forms)

- Land for sport, recreation and tourism (which may expand and diversify employment in many towns and rural areas close to large cities).
- Water for urban uses (often competing with or pre-empting sources previously used by rural enterprises or households).
- More diverse and often higher value foodstuffs (although many of these come from distant areas, especially where transport networks are well developed and there is a demand for foodstuffs for the production of which the local ecology is not well suited).
- Locations where city wastes can be disposed of cheaply, often giving rise to a concentration of households and enterprises based on waste recovery, reuse

and recycling, and with serious environmental consequences, especially for water bodies.
• Building materials (seen in quarries, sites from which aggregate is drawn, cement plants, timber yards, brick-making units, and so on).

These demands also transform occupational structures. The statistics on employment or enterprises in rural areas around cities often highlight the importance of non-farm employment and non-agricultural activities and the coexistence of agriculture, cottage industry, industrial estates, suburban developments, large commercial enterprises, sport and recreation and other types of land use (see, for instance, Jones, 1983; McGee, 1987). There may also be a considerable undercount of non-farm or off-farm employment, if employment surveys only allow each person to be registered in one occupation, so the non-agricultural work undertaken by farmers and agricultural labourers is not registered.

The implications of these economic and land-use changes for poverty are complex and likely to be very location-specific. For existing rural inhabitants, they are influenced by the distribution of land ownership (or rights to use land), the extent to which those with rights to land can benefit from changing demands, and the responsiveness of political and bureaucratic systems to poorer groups' rights and demands. The benefits for those who own (or acquire) land can be very considerable, as the value of land multiplies manyfold as it changes from agricultural to non-agricultural use. Land availability for poor rural dwellers who do not own land – for instance, tenant farmers, share-croppers and those who draw resources from open access or common property resources – is likely to diminish. In many countries, traditional land allocation systems, which had long permitted local populations to acquire land for agriculture, usually become more commercialized and more oriented to urban demands. However, rural households with small or no land holdings may also benefit from increased employment opportunities. In general, those who are most at risk are those who have little or no land, are dependent on wage or casual labour on other farms for part or all of their income and are unable to take advantage of alternative economic opportunities in the urban labour market because households and their members lack skills, contacts, capital or freedom of movement (Rakodi, 1998).

Many farmers with sufficient land holdings benefit from urban demand or more accessible markets – for instance, around Kumasi (Sarfo-Mensah and Adam, 1997) and Yogyakarta (Douglass, 1998). Agricultural production may respond to external demand (including international demand) as urban expansion improves farmers' access to roads, ports, airports, credit and information about market opportunities. It is also common for many low- and middle-income urban households to find better possibilities for acquiring land and building their own homes outside the main built-up area (including possibilities for illegal occupation or purchasing a plot in an illegal or legal subdivision).

Although there is a tendency to refer to the rural–urban interface as 'peri-urban', it is generally more complicated spatially than the term peri-urban implies – that is, it is not simply a circular zone around the built-up area of an urban centre in which rural and urban land uses and agricultural and non-agricultural activities are mixed. For instance, it is common for there to be more intense urban-type development along major transport corridors or around transport nodes. Around larger cities, it is also common for there to be a considerable range of activities and residential communities that are spatially scattered – for instance, factories, quarries, airports and residential communities from which most of the workforce commute. Particular settlements spatially separate from the city's built-up area but within a peri-urban zone often develop diverse employment bases with enterprises strongly connected to the main city. Certain natural features, the preferences of particular landowners or existing road systems can also keep some peri-urban areas undeveloped, while others that are not contiguous with or close to the built-up area become highly urbanized.

One of the most difficult issues in the rural–urban interface, especially around or close to prosperous cities, is how to manage the rapid economic and land-use changes in ways that enhance prosperity while controlling environmental costs, bringing forward sufficient land for housing (so prices are kept down) and ensuring secure livelihoods for poorer groups. Local government structures are often particularly weak and ineffective on the edge of large cities' built-up areas. For instance, they may fall within the boundaries of a large predominantly rural provincial or district authority (whose headquarters may be some distance from the large city) or may be part of a newly formed municipality that remains weak and ineffective. Reviews of growth rates for the districts or municipalities that make up large cities or metropolitan areas often reveal rapid population growth rates in peripheral municipalities or districts where local authorities are particularly weak and household incomes are well below the city average.

In the absence of an effective land-use plan or other means to control new developments, cities generally expand haphazardly. Uncontrolled physical growth impacts most on the immediate hinterland of a city; much of this cannot be described as urban or suburban and yet much of it is no longer rural. Within this area, agriculture may disappear or decline as land is bought up by people or companies in anticipation of its change from agricultural to urban use and the (often very large) increases in land value that result. There is usually a lack of effective public control of such changes in land use and no means of capturing a share of the increased land value, even when it is public investment (for instance, the expansion of road networks) that creates much of the increment.

Unplanned city expansion produces a patchwork of developments, including businesses and high-density residential settlements, interspersed with land that remains undeveloped in anticipation of speculative gain. These include legal subdivisions for houses or commercial and industrial use that have been approved without reference to any city-wide plan. Around more prosperous cities, low-density high-income residential neighbourhoods may also develop, along with commercial developments and leisure facilities for higher income groups. In many cities, especially those with high levels of crime and violence, such residential developments may be enclosed within walls and protected by private security firms – the gated communities or *barrios cerados*. There are usually unauthorized subdivisions as well and where regulation is lax, these may also cater for middle- and upper-income housing. There are usually illegal squatter communities too, which originally located here because inaccessibility and lack of infrastructure gave more chance of not being evicted. In many cities (including Buenos Aires, Delhi, Santiago, Seoul and Manila), this hinterland also contains settlements formed when their inhabitants were dumped there after being evicted from their homes by slum or squatter clearance (Hardoy and Satterthwaite, 1989; *Environment and Urbanization*, 1994). The inhabitants of these settlements may find themselves again under threat of eviction as the physical expansion of the urban area and its road network increases the value of the land on which they live (see, for instance, ACHR, 1989).

The uncontrolled and unregulated physical expansion of a city's built-up area usually has serious environmental and social consequences, including soil erosion which contributes to the silting up of drainage channels, and the segregation of low-income groups in the worst located and often the most dangerous areas. The haphazard expansion of settlements may bring greatly increased costs for providing basic infrastructure, public transport and social services, as new developments spring up far from existing networks. It is also more expensive to provide public transport and social services. Around cities, one often sees the paradox of overcrowding, housing shortages and inadequate infrastructure and services in particular areas, and yet large amounts of land left vacant or only partially developed. Informal settlements are often concentrated on sites that are subject to flooding or at risk from landslides or other natural hazards, especially where these offer the best located sites on which low-income settlers have the best chance of establishing a home or simply avoiding eviction. But these are also sites to which it is more difficult and expensive to extend basic infrastructure.

Environmental health problems may become particularly serious for certain groups within the rural–urban interface, in part because of the increased concentration of population and activities, in part because government controls are less effective, which is one reason why polluting activities locate there and why land subdivisions and developments do not conform to official regulations.

Urban land markets can also disrupt agricultural production and the livelihoods of those who depend on it in areas that stretch far beyond the sites developed for urban use. Conflicts over land-use priorities between urban-based demands and environmental perspectives include the loss of agricultural land, forests, wetlands and other undeveloped sites to industrial estates and residential developments or to golf-courses and country-clubs. These conflicts generally involve social conflicts too, as the livelihoods are threatened by urban-based demands (see, for instance, Douglass, 1998). Kelly (1998) analyses such conflicts in the zone to the south of Manila, describing how national, local and personal forces ensure that land for residential, industrial or other urban developments is favoured over the protection and continued use of highly productive farmland.

Some Conclusions

1 *To understand the particular deprivations that poor people face and the best means to address them, we need to understand local contexts and the diversity of livelihoods within these contexts.* There is also great diversity in local contexts both between different urban areas and different rural areas and between rural and urban areas. Rural–urban differences include sources of income, the range and nature of environmental hazards and the form and relative importance of

different kinds of deprivation. However, the lines between what is rural and what is urban are fuzzy, in part because the economic and spatial boundaries between urban and rural areas are not clear-cut, and in part because of the many rural–urban interlinkages.

2 Most governments and international agencies still act as if urban and rural economies and societies are not connected and as if agriculture only affects rural populations and non-agricultural production only takes place in urban areas. However, strong rural–urban links at the household level (including livelihoods that have rural and urban components) mean that increased poverty in rural areas often impacts negatively on urban areas, and vice versa. As noted earlier, it is common in the literature to see statements that rural poverty increased more than urban poverty or (although less often) urban poverty increased more than rural poverty. But increasing urban poverty will usually mean that there are fewer job opportunities in urban areas for rural dwellers, reduced remittance flows from urban to rural areas, less urban demand for rural products and possibly more urban to rural migration, which could increase dependency burdens in rural areas. There are tens of thousands of urban centres in low- and middle-income countries whose economic and employment base is strongly connected to agriculture, yet most governments and international agencies operate as if agricultural and urban development are independent of each other or in conflict. In addition, rural–urban interlinkages are intensifying, partly because of increased opportunities (for instance, improved transport and communication facilities which increase access to information on new employment opportunities in expanding export-oriented industrial sectors) and partly because of stronger constraints (for example, population pressure on agricultural land but also, importantly, decreasing agricultural incomes). The nature and scale of rural–urban linkages are affected by the predominant production base and urbanization patterns of specific regions and countries. A country's position in global markets is also important in rural–urban linkages.

3 Most national government departments or ministries and international agencies know little about the local contexts in which their projects and programmes operate. Local contexts have a strong influence on the scale and nature of poverty and the most effective means of reducing it. Many studies show the complexity and diversity of urban livelihoods, rural livelihoods and rural–urban linkages, but almost everywhere, the projects and programmes of governments and international agencies are planned with relatively little knowledge of local contexts and what these imply for the best means to address poverty.

4 Appropriate responses to diversity and complexity within each local context. The only possible way to operate effectively, given such diversity between localities and such complexity within each locality, is to ensure that the interventions of external agencies are influenced by the priorities of those who face deprivation and build on their knowledge and resources. Also, it is necessary to ensure the effective functioning of institutions that protect poorer groups' civil and political rights, and to ensure that they have access to basic services. This is likely to require institutional innovation, so that the organizations that allocate resources and plan and implement interventions can respond to local needs and demands. This implies the use of more participatory approaches, less to increase the knowledge of external agencies about local contexts than to allow those suffering deprivation a greater voice in setting priorities, influencing resource allocation, preventing measures that threaten their livelihoods and gaining access to justice. It also means that external agencies must work with and support local organizations that can implement poverty-reduction measures that respond to local contexts and work with disadvantaged groups in participatory and accountable ways. These may include local governments and local NGOs, although with care taken to ensure that the latter are accountable to low-income groups since many NGOs work in ways that are non-transparent and non-participatory (see, for instance, Anzorena et al, 1998). Finally, it implies a better understanding of how best to support the development of a stronger economic base, while ensuring that this maximizes livelihood opportunities for those with the least incomes and assets, despite the difficulty of ensuring pro-poor economic growth when poor groups have few assets and little political influence (see, for instance, Benjamin, 2000). Perhaps only in these rather general principles are there points that have the same relevance for all urban and rural areas.

NOTE

1   This section draws primarily on Chapter 5 of Hardoy et al, 2001

REFERENCES

ACHR (Asian Coalition for Housing Rights) (1989) 'Evictions in Seoul, South Korea', *Environment and Urbanization,* vol 1, no 1, pp 89–94

Afsar, R (1999) 'Rural–urban dichotomy and convergence: emerging realities in Bangladesh', *Environment and Urbanization*, vol 11, no 1, pp235–246

Afsar, R (2000) *Urbanization in Bangladesh*, Institute for Environment and Development, Working Paper on Urban Change, London

Amis, P (1999) *Urban Economic Growth and Poverty Reduction*, Urban Governance, Partnership and Poverty WP 2, International Development Department, School of Public Policy, University of Birmingham, Birmingham

Anzorena, J, Bolnick, J, Boonyabancha S et al (1998) 'Reducing urban poverty: some lessons from experience', *Environment and Urbanization*, vol 10, no 1, pp167–186

Bebbington, A (1999) 'Capitals and capabilities: a framework for analyzing peasant viability, rural livelihoods and poverty, *World Development*, vol 27, no 12, pp2021–2044

Benjamin, S (2000) 'Governance, economic settings and poverty in Bangalore', *Environment and Urbanization*, vol 12, no 1, pp35–56

Blitzer, S, Davila, J, Hardoy, J E and Satterthwaite, D (1988) *Outside the Large Cities: Annotated Bibliography and Guide to the Literature on Small and Intermediate Urban Centres in the Third World*, Human Settlements Programme, International Institute for Environment and Development, London

Bryceson, D, Kay, C and Mooij, J (2000) *Disappearing Peasantries? Rural Labour in Africa, Asia and Latin America*, IT Publications, London

Cairncross, S (1990) 'Water supply and the urban poor', in Hardoy, J E, Cairncross, S and Satterthwaite, D (eds) *The Poor Die Young: Housing and Health in Third World Cities*, Earthscan, London, pp 109–126

Cairncross, S, Hardoy, J E and Satterthwaite, D (1990) 'The urban context' in Hardoy, J E, Cairncross, S and Satterthwaite, D (eds) *The Poor Die Young: Housing and Health in Third World Cities*, Earthscan, London, pp1–24

Carney, D (1998) 'Implementing the sustainable rural livelihoods approach', in Carney, D (ed) *Sustainable Rural Livelihoods: What Contribution Can We Make?* Department for International Development, London, pp3–23

Carney, D, Drinkwater, M, Rusinow, T, Neefjes, N, Wanmali, S and Singh, N (2000) *Livelihoods Approaches Compared*, Department for International Development, London

Chambers, R and Conway, G (1992) *Sustainable Rural Livelihoods: Practical Concepts for the 21st Century*, Discussion Paper 296, Institute of Development Studies, University of Sussex, Brighton

Douglass, M (1998) 'A regional network strategy for reciprocal rural–urban linkages: an agenda for policy research with reference to Indonesia', *Third World Planning Review*, vol 20, no 1, pp1–34

Ellis, F (1998) 'Household strategies and rural livelihood diversification', *Journal of Development Studies*, vol 35, no 1, pp1–38

Environment and Urbanization (1994), Special issue on evictions, vol 6, no 1

Hardoy, J E and Satterthwaite, D (eds) (1986) *Small and Intermediate Urban Centres: Their Role in National and Regional Development in the Third World*, Hodder & Stoughton, London and Westview, Boulder, CO

Hardoy, J E and Satterthwaite, D (1989) *Squatter Citizen: Life in the Urban Third World*, Earthscan, London

Hardoy, J E, Mitlin, D and Satterthwaite, D (2001) *Environmental Problems in an Urbanizing World: Finding Solutions for Cities in Africa, Asia and Latin America*, Earthscan, London

Hataya, N (1992) 'Urban–rural linkage of the labour market in the coffee growing zone in Colombia', *The Developing Economies*, vol XXX, no 1, pp63–83

Jones, G W (1983) *Structural Change and Prospects for Urbanization in Asian Countries*, Papers of the East–West Population Institute, no 88, East–West Centre, Honolulu

Kamete, A Y (1998) 'Interlocking livelihoods: farm and small town in Zimbabwe', *Environment and Urbanization* vol 10, no 1, pp23–34

Kanji, N (1995) 'Gender, poverty and structural adjustment in Harare, Zimbabwe', *Environment and Urbanization*, vol 7, no 1, pp37–55

Kellett, P and Tipple, A G (2000) 'The home as workplace: a study of income generating activities within the domestic setting', *Environment and Urbanization*, vol 12, no 1, pp203–14

Kelly, P F (1998) 'The politics of urban–rural relationships: land conversion in the Philippines', *Environment and Urbanization*, vol 10, no 1, pp35–54

Krüger, F (1998) 'Taking advantage of rural assets as a coping strategy for the urban poor', *Environment and Urbanization*, vol 10, no 1, pp119–134

Manzanal, M and Vapnarsky, C (1986) 'The development of the Upper Valley of Rio Negro and its periphery within the Conahue Region, Argentina' in Hardoy, J E and Satterthwaite, D (eds) *Small and Intermediate Urban Centres: Their Role in Regional and National Development in the Third World*, Hodder & Stoughton, London and Westview, Boulder, CO, pp18–79

McGee, T G (1987) *Urbanization or Kotadesasi – the Emergence of New Regions of Economic Interaction in Asia*, Working Paper, East West Center, Honolulu

Pryer, J (1993) 'The impact of adult ill-health on household income and nutrition in Khulna, Bangladesh', *Environment and Urbanization*, vol 5, no 2, pp35–49

Rakodi, C (1998) *Review of the Poverty Relevance of the Peri-Urban Interface Production System Research*, Report for the DFID Natural Resources Systems Research Programme, London

Sarfo-Mensah, P and Adam, M (1997) *Kumasi Natural Resource Management Project: Highlights of the Findings of the PRA Study on Agriculture*, Bureau of Integrated Rural Development, Kumasi, Ghana and Natural Resources Institute, London

Scoones, I (1998) *Sustainable Rural Livelihoods: A Framework for Analysis*, WP 72, Institute for Development Studies, University of Sussex, Brighton

Smit, W (1998) 'The rural linkages of urban households in Durban, South Africa', *Environment and Urbanization*, vol 10, no 1, pp77–87

Smit, J, Ratta, A and Nasr, J (1996) *Urban Agriculture: Food, Jobs and Sustainable Cities*, Publication Series for Habitat II, volume 1, UN Development Programme, New York

Tacoli, C (1998) *Bridging the Divide: Rural–Urban Interactions and Livelihood Strategies*, Gatekeeper Series no 77, IIED Sustainable Agriculture and Rural Livelihoods Programme, International Institute for Environment and Development, London

UNCHS (Habitat) (1996) *An Urbanizing World: Global Report on Human Settlements, 1996*, Oxford University Press, New York

WHO (1992) *Our Planet, Our Health*, Report of the WHO Commission on Health and Environment, World Health Organization, Geneva

World Bank (2000) *Attacking Poverty. World Development Report 2000/1*, Oxford University Press, New York

Zoomers, A E B and Kleinpenny, J (1996) 'Livelihood and urban–rural relations in central Paraguay, *Tidschrift Economische voor Geografie*, vol 87, no 2, pp161–74

Chapter 5

Living in the Present, Investing in the Future – Household Security Among the Urban Poor

Jo Beall

INTRODUCTION

The chapter begins by providing a response to the exponential growth of frameworks and debate on livelihoods in general. It goes on to make a case for an integrated framework for thinking about urban livelihoods that focuses on the interplay between access and resources, starting at the household level. The chapter then analyses the efforts of poor urban dwellers to survive and cope – the matter of living in the present. It does so by focusing on how urban people in poverty make a living and maintain affordable levels of consumption. It goes on to examine ways in which urban dwellers try to move beyond survival or simply coping and seek longer-term security – the business of investing in the future. These strategies include individual and household investments, such as in tenure security and children's education, investments in social relations of mutual support and organized collective strategies, often around struggles for urban services and area-based improvements. The chapter concludes by addressing the linkages between smaller urban units such as households and communities, and the larger-scale social, economic and political processes operating in and on the city.

REFRAMING URBAN LIVELIHOODS

Since the publication of earlier papers on sustainable rural livelihoods (for example, Chambers and Conway, 1992), there has been rapid take-up of the concept in development studies and practice. This is testimony to the resonance that it has for those concerned to move beyond a money-metric approach to poverty analysis. The livelihoods perspective is appealing too because it promises to capture the dynamic, historical and relational processes that inform the 'diverse ways in which people make a living and build their worlds' (Bebbington, 1999, p2021). For this reason the perspective warrants an important role for the social sciences, well versed as they are in investigating the complexity of social relations and institutional interactions. However, for policy-makers to engage with this rather messy reality, some organizing principles are required. It is for this reason that a proliferation of livelihood frameworks has emerged.

Analytical contributions include Bebbington's (1999) 'capitals and capabilities' framework, Moser's (1998) 'assets and vulnerability framework' and Rakodi's 'capital assets' framework (1999), with the two latter contributions paying some attention to the urban condition. Frameworks can be a useful mechanism for the frequently perplexing understanding derived from detailed social analysis. However, they can also become straitjackets, rigid grids that awkwardly accommodate the micropolitics of everyday life and the realities of policy and planning processes. This in turn renders a livelihoods approach open to criticisms of rigidity and of trying to codify complexity.

Problems include those of language, discipline and analytical starting points. As Whitehead (2000, p7) has argued, there is a problem with conceptualizing social relations, processes and institutions in terms of 'assets' or 'capitals' when using ideas from anthropology, sociology or political economy. This does not necessarily mean eschewing the terms that have become intrinsic to a livelihood approach. Rather it is about preserving their more complex meaning. Whitehead elaborates:

> From the perspective of the latter [political economy], assets are of course relational: systems for access and distribution and systems of exclusionary access are intrinsic to the idea. They become torn out of their relational context in the shift to the language of neoclassical economics to explore livelihoods.

The livelihoods debate would do well to take note of Fine's (1999) recent argument in relation to social capital, that there is a colonization of the social sciences by economics that tends to drive out approaches that are 'inhospitable' to a functionalist and reducible view of social interactions. To this end, therefore, rather than seeing the poor as 'strategic managers of complex asset portfolios' (Moser, 1998, p5), it is perhaps more helpful 'to have a wide conception of the *resources* that people need to *access* in the process of *composing* a livelihood' (Bebbington, 1999, p2022, emphasis added).

As Bebbington has cogently argued, a livelihoods perspective offers an integrated framework for thinking about access to resources. He makes the case that in the context of livelihoods 'the distinction between *access* and *resources* breaks down, because *access* becomes perhaps the most critical resource of all' (Bebbington, 1999, p2022). Although developed in respect of rural livelihoods, Bebbington's emphasis on the relationship between access and resources is particularly useful for understanding the urban context, for investigation of urban poverty processes in cities quickly reveals that proximity to resources means very little when access to them is denied (as noted in Chapter 3). The experience of many poor people in cities is as much of doors closing on them as of open windows of opportunity.

Nowhere is the complex relationship between access and resources more acutely observed than in relation to intra-household dynamics. Yet many livelihoods analysts, including Bebbington, largely ignore the role played by gender and generation in influencing differential access and ability to command resources on the part of individual household members. This stems from the fact that most livelihoods approaches take their cue from the contribution of Chambers and Conway (1992) who do not point up explicitly the gender dimensions of livelihood strategies. It is also due to the fact that current livelihoods frameworks have not fully recognized studies of livelihoods where gender and intra-household relations are intrinsic to the analysis. Contributions such as that by Grown and Sebstad (1989, p941) see livelihoods systems as 'the mix of individual and household survival strategies developed over a given period of time that seeks to mobilise available resources and opportunities'. They provide a strong rationale for incorporating an understanding of intra-household relations into analysis of livelihoods but perhaps lacking the same propitious audience as the sustainable livelihoods framework. As a result, this more nuanced understanding has remained largely confined to gender and development debates.

The problem of gender getting lost in translation extends to the operational sphere as well. It has been noted that UNDP's sustainable livelihoods work has seen gender analysis and intrahousehold relations as being 'somewhat neglected' (Carney et al, 1999, p16) and in the case of DFID it has been argued that:

> *Some important concepts (e.g. power relations, gender concerns) seem to be under-emphasised in the SL framework and are not made explicit in the underlying principles. It is important to use other tools to ensure that these 'missing ideas' are reflected in practice* (Carney et al, 1999, p10).

However, as argued elsewhere (Beall and Kanji, 1999) a livelihoods perspective by definition needs to embrace both productive and reproductive activities and the social relations accompanying them, notably of gender and generation. Thus 'additional tools' to bring back in these 'missing ideas' should not be necessary, as they are in principle intrinsic to the livelihoods perspective itself.

As suggested above, a key issue that is often missing from the various livelihoods frameworks on offer is a recognition of social asymmetries and relations of power, a useful proxy which might include an understanding of how things are distributed within urban households and communities. The advantage of a livelihoods approach that both recognizes intrahousehold relations and starts from an analysis of the relationship between access and resources, is that it makes possible a more layered view of low-income urban households according to their different and most urgent pursuits. These may be to survive, to cope, to seek security or to increase wealth. A consideration in the concluding section of this chapter is the extent to which the policy frameworks in use accommodate pursuits at all these levels. Second, this approach to livelihoods analysis allows for the illumination of processes not only of production and reproduction but also of distribution, for while accessing resources is crucial, sharing them is also important. As Moore (1994) has suggested, it is the mechanisms of redistribution in society, rather than the processes of production and reproduction, which are crucial for understanding the relationship between households and larger-scale socio-economic processes and institutions.

Composing Livelihoods in an Urban Context

Although, as noted in Chapter 1, there is some concern that the term 'strategy' is inappropriate for the very poor, given that it risks overemphasizing the options available and negotiations possible, clearly, urban people in poverty engage in multiple and resourceful efforts at survival and betterment. What follows in this section is an examination of different dimensions of urban household livelihood strategies against a review of relevant literature and debates analysing the lives of the urban poor at work, at home and in the community.

At Work

Conventional wisdom would see a discussion of livelihoods beginning with a focus on people's productive activities. In an urban context these refer primarily to labour market participation, engagement in entrepreneurial activities or involvement in the informal economy. The urban poor are generally to be found in casual wage labour or as workers in the informal economy, with the division between formal and informal economic activity becoming increasingly blurred. However, changes in the world economy such as global trade expansion, increased international competition, economic reforms, technological changes, the precariousness of employment and deterioration in the quality and conditions of work have led to an increase in the number of people contributing to the resources of a single household. As Moser (1998, p4) has pointed out:

> *The highly 'commoditized' nature of the urban sector means that labor is the urban poor's most important asset, generating income either directly in terms of its monetary exchange value through wage employment, or indirectly through the production of goods and services which are sold through informal sector self-employed activities.*

It is this aspect of urban life, the earning of income to purchase the essentials for life, that is generally most flexible, providing the greatest opportunity for poor households to improve their well-being or adapt to a deterioration in life circumstances. It is, therefore, the area of urban livelihoods that has received most academic attention over the longer term.

Investigation of the informal economy, for example, dates back to the mid-1970s, following the report of the 1972 ILO mission to Kenya (ILO, 1972) which made the point that outside the 'modern sector' people were 'not only working but working hard' (Allen, 1999, p3). Despite a strong materialist critique which saw the informal sector as subordinate to the formal sector and global accumulation processes (Arrighi, 1970; Quijano, 1974), by the end of the 1970s a broad consensus had emerged that the informal sector was benign. Activities in the informal economy were seen not so much as the result of evasion or illegality but of necessity (Bromley, 1978). The view that prevailed praised the ingenuity of the poor to survive and sometimes prosper in situations where they lacked resources and access to markets, information and above all connections (Hart, 1973). Reference to this enduring and extensive body of literature provides a useful foundation for any analysis or framing of secure urban livelihoods.

During the 1980s a combination of economic recession and the accompanying reform measures served to entrench the informal economy throughout much of the urban South. Virtually everywhere, the rate of urbanization outstripped the ability of urban industrial and service sectors to absorb the vast and growing numbers of unskilled workers seeking work. Moreover, economic growth strategies were not solving the problems of unemployment or poverty. By the 1990s de Soto (1989) had endorsed informality as 'the other path', and governments and agencies were pointing to the 'creativity and rugged self-reliance' of the working poor (Allen, 1999, p7), so that informality was increasingly endorsed and even tacitly promoted. The drift towards informalization, which, as Meagher (1995) has pointed out, serves multiple interests globally, means that historical debates on the informal sector have never been more relevant than they are today. Moreover, they are crucial for understanding urban livelihood strategies aimed at increasing well-being through use of household labour resources.

A livelihoods perspective, with its emphasis on agency and on what the poor can do for themselves, follows in the tradition of this latter-day approach to the informal economy. In policy terms, if one can talk of 'strong' and 'weak' approaches to analysis of urban livelihoods, then a 'weak' approach would sit comfortably with the view that emphasizes the resilience and agency of the working poor in the informal economy. A 'strong' approach, by contrast, would be concerned with structural constraints, as well as the fact that 'in the context of current "flexible labour" strategies, self-employment becomes a dubious category, which may often include unprotected labour treated as self-employed workers' (Meagher, 1995, p267). A strong approach would be concerned not just about the fate of the working poor, living in the present, but with the perpetuation of their insecurity into the future.

At Home

People best pursue urban livelihood opportunities and embed themselves in urban communities and city life from a secure domestic unit.[1] As noted in Chapter 1, an important issue in defining urban households is to recognize that the process of household consolidation is often a lengthy and dynamic process, particularly for migrant households and younger families. This means that urban households often remain fluid in size, composition and location for a long time, as members seek security in the city. Thus it can be argued that the formation and maintenance of urban households is often in itself a livelihood strategy. Urban household consolidation involves, above all, the accumulation of resources, achieving security of tenure and becoming engaged and networked in area-based or interest-based communities in the city. Moreover, in addition to increasing income-earning activities, the pursuit of livelihoods can include a swathe of responses within households. Such responses are put under severe strain during periods of wider economic stress, as real incomes fall and as welfare services, however inadequate, are replaced by increased reliance on the caring capacity of families and communities. There is evidence that structural adjustment policies, such as liberalization and cuts in social sector spending, at least in the short term, have had a particularly negative impact on urban poverty (Moser, 1996).

It is difficult to generalize about household level responses to poverty, vulnerability and stress because impact and outcomes are always context specific, but common external factors relate to the state of the urban and national economies and the extent to which these are incorporated into the global economy. There are an almost infinite number of variables that determine the responses of poor urban households themselves. Their strategies depend, for example, on individual characteristics of household members, including gender, age and human capital endowments. They also depend on household profiles, such as size, composition, the status of different members and the stage of the family life cycle.

City-level studies (Beall, 1995; Beall, Crankshaw and Parnell, 2000; Chant, 1991, 1997; Kanji, 1995; Moser, 1996; Thorbek, 1987, 1994) have revealed a range of social responses to economic crises and austerity. In terms of labour force participation, these include the long-term or seasonal out-migration of men to work abroad or in rural areas, and more women and children in the family taking up paid work. Those household members already in employment work longer hours and older people work for years longer than they should. Changes in production processes have in some contexts seen a decline in regular male employment, while in many places women have entered the labour market in increasing numbers. The involvement of children in household strategies to increase resources is particularly worrying and, for many urban children, this involves long hours of labour and life lived on the streets (Szanton Blanc, 1994). For 70 per cent of urban children in the developing world this means conditions of continuous poverty, inadequate housing and food, lack of basic services and an institutional and legislative framework that is rarely supportive and often hostile to them (Curtin et al, 1997).

Household responses also extend to strategies once removed from urban labour markets, such as changing expenditure patterns, reducing overall consumption, changes in family diet, increased indebtedness and a rise in self-production of food, shelter, child care and healthcare. Efforts to hold back on consumption include reducing expenditure on housing (squatting rather than renting), on transport (walking rather than catching a bus or train), or on clothing (less quantity, quality and diminished choice). Other instances of belt-tightening exercises reported are labour-intensive solutions to housework and reducing costs by use of fossil fuels for cooking, even in electrified areas. Even more harmful are strategies associated with reduced consumption of food, resulting in child malnutrition, and social services, such as avoiding seeking medical treatment or keeping one or more children out of school.

Many households engage in risk-spreading behaviour, such as diversifying income sources. Specific urban strategies include increasing household size to enhance income (by providing assistance with child care or domestic work) or to reduce expenditure (co-residence of different household units). The practice of *allegamiento* (more than one household sharing the same house or site) is common in parts of Latin America. Household strategies can also involve reducing the number of dependants in the household, as in Southern Africa, where child-fostering arrangements are common, calling on family members in villages (Jones, 1994) or the migration of older urban dwellers back to the rural areas (Bozzoli, 1991). Such arrangements support the argument that the livelihood strategies of urban households cannot be seen in isolation from their wider context. As Murray (1981) argues, the notion of the nucleated urban household ignores both the developmental cycle of household units and the urban linkages of household members and their kinsfolk (Tacoli, 1998).

The intergenerational strategies employed by urban households are not only about surviving but are also about investment in security and human capital. Spacing births or ceasing childbearing altogether is a strategy to reduce consumption and is more a feature of urban than rural areas. However, where a thriving market for child labour exists, along with the absence of state pensions, it may still be strategic, in urban as much as in rural areas, to have more children to increase family income and security in old age. Either way, policy-makers would do well to heed Murray's caution (1981) against lamenting the growth of nuclear households in urban areas and glorifying the extended family in the countryside. To do so, he argues, falls into the trap of seeing the latter in a residual sense as 'something that allegedly accommodates everyone (the sick, the unemployed, older people) in default of decent wages or social security arrangements'.

In urban households, strategies to achieve long-term security involve investment in human capital and commonly this is directed at the education of children. When this is not possible for all the children in a household, a common pattern in poorer families is for older children to leave school early and engage in paid work. Often this is to fund a younger sibling in completing primary or secondary education, the hope being that the younger child may find a better job in due course and bring greater benefits to the household in the long-run. In many contexts girl children leave school very young. This is often so they can help with the increased burden of domestic chores arising out of adult women of the household going to out to work or additional members joining the household. Alternatively, girls drop out of school because in patrilocal cultures investment in girls' education is seen as wasteful, as they are regarded only as temporary members of a household.

In cultural contexts where dowry or bride-wealth are common, opting for consensual unions to avoid the costs associated with getting married is sometimes an option. However, the tenacity with which the urban poor hold on to conventions such as marriage is testimony to the perception of their importance in maintaining social probity, respect and networks of support and reciprocity. For example, although women-headed households in the South are more common in urban than in rural areas, in much of South Asia women still go to extraordinary lengths to enter into or remain in conjugal relationships for the sake of respectability. To do so, they may endure domestic violence, abuse by in-laws or frivolous expenditure of scarce resources by their spouses (Thorbek, 1994). However, lone parents face less stigmatization in some contexts and here Chant (1997) asserts that single-parent households are often the outcome of a positive choice by women. Whether or not this is the case, she shows that family life can be more secure and stable for women-headed households than those headed by men in cities, and that in such households income and resources may be distributed more equitably among household members.

It is common to portray older urban dwellers as a burden and a drain on their families' resources and indeed they often are regarded as such. However, commensurate with a livelihoods approach, there is an emerging literature that does not see older people as a liability but that emphasizes their contribution to development (Box 5.1).

BOX 5.1 *OLDER PEOPLE AND THEIR HOUSEHOLDS*

In his study of older people in the shantytowns of Buenos Aires, for example, Lloyd-Sherlock (1997) shows that older people significantly augment household well-being and urban life. Rather than portraying older people as the passive recipients of economic support from pensions, social security systems or their families, he paints a picture of their pensions providing a valuable source of guaranteed income in households where younger members are forced to rely on casual or poorly remunerated work. Work in South Africa also points up the important role played in particular by older women, in terms of supplementing household income and providing domestic work, child care and security, simply by being at home all day in crime-rife areas.

This more up-beat perspective on older people reinforces the value of acknowledging the importance of intra-household relationships in livelihoods analysis and of recognizing that the struggle for urban livelihoods involves decisions not only about production but about household-level consumption and distribution as well. However, it should not distract from the fact that older people often face terrible abuse and neglect or that they have very specific welfare needs of their own. This latter perspective opens up the opportunity for addressing the issue of gate-keeping and power relations, whether around household consumption, community-level distribution or access to city-wide resources.

Care in the Community

Development debates evolving mainly out of a rural context have long explored the prospects for broader mutual support strategies. Scott's (1976) 'moral economy' thesis saw rural communities insure collectively against social risk and many authors since have explored examples of sharing, risk-pooling and reciprocal relations. There has been a tendency to argue that mutuality and social networks are not as entrenched in urban contexts and that institutions of social support are, as a result, less robust. Reasons offered have ranged from length of residence in the city or degree of commitment to urban life, to pernicious corruption and clientelism, or the prevalence of violence and crime (Beall, 1997a; Moser, 1996; Moser and Holland, 1997; Rakodi, 1999). This view risks falling prey to the same essentialism about which Murray (1981) cautions with respect to seeing rural households as eternally supportive and repositories of social care. However, as González de la Rocha (1994, p13) has argued in respect of poor urban dwellers in Mexico City, '. . . it is precisely because of poverty that individual survival is not possible and people need to rely on others in their house-holds and their social networks to make ends meet'.

Thus urban livelihood systems can and do involve wider cooperative behaviour beyond the household. Many examples of urban norms of reciprocity parallel those to be found in rural areas, such as gift exchanges and voluntary labour pooling. Others are more closely linked to urban lifestyles, such as the provision of rent-free accommodation. As in rural areas, such acts may be motivated purely by altruism or may be seen as social credit. Moreover, social networks can be just as asymmetrical in urban as in rural areas and there are many examples of vulnerable groups trying to increase their security within the urban system by entering into dependency relations with social superiors such as labour touts or middle dealers (Beall, 1997b; Sicular, 1992). Sometimes urban social groupings mobilize around rural linkages and identities, such as home-town associations or job-securing networks (Breman, 1985; Cohen, 1969). Alternatively, collective action in cities can take on a specifically urban mantle (Box 5.2).

BOX 5.2 *THE COMMUNITY SPHERE: SOCIAL NETWORKS AND COLLECTIVE ACTION*

In Colombo, traditional funeral societies (*Maranadara Samiti*) and savings groups (*sittu*) exist alongside sports clubs, trade unions and community development organizations (Fernando et al, 1999). In Bangalore, customary savings mechanisms such as *chit* funds play a critical role in the livelihood structures of poor groups and feed into complex informal land markets (Benjamin and Bhuvanes-hari, 1999). In Johannesburg there are a range of collective strategies adopted by people who want to survive, cope and modestly prosper, such as membership of religious organizations and informal savings clubs (*stokvels*), bulk-buying schemes and communal eating arrangements (Beall, Crankshaw and Parnell, 2000).

When these communal strategies extend into concerted action, this is often around efforts to get access to land, housing or infrastructure such as electricity, water and other basic services. Moser (1992, p24) has argued in relation to Guayaquil, Ecuador, for example, that frequently it is to obtain basic infra-structural services in squatter settlements that community organizations are first formed. She goes on to say that although '. . . women do not necessarily see themselves as natural leaders they play an important role in the formation of such organisations'. It has been pointed out with reference to the celebrated communal kitchens in Lima, Peru, that collective action at community level, particularly by women, does not link usefully into the broader political picture because such organizations are geared towards meeting immediate needs and tend not to be transformative (Barrig, 1996). However, this is a contested view and Lind and Farmelo (1996) have argued that some affiliates to the communal kitchen movement have played an effective role in community- and local-level politics. What is clear is that without coordination (coalitions) or aggregation (scaling up) and a sustained advocacy focus, community-based initiatives and concerted action cannot on their own influence policy (Beall and Kanji, 1999).

Moreover, the point here is no more to romanticize communities than to romanticize households. Cites are not cosy places and care in the community can be hard to find. Reciprocity entails obligations, often not equal in outcome, and can result in relationships that are not always harmonious. They can involve, for example, the exploitation of child labour, the prostitution of women and life-long indebtedness or labour bondage (Beall, 1997a). People become embroiled in social networks, such as mafias, criminal syndicates and street gangs, which engage in harmful and anti-social activities. In terms of the impact of these networks and behaviours, in a study of urban violence in Jamaica, Moser and Holland (1997) show how social capital can be eroded through their effect. It is up for debate whether the alcoholism, drug-addiction, prostitution, gambling and crime in which unemployed people can get involved are to be regarded as specific strategies for coping with extreme adversity or merely as the undesirable and perhaps inevitable outcomes of urban poverty. We may not wish to regard such activities as sustainable urban livelihoods, but they do persist over a long time. One reason for this is that they constitute not only economic dealings but also social exchanges, which in turn constitute considerable investment in social capital, however perverse.

Even social norms and networks, typically understood in a livelihoods framework as social capital, that are benign, helpful or redistributive need not necessarily be sustainable, especially in the case of very poor households and communities. As an elderly informant said in the context of research on social networks in urban Pakistan, 'If one man is hungry and does not have any food then how can he help another hungry man?' (Beall, 1995, p435). As I have argued elsewhere:

> *... from a policy perspective, it is important to remain clear that reciprocal relations among the very poorest are particularly fragile and provide an unstable base for long-term security. For social networks to constitute viable and sustainable survival strategies, people require at least a minimum degree of economic stability, social respect and organisational capacity* (Beall, 1995, p435).

Thus acknowledging the importance of social resources, or what in a livelihoods perspective is referred to as social capital, should not imply that policy-makers and planners be allowed to rely exclusively on the initiatives of poor urban dwellers for solutions to problems of poverty and social development in the city.

DRAWING THE LINKS

This concluding section addresses the linkages between smaller urban units such as households and communities and the larger-scale social, economic and political processes operating in and on the city. It does so by looking at macro–micro linkages in terms of the livelihood strategies of the urban poor respectively at work, at home and in the community.

Over the last half century the world economy has changed drastically, deeply affecting cities of the South. The changes that have taken place have been characterized as globalization, the physical manifestation of which Mittelman (1994, p427) has defined as '. . . the spatial reorganization of production, the interpenetration of industries across borders, the spread of financial markets, the diffusion of identical consumer goods to distant countries'. Some cities have found a niche for themselves in this changing global economy, while others are still seeking a viable place in an increasingly unequal world. Many fail because they maintain relatively weak positions within world markets and are bypassed by the digital highways that connect the older major cities (Sassen, 1991), leading Rakodi (1998) to conclude for the case of Africa, for example, that no 'world city' as yet exists on the continent.

Some in poor urban households have found a niche for themselves too, often by turning their homes into sweatshops as they participate in the global economy as homeworkers or by taking advantage of jobs opening up in export-oriented manufacturing industry. Overall, however, the impact of global processes on the lives of ordinary people has made the struggle for urban livelihoods more competitive and precarious. The impact of the phasing out of the Multi-Fibre Arrangement in Bangladesh serves by way of illustration (Box 5.3).

BOX 5.3 *GLOBAL COMPETITIVENESS AND HOUSEHOLD LIVELIHOOD STRATEGIES: THE GARMENTS INDUSTRY IN DHAKA, BANGLADESH*

The impact of the phasing out of the Multi-Fibre Arrangement between 1995 and 2005 in Bangladesh is to remove the quota advantage held by the Dhaka-based Bangladesh garments industry, leaving it at the mercy of the free market and competition from other garment producers. In such an event the industry may be tempted to manipulate its remaining comparative advantage by reducing the wages of the young single women who make up its labour force or by cutting production. If such employees lose their jobs, there is nothing else for them and the families they help to support (Beall, 2000, p434). As Seabrook (1996, p130) has argued, Dhaka is part of a global putting-out system and yet these young women do not know that they are in competition with workers in the cities of Indonesia, Thailand, India or Vietnam.

Another key area of significance for urban households has been recession, economic crisis and the overriding concern of international financial institutions and many governments since the 1980s to ensure macroeconomic stability and address budget deficits by cutting public expenditure and focusing on economic growth. The qualitative impact of these macrolevel trends at the household level has been discussed above and some of the linkages are elaborated here, although it is difficult to quantify the impact of macroeconomic, fiscal and monetary policies on the poor, both because they are not a heterogeneous group and because of the complexity of the effects, both direct and indirect, which change over time (Killick, 1995).

In many countries, adjustment policies involved a redefinition of the role of the state, which in turn impacted on mesopolicies linked to fiscal and public expenditure. In terms of public expenditure, some sectoral policies were impacted more than others. An important impact in terms of household strategies was a much reduced emphasis on direct poverty reduction and a reliance on the market to promote economic growth, with the benefits trickling down to low-income groups. Mainstream development agencies moved towards more residual approaches to social policy, supporting limited safety nets, usually basic income-maintenance programmes, to protect the most vulnerable individuals or households against adverse outcomes, the rationale being to compensate for retrenchments and cutbacks in the social sector. These policies were expected to exacerbate poverty in the short-term, until export-oriented growth and liberaliza-tion provided the impetus for poverty reduction. Urban populations were seen to be more affected by structural adjustment because they were more integrated into cash and wage economies and more dependent on food and other social sector subsidies which were lifted. Retrenchment packages were specifically directed to urban workers who had lost jobs, sometimes defined as the 'new poor' (Beall and Kanji, 1999).

The 1990s also saw trends in policy implementation, first towards com-munity participation and then towards decentralization. The latter in particular implied a shift in the role of central governments, from direct providers of services to regulators and enablers (World Bank, 1991), with responsibilities being shifted to local (public and private) levels. While decentralization has the potential to provide new opportunities for previously excluded groups to participate in and to gain access at the local level, much depends on local power structures and the mobilization of resources remains a critical problem. Rakodi (1999, p323) has pointed out that:

> At subnational (regional/local) levels, the incidence and character-istics of poverty result from the interaction between macro- or meso-processes and policies and the particular circumstances of regional/local economies, settlements and households.

As argued elsewhere (Beall and Kanji, 1999), too often the shifts have implied transferring the costs of social reproduction to individual households and there-fore to women.

Much of the research on macro–micro linkages in relation to urban poverty has focused on impact – in other words, how large-scale processes determine or constrain the workings of smaller units such as households and communities. Less attention has been paid to how smaller units influence larger-scale economic, social and political processes (Beall and Kanji, 1999). An important contribution of the livelihoods perspective, with its emphasis on the agency of the urban poor, might be to demonstrate how initiatives by less powerful and microlevel groups in society can and do influence decisions, access and the allocation of resources at higher levels.

To illustrate this point, an obvious example for the urban context can be found in relation to rural–urban migration. Despite sometimes draconian efforts on the part of governments – for example, in China and South Africa – to curb population movement, they have been largely unsuccessful. In South Africa, the infamous 'pass laws' were abandoned in the late 1980s as much because they were being so blatantly flouted as due to a change of political heart on the part of the apartheid regime. The question is whether the flouting of migration controls or the illegal construction of houses are isolated reactions or whether collectively they have a wider impact. The answer depends on context. For example, people in a minority community in Karachi, Pakistan, have repeatedly seen their homes bulldozed and torched over the last decade, but have doggedly rebuilt them on the land they have occupied for almost 30 years and to which they have rights (Beall, 1995). However, there is no evidence to suggest that the political or policy environments have changed in respect of their status in society or their security of tenure. Writing on urban Brazil, Scheper-Hughes (1992, pp472–473) emphasizes the futility of collective action by the urban poor:

> *Their daily lives are circumscribed by an immensely powerful state and by local economic and political interests that are openly hostile to them ... It is too much to expect the people of the Alto to organize collectively when chronic scarcity makes individually negotiated relations of dependency on myriad political and personal bosses in town a necessary survival tactic ... Staying alive in the shantytown demands a certain 'selfishness' that pits individuals against each other and that rewards those who take advantage of those even weaker.*

By contrast, Cole's (1987) touching account of the struggles of the Crossroads squatter community in Cape Town under apartheid and subsequent events tells a different story. Cole testifies to the vanguardist role of women in this squatter settlement, in securing for themselves and their families a permanent place in the city.

CONCLUSION

An essential point of departure for understanding livelihoods in any context must be the analysis of social relations in households and the communities of which they are a part. People's working lives feed off and into complex webs of domestic and local-level social relations. These in turn determine how they gain access to resources and relate to the wider economy and higher level social and political institutions.

The great value of a livelihoods perspective as it has emerged in development theory and practice is that it has opened up the discursive space for addressing in interdisciplinary and policy relevant terms, the multiple, fluid and often convoluted ways that people manage their lives. What this chapter seeks to emphasize is that household relations provide an essential starting point for understanding the attempts by disadvantaged and less powerful groups to get by, to advance themselves and to influence policy agendas. Moreover, differences based on gender and generation, among others including urban identity, are important to factor into any analysis of livelihoods, as they encode ideas about the needs of poor people and their rights of access in the city (Beall, 1997b).

The 'urban poor' cannot be viewed as an undifferentiated mass. Especially when understood in terms of dynamics and processes, among people classified as low-income or poor, there are those for whom actual day-to-day survival is a struggle, those who cope, those who attain security and those who prosper. And yet a potential danger with the livelihoods perspective is that it aggregates these groups, resulting in policies that build only on their proactive energy and endeavour. Urban people in poverty are indeed active agents who respond to social and economic change and sometimes effect it. But there is also a problem in the livelihoods approach taking as its analytical starting point the 'wealth of the poor', even if the vulnerability context is acknowledged analytically and addressed in policy terms – for example, through compensatory measures.

What the livelihood perspective does not address is the inefficiency of poverty. Poverty is everywhere expensive (buying things in small quantities always costs more), time-consuming (standing in queues for bargains takes many hours out of women's days), a waste of people's creativity and potential or, to put it another way, a waste of human and social capital. Lastly, and this bears repeating, the inefficiency of poverty is uneven in its impact, not least across gender and generation, reinforcing existing social relations based on unequal access to and control over resources. As long as this is the case and without broad and effective redistributive policies, such as national and citywide transfers and investment in accessible and affordable infrastructure, we have to ask whether a lasting reduction in poverty can be achieved. The policy challenge for promoting secure urban livelihoods and longer-term improvements in well-being is to ensure that people are not simply condemned to living forever in the present, but that they can invest in their futures.

NOTE

1   How these units are defined and analysed presents difficulties for both rural and urban contexts, although the concept of 'household' is most commonly used and is employed here as a matter of convenience. It is recognized, nevertheless, that it is an analytical category and covers a wide range of residential forms, groupings of people and functions. The concept 'family' is used to imply a broader and more complex set of relationships and normative assumptions

REFERENCES

Allen, T (1999) 'From "informal sectors" to "real economies": changing conceptions of Africa's hidden livelihoods', mimeo
Arrighi, G (1970) 'International corporations, labour aristocracies and economic development in Tropical Africa', *Journal of Modern African Studies*, vol 6, pp141–169
Barrig, M (1996) 'Women, collective kitchens and the crisis of the state in Peru', in Friedman, J et al (eds) *Emergencies, Women's Struggles for Livelihood in Latin America*, UCLA Latin American Studies Center, Los Angeles
Beall, J (1995) 'Social security and social networks among the urban poor in Pakistan', *Habitat International*, vol 19, no 4, pp427–445

Beall, J (1997a) 'Assessing and responding to urban poverty: lessons from Pakistan', *IDS Bulletin*, vol 28, no 2, pp58–67

Beall, J (1997b) 'Thoughts on poverty from a South Asian rubbish dump: gender, inequality and household waste', *IDS Bulletin*, vol 28, no 3, pp73–90

Beall, J (2000) 'Life in the cities', in Allen, T and Thomas, A (eds) *Poverty and Development into the 21st Century*, Oxford University Press, Oxford, pp 425–442

Beall, J, Crankshaw, O and Parnell, S (2000) 'The causes of unemployment in post-apartheid Johannesburg and the livelihood strategies of the poor', *Tijdschrift voor Economische en Sociale Geografie*, vol 91, no 4, pp379–396

Beall, J and Kanji, N (1999) *Households, Livelihoods and Urban Poverty*, Urban Governance, Partnership and Poverty WP 3, International Development Department, School of Public Policy, University of Birmingham, Birmingham

Bebbington, A (1999) 'Capitals and capabilities: a framework for analyzing Peasant viability, rural livelihoods and poverty', *World Development*, vol 27, no 12, pp2021–2044

Benjamin, S and Bhuvaneshari, R (1999) *Bangalore*, Urban Governance, Partnership and Poverty WP 15, International Development Department, School of Public Policy, University of Birmingham, Birmingham

Bozzoli, B (1991) *Women of Phokeng, Consciousness, Life Strategy and Migrancy in South Africa, 1900–1983*, Ravan Press, Johannesburg

Breman, J (1985) *Of Peasants, Migrants and Paupers: Rural Labour Circulation and Capitalist Production in West India*, Oxford University Press, Delhi

Bromley, R (1978) 'The urban informal sector: why is it worth discussing?' *World Development*, vol 6, no 9/10, pp1033–1039

Carney, D with Drinkwater, M, Rusinow, T, Neefjes, K, Wanmali, S and Singh, N (1999) *Livelihoods Approaches Compared*, DFID, London

Chambers, R and Conway, G (1992) *Sustainable Rural Livelihoods: Practical Concepts for the 21st Century*, IDS Discussion Paper 296, Institute of Development Studies, University of Sussex, Brighton

Chant, S (1991) *Women and Survival in Mexican Cities: Perspectives on Gender, Labour Markets and Low-income Households*, Manchester University Press, Manchester

Chant, S (1997) *Women-headed Households: Diversity and Dynamics in the Developing World*, Macmillan, Basingstoke and London

Cohen, A (1969) *Custom and Practice in Urban Africa: A Study of Hausa Migrants in Yoruba Towns*, Routledge and Kegan Paul, London

Cole, J (1987) *Crossroads, The Politics of Reform and Repression, 1976–1986*, Ravan Press, Johannesburg

Curtin, M, Hossain, T and Verghese-Choudhury, A (1997) 'Children living, learning and working in the city', in J Beall (ed) *A City for All*, Zed Books, London, pp66–78

de Soto, H (1989) *The Other Path: The Invisible Revolution in the Third World*, Harper & Row, New York

Fernando, A, Russell, S, Wilson, A and Vidler, E (1999) *Colombo*, Urban Governance, Partnership and Poverty WP 9, International Development Department, School of Public Policy, University of Birmingham, Birmingham

Fine, B (1999) 'The World Bank and social capital: a critical skinning', mimeo

González de la Rocha, M (1994) *The Resources of Poverty, Women and Survival in a Mexican City*, Blackwells, Oxford

Grown, C A and Sebstad, J (1989) 'Introduction: toward a wider perspective on women's employment', *World Development*, vol 17, no 7, pp937–952

Hart, K (1973) 'Informal income opportunities and urban unemployment in Ghana', *Journal of Modern African Studies*, vol 11, no 1, pp61–89

ILO (1972) *Employment, Incomes and Equity: A Strategy for Increasing Projective Employment in Kenya*, International Labour Organization, Geneva

Jones, S (1994) *Assault on Childhood*, Witwatersrand University Press, Johannesburg

Kanji, N (1995) 'Gender, poverty and economic adjustment in Harare, Zimbabwe', *Environment and Urbanization*, vol 7, no 1, pp37–55

Killick, T (1995) 'Structural adjustment and poverty alleviation: an interpretative survey', *Development and Change*, vol 26, no 2, pp305–331

Lind, A and Farmelo, M (1996) *Gender and Urban Social Movements: Women's Community Responses to Restructuring and Urban Poverty*, UNRISD Discussion Paper 76, United Nations Research Institute for Social Development, Geneva

Lloyd-Sherlock, P (1997) *Old Age and Urban Poverty in the Developing World, the Shanty Towns of Buenos Aires*, Macmillan, Basingstoke and London

Meagher, K (1995) 'Crisis, informalization and the urban informal sector in sub-Saharan Africa', *Development and Change*, vol 26, pp259–284

Mittelman, J H (1994) 'The globalization challenge: surviving at the margins', *Third World Quarterly*, vol 15, pp427–443

Moore, H (1994) *A Passion for Difference*, Polity Press, Cambridge

Moser, C (1992) 'Adjustment from below: low-income women, time and the triple role in Guayaquil, Ecuador', in Afshar, H and Dennis, C (eds) *Women and Adjustment Policies in the Third World*, Macmillan, Basingstoke and London

Moser, C (1996) *Confronting Crisis: A Comparative Study of Household Responses in Four Poor Urban Communities*, Environmentally Sustainable Development Studies and Monograph Series No 8, The World Bank, Washington, DC

Moser, C (1998) 'The asset vulnerability framework: reassessing urban poverty reduction strategies', *World Development*, vol 26, no 1, pp1–19

Moser, C and Holland, J (1997) *Urban Poverty and Violence in Jamaica*, The World Bank, Washington, DC

Murray, C (1981) *Families Divided: The Impact of Migrant Labour in Lesotho*, Ravan Press, Johannesburg

Murray, C (1999) *Changing Livelihoods: The Free State, 1990s,* Working Paper Four, Multiple Livelihoods and Social Change Working Papers, Institute for Development and Policy Management, University of Manchester, Manchester

Quijano, A (1974) 'The marginal pole of the economy and the marginalised labour force', *Economy and Society*, vol III, pp393–428

Rakodi, C (1998) 'Globalization trends and sub-Saharan African cities', Lo, F-C and Yeung, Y-M (eds) *Globalization and the World of Large Cities*, United Nations University Press, Tokyo, pp314–51

Rakodi, C (1999) 'A capital assets framework for analysing household livelihoods strategies: implications for policy', *Development Policy Review*, vol 17, no 3, pp315–42

Sassen, S (1991) *The Global City: New York, London, Tokyo*, Princeton University Press, Princeton, NJ

Scheper-Hughes, N (1992) *Death Without Weeping: The Violence of Everyday Life in Brazil*, University of California Press, Berkeley

Scott, J (1976) *The Moral Economy of the Peasant, Rebellion and Subsistence in Southeast Asia,* Yale University Press, New Haven and London

Seabrook, J (1996) *In Cities of the South: Scenes from a Developing World*, Verso Press, London

Sicular, D (1992) *Scavengers, Recyclers and Solutions for Solid Waste Management in Indonesia*, Centre for Southeast Asian Studies, University of California, Berkeley

Szanton Blanc, C S (ed) (1994) *Urban Children in Distress: Global Predicaments and Innovative Strategies*, UNICEF, New York

Tacoli, C (1998) 'Rural–urban linkages and sustainable rural livelihoods', in Carney, D (ed) *Sustainable Rural Livelihoods: What Contribution Can we Make?* DFID, London, pp67–80

Thorbek, S (1987) *Voices from the City, Women of Bangkok*, Zed Books, London

Thorbek, S (1994) *Gender and Slum Culture in Urban Asia*, Zed Books, London

Whitehead, A (2000) 'Continuities and Discontinuities in Rural Livelihoods in Northeast Ghana between 1975 and 1989', Workshop Paper to Multiple Livelihoods and Social Change Project, Institute for Development Policy and Management, University of Manchester, Manchester

World Bank (1991) *Urban Policy and Economic Development: An Agenda for the 1990s*, World Bank, Washington, DC

Part 3
The Policy Implications of Urban Livelihoods Analysis

The aim of Part 3 is to analyse the policy implications of what we know about urban livelihoods, taking into account both the situation of poor people and the strategies they adopt to cope with impoverishment, maintain their security or improve their well-being.

INTRODUCTION

Carole Rakodi

The crucial determinants of households' ability to achieve improved livelihoods are their access to assets and the effects of external conditioning variables that constrain or encourage the productive use or accumulation of such assets and that expose households to risks or threats. A variety of levels and categories of policy may impact on these and the policy 'cake' may be cut in various ways. Policies are generally categorized in a vertical sense as macroeconomic, meso- or local policies. But there are cross-cutting distinctions, too: they may be sectoral or multisectoral/integrated; and they may aim to address directly the causes of poverty/the needs of poor households or to reduce poverty by indirect means (Rakodi, 1999).

International and national economic conditions and national macroeconomic and mesopolicies are of critical significance to many aspects of urban livelihoods. The effects of macroeconomic fiscal and monetary policies are transmitted to the micro-/household level by the conduits of markets and infrastructure (Behrman, 1993). It is difficult to assess their impact on the poor because of the complexity of the effects, which are both direct and indirect and also change over time, and the heterogeneity of poor groups (Killick, 1995). Care must be taken to separate the effects of economic crises and the policies which help to precipitate them and the impact of economic reforms themselves. Views about the effects of economic reforms on the livelihoods of poor rural people differ: Sahn et al (1996) suggest that, because of improvements in rural terms of trade as a result of devaluation, liberalized marketing, higher producer prices and lower taxes, the incomes of the rural poor, in general, have increased marginally (see also Faruqee and Husain, 1996). However, they acknowledge that export crop producers, especially of non-traditional crops, have gained more than other producers and that only some food producers have benefited. They also argue that the rural poor have not suffered from cutbacks in public sector employment, increased prices for inputs, or reduced subsidies, as they generally did not have access to these previously (Sahn et al, 1996). Not all analysts would agree.

The policies that aim at economic stabilization and reform (structural adjustment) are closely related, so that it is difficult to disentangle their effects. Moreover, outcomes may be different in the short term from those in the medium or long term, and are affected by policy design, timing and sequencing. In most countries, wage freezes, subsidy reductions and public sector downsizing were part of the policy package, leading, at least in the short term, to falling real wages, increased prices for some wage goods and loss of public sector jobs, with knock-on effects on the rest of the economy. These outcomes have had a particularly adverse effect on the urban working poor (Moser et al, 1993; Killick, 1995).

In addition, over-rapid liberalization has led in some countries to deindustrialization (Hoeven, 1995). Thus real wage reduction has often been associated with job shedding and the liberalization of government controls, with increased casualization of work, rather than increased full-time wage employment, at least in the short term. While initially demand for goods produced in the informal sector may increase because of their lower prices, later aggregate demand falls and too many people are competing for opportunities in the sector. As a result, the open unemployment rate has increased in many urban areas (Jamal, 1995; Zeleza, 1995; UNCHS, 1996). To the extent that the urban poor were buying their essential goods (including food) in parallel markets before the start of adjustment, their welfare was not adversely affected. But where they had access to cheaper goods, they were adversely affected by increases in the price of food and other goods and services (Faruqee and Husain, 1996). Although in some countries, especially in Asia, real wages were restored to former levels after stabilization (and even increased), in many countries (especially in Africa) they have not recovered to earlier levels.

Increasingly, it is recognized that, for economic growth to be accompanied by poverty reduction, it needs to be 'pro-poor', although what is meant by this is by no means clear (Hanmer et al, 1997). Questions of equity are not considered to be as important as growth by the World Bank (see also, Lipton and Ravallion, 1995), although the Bank does acknowledge that the design of structural adjustment policies, including sequencing, and the type of economic growth achieved ('broad-based', 'labour-intensive') matter. Others, for example Watt (2000, p13), consider that:

> *Inequality has two effects on poverty levels: it slows economic growth, and it makes a given rate of economic growth less effective in reducing poverty. While equity and economic growth are mutually reinforcing, inequality is socially destabilising, bad for growth, and of its nature restricts the capabilities of marginalised groups. Conversely, equitable access to markets, political power, and social provision, on the basis of needs, is the fastest and most effective route to poverty eradication.*

In order to reduce poverty, therefore, policies designed to achieve economic growth need to be accompanied by redistribution of income and/or assets. Income redistribution can be achieved either *ex ante*, by designing growth strategies that increase disproportionately the incomes of the poorest, or *ex post facto*, by redistributing income through taxation (see below) (Maxwell and Hanmer, 1999; Watt, 2000). Growth might be expected to be pro-poor if it takes place in sectors in which the poor work, but opportunities for urban wage employment arising from economic growth are often not accessible to the poor because of their lack of education and appropriate skills. Redistribution of assets is necessary to enable poor people to take advantage of opportunities, but which assets are critical varies according to the context. In urban labour markets, redistribution of human capital assets (education, knowledge, skills, health) may be as important as the redistribution of productive assets, especially land. However, some consider the latter to be a prerequisite for reducing poverty and inequality, raising efficiency and growth levels and providing a basis for secure livelihoods (Stewart, 1995; Watt, 2000). These questions, among others, are discussed further in Chapters 6 and 7.

Ex post strategies, or redistribution on the margins through tax and subsidy policies and public investment, may be adopted because they are less politically risky than *ex ante* redistribution. However, they may not have significant equalizing effects, may have efficiency costs, and may not benefit the poorest. This argument is not against such policies, but in favour of their careful design, but also implies recognition that tackling inequality solely at the level of income is insufficient, as income levels are more a symptom than a cause of the inequalities of asset distribution, educational attainment and political power (Watt, 2000).

Fiscal and public expenditure mesopolicies have an impact on secondary incomes (incomes after tax) and tertiary incomes (incomes after tax and public expenditure), and also affect the stock and distribution of assets, broadly defined. They may reinforce, or compensate for, the possible poverty-increasing effects of macropolicies by (Stewart, 1995):

- Their impact on disposable incomes, by direct taxes, transfers and schemes to generate employment or raise productivity.
- Their influence on the prices of goods and services consumed by the poor by means of indirect taxes and subsidies. Taxation of goods consumed by the poor is regressive, as are reductions of food and other subsidies. Replacing general by targeted subsidies may increase the proportion of the total subsidy received by lower income households, but targeted subsidies also tend to leave out more eligible people than general subsidies.
- Their influence on the availability (and price) of publicly provided goods, especially health, education and water.

Public expenditure mesopolicies are typically sectoral and may have a significant impact on the context in which poor people live and work, the assets available to them and their livelihoods. In practice, taxes may be regressive and subsidies and public expenditure may not be well targeted to the poor. Some policies may benefit the poor about as much as middle- and upper-income groups (primary education and non-hospital health services), but are generally allocated only a small share of total budgets. Policies that disproportionately benefit the poor are rare. In addition, reforms may adversely affect access by the poor to publicly provided services. A wide range of public expenditure policies, generally decided at the national level, are relevant to the context, vulnerability and assets of the poor: infrastructure, safety nets, education and training, health, etc. In this volume there is only limited scope for discussing mesopolicy issues in depth, but they are referred to in Chapters 7, 10 and 11.

At subnational (regional/urban) levels, the incidence and characteristics of poverty result from the interaction between macro- or mesoprocesses and policies and the particular circumstances of regional/urban economies, settlements and households. Local policies are constrained both by the effects of these processes and policies and by the allocation of responsibilities for social and infrastructure expenditure (Dillinger, 1993). The potential for action depends on the extent of local autonomy, which is limited in most countries so that, although there may be scope for local decision-making on expenditure priorities and pricing/subsidy policies, the design of social policies and safety nets, and measures to support economic activities, the impact of local policies is likely to be outweighed by the effects of national policies. Nevertheless, devolution of decision-making to the local level potentially allows the initiation and design of policy packages that are appropriate to local conditions, the adaptation of national policies to local circumstances, and the adoption of a coordinated multisectoral approach to poverty reduction (de Haan, 1998; Rakodi, 1999). The implications for urban governance and management of policies to support the livelihoods of the poor are explored in Chapter 13.

The aim in this part of the book is to assess the implications of the livelihoods framework for the identification and implementation of policy. Policies designed to increase poor households' access to assets may focus on enabling them to take advantage of opportunities by increasing their capabilities, removing constraints and assisting them to accumulate assets. Thus human capital is considered in Chapters 7 and 10, social and political capital in Chapters 8 and 13, physical capital in Chapters 9, 11 and 12, financial capital in Chapter 7 and natural capital in Chapter 9.

The scope for individuals or households to increase their stocks of assets depends on the opportunities for, and relieving constraints on, accessing and using assets and resources, many of which may also be affected by policy and amenable to intervention. Enabling and regulatory policies may be as important in this respect as public expenditure programmes. In turn, the scope for and outcome of each of the above are conditioned by the broader context, including national macroeconomic and mesopolicies, political rights and national political regimes, and processes of social and cultural change. Therefore an attempt will be made to set the policy discussion in this wider framework. In addition, policy issues such as prioritizing and sequencing will be discussed.

The policy areas selected for discussion are those which have been demonstrated in Part 1 to be the most salient to the livelihoods of poor urban people. They are those that can be addressed within the scope of 'national urban policy', and particularly those with respect to which there is potential for action at the urban level by local governance actors. Attention will be paid to the policy formulation process, because:

> *What is at issue is not just the type or quality of policy that a government is willing to 'sign up' to but also the quality of its domestic political and bureaucratic processes. The underlying presumption is that an open and accountable process, in which the poor have a voice and on which some sustainable coalition has been built, stands more chance of being sustained* (Healey et al, 2000).

REFERENCES

Behrman, J R (1993) 'Macroeconomic policies and rural poverty: issues and research strategies, in Quibria, M G (ed) *Rural Poverty in Asia: Priority Issues and Policy Options*, Oxford University Press, Hong Kong, pp124–215 de Haan, A (1998) 'Social exclusion in policy and research: operationalizing the concept, in Figueirendo, J B and de Haan, A (eds) *Social Exclusion: An ILO Perspective*, International Institute for Labour Studies, Research Series 111, Geneva, pp11–24

Dillinger, W (1993) *Decentralization and its Implications for Urban Service Delivery*, Urban Management Paper 16, World Bank, Washington, DC

Faruqee, R and Husain, I (1996) 'Adjustment in seven African countries, in Husain, I and Faruqee, R (eds) *Adjustment in Africa: Lessons from Country Case Studies*, Avebury, Avebury, pp1–10

Hanmer, L, Pyatt, G and White, H (1997) *Poverty in Sub-Saharan Africa: What Can We Learn from the World Bank's Poverty Assessments?*, Institute for Social Studies, The Hague

Healey, J, Foster, M, Norton, A and Booth, D (2000) 'Towards national public expenditure strategies for poverty reduction', *ODI Poverty Briefing 7*, March

Hoeven, R van der (1995) 'Structural adjustment, poverty and macro-economic policy', in Rodgers, G and Hoeven, R van der (eds) *The Poverty Agenda: Trends and Policy Issues*, International Labour Office, Geneva, pp177–205

Jamal, V (1995) 'Changing poverty and employment patterns under crisis in Africa', in Rodgers, G and van der Hoeven, R (eds) *The Poverty Agenda: Trends and Policy Issues*, International Labour Organization, Geneva, pp59–68

Killick, T (1995) 'Structural adjustment and poverty alleviation: an interpretative survey', *Development and Change*, vol 26, no 2, pp305–331

Lipton, M and Ravallion, M (1995) 'Poverty and policy', in Behrman, J and Srinavasan, T N (eds) *Handbook of Development Economics*, vol III, Elsevier Science, Amsterdam, pp2251–2637

Maxwell, S and Hanmer, L (1999) 'For richer, for fairer: poverty reduction and income distribution', *Development Research Insights*, Issue 31, September, pp1–2

Moser, C O N, Herbert, A J and Makonnen, R E (1993) *Urban Poverty in the Context of Structural Adjustment: Recent Evidence and Policy Responses*, Urban Development Division, TWU DP 4, World Bank, Washington, DC

Rakodi, C (1999) 'A capital assets framework for analysing household livelihood strategies', *Development Policy Review*, vol 17, no 3, pp315–342

Sahn, D E, Dorosh, P and Younger, S (1996) 'Exchange rate, fiscal and agricultural policies in Africa: does adjustment hurt the poor?' *World Development*, vol 24, no 4, pp719–747

Stewart, F (1995) *Adjustment and Poverty: Options and Choices*, Routledge, London

UNCHS (1996) *An Urbanizing World: Global Report on Human Settlements, 1996*, Oxford University Press, New York

Watt, P (2000) *Social Investment and Economic Growth: A Strategy to Eradicate Poverty*, Oxfam, Oxford

Zeleza, T (1995) 'The unemployment crisis in Africa in the 1970s and 1980s', in Osaghae, E (ed) *Between State and Society in Africa: Perspectives on Development*, CODESRIA (Council for the Development of Social Research in Africa), Dakar, pp75–122

Chapter 6

Municipal Government, Urban Economic Growth and Poverty Reduction – Identifying the Transmission Mechanisms Between Growth and Poverty

Philip Amis

INTRODUCTION

This paper has two aims: first to explore the relationship between urban economic growth and poverty reduction within a livelihoods framework, and second to identify what room for manoeuvre there is for municipal governments to intervene in this process.[1] Many of the policy implications are wider than the municipal level, but it was not felt appropriate, nor is there the space, to become involved in a wider discussion of the macro policy options around growth and poverty. The focus is to explore the 'black box' of how growth actually does 'trickle down' to the poorest in an urban context.

Research in this field characteristically works using aggregate data such as GDP per capita which is then compared with poverty indicators such as the proportion of population which is below the poverty line or social indicators like under-five mortality. This is the method adopted in the World Bank's reports on poverty (World Bank, 1990; World Bank, 2000). However, almost all economic data is collected at the national level and it is difficult to get figures for economic growth or poverty incidence for specific urban areas. Also, in most cases poverty analysis in specific urban areas requires the use of proxy indicators, often the 'urban' component of a national figure. Generally, there is no single indicator of urban economic growth that is equivalent to GDP. We are left therefore with an awkward position in terms of the data because we are unable to determine either of our two variables.

As a result, in this chapter, rather than examining the relationship between the health of an urban economy and poverty incidence, the possible 'transmission mechanisms' through which urban economic growth may trickle down to the urban poor will be analysed. Our concern is also with the question of how public sector agencies can facilitate and/or enable the poor to benefit from a process of economic growth. The focus of the analysis is on the role of local government in these processes.

At the urban level, flexibility in responding to a changing environment, the provision of physical infrastructure, often on a large scale, and investment in human capital are all important to economic growth. The drivers for such policies are often at a national rather than municipal level, in terms of macro-economic, labour, trade and industrial policies, although there is also an important role for local government. Policies to facilitate urban economic growth are, in many respects, top-down policies. Where appropriate, we shall also attempt to address the question in a more bottom-up and negative way – namely, 'Why can the poor not participate in such a growth process?'.[2] This will involve us in considering 'barriers' to the involvement of poor people, as well as 'transmission mechanisms'.

Finally, we should perhaps acknowledge the irony of discussing the theme of urban economic growth in the post-1997 financial meltdown in South East Asia and elsewhere. First, the initial work on which the chapter is based was conceived a few years earlier, which illustrates the current speed of global change.[3] Second, it was inspired by work in India – most notably the experience of Visakhapat-nam, where it was discovered that casual wages had doubled in the second half of the 1990s (Amis and Kumar, 2000, p188). To acknowledge these contrasts, in the section on transmission mechanisms we shall also look at how both economic decline and economic growth are transmitted. A related theme that emerges is the extent to which municipal governments are able to facilitate or ameliorate such processes. Municipal governments can be seen as having both an 'attacking' role in enabling the poor to participate in economic growth and also a 'defensive' role in protecting them from the impacts of economic decline. As we shall see, urban local government may be able to make a more significant contribution in the latter than the former role.

Tables 6.1–6.4 and the accompanying text map out the relationship between urban economic growth and assets/capital, which is categorized into four types: labour capital, human capital, social capital and productive capital. This is an extension and adaptation of the asset vulnerability approach used to explain household and community behaviour in four communities in Lusaka, Zambia; Guayaquil, Ecuador; Metro Manila in the Philippines; and Budapest, Hungary, when faced with deteriorating macroeconomic and labour market conditions (Moser, 1998). It was felt that Moser's framework, which separates labour resources from human capital, and also identifies productive assets such as housing, household relations and social capital as the assets on which households draw in reducing their vulnerability, was particularly appropriate because of its specifically urban background.

The tables seek to map the impact of economic growth as well as decline, and to explore in schematic form the potential role of local government. For each form of capital or asset, the first row in each table outlines which dimension or aspects of poverty it captures. The second row is concerned to highlight briefly the impact of urban economic growth and decline on this aspect of poverty. In addition, an attempt is made to explain the speed with which the transmission takes place. The third row is concerned with household responses to urban economic change. This includes responses to both positive and negative changes. The latter was the main focus of the Moser study. The next two rows are concerned with the potential roles of municipalities in facilitating positive impacts of urban economic growth on the urban poor and ameliorating its negative impacts.

LABOUR CAPITAL RELATIONSHIP TO URBAN ECONOMIC GROWTH

Income measures and the related use of 'poverty lines' are often criticized as representing a narrow definition of poverty. There are many problems in measurement and in certain quarters a tiresome debate has taken place about poverty lines, which is best illustrated by the endless reworking of Indian poverty lines in the journal *Economic and Political Weekly*. Nevertheless, recent participatory work in India suggests that the income dimension remains very important to the poor; thus, approximately half the statements made by poor households in an impact assessment study of DFID supported slum improvement projects related to incomes, assets and livelihoods. (Amis, 2001, p105). The main asset on which poor households are able to draw is their labour.

The relationship between urban economic growth and income-based dimensions of poverty is the most well researched; this is particularly the case in terms of the negative impact of economic decline – with or without structural adjustment. The transmission mechanisms are via the labour market through a reduction in wages and/or employment and through increases in the cost of living (Moser et al, 1993). Such changes are transmitted very quickly to households, their impact depending on the type of growth and the condition of the labour market. There are also examples of successful trickle-down from economic growth. In Bogota, poverty fell from 57 per cent of the population in 1973 to 17 per cent in 1991 as a result of large-scale employment growth, much of it in construction (Gilbert, 1997, pp30–31). In certain situations wages can be bid up quite quickly. For example, wages in the coastal districts of South China (Guangdong) are now 50 per cent higher than in inland China (Watkins, 1998, pp118–119).

Successful local municipal management can facilitate local economic development. This requires a new role in 'enabling' such development, as well as providing services. Indeed, it has been argued that the major impediment to successful urban development is that urban managers have consistently focused their interventions on consumption rather than considering cities' productive roles. Thus it is argued that local governments should see the development of the local economy as an important objective. The need for such a focus – for large urban centres – has been greatly increased by processes of globalization; cities perforce must be as much engaged in reorganizing their economies as in planning to accommodate changes (Harris, 1996).

Inadequate provision of infrastructure can be a major constraint on urban economic growth and employment creation. It is now widely accepted that a lack

Table 6.1 *Labour capital relationship to urban economic growth*

Labour capital (characteristics)	Households draw on labour capital to generate the income that is crucial in cash-based urban economies. Income is the classic dimension of poverty associated with household expenditure and consumption. Well-known measurement problems, but income remains the central component of urban poverty.
Impact of urban economic change (top-down)	Changes are entirely driven through and by position within the labour market and prices (especially food). Involvement depends on the type of growth (capital/labour intensive). Positive changes can in theory happen quickly but depend to a very large extent on the state of demand. Negative impacts associated with structural adjustment are transmitted very quickly. These are very rapid transmission mechanisms.
Household responses to urban economic change (bottom-up)	*Positive:* the ability to respond to positive economic changes is dependent on skill/education and health levels. The importance of the absence of barriers (physical and social) in preventing groups and individuals benefiting from urban economic change. *Negative*: the critical importance of being able to increase labour within the household and utilize other sources.
Role for municipality in facilitating (positive)	Limited role in encouraging economic growth. Important role in providing infrastructure for industrial growth. Ability is dependent on local government revenue sources. Major role in not restricting informal and small-scale enterprise activity. An appropriate regulatory framework is key and becoming more important for local government.
Role for municipality in ameliorating (negative)	Major local employer with the potential to maintain employment by changing investment priorities. Potential involvement in implementing temporary labour creation (for example, food for work schemes). The provision of support (training, premises) to small-scale enterprise. Moderate ability to influence housing market to reduce costs. De facto acceptance of urban farming as a survival strategy.

of infrastructure provision hinders economic development. Research in Lagos, Bangkok and Jakarta has clearly shown the costs to manufacturing of inadequate infrastructure (World Bank, 1991). The poorer the public infrastructure the more the private sector itself has to carry extra costs. Thus the provision and renewal of infrastructure remains one, if not the most, important intervention that municipalities can make, whether as providers, enablers or lobbyists (Harris and Fabricus (eds), 1996).

The financing of infrastructure, whether from local revenues, grants, loans or bonds, is a critical element in urban governance. The politics that underlie resource allocation for this purpose is an important element in urban governance and in potential growth coalitions. Whether the industrial sector and/or the middle class seeks to stay in the system and improve local delivery or effectively exits and provides its own services is important.[4] The latter strategy is likely to hurt small businesses and the poor as a) the system declines, and b) the powerful no longer have an interest in the system working. In Nairobi the provision of roads and services became so poor in the industrial area that industrialists, over the last five years, have refused to pay local taxes and have paid their own agency to improve the facilities. Inevitably, given limited resources, there will be conflicts between priorities: the demands of large employers may be very different from those of low-income residents and small and microenterprises, with respect, for example, to transport infrastructure. There is no clear evidence to guide resource allocation between promoting large-scale formal sector economic development and poverty reduction, or between attracting foreign direct investment and supporting indigenous enterprises – ultimately the decisions are likely to depend on the balance of political power (see Chapter 13).

An additional role for the municipality is the regulatory framework. It is much easier to destroy jobs than to create them, especially in the informal and/or small-scale enterprise sector. Relocation and/or 'city pride' initiatives can easily destroy local economic activities, often by pushing them to the urban periphery and reducing their profitability. This practice often affects hawkers.

The opposite is also true: a municipality adopting a laissez-faire approach can 'create' employment opportunities. The clearest examples come from South Africa after the abandonment of restrictive planning and regulatory practice with the end of apartheid in the 1990s. In the early 1980s, there were estimated to be only 300 hawkers functioning in Johannesburg's inner core; the estimate for the mid-1990s was 4000 hawkers in the inner core and 15,000 in the Greater Johannesburg area. There is an international dimension to this dramatic growth in informal activity: it is estimated that 7000 of the hawkers were from outside South Africa. The change in official policy from repression to greater tolerance is the main explanation for this growth (Tomlinson, 1996, pp188–189).

Within India the importance of a flexible and non-master plan approach to urban planning has been noted in East Delhi, where an area of mixed use became the main location for Indian suppliers of coaxial TV cables. This, it is argued, was based upon mixed land use in the neighbourhood, community networks (or social capital), the use of land and housing as an asset – the concept of 'neighbourhood as factory'. It was underpinned by a process through which the community was able to obtain incremental infrastructure installation through political interaction with local agencies and politicians. Such patronage to provide legality and security contrasts with more formal planning processes (Benjamin, 1991, 1993). Thus:

> *Attempting to attract and sometimes divert public investment, local development also relates to thwarting centrally planned projects that conflict with local interests. Often the only way these areas can get development to happen is by subverting development (or getting there before it does) and mustering political support* (Benjamin, 1993, pp144–145).[5]

The emphasis throughout is on the importance of the local economy, flexibility and diversity. There is also a clear implication that social capital contributes to urban economic growth (see below). The role of the municipality is first, not to destroy the neighbourhood economy through formalization or over-regulation and second, to provide incremental infrastructure when it is needed to support economic activity.

HUMAN CAPITAL RELATIONSHIP TO URBAN ECONOMIC GROWTH

The importance of human capital – education and health – to economic growth has been well documented, but is worth underlining, especially when women are included. The literature focuses on primary education, but as development occurs secondary education is also important (Watkins, 1998, pp56–57), as well as vocational skills (see Chapter 7). Health status depends on a variety of factors, including incomes (to purchase food and medical treatment), access to healthcare services and environmental standards (see Chapter 10). The effective delivery of these services has very powerful synergies for overall economic development; they are important, regardless of whether a 'growth-mediated security' or 'support-led security' strategy is adopted (Dreze and Sen, 1989). Increased education, especially of girls, has been shown to be one of the most effective ways of tackling gender inequality (Dreze and Sen, 1996). Similarly, increased resources in health – especially in the public sector – begins to address one of the main causes of urban poverty – namely, the negative impact on earning capacity and security of health-related shocks (Amis, 1997).

The provision of access to education and healthcare has been a particular failure in India. Thus, as Sen notes:

> Four decades of allegedly 'interventionist' planning did little to make the country more literate, provide a wide-based health service, achieve comprehensive land reforms or end the rampant social inequalities that blight the material prospects of the underprivileged. Second, while successive Indian governments have been only minimally active in social development, they have been superactive in tying the economy up in knots of bureaucracy, control and regulations, – the so-called 'licence raj'. The power of government policy had been unleashed not on behalf of goals such as providing schooling for every villager [and slum dweller] but in interference aimed at restricting people's initiatives (Sen, 1995, pp28–29).

The government in India has traditionally intervened too much in some sectors (tradeables), but has often not intervened enough in others (non-tradeables). Furthermore, India has devoted more attention to direct poverty initiatives, like Integrated Rural Development Programmes, than most countries, yet has ignored, despite its rhetoric, the provision of basic needs. Thus Indian government expenditure on health and education, at 2 per cent each of central government

Table 6.2 *Human capital relationship to urban economic growth*

Human capital (characteristics)	Human capital is the classic dimension of poverty concerned with human potential. This is closely associated with the provision of health, education and physical infrastructure (water, sanitation and services). Measured by indicators of health (infant mortality rate, under-five mortality rate), literacy, and access to water and sanitation. UNDP has developed a single human development index.
Impact of urban economic change (top-down)	Growth is seen as a necessary but not sufficient condition, depending on the extent to which growth is translated into higher actual allocations *and* the efficient use of funds. Dependent upon allocation procedures and local control. The reverse argument, that human capital improves growth, has been strongly made from Asia. The positive impact is long term (>ten years). The negative impact can be felt in both the short and medium term: expenditure is sometimes cut during structural adjustment.
Household responses to urban economic change (bottom-up)	*Positive:* more resources for extra education; increased attendance at health outlets. Increased perceived return to improvements in education (secondary) and improved health status. More funds for water and sanitation. *Negative:* withdrawal of children – usually girls first – from school. Non-attendance at health centres and/or switch to private or traditional healers, postponement of treatment. Increased debt to maintain fees (education and/or health) Substitution with cheaper but unclean forms of water and sanitation.
Role for municipality in facilitating (positive)	Human capital (primary education, health and infrastructure) is the major responsibility of municipal governments. This is usually more the case with implementation than policy formulation. Impact is therefore related to local government efficiency. Total spend is dependent upon local government revenue sources and the degree of earmarking of funds.
Role for municipality in ameliorating (negative)	A potentially important role in protecting the sector from the worst impacts of structural adjustment. The possibility for targeting and/or access mechanisms to protect delivery to the poor. Introduction of user fees can have a very strong and quick impact on services for the poor.

spending, is exceptionally low, especially when compared with countries at similar economic levels (Indonesia, 3 per cent and 10 per cent; Sri Lanka, 6 per cent and 10 per cent; Kenya, 5 per cent and 19 per cent; the Philippines, 3 per cent and 16 per cent) (UNICEF, 1998, pp114–117).

The importance of the human capital dimension of poverty has been confirmed by the use of panel data from the Côte d'Ivoire. Panel data involves interviewing the same households repeatedly and therefore allows us to consider poverty dynamics – namely, what are the processes that are moving some households into poverty and facilitating some to escape? Through this method it is possible to distinguish between those in temporary and chronic (permanent) poverty and to consider different policy options. The analysis of this panel data suggests that, in urban areas, human capital is the most important endowment that explains welfare changes over time. Households with well-educated members suffered less loss of welfare over time than other households. What seemed to matter were skills learnt through education rather than diplomas obtained. Indeed, diplomas may even have worked against some households in having orientated workers too much towards a formal sector job when employment growth came almost exclusively from small enterprises (Grootaert et al, 1995).

The provision of those services that enable households to develop their human capital is therefore a major responsibility of government, in which local government may have a significant policy-making or, more commonly, operational role. The positive impacts of increases in human capital on the poor are medium to long term. The failure to provide regular and efficient services particularly hits the poorest because, as with infrastructure, they are unable to exit to the private sector.

SOCIAL CAPITAL RELATIONSHIP TO URBAN ECONOMIC GROWTH

Social capital is the dimension of assets concerned with households, networks and community. It is seen as important for facilitating local solutions to problems, but is very difficult to measure. Indicators usually look at 'civicness' and the outputs of social capital. These are the reciprocal exchanges that exist between individuals and households which allow 'local citizens to work together in identifying and acting on local problems or in taking local initiatives' (UNCHS, 1996, p419). These are very important in India – for example, the Self-Employed Women's Association (SEWA) in Ahmedabad or the Society for the Promotion of Area Resource Centres (SPARC) in Bombay. What is critical is that the local authority provides an environment in which such initiatives can take place. The above are examples of positive aspects of social capital. Social capital is also important in providing the networks that support the economic activities of the poor. This has been clearly illustrated, mainly from South Asia, in the case of local savings clubs and finance groups that form an important mechanism to allow limited asset accumulation and to encourage small and/or microenterprises (Rutherford, 2000, pp31–58; see also Chapter 7). Recent research in Kampala, Uganda, has also clearly shown the importance of trust and complex networks between households in allowing small businesses headed by women to develop. This is in sharp contrast to previous periods in Ugandan history during which the lack of trust profoundly limited both available credit and economic activity.[6]

Research has shown that it is the maintenance of security or the absence of intimidation and violence that is critical in allowing such initiatives to flourish. The impact of violence on the urban poor, in terms of limiting the development of enterprises, community activity and social capital, has been well documented.

Table 6.3 *Social capital relationship to urban economic growth*

Social capital (characteristics)	Social capital is the dimension of assets concerned with households, networks and community. It is seen as very important for facilitating local solutions to problems. Measuring stocks is difficult (indicators usually look at 'community-ness') or the results of differing levels of social capital.
Impact of urban economic change (top-down)	Urban economic growth usually has a positive effect on social capital, but stratification can reduce it. Economic decline tends to weaken social capital, especially dramatic decline, which is likely to fracture communities and households. Nevertheless, there is no clear direct relationship between growth and strengthening social capital; the local context is important. Changes are likely to come in the medium term. Infrastructure changes can change social capital quite quickly.
Household responses to urban economic change (bottom-up)	*Positive:* increased time and money to support CBOs and other community activities. This is especially important for women as they tend to be more involved with community action. Funds to start credit unions or other activities. It may be easier in a buoyant situation to forge political alliances, lessening dependence on patronage/patriarchy structures. The strengthening of extended families. *Negative:* lack of attendance at and involvement in activities of CBOs, especially by women. Increases in youth gangs, crime and murder. Increased dominance of illegal activities. Increased domestic violence. Lack of activity at night.
Role for municipality in facilitating (positive)	Very important role in setting the scene, and providing a facilitating environment and funds. The success of community organizations (and participation) is often conditional on flexibility in delivery by governmental agencies. Providing for law and order is critical. Street lighting is important.
Role for municipality in ameliorating (negative)	Potentially critical role in supporting community initiatives. Importance of preventing violence and destruction of social capital, with subsequent increases in poverty.

Work in Jamaica – admittedly, a very violent society – makes it clear that endemic violence undermines local initiatives and any chance of local economic growth (Moser and Holland, 1995). Communal violence, crime and protection racket-type patronage in urban India, much of which is concerned with controlling access to informal sector employment opportunities, may have similar outcomes (Das, 1990). Thus Das, in a study of the riots in New Delhi after the assassination of Mrs Gandhi, noted in relation to economic activity, '. . . that the fencing mechanisms and the regulation of entry into most sectors of the informal economy were a product of several factors – caste and kinship networks, defined by spheres of influence by politicians and local Big Men, and the constant threat of violence to regulate behaviour' (Das, 1996, p188). These are examples where negative social capital (gangs) can have very negative effects on development. Mechanisms for controlling access to the informal sector by kinship, but underpinned by violence, have also been observed in sub-Saharan Africa (Chabal and Daloz, 1999). The maintenance of law and order and a safe urban environment is therefore an important governmental function.

PRODUCTIVE CAPITAL RELATIONSHIP TO URBAN ECONOMIC GROWTH

Municipalities, through their planning and regulatory processes, can make significant impacts on the access of the poor to productive capital, especially through interventions in housing markets. As highlighted in Table 6.4, it is important for households to be able to use their houses as productive assets in periods of decline (but also growth), as a base for household enterprise, for renting and for other activities (Moser, 1998). Indeed, Moser asserts that, in some circumstances, access to secure tenure is one of the major poverty-reduction tools, which is, moreover, almost exclusively de facto controlled at the local level regardless of national legislation.

An impact assessment study of slum projects supported by DFID in India highlighted the relationship between improvements in infrastructure provision and environmental conditions, income-earning activities and the development of productive capital (Amis, 2001). The infrastructure components of the projects were greatly appreciated by the inhabitants in improving their overall environment (through reducing flooding, making roads passable and reducing the burden of collecting water); this was particularly liked by women. In addition, there was some evidence that these improvements, through effectively increasing the length of the day (by street lighting) and increasing the use of outside space, had resulted in increases in economic activity.

One of the main differences between cities, in policy and implementation terms, is their responses to informal housing and trade. Furthermore, this varies over time. This, then is a major policy area for municipal intervention.

A longitudinal analysis of informal rents in Nairobi between 1970 and the mid-1990s showed, contrary to expectations, that they had gone down in real terms. In this process they followed urban wages down. Given the ruthless nature of Nairobi landlords, this is startling. Furthermore, because of the dramatic increase in the supply of informal sector housing, there had been no corresponding increase in overcrowding. The Nairobi authorities, in sharp contrast to their repressive approach of the 1960s and 1970s, have allowed, whether consciously or not, the informal sector to build extensively. Kibera, Nairobi's largest unauthorized settlement, has grown at 12 per cent per annum since 1980. It is therefore possible to assert that the impact that informal housing has had on the urban poor is neutral or even positive, although this is in terms of a reduction in rents rather than an increase in ownership, which would allow households to benefit from using the house as a productive asset (Amis, 1996).

Table 6.4 *Productive capital relationship to urban economic growth*

Productive capital (characteristics)	Within productive capital, Moser suggests that the use of housing as a productive asset is the most significant in urban areas. The extent to which this is so, clearly depends on the nature of the housing market – in particular, the extent of ownership as opposed to tenancy.
Impact of urban economic change (top-down)	Urban economic growth is likely to increase the use of houses as productive assets; furthermore, it is likely to increase property values. This is particularly important for women and for home-based enterprises. In periods of economic decline, housing can act as a very important cushion.
Household responses to urban economic change (bottom-up)	*Positive:* uses additional resources to invest in housing as an asset, either for renting out or improving the existing structure – for example, improve the roof or provide infrastructure on site (water/toilet). Uses more to housing resources for family and own benefit. *Negative:* diversify income through home-based enterprises and renting out.
Role for municipality in facilitating (positive)	Potentially very important. 'In those urban contexts where the poor are . . . excluded from formal sector jobs and the capacity to generate additional jobs is limited, the removal of tenure-insecurity related obstacles that prevent or constrain households from using their housing effectively as a productive asset is possibly the single most important critical poverty reduction intervention' (Moser,1998, p11). In addition the municipality can strongly influence this process by the provision of basic infrastructure.
Role for municipality in ameliorating (negative)	The activity of the municipality is critical in influencing the housing market. A restrictive regulatory environment and/or policy of eviction of informal settlements can prevent the use of housing as a productive asset. This is an area in which, as far as enforcement is possible, local government has control over implementation. The legislation is usually drawn up at national level, but most research suggests that local implementation is more important than the formal legislation.

The reverse situation has been noted in Harare, where informal housing has not been tolerated and the result has been increases in rents, overcrowding and the development of increasing numbers of backyard shacks in formal low-income housing areas (Potts and Mutambirwa, 1991; Rakodi, 1996). In Latin America during a period of recession in the 1980s a similar contrast was found between Chile, in which self-help housing was restricted and overcrowding increased, and Brazil and Venezuela, where there was a proliferation of poor quality (informal) accommodation (Gilbert, 1989).

In policy terms there are two divergent options regarding housing markets: an 'informal sector' option and an 'overcrowding' option. The former is characterized by rapid informal sector growth and low-quality accommodation with no increase in overcrowding or real housing costs. The second option implies state intervention to provide relatively high-quality public housing and to limit the growth of the informal sector. The result tends to be increased overcrowding and rent inflation in relatively high standard accommodation. At a policy level it is not possible at present to weigh up definitively the advantages and disadvantages of the two options. This will clearly vary with local circumstances. However, what is clear is that, in the short to medium term, it is possible for municipal governments, through their actions in preventing or facilitating access to land and services, to exacerbate or mitigate urban poverty and deprivation (see also Chapters 9–12).

CONCLUSION: TOWARDS A REINVENTION OF PLANNING

From the above discussion it is clear that municipalities have varying potential for facilitating and mediating the effects of urban economic growth or decline upon the poor. This chapter has tried to map out this potential in terms of a livelihoods or asset vulnerability framework (Moser, 1998) and to consider the role for the municipality in each case. The strongest findings are highlighted below.

In relation to labour capital, the main observation concerned the importance of the provision of infrastructure for successful economic growth. Poor households and small and microenterprises suffer the most from the non-delivery of infrastructure, both because they cannot provide their own facilities and because inadequate infrastructure itself restricts growth. Furthermore, infrastructure deficiencies accentuate any tendency towards capital-intensive industrialization. The second area where the municipality makes an impact is through inappropriate planning, and by laws and restrictive practices which can substantially destroy employment opportunities. The provision of infrastructure is necessary but not sufficient for urban economic growth and many of the other influencing factors are beyond the control of local government. Therefore not destroying economic activity is more important than facilitating it; the negative levers are so much more effective than the positive.

The poverty literature stresses the importance of human capital, built up through access to services (primary health and education) that are often mediated and delivered by local government. While the circumstances vary, the effective delivery of these services is a function of funding mechanisms that depend on central–local relations of government and also local revenue systems. The resources available are determined by local governance, revenue structures (whether they are buoyant or not) and also by local political coalitions. Furthermore, accountability is a very important component in determining successful local delivery. Again the poor suffer most from the non-delivery of these services both by not being able to exit and by not being able to participate in growth due to illiteracy, lack of education and skills, or poor health.

The strengthening of social capital is increasingly seen as an important aspect of development and relevant to household strategies – for example, in accessing employment opportunities and underpinning relations between small and micro-enterprises. However, research has shown the devastating effect that crime, violence and the lack of security have on its formation and on urban economic growth. Participatory research methods often highlight crime and violence as one of the main problems experienced by poor people. Here the key role for the public sector is in law and order to limit these problems. Not letting criminality take hold in the first place seems particularly important.

The final asset considered is productive capital. In the urban sphere this is primarily associated with housing and household enterprise. It was noted that lifting restrictions on using housing as an asset is one of the most important interventions that municipalities can do for the poor. Regulations, land-use policy and attitudes to the informal sector can significantly affect access to land and thus the costs of house acquisition or the rents that poor households have to pay. In addition, the positive impact at a neighbourhood level of improvements in urban infrastructure in encouraging and facilitating economic activity was noted. These are all areas where municipalities can and do actively intervene, as Wu explains:

> *To compete effectively, a city's governing coalition needs to crystal-lise and endorse a vision of the future that is acceptable to both businesses and citizens. Private and public sectors must collaborate so as to share the burden of risk. The public sector should return to what it does best: keeping urban infrastructure in good mainte-nance and repair, building new facilities to accommodate new needs, and policing the public environment* (Wu, 1996, p149).

The main policy implication is first, to recognize the importance of municipal governments and second, to emphasize that they should 'stick to their knitting'. Municipalities should concentrate on their traditional roles of providing infra-structure, ensuring health and education, and appropriate planning and regula-tion. Despite the hype about city marketing and mega projects, traditional service delivery may be more critical. For policy-makers this means concentrating on not destroying employment opportunities as well as undertaking traditional functions as efficiently and equitably as possible. The poor benefit disproportionately from the efficient and inclusive delivery of services.

NOTES

1   This is an edited version of a theme paper on *Urban Economic Growth and Poverty Reduction* which forms part of a DFID-funded research project on Urban Govern-ance, Partnership and Poverty that was recently completed at the University of Birmingham, London School of Economics, Cardiff University and the International Institute for Environment and Development
2   I am grateful to Rakesh Mohan for this comment in January 1997
3   The speed of the subsequent 'melt-up' in certain Asian economies – South Korea and Thailand – is already challenging this crisis perception

4   Exiting out of the economic and political system is one of the clearest developments in contemporary urban India. Even a cursory look at the advertisements in *India Today* for privately run housing and industrial complexes, where the entire infrastructure is privately provided, illustrates this development

5   Given present-day regulation, except for a very specific range of 38 land uses (which assume that home-based activities are 'handicrafts' and not of any serious consequence), income-generating enterprises within planned neighbourhoods are considered illegal, requiring some form of political patronage for legalization

6   Personal communication from Julie Gifford, PhD student in the International Development Department, Birmingham University, May 2001

REFERENCES

Amis, P (1996) 'Long run trends in Nairobi's informal housing market', *Third World Planning Review,* vol 18, no 3, pp271–285

Amis, P (1997) 'Indian urban poverty: where are the levers for its effective alleviation?' *IDS Bulletin,* vol 28, no 2, pp94–104

Amis, P (2001) 'Rethinking UK aid in urban India: reflections on an impact assessment study of Slum Improvement Projects', *Environment and Urbanization,* vol 13, no 1, pp101–113

Amis, P and Kumar, S (2000) 'Urban economic growth, infrastructure and poverty in India: lessons from Visakhaptnam', *Environment and Urbanization,* vol 11, no 2, pp185–196

Benjamin, S (1991) *Jobs, Land, and Urban Development: The Economic Success of Small Manufactures in East Delhi, India*, Lincoln Institute of Land Policy, Boston, Mass

Benjamin, S (1993) 'Urban productivity from the grassroots', *Third World Planning Review,* vol 15, no 2, pp143–173

Chabal, P and Duloz, J (1999) *Africa Works,* James Currey, London

Das, V (ed) (1990) *Mirrors of Violence. Communities, Riots and Survivors in South Asia,* Oxford University Press, Delhi

Das, V (1996) 'The spatialization of violence: case study of a "Communal Riot"', in Basu, K and Subrahmanyam, S (eds) *Unravelling the Nation: Sectarian Conflict and India's Secular Identity,* Penguin, New Delhi, pp157–203

Dreze, J and Sen, A (1989) *Hunger and Public Action,* Clarendon Press, Oxford

Dreze, J and Sen, A (1996) *India: Economic Development and Social Opportunity,* Oxford University Press, Delhi

Jones, S and Nelson, N (eds) (1999) *African Urban Poverty,* IT Publications, London

Gilbert, A (1989) 'Housing during recession: illustrations from Latin America', *Housing Studies,* vol 4, no 3, pp156–166

Gilbert, A (1997) 'Work and poverty during economic restructuring: the experience of Bogota, Colombia', *IDS Bulletin,* vol 28, no 2, pp24–34

Grootaert, C, Kanbur, R and Oh, G-T (1995) *The Dynamics of Poverty: Why some People Escape form Poverty and Others Don't. An African Case Study,* World Bank Working Paper No 1499, Washington, DC

Harris, N (1996) *Preparatory Work for Defining an ESCOR Research Programme on Sustainable Cities and Urban Living,* Development Planning Unit, University College London, London

Harris, N and Fabricus, I (eds) (1996) *Cities and Structural Adjustment,* UCL Press, London

Moser, C (1998) 'The asset vulnerability framework: reassessing urban poverty reduction strategies', *World Development,* vol 26, no1, pp1–19

Moser, C, Herbert, A and Makonnen, R (1993) *Urban Poverty in the Context of Structural Adjustment*, Urban Development Division Discussion Paper, World Bank, Washington, DC

Moser, C and Holland, J (1995) *A Participatory Study of Urban Poverty and Violence in Jamaica,* Urban Development Division, World Bank, Washington, DC

Potts, D and Mutambirwa, C (1991) 'High density housing in Harare: commodification and overcrowding', *Third World Planning Review*, vol 13, no 1, pp1–25

Rakodi, C (1996) 'The household strategies of the urban poor: coping with poverty and recession in Gweru, Zimbabwe', *Habitat International*, vol 19, no 4, pp447–471

Rutherford, S (2000) *The Poor and Their Money*, Oxford University Press, New Delhi

Sen, A (1995) 'Wrongs and rights in development', *Prospect*, Issue no 1, pp28–35

Tomlinson, R (1996) 'The changing structure of Johannesburg's economy', in Harris, N and Fabricus, I (eds) *Cities and Structural Adjustment*, UCL Press, London, pp175–199

UNCHS (1996) *An Urbanizing World: Global Report on Human Settlements*, Oxford University Press, New York

UNICEF (1998) *The State of the World's Children*, Oxford University Press, New York

Watkins, K (1998) *Economic Growth with Equity: Lessons from East Asia*, Oxfam Publications, Oxford

World Bank (1990) *World Development Report*, Oxford University Press, New York

World Bank (1991) *Urban Policy and Economic Development: An Agenda for the 1990s*, World Bank Publications, Washington, DC

World Bank (2000) *World Development Report 2000/2001: Attacking Poverty*, Oxford University Press, New York

Wratten, E (1995) 'Conceptualising urban poverty', *Environment and Urbanization,* vol 7, no 1, pp11–36

Wu, W (1996) 'Economic competition and resource mobilisation', in Cohen, M, Ruble, B, Tulchin, J and Garland, A (eds) *Preparing for the Urban Future,* Woodrow Wilson Press, Washington, DC, pp123–154

Chapter 7

Support for Livelihood Strategies

Stuart Rutherford, Malcolm Harper and John Grierson

Urban livelihood strategies centre on income-earning activities in either the formal or informal sectors, and as wage employees, unpaid family workers or in self-employment. In this chapter, a variety of ways in which people's efforts to increase their incomes and make them more secure are reviewed. In the first section, Stuart Rutherford considers ways in which access to financial capital by the poor can be improved, not just for microenterprise development but for household financial management more broadly. Malcolm Harper considers the non-financial constraints on small businesses and suggests ways in which they can be alleviated. Finally, John Grierson discusses how those aspects of human capital that are most relevant to income earning activity (education and skills) might best be developed.

FINANCIAL SERVICES AND THE LIVELIHOODS OF THE POOR[1]

Introduction: Rural Credit and Microcredit

One of the strengths of the livelihoods approach to policy-making is that it encourages its users to examine in detail how poor people manage their lives. Unsurprisingly, this reveals complexity and diversity. We see this when we look at how poor people manage their money.

However, the diverse ways in which poor people do manage their money, and how they may be helped to do it better, has surfaced only recently as an important issue in the development of formal services for the poor. It was notably absent from the analyses that supported the two most important experiments in financial services for the poor in post-colonial times – 'rural (agricultural) credit' and 'microcredit'. Each of these was aimed at a particular subset of the poor for whom particular objectives were set (Matin et al, 1999). From the 1950s through the 1970s the focus was on helping poor male farmers, through credit, to adopt more productive farming techniques. Starting in the late 1970s and building up to a crescendo in the 1990s, the focus shifted to helping the poor – mostly women and not necessarily farmers – to develop off-farm 'microenterprises', again through credit. In each case, support from donors was based on the potential of such schemes to alleviate or eliminate poverty, and to promote economic growth. In the more recent case, gender considerations were also important in donor policy.

The 'microcredit' approach has enjoyed many successes. In Asia, especially in Bangladesh, where the movement began in the rural areas, it brought organized financial services to millions of poor people who had never before had access to them. By the 1990s, microcredit in Bangladesh had expanded from the villages into the urban slums. In Latin America, especially in Bolivia, where microcredit had from the start been an urban as much as a rural phenomenon, it led to the emergence of highly sophisticated specialist providers of microenterprise credit. However, by the mid-1990s it was clear that the financing of women-owned enterprises was touching only the surface of the myriad financial needs of the poor. In Africa, for example, where both the Asian and Latin American models had been taken up enthusiastically, microcredit's failure to penetrate into the countryside or to reach the poorer urban households showed that the number of households that could benefit from just one form of financial intermediation – credit – for just one use – microenterprise – was limited.

The livelihoods perspective should broaden our understanding of the poor, helping us to see them not just as farmers or microentrepreneurs but as individual men and women struggling with the day-to-day business of managing the opportunities and risks of diverse and complex survival and development strategies. So far, the livelihoods literature has not contributed much to people's understanding of the role of financial services in the lives of the poor.

Financial Services and the Poor

Attention has in recent years switched to the question of the role of financial services in the lives of the poor. One stream of research investigates the risks and vulnerabilities in the lives of the poor, and the degree to which these are and can be mitigated through financial service provision (Platteau and Abraham, 1984; Alderman and Paxson, 1992; Fafchamps, 1995; Morduch, 1997; Udry, 1994; Zeller et al, 1996). This has led recently to an examination of the scope for 'microinsurance' for poor people, and some donors have funded appraisals of such services (Brown and Churchill, 2000). Another looks more directly at how poor people create and use informal financial services (Bouman, 1989; Rutherford, 1996, 2000; Brink and Chavas, 1991). In contrast to 'rural credit' and 'microcredit' with their large objectives (poverty alleviation and economic growth) and their specification of a particular form of financial service (credit) with a specific use (farm inputs and microenterprise financing), informal and indigenous financial services respond to a much more basic and general demand from the poor. They have evolved everywhere a general-purpose intermediation function in response to the difficulties that poor people have in matching their cash resources with their expenditure needs.

Poor people tend to have small and uncertain incomes, of which a large proportion is spent on food and cooking fuel. The inevitable consequence is that much non-food expenditure, even for some low-cost items, cannot be met from current cash resources. They must be financed therefore from past income (through saving), or from future income (through loans which are essentially advances against future savings), or by some combination.

In short, the poor need financial services. The only alternative is that they must go without, an all-too-common outcome. The smaller the cash surplus left over after basic food and fuel have been obtained, the greater will be the need for this basic financial service, so it can be argued that the poor need financial services more frequently and more urgently than other groups – and the poorest most of all (Sinha and Lipton, 1999). This argument appears to be borne out by observations of the way in which poor people manage their money, as a few examples given below will show (Rutherford, 2000).

Indigenous General-purpose Financial Services

Deposit collectors in southern India collect tiny savings daily from their slum clients, and then charge them for storing their money. Users of the service in effect accept negative rates of return on their savings, and do so willingly, since the productivity of the investment is a secondary consideration compared with the overwhelming need to find a safe way to turn savings into a usably large sum. A typical case is a housewife wanting to save up a few hundred rupees for school fees. She saves 5 rupees a day for a hundred days and then gets back, from her deposit collector, nine-tenths of the amount saved, forfeiting 50 rupees which the collector keeps as a fee for the service. The daily collection ensures that she maximizes her savings potential despite her tiny income, and the discipline of daily collection gives her the confidence of knowing that the school fees will be paid on time. Women around the world see this as a service well worth paying for, since savings stored at home (something which almost every woman tries to do, no matter how poor) are notoriously difficult to defend from pressing expenditure needs.

These informal 'saving up' collection services are not always available in slums and villages for the lack of a suitable collector. In such circumstances poor people may resort to 'saving down' – taking the lump sum from a moneylender and then repaying it through a series of small savings over the following days or weeks. The basic intermediation function – turning savings into a lump sum – is the same, but the fact that it is future savings that are being tapped makes this service more expensive than those of a deposit collector because the moneylender bears the risk of default and has to put up the capital in the first place.

Many savings clubs run by poor and not-so-poor groups turn savings into lump sums using what I have called a 'savings through' strategy (Rutherford, 2000). The Rotating Savings and Credit Association (ROSCA) is the clearest example. A ROSCA's members agree a timetable of meetings – say, weekly – and agree to deposit an equal amount of money at each meeting for as many meetings as there are members. At each meeting one of their number receives the total deposited on that occasion. The general-purpose financial services function could hardly be clearer: each member has withdrawn the same amount as they deposited, so the benefit they receive from conducting this elaborate exercise is nothing more or less than the conversion of a series of small savings into a lump sum at some point in the process. The enduring worldwide popularity of ROSCAs is evidence that the ability to manage this basic swap is of vital concern to many poor and not-so-poor people.

These three examples merely illustrate three basic 'swap' patterns and barely hint at the richness of informal devices. Work now in progress in villages and slums in Bangladesh is shedding light on the financial behaviour of slum dwellers and villagers.[2] Early results confirm the wide variety of indigenous intermediation devices, and the frequency and intensity with which they are used. It is rare to find households that are not users: such cases are either richer households whose surpluses are stored with formal service providers or the extreme poor who are virtually outside the cash economy – the elderly disabled who survive by begging. In Bangladesh it was found, for example, that in a sample of 42 poor, upper-poor and 'near-poor' households whose financial service transactions were tracked for a full year, none had used less than 5 different types of financial services (informal or formal) during the year, one had used 18, and the average was 10. These households were found to have pushed some two-thirds of their total income through financial services and devices, lodging it with money guards, borrowing from and lending to neighbours and family, borrowing from moneylenders, using it in various forms of saving club, or by joining microfinance institutions.

The study also confirms the wide range of needs and opportunities for which poor people seek to turn savings into lump sums (Rutherford, 2000; Holzman and Jorgensen, 1999). They include life-cycle needs (birth, education, marriage, homemaking, old age, widowhood, death, bequests), emergencies (personal ones like illness or desertion and impersonal ones like floods, fires and the bulldozing of squatter settlements) and opportunities (to buy various assets or to start or run businesses). Many of these occur repeatedly. Some can be anticipated while others arrive unexpectedly. Their timescales vary from the very short (borrowing a few coins to get some food on the table for guests) to the life-long (making arrangements for financial support in old age).

Clearly, loans for agricultural production and microenterprise, important though they are, are merely two among many competing needs for financial services. Where the poor have access to modern (microenterprise) 'microcredit', they commonly find ingenious ways to 'bend' the credit on offer to their actual needs of the moment and/or to continue using informal devices in parallel. Conversely, where farming inputs or small businesses are the need of the moment, poor people may try to assemble a full set of financial service devices to meet the need, of which the modern microcredit loans may be merely one element. Thus, having a microenterprise as a component of one's livelihood strategy makes it more, rather than less, important for poor people to have access to financial services, not just to provide capital for the enterprise, but to cater for the many contingent needs and opportunities that inevitably arise. One of the most common causes of enterprise failure is the unavoidable erosion of business capital to meet other demands on household cash-flow.

General-purpose Financial Services and Sustainable Livelihoods

Seen from the sustainable livelihoods perspective, indigenous general-purpose financial intermediation is one of 'policies, institutions and processes' and is crucial for creating, enhancing, employing and protecting natural, physical and social capital. Among the expenditures that most commonly require poor people to seek financial intermediation are those that enhance or protect human capital – education and healthcare. Maintaining social capital, especially through saving up or borrowing to pay for visiting or entertaining relatives, patrons and other potential allies is another common example. A record kept by a Dhaka-based savings bank for slum dwellers showed that one-third of withdrawals were made for transportation and food costs so that people could visit (or entertain visitors from) their home villages.

Because of its reciprocal nature, the link between financial services and social capital is particularly strong. Financial service devices enable people to exploit their savings to create the financial capital needed to form or maintain social capital. In return, social capital provides the means through which financial capital can be formed, by providing partners for reciprocal or contractual money management behaviour, links to service providers like moneylenders and deposit collectors, or providing fellow members for savings clubs such as ROSCAs.

By not emphasizing the difference that access to financial services makes to a household's ability to secure and use other forms of capital, the livelihoods literature in the past may have underestimated the significance of financial services. The Finance and Development researchers (see Note 2) have been running interviews that focus on episodes in their respondents' lives during which they felt a pressing need for a lump sum (whether they actually obtained it or not), and the resulting stories vividly demonstrate how human capital (life, health, education) and social capital (marriage and employment alliances) were won or lost simply as a result of the presence or absence of reliable ways of turning savings into lump sums.

The research has shown how informal general-purpose financial service devices are similar in nature in urban and rural settings, at least in Bangladesh. However, in any given urban area there tends to be a greater range of devices than in any village. Their urban use is not necessarily more intensive – indeed, the most common of all devices, reciprocal borrowing and lending between neighbours and relatives, is, if anything, practised more frequently by rural households. But values tend to be higher in the town. In urban slums livelihoods are often more monetized. In town the proportion of income gained, in cash, from paid labour, trading and other services is higher than in the countryside, and the proportion gained, in kind, from primary production is lower. Basic goods (food, fuel, shelter and transport) are more likely to be purchased (for cash) than produced or found. Above all, the range of employment and self-employment opportunities is greater, and livelihoods that rely on multiple and frequently changing suboccupations need to be lubricated more frequently with cash.

Policy Implications

A livelihood perspective helps us to understand the frequency and intensity of demand for financial services from the poor and the myriad ways in which informal attempts have been made to meet that demand. It should not, however, romanticize informal services. On the contrary, there is ample evidence of the weakness and failures of savings clubs, ROSCAs and deposit collections, and of the high costs, unreliability and unavailability of moneylenders. Prices in the informal market everywhere point to severe supply-side constraints on informal financial services of all kinds. In this competition for access to services, the very poor are the least well served (Rutherford and Arora 1997; Jalan and Ravallion, 1997; Sinha and Lipton, 1999; Dercon, 1999; Wright, 2000). Their incomes are more often irregular and unreliable, making it harder for them to join clubs that require equal and regular pay-ins, and they may lack social or kinship links to potential informal moneylenders. They may not own their home, a key asset used as collateral for loans from informal as well as from formal sources, and their insecure tenure rights to rented or squatted homes may make it harder for them to settle in one place for long enough to establish residency as a qualification for joining clubs or using commercial services. Moreover, financial service needs and opportunities vary with age, gender, social and ethnic group and wealth (among other factors), and existing informal services do not serve this diversity even-handedly. For example, in many societies women marry older men and then outlive them, but informal devices that help women to manage their almost inevitable widowhood are poorly developed.

The case for supporting the establishment of flexible general-purpose financial service provision for the poor on a formal or semi-formal basis is therefore strong (Sebsted and Cohen, 1999). This task has only just begun. A handful of initiatives are beginning to show that flexible services can be delivered to the poor. One such is *Safe*Save, which operates in the slums of Dhaka, Bangladesh (see Box 7.1). Grameen Bank, the microcredit pioneer, now has plans to offer long-term accumulating-deposit savings plans to its clients, as well as the opportunity to invest their savings long term, through the Bank, in the Dhaka stock exchange. Encouragingly, many donors, including CGAP (Consultative Group to Assist the Poorest, a consortium of microfinance donors),[3] are now seriously examining the arguments for flexible general-purpose financial services for the poor.

BOX 7.1 *FINANCIAL SERVICES FOR THE POOR:* SAFE*SAVE IN DHAKA*

*Safe*Save recruits clients as individuals, eschewing the constraints of group formation, and serves them through a daily visit to their home or workplace. On each occasion, clients can save, or withdraw, or pay down loans, in any sum they choose, including zero. *Safe*Save is still very small, with fewer than 6000 clients in mid-2001. Thus, although three of its four branches are covering their costs already from income earned on loans, it is by no means clear that such a service could be offered sustainably – or even offered at all – on the grand scale already achieved by the much more restricted services delivered by microcredit organizations in Bangladesh. However, pushed by the healthy need to improve their products to keep or extend their market share, some of these large organizations are now themselves experimenting with more flexible services. The ASA (Association for Social Advancement), a large nationwide MFI, for example, with 1.5 million clients, has been experimenting with two new savings products in addition to its basic diet of microenterprise lending.
Source: www.safesave.org

SUPPORT FOR ENTERPRISE: BUSINESS DEVELOPMENT SERVICES AND THE POLICY ENVIRONMENT

The Relevance of Enterprise Development to Livelihoods

Microfinance was originally conceived as a solution to the problem of capital shortage for the microenterprises of the poor. Rutherford and others have now shown that poor people need a full range of financial services, just like the readers of this book. Not many of us own our own businesses, but we do all need ways of intermediating between the times we get money and the times we spend it. This is common sense, but the sustainable livelihoods approach may have played some part in making development practitioners realize that it is as true for poor people as it is for themselves.

Banking is not only for business, but business people also need more than banking. It is not easy to draw the line between the familiar commercial relationships between businesses and their customers and suppliers, whether of goods or services, and so-called 'business development services' (BDS) which are intended to help businesses to start, to survive and to grow. This term is understood to cover non-financial services. The most familiar types of such service are listed in Table 7.1, roughly classified under the five types of asset which people need for their livelihoods, as identified by Carney (1998, p6), but excluding financial assets since these have been covered in the previous section of this chapter.

Table 7.1 *Business development services and building assets*

Capital asset	Relevant business development services
Physical	The provision of home-based business space, power, water, factory sheds, business incubators, land tenure, roadside rights, transport
Social	The development of cooperatives, self-help groups, associations, clusters, chambers of commerce. Assistance with linkages to customers and to suppliers
Natural	Promotion of sustainable use of raw materials, recycling, pollution reduction, waste disposal
Human	Training, advice, counselling, consultancy, in technical skills, entrepreneurship and management, the provision of information

Some of these services are directly related to the policy environment, and particularly to policies as they are implemented by local authorities, at the city, ward or even more local level. The 'service', in fact, may be the withdrawal of inappropriate rules or other forms of harassment; officials may have to be persuaded to do less, not to do more (see also Chapter 6).

Many of the other services are also routinely provided to small enterprises by other small enterprises, at a profit. The only way by which BDS can be distinguished from other interbusiness relationships may be that BDS are often provided by government or NGOs and are free or subsidized.

The aim of this section is to examine whether, if at all, the sustainable livelihoods approach can inform and improve the provision of services of this type to urban enterprises. Since we are concerned with livelihoods and the alleviation of poverty, our focus is on microenterprises, in which poor people are engaged as part of their attempt to earn a living, rather than with larger, more formal businesses, which may employ poor people, but whose owners are not usually poor. Many of those who engage in microenterprise would prefer to be employed rather than to be self-employed, and the search for a job may have been the main reason they are in a city. The option is not available, however, for many people; self-employment of some sort has to be part of their livelihood strategy.

Much of the more recent BDS literature is about services for small and medium enterprises, with the potential to grow and to employ large numbers (see, for example, Tanburn, 1999, p55; Gibson, 1997, p12). It is hoped that the poor will benefit indirectly from their growth by being employed. It is more difficult to deliver BDS for microenterprises; their owners are less likely to be able to spend time away from their businesses, so that the services probably have to be delivered on site. This means that the cost per client reached is higher, while the benefits in increased incomes, or numbers of jobs created, will almost inevitably be smaller. Microenterprise clients are less likely to be able to pay even a small part of the costs, and BDS are also themselves increasingly expected to be sustainable (Goldmark, 1999, p5). This is unlikely to be possible for most types of services, if their clients are predominantly microenterprises.

Business development services, as the title suggests, are intended to develop businesses. This may or may not mean more jobs; a business owner may be advised to improve quality by replacing a labourer with a machine, or s/he may learn how to cost the different activities and conclude that s/he should close down one which is unprofitable and focus on expanding what remains. The business will have been 'developed' in both cases, but jobs may have been lost. Development may mean growth in profits, or sales, or exports, or it may mean improved technology, reduced pollution or better management systems. The owners' or the employees' incomes may or may not increase, but the sustainability of any increase, or the equity of its distribution, is not usually considered. Business growth is an end in itself, which is deemed likely to lead to greater well-being for all.

The livelihoods approach requires us to take a holistic view of the lives of those who own, or are in some way dependent on, microenterprise. It is odd that it should be necessary to state that people should be at the centre of the development process, but enterprise development does aim to develop the enterprise and thus to benefit its owners; benefits to employees, customers, suppliers or society in general are incidental. We should look beyond the enterprise and its owners, to the wider context in which it operates.

Perhaps the most important aspect of the livelihoods approach is its emphasis on vulnerability and the reduction or mitigation of risk. Self-employment is often perceived as being more risky than being employed by someone else, and formal employment may also include some form of legal protection against dismissal and compensation for loss of employment. These generalizations apply mainly to jobs in formal large-scale businesses, or, more typically, in government organizations. In the contemporary climate of 'down-sizing' and casual employment, it is as or more difficult to get a job with someone else. Nevertheless, and despite reductions in the power of trade unions, such wage employment is still more secure when you have got it than self-employment.

Only a minority of new businesses anywhere survive for more than a year or two, and this seems to be essential to the nature of a competitive free-enterprise economy. Their vulnerability can be reduced by attempts to mitigate 'artificial' causes of failure, such as official harassment and destruction, but it cannot be eliminated. The livelihoods approach suggests that it may be more realistic to try to mitigate the effects of failure through means such as the provision of financial services, such as those advocated by Rutherford in the previous section.

Business development usually means expansion and innovation, which may mean that the business becomes more risky, not less. However, microenterprise failure, even for a poor person, does not necessarily mean total destitution, any more than the failure of a large business leads to poverty for its owners. The owner may find another business opportunity elsewhere, or s/he she may find a job. The occupational biography of Miguel in Cali (Bromley and Gerry, 1979, p209) shows that he was involved in 24 different enterprises in about 28 years, some of them on several different occasions. Some failed dramatically, most often because of theft or official action, and others merely proved unremunerative; in either case, Miguel lost money and had to change. Enterprise is risky.

It would be less risky, and more to the taste of most microentrepreneurs, if they could be employed instead of self-employed. Since this is not possible, the main lesson that the livelihoods approach can teach BDS practitioners is that they should devote more attention to risk reduction.

Appropriate Support for Business: Service Provision and the Policy Environment

This book aims to look at the implications of the livelihoods approach for enterprise development in towns and cities rather than in the countryside where the approach was evolved and has thus far been most commonly applied. We should not exaggerate the differences. Many of the same people are involved in both, there are many 'rural' enterprises in cities, such as dairies, vegetable farms and poultry units, and many household livelihood strategies depend on exchanges and movement between the two (see Chapter 4). Nevertheless, there are some critical differences which have important implications for the design and delivery of BDS. Some of these differences are summarized in Table 7.2, with relevant broad types of business services grouped again under the five asset headings of Carney's pentagon (see Chapter 1), but omitting financial services and with the addition of risk reduction.

Poor urban people cannot always access these services and facilities, such as healthcare, markets and training, but they are more available, even to the poor, in urban than in most rural areas.

Chambers' seminal discussion paper includes three agenda items which he suggests can be 'livelihood intensive' without economic growth (Chambers, 1995, pp33–34). These are secure rights to common property resources, removal

Table 7.2 *Appropriate business services*

Type of business service	Rural situations	Urban situations
Physical facilities, home-based or elsewhere, transport, etc	Homestead and business premises usually secure, small but secure landholdings, land leasing possible, transport and utilities often unavailable	Insecure tenure of home and business locations, need for flexibility, utilities more accessible but often inadequate
Social grouping, cooperative development associations, market linkages, etc	Cohesive small discrete communities, long-standing traditions of informal group working, formal cooperatives often fail because of official interference, linkages to outside markets and suppliers weak	Individualistic, insecure and rapidly changing mixed communities, few formal groupings, many temporary groups for particular purposes, markets and suppliers accessible, markets dynamic and highly competitive
Natural resources, environmental services	High dependency on commons, intense competition for farming resources, space usually adequate for non-farm enterprise	Desperate competition for living and working space, high levels of pollution, locations of all kinds insecure
Human capital, training, advice and information about business opportunities and techniques	Few training opportunities, on-site advice available only for farming, little information about non-farm business opportunities	Apprenticeships, informal training and official training facilities are available, rapid spread of information, new opportunities quickly become overcrowded
Risk reduction	Major risks from drought, flood and pests. Also price fluctuations, input shortages. Few opportunities for risk diversification. Few healthcare facilities	Major risks man-made, from theft and official harassment, although environmental risks also significant in many locations where the poor live. High and continuous physical insecurity. Healthcare facilities usually available, but may be costly

of restrictions and access to health services. His paper was concerned with the rural poor and their livelihoods, but these items may provide some clues as to areas with which urban business development services should be concerned, if they are to go beyond their present business focus and 'place people at the centre'. Although enterprise development has not focused on health services, except as one type of business, the removal of burdens and the improvement of access to property has been a central theme almost as long as small enterprise has been a development concern.

In 1977 a senior adviser at the British Overseas Development Administration stated that small business was irrelevant to 'third world' development, and his view was not unrepresentative of the institution as a whole at that time. Other donors, and national and local governments, however, had for some time been involved in urban microenterprise development, and the whole issue of harassment and irrelevant regulation was already at the centre of the agenda over 25 years ago. In spite of their efforts, however, the situation in many countries is unchanged. In India (Reid, 1993) and worldwide (Harper, 1992, 1996), urban microenterprises are routinely harassed and forcibly removed from their places of business in the interests of urban 'beautification' and the faster movement of motorized vehicles which many poor people cannot afford to use.

Table 7.2 shows that urban microenterprises already have relatively better access than those in rural areas to most forms of BDS, through formal or informal channels. It may be difficult to find a useful niche for publicly provided subsidized BDS 'products', where the subsidy will not damage existing commercial providers, many of which may be microenterprises themselves. DFID itself recognized the difficulty in India in the context of its major programme of slum improvements. Income and asset creation was seen as an important part of any slum improvement project, but it was less clear how support in this direction could be implemented (Buckley, 1997, item 1). It may be better for governments and the donors who assist them to focus on their distinctive competence, which is their money. They should not pay for physical improvements, but should demand that their planning and implementation be informed by a recognition that the reason for the existence of a slum is people's need for a home and a base for microenterprise.

There are, however, ways in which microenterprises can be assisted in a manner which goes beyond the enterprise itself and positively affects the sustainability of the livelihood to which it contributes.

The first is by improving the policy environment which has been referred to above. Many of the serious shocks which affect farmers are not amenable to direct policy intervention, except possibly through major investments in irrigation or flood control which go beyond BDS as it is commonly perceived. Urban shocks, however, are usually man-made. Some of the men who make them are thieves and other law-breakers. Policing is notoriously more effective in the rich than in the poorer parts of cities, and improvements to the quality and the equity of the security services can reduce the vulnerability of the poor substantially. Other instigators of shocks, however, are city employees. Some of these, such as the police, or hygiene, weights and measures or buildings inspectors, may harass microenterprises on a day-to-day basis, as a part of their own livelihood strategies. Others, such as planners and policy-makers, may be quite unaware of the damage they do to the livelihoods of the urban poor, but can also be susceptible to donor influence. This may be through appropriate conditionalities, or through training and exposure to cities where microenterprises have been allowed to flourish, and where the community as a whole has benefited rather than suffered.

A group of street traders in Hyderabad have reduced their vulnerability to the depredations of thieves and to the often more serious threat posed by the city authorities, by providing themselves with a group-managed lock-up facility for their stocks. This initiative owes nothing to official support and is, in fact, designed to protect the traders from officials (Puroshotham, 1999). This is a very modest undertaking, but it demonstrates that there is a role for BDS in the context of urban microenterprises. It is difficult, however, for government authorities or the donors which support them to recognize that the main threat to sustainable urban livelihoods may often be their own activities.

Informal conversations with urban microentrepreneurs and more formal surveys show quite clearly that one of their main problems is harassment from the authorities. It is always easier for public officials to do new things than to stop doing old ones, particularly when the activities which they are told to stop are often unofficially remunerative. External donors also are ill-equipped to promote city-level liberalization since they lack the levers of conditionality which are available at the level of central government. Nevertheless, there are positive ways of promoting urban microenterprises, particularly when city authorities are short of funds, and donors can play a role in this.

One useful approach is through 'microprivatization' (Harper, 2000). Local authorities, or national governments, with or without subsidy from national or international sources, can employ microenterprises to deliver urban public services which are presently costly, ineffective and inequitably distributed. This creates and sustains microenterprises, and also reduces the cost and improves the outreach of services such as urban transport and waste removal, which themselves serve other microenterprises. It is often argued that it is better to improve the outreach services of the large formal providers themselves by resisting the pressure for economies and creating more jobs. Not only would this be very difficult in today's climate, but there is also strong evidence, from experiences as diverse as public telephones in India, community schools in Denmark and irrigation management in the United States, that small local community or privately owned enterprises can manage the retail provision of public services more effectively, and less expensively, than the large-scale service providers, whether they are themselves in the public or the private sector.

This approach has been successfully introduced for many different activities throughout the world, sometimes with donor support. More effective and efficient street cleaning and waste removal in Dar es Salaam, personal health services in Managua and waste recycling in Manila, have all been achieved in this way. This has created large numbers of new microenterprise opportunities and has also improved conditions for existing businesses. This approach is particularly effective for the delivery of health services which Chambers identified as being critical to the reduction of poor people's vulnerability.

The livelihoods approach thus suggests a more focused policy for interventions to assist urban microenterprises. Efforts should be concentrated on improving the policy environment and using microenterprises to deliver public services. For external funding agencies, both methods involve working closely with and through city authorities, rather than setting up special local projects; the results may come more slowly, but they are likely to reach more poor people, more sustainably, and thus to enable them to make long-term and sustainable improvements to their own livelihoods.

Developing Human Capacity for Accessing Employment by Education and Training

The livelihoods framework encapsulates a process of reducing vulnerabilities and building capacities, largely through the enhancement of assets. This conceptualization is inherently positive. It is people-centred, it takes as its starting point existing strengths rather than existing needs and it seeks to understand how relatively modest increments of support can leverage large-scale improvements in livelihood outcomes. The focus of this section is on human capital, specifically on human capital development for employment through education and training.

Reflecting the multidimensional characteristic of livelihoods and the realities of increasingly informalized economies, education and training for employment resists tidy packaging in the traditional preparation-for-employment box. Employment, part-time and seasonal employment, self-employment and enterprise are intertwined in the lives of the poor. This is for the most part a positive thing, although the circumstances that have brought it about may be less so.

Getting to Work

In the preceding sections of this chapter, Rutherford and Harper have described an array of financial, BDS and policy options in support of those seeking their livelihoods as entrepreneurs, albeit often reluctant ones. This section focuses on employment while stressing that employment and enterprise are seldom discrete and are often intimately interrelated. There are many paths to employment and enterprise. These intersecting, overlapping and complementary paths have long been celebrated in literature:

> *My mama say that if I am apprentice to this driver, after some time I will get my own licence and then I can get my own lorry to drive. And if I save my salary and my chop money, I can buy my own lorry and then I will be big man like any lawyer or doctor. So I like that and after we have paid money to the driver of 'Progres' plus one goat, and one bottle of Gordon gin and one piece of cloth, I become his apprentice* (Saro-Wiwa, 1994).

Life imitates art at least as much as the reverse, as the case of Said Ahmed Elmi attests (Box 7.2).

Intertwined and interrelated pathways to work are reflected increasingly in the research that underpins education and training best practice. Over a lifetime, the work of the poor commonly proceeds in stages or cycles of employment, self-employment, enterprise and myriad combinations of these. McGrath et al (1995), in looking at education and training for the informal sector, identified six pathways to work. With some risk of oversimplification, these can be summarized as two:

> **BOX 7.2** *SAID AHMED ELMI, SHOEMAKER: CYCLES OF*
> *EMPLOYMENT AND SELF-EMPLOYMENT*
>
> Said Ahmed Elmi is a 34-year-old Somali shoemaker currently living in Hargeisa,
> the capital of Somaliland (formerly Northwest Somalia). Said has lived and
> worked in many places in the past 15 years, for the most part compelled by
> circumstance to stay ahead of the shifting tides of war and civil war. Said's
> livelihood strategies have been as diverse as the pathways he has followed
> across the Horn of Africa.
>
> When Said was 14 years old he lost the use of his left leg as the result of an
> allergic reaction to medical treatment. As a poor youth in a nomadic culture, with
> little education and no obvious skills, his livelihood prospects appeared severely
> limited. However, Said's assets included a willingness to work with his hands, an
> entrepreneurial sense of what he might do and sufficient social capital to get
> access to training. In 1986 he joined a donor-funded shoemakers' apprenticeship
> programme taught by Omar Ayeda, a master shoemaker from Mogadishu. After
> training, Said became a self-employed shoemaker, working as a junior member
> of a shoemakers' cooperative. In 1988, following the outbreak of war, he fled to
> Mogadishu and joined his former teacher as an employee. When the war came
> to Mogadishu in 1991, Said returned to Hargeisa and again established himself
> as a self-employed shoemaker, now working independently. When civil war
> broke out in Hargeisa in 1994, he fled for a time to Jigjiga, Ethiopia, where he was
> again self-employed. In 1996 he returned to Hargeisa. He is now a member of
> the workers' cooperative of the Somaliland Handicapped Training Centre, where
> he both produces shoes and trains others. Said Ahmed Elmi initially used a form
> of employment-based training (apprenticeship) in order to become self-employed.
> When the need arose he then used his enhanced capacities to gain secure
> employment. He is currently self-employed and a trainer as well. Said has a solid
> base of human and social capital, a demonstrated capacity to overcome advers-
> ity, and the willingness and ability to help others to build their livelihood assets.
>
> *Source:* Grierson, 1997

- from school to employment to self-employment/enterprise; and
- from school to self-employment/enterprise to employment.

Each of these broad avenues subsumes a number of alternative pathways.

Over time, livelihood demands often compel cyclical changes in work status
and encourage opportunistic combinations of employment, self-employment and
enterprise. It is not uncommon to find both pathways used cyclically as well as
simultaneously. This is particularly characteristic of those who are compelled to
start work early in life. Many, such as Said Ahmed Elmi, alternate between
employment and self-employment as their working life progresses. The fluid and
multidimensional reality of livelihoods is such that support for employment must
anticipate that people may prefer either waged work or self-employment, but
may also take up one in the hope that they can transfer to the other in the longer
term.

Supporting Multiple Options

The flexibility implicit in diverse working lives is both a reaction to insecurity and a means of reducing it. However, accessing work opportunities is a formidable challenge. It is increasingly recognized that systems intended to support one form of work – for example, employment – must at least understand and provide for other forms of work as well. Livelihoods are multidimensional as well as both linear and cyclical, as the livelihoods framework makes clear. Education and training systems are only now coming to terms with the reality that they can no longer live within the comfortable confines of an homogenous 'clientele' and narrowly defined outcomes. Education and training systems must help to impart capacities that can both cope with stresses, such as loss of work, and recognize and create opportunities, such as self-employment in lieu of readily available employment.

'Education' and 'training', respectively, need to respond in quite different ways. The fundamental difference between them, from the livelihoods perspective, is that education makes a broad general contribution to asset enhancement, while training usually makes a specific and more immediately applicable one. Each wields a considerable 'transformation' potential, although in very different ways.

Education is in a very real sense the basic element in human capital. Moreover, a solid foundation of basic education enhances all other efforts to build human capital. Hence the urgency and practicality of calls for education for all. Support for education works best when it is delivered early, when most other options for young people are either impractical (for example, many types of training) or undesirable (for example, child labour). Even basic education results in general capacities that can be widely applied over time. Education lends itself to large-scale systematic delivery of standardized products. Even if only in the basics – reading, writing and arithmetic – education results in a sustained positive effect in many civic, social and economic areas. The ability to access, absorb and apply virtually all employment-related skills is a function of the educational base of those undergoing training.

Due to the very different nature of 'training', it is unlikely that there will be calls for training for all. With few exceptions, training needs to be both specialized and situation specific. It is specialized in the sense that it seeks to impart a precise set of skills which can then be applied to a narrow range of tasks. The application of such training-acquired skills is most effective when the training-to-work transition is short. Training must be situation specific in the sense that it is most effective when it responds to both the aspirations and the ideas of those undergoing training and to the opportunities currently available in highly differentiated fast-changing local labour markets. Due to the high levels of specialization and specificity '. . . the large-scale delivery of standardized training programmes is not likely to be viable' (Middleton et al, 1993).

The report of a recent Population Council/International Council for Research on Women (2000) workshop summarizes the elements of good training for livelihoods:

- recognizes the wider economic environment;
- offers training in new, demand-led growth areas and is wary of training in already crowded sectors;
- ensures that skills offered are matched to the needs of communities;
- encourages women and girls to train in new and growing sectors that are not characterized by gender stereotypes;
- keeps programmes simple and consistent;
- exploits traditional knowledge while being wary of traditional barriers; and
- recognizes that a business-like approach is both realistic and holds far greater potential for long-term success.

While the respective contributions of education and training remain sharply differentiated, the roles and responsibilities of education and training systems are becoming less and less so. It is not uncommon to find education programmes that include 'entrepreneurship' components and experiments with 'vocationalizing' primary and secondary curricula. Neither of these approaches as yet has proved themselves in practice, in part due to the very lack of the specificity of generalized approaches to enterprise and vocational training. Correspondingly, '. . . it has become very common to regard a re-orientation towards self-employment as a major contribution towards revitalising' training programmes (Hoppers, 1994). Vocational training in developing countries is now at least as much about enterprise development and self-employment as it is about its traditional role of preparation for employment (Grierson, 2000). These very recent reforms are for the most part crisis driven; they have yet to be tested and proved.

Responding to Need Amid Crisis

Worldwide, many education and training systems are in crisis; they are failing to respond to the needs of growing populations and stagnant economies facing the challenges of globalization (UNESCO, 1996). In all cases the crisis is largely one of outreach and equity. Globally, education for all, although deemed a useful and attainable goal, falls far short of even its quantitative objective. Although many countries have achieved universal primary education and are now concentrating on secondary education, in the poorest parts of the world as few as one in four girls complete primary school (Madavo, 2000). In training, the crisis is one of relevance and equity; there is a mismatch between the training on offer and the demand in local labour markets, as well as greatly restricted access for those most in need of productive skills. In both cases there is a crisis of cost. The funds available for education and training have declined in real terms in many countries, certainly relative to population growth, and increased charges for public services have often had inequitable outcomes.

There are no models or proven approaches to mark the way forward. Hence, it is thought most useful at this juncture to offer a general sense of the factors that influence design, implementation and assessment rather than descriptions of particular approaches or programmes. Table 7.3 summarizes the key factors that influence education and training interventions in support of employment.

The four influencing factors are interrelated. In virtually all cases, modifying any single factor will affect one or more of the other factors. The art of designing

Table 7.3 *Factors influencing education and training for employment*

Factor	Problem Description/Remedies
Relevance	There is a mismatch between the available education and training opportunities on offer and the skills and capacities in demand in local labour markets: • Education should provide the base on which livelihood-oriented human capital assets are built. • Training should respond to local labour market demand and result in work (employment, self-employment or enterprise).
Cost	Education and training are expensive; education due to the outreach needed to yield broad-based positive outcomes, training due to specialization and relatively high unit costs: • The social and economic returns to basic education are well established; support for education, particularly basic education, should be increased to reflect this. • Training can be made more efficient by greater cost sharing and by making better use of traditional knowledge and available facilities, particularly those of local enterprises.
Equity	Education and training are often difficult to access and difficult to use, especially for those who, due to social or economic disadvantage, are in greatest need of work-related skills: • Education: provision should be made to overcome economic and social barriers to access and participation by, *inter alia*, adequate funding for basic provision, scholarships/vouchers for those in greatest need, and restructuring schooling in terms of, for example, location, vernacular languages and class schedules, in order to accommodate the circumstances and multiple obligations of those in need. • Training programmes should reflect and accommodate the backgrounds and customs of those they serve. Training schedules and structures should accommodate the circumstances and multiple obligations of those they are intended to serve.
Asset enhancement	Education and training initiatives should be designed and assessed in terms of the degree to which they enhance the human (and social) capital of those participating: • Education at all levels should be structured to provide a sound (even if modest) general basis for the acquisition of specific work and income-related skills. • Training should provide the skills needed to grasp existing work opportunities and to identify future opportunities; asset enhancement should be assessed in terms of increased income, greater flexibility, reduced vulnerability to crisis and enhanced access to economic support networks.

Source: Derived from Grierson and Schnurr, 2000

useful employment support interventions is that of finding an appropriate balance of factors in relation to local resources and circumstances.

Making Best Use of the Tools Available

Large-scale unemployment and underemployment is a function of three inter-related problems: skills shortages, the lack of equitable access to employment opportunities and a severe shortage of employment (Crump et al, 2000). The near universal response in low-income cities has been a structural shift in the direction of self-employment and the informal sector, followed by belated attempts to make the best of this largely unwelcome situation. Education and training can do little to resolve the underlying problem – the dearth of jobs. Appropriately structured economic growth is the key to solving the job shortage problem. Human capital development initiatives, however, can do much to expand the diversity and quantity of relevant training and to improve equitable access.

Support for education and training is likely to be most effective and efficient when cast within a context of pro-poor growth. Overall employment must be growing if further subdivision and displacement is to be avoided. Initiatives intended to '. . . enhance welfare and employability . . . should be undertaken in the broader context of policies aimed at enhancing overall labour absorption capacity' (ILO, 1999). John Mellor, in surveying the literature on pro-poor growth, found that expanding education for the poor is an important contribut-ing factor. In his analysis the '. . . facilitation of the growth of small scale non-farm enterprises, largely producing non-tradable (i.e. locally consumed) goods and services' is central to pro-poor growth (Mellor, 1999). These small enter-prises are, he suggests, the key to tomorrow's employment.

Urban enterprises and urban employment manifest characteristics that reflect the density, diversity and dynamism of urban areas. Hernando de Soto makes a compelling case for the role and potential of urban housing as an economic asset, an aspect that can complement without diminishing housing's shelter function (de Soto, 2000). Pro-poor urban livelihoods initiatives are most likely to be effective when they focus on sectors that offer good growth prospects (such as transportation and waste management), many entry-level microenterprise and self-employment opportunities (such as housing) and good prospects for dis-aggregation rather than economies of scale (such as light construction and many types of services, from appliance repair to hairdressing). Many sectors, such as waste collection and sorting, tend by their nature to favour local (that is, community-based) enterprises. New sectors, the bulk of which are urban or urban based (such as electronic assembly), may be ungendered at the outset. Similarly, traditional sectors may lower gender barriers when they modernize and adopt new technologies (such as machine-based shoe manufacture). Many rural–urban differences are pronounced and significant in terms of livelihoods generally and human capital development specifically. Training initiatives in support of urban livelihoods work to best effect when they are designed to identify and increase access to opportunities in urban growth sectors that have significant pro-poor growth potential.

Beall closes Chapter 5 with the thought that support for urban livelihoods should help people to invest in their own futures. Education and training, when set within the context of pro-poor growth opportunities, can do much to encourage and reward such investments.

NOTES

1   Financial services that allow money to be transferred across national or local boundaries, or currencies to be exchanged, are also very important for many poor people, but are ignored in this brief treatment
2   By the Institute for Development Policy and Management at Manchester University for the Finance and Development project funded by DFID (www.man.ac.uk/idpm)
3   Consultative Group to Assist the Poorest (www.cgap.org), based at the World Bank and including DFID as one of its leading members

REFERENCES

Alderman, H and Paxson, C (1994) 'Do the poor insure? A synthesis of the literature on risk sharing institutions in developing countries', in proceedings of the *International Economic Association Moscow Conference*, vol 4, Moscow
Bouman, F J A (1989) *Small Short and Unsecured: Informal Rural Finance in India*, Oxford University Press, Delhi
Brink, R and Chavas, J-P (1991) *The Microeconomics of an Indigenous African Institution*, Cornell University, Cornell Food and Nutrition Policy Programme, Working Paper 15, Cornell, NY
Bromley, R and Gerry, C (1979) *Casual Work and Poverty in Third World Cities*, John Wiley, Chichester
Brown, W and Churchill, C (2000) *Insurance Provision for Low-Income Communities*, USAID, Washington, DC
Buckley, G (1997) 'An options paper on enterprise development in India', DFID, New Delhi
Carney, D (ed) (1998) *Sustainable Rural Livelihoods, What Contribution Can We Make?* DFID, London
Chambers, R (1995) *Poverty and Rural Livelihoods: Whose Reality Counts?*, Discussion Paper 347, Institute for Development Studies, University of Sussex, Brighton
Crump, P, Grierson, J and Wahbah, M (2000) *Tradition and Change: Enterprise-based Training in Egypt*, CEOSS (Coptic Evangelical Organization for Social Services), NCNW (National Council of Negro Women), USAID, Cairo
Dercon, S (1999) *Income Risk, Coping Strategies and Safety Nets*, World Development Report 2000 Background Paper, World Bank, Washington, DC
de Soto, H (2000) *The Mystery of Capital: Why Capitalism Triumphs in the West and Fails Everywhere Else*, Basic Books, New York
Fafchamps, M (1995) 'Risk Sharing, Quasi-credit and the Enforcement of Informal Contracts', Stanford University, Stanford, CA, draft
Gibson, D (1997) 'Business development services – core principles and future challenges', *Small Enterprise Development*, vol 8, no 3, pp4–14
Goldmark, L (1999) 'The financial viability of business development services', *Small Enterprise Development*, vol 10, no 2, pp4-16
Grierson, J (1997) *Where There Is No Job: Vocational Training for Self-employment in Developing Countries*, SKAT, St Gallen; University of Edinburgh Centre of African Studies; Swiss Development Cooperation, Bern

Grierson, J (2000) 'Vocational training for self-employment: learning from enterprise development best practice', *Small Enterprise Development*, vol 11, no 3

Grierson, J and Schnurr, J (2000) *Youth, Enterprise, Livelihoods and Reproductive Health: Can Small Enterprise Help Address the HIV/AIDS Crisis in Africa?* Report by FTP International, Helsinki, to International Development Research Centre, Ottawa

Harper, M (1992) 'The city as a home for enterprise: has anything changed for the informal sector?', *Habitat International*, vol 16, no 2, pp143–148

Harper, M (1996) 'Urban planning and the informal sector', *Regional Development Dialogue*, vol 17, no 1, pp97–112

Harper, M (2000) *Public Services Through Private Enterprise – Micro-privatisation for Improved Delivery*, Sage Publications, New Delhi; ITDG Publications, London

Holzmann, R and Jorgensen, S (1999) *Social Protection Sector Strategy Paper*, World Bank, Human Development Network, Washington, DC, mimeo

Hoppers, W (1994) *The Promotion of Self-employment in Education and Training Institutions: Perspectives in East and Southern Africa,* Discussion Paper, International Labour Office, Geneva

Hulme, D, Rutherford, S, Matin, I and Maniruzzaman, forthcoming reports on financial services for the poor and poorest, Institute for Development Policy and Management, Manchester

ILO (1999) *Strategies to Combat Youth Unemployment and Marginalisation in Anglophone Africa*, International Labour Office/SAMAT, Geneva, draft, May

Jalan, J and Ravallion, M (1997) 'Risk, financial markets and human capital in a developing country', *Review of Economic Studies,* vol 64, no 3, pp311–335

Madavo, C (2000) 'Stand back and take a more positive look at Africa', *International Herald Tribune*, Paris, 6 June

Matin, I, Hulme, D and Rutherford, S (1999) *Financial Services for the Poor and Poorest: Deepening Understanding to Improve Provision*, Finance and Development Paper 9, Institute for Development Policy and Management, Manchester University, Manchester

McGrath, S and King, K with Leach, F and Carr-Hill, R et al (1995) *Education and Training for the Informal Sector,* Education Research, Serial No 11, DFID, London

Mellor, J M (1999) 'Pro-poor growth: the relation between growth in agriculture and poverty reduction', Report to USAID, John W Mellor Associates, Inc., 11 November

Middleton, J, Ziderman, A and Van Adams, A (1993*) Skills For Productivity*, World Bank, Washington, DC

Morduch, J (1997) 'Between market and state: can informal insurance patch the safety net?', Princeton University, Princeton, NJ, mimeo

Platteau, J P and Abraham, A (1987) 'An inquiry into quasi-credit contracts: The role of reciprocal credit and interlinked deals in small-scale fishing communities', *Journal of Development Studies*, vol 23, no 4

Population Council/ICRW (2000) *Adolescent Girls' Livelihoods: Essential Questions, Essential Tools,* Workshop Report, Population Council, New York; International Council for Research on Women, Washington, DC

Purushotham, P (1999) 'The case for lock-up storage facilities for micro-enterprises in India', *Small Enterprise Development*, vol 10, no 2, pp49–54

Reid, M (1993) 'Business regulation and poor entrepreneurs in urban India', *Small Enterprise Development*, vol 4, no 1, pp34–42

Rutherford, S (1996) *A Critical Typology of Financial Services for the Poor*, ActionAid Working Paper 1, London

Rutherford, S (2000) *The Poor and Their Money*, Oxford University Press, Delhi

Rutherford, S and Arora, S (1997) 'City Savers', Urban Poverty Office, DFID, Delhi

Saro-Wiwa, Ken (1994) *Sozaboy,* Longman, Harlow

Sebsted, J and Cohen, M (1999) *Micro-finance, Risk Management and Poverty*, background paper for World Development Report 2000, USAID, Washington, DC

Sinha, S and Lipton, M (1999) *Damaging Fluctuations, Risk and Poverty: A Review*, World Development Report 2000 Background Paper, World Bank, Washington, DC

Tanburn, J (1999) 'How sustainable can business development services really be?' *Small Enterprise Development*, vol 10, no 1, pp53–57

Udry, C (1994) 'Risk and insurance in a rural credit market', *Review of Economic Studies*, vol 61

UNESCO (1996) *Analyses, Agendas and Priorities for Education in Africa*, Working Series No ED-96/WS/13, UNESCO, Paris

Wright, G (2000) 'Relative Risk in Mount Elgon', MicroSave Africa, Kampala, mimeo

Zeller, M, Schrieder, G, von Braun, J and Heidhues, F (1996) *Rural Finance for Food Security for the Poor: Implications for Research and Policy*, Food Policy Review No 4, International Food Policy Research Institute, Washington, DC

Chapter 8

Social Capital, Local Networks and Community Development

Sue Phillips

INTRODUCTION

The last two decades have seen an increasing emphasis on community participation in urban development programmes. As experience has grown, approaches to participation have evolved and become more sophisticated and central to such programmes. While generally not explicit, the purpose of participatory development initiatives is often to help build social capital among the urban poor. Social capital – that is, the relationships and networks developed and drawn upon by the urban poor to survive and improve their livelihoods – is now recognized as a vital part of their livelihood strategies.

The following chapter draws on the author's own experience of state-funded urban development projects in South Asia, many of which were funded by DFID (see also Chapter 14). The projects analysed stretch over a 15-year period. The analysis examines the approaches to participation used by these projects, explores the extent to which these approaches have increased social capital and draws some implications for urban policy and practice from the findings.

The analysis uses a livelihoods framework to analyse social capital. As the following analysis shows, social capital is indeed a highly useful concept. One of its most valuable aspects is that it forces the user to take existing networks, relationships and organizations used by poor people as a starting point. What works and doesn't work? Who benefits and who is excluded? What are the constraints which prevent the accumulation of social capital, particularly among poorer groups? The critical question then becomes for outsiders: how can external agencies (governmental, NGO or donors) support the processes and structures used by poor people to improve their livelihood opportunities?

WHAT IS SOCIAL CAPITAL AND WHY DOES IT NEED STRENGTHENING?

The Habitat Agenda that emerged from Istanbul in 1996 commits the international community to supporting the development of social capital as an important strand of urban poverty reduction:

> *We commit ourselves to . . . encouraging the establishment of community-based organisations, civil society organisations and other forms of non-governmental entities that can contribute to the efforts to reduce poverty to improve the quality of life in human settlements* (Habitat Agenda Commitment C: Enablement and Participation).

This commitment reflects a long tradition in urban policy that can be traced back to John Turner and the self-help movement of the 1970s which influenced the emergence of sites and service, and slum and squatter upgrading projects during the 1970s and 1980s. The concept of participation took on a new importance in the late 1980s and 1990s with the broader shift towards mainstreaming people's participation in development. This period saw the emergence and evolution of urban development programmes which focused initially on involving community groups in the implementation and maintenance of projects and, later on, the involvement of people from the outset of project planning and design. The distinction is often made between participation as a means to an end and participation as an end in itself. Much of the emphasis of the last two decades, particularly within government programmes, has been on building community groups as a means to an end, in order to achieve more effective and efficient outcomes. Since the late 1990s the emphasis of urban policy and programmes has been increasingly on governance and a belief that poor people have a right to participate. The empowerment of poor people has become an important end in its own right and a means of obtaining accountable government. 'Partnership' has become the buzz word. Associated with this shift towards governance we have seen the re-emergence of the concept of civil society and a belief that accountable and responsible government can be achieved by strengthening civil society.

While it is not new, social capital re-emerged in the late 1990s as an analytical concept in development theory and practice. Although commonly used, the term is often confused and has many definitions. As defined in Chapter 1, social capital is regarded as a resource that people use to achieve certain ends. It is argued that social capital is particularly important to the poor as a survival mechanism. In the absence of other assets, poor people rely on their relationships, associations and networks to survive on a day-to-day basis – for example, sharing and reciprocating labour, cash, food, information, friendship and moral support. In times of crisis, such as ill health, death, land clearances or fire, social capital is one of the few resources upon which poor people can draw (see also Chapter 5).

The relationships and networks formed by the poor are, of course, not just with other poor people. They also draw on relationships with better off groups (for example through caste, kinship or political links). Furthermore, social capital may not always be harmonious. The poor utilize patronage networks that may be highly exploitative but nonetheless a vital part of their livelihood strategies, providing access to land, housing, credit and jobs. (See, for example, Chapter 6 on the relationship between social capital and economic growth.) Some forms of social capital, such as gangs, are referred to as 'negative'. This terminology belies the fact, however, that there are often both costs and benefits deriving from participation in any network or relationship. Both the poor and their patrons use patron–client relationships for their own advantage, as illustrated by the recognition by politicians that the urban poor constitute an important source of electoral support and that political control of an urban area can often be won or lost by the support or absence of support of the poor population.

What do we Know about Social Capital in Urban Areas?

There is much debate in the literature and in development practice around the question of whether social capital is weaker or stronger in towns and cities than it is in rural areas. Boxes 8.1 and 8.2 list typical social networks in urban areas and the factors influencing the formation of social capital. The opportunities for and barriers to its formation are discussed below.

Box 8.1 *Examples of Social Networks in Urban Areas*

Neighbourhood-based groupings
Gender- and age-based networks and associations
Kinship-based associations (including rural–urban linkages)
Networks based on a common area of origin
Political-based networks
Religious and ethnic linkages and associations
Savings and credit groups
Employment-based networks and associations (such as trade unions, informal associations, trading networks)
Linkages with NGOs and other external civil society organizations

---

Opportunities

Some of the main opportunities for social capital formation in urban areas arise from the following:

- Reciprocal relations and social networks and associations in urban areas are diverse, drawing on rural–urban family linkages (Tacoli, 1998), networks based on kin and place of origin, and more recently formed local networks. Relationships form around short-term reciprocity, centred mainly on money and responding to crises such as death and illness, and longer-term reciprocity

---

Box 8.2 *Factors Known to Influence the Formation of Social Capital in Urban Areas*

Barriers	Opportunities
Heterogeneity of populations	Richness of social contacts
Mobility	Links with rural areas
Breakdown of traditional networks	New networks needed for survival
Cultural norms	Cultural norms
Social exclusion	Social change
Relative poverty	Common struggles
Exploitation	Resisting exploitation
Crime and violence	Common adversity
Restrictive policies	Supportive policies
Restrictive laws	Supportive laws

---

with respect to food, water, space and child care (Moser, 1996). Networks and associations are not just based on neighbourhood, but also religion, ethnicity, politics (Mitlin, 1999) and labour (Beall and Kanji, 1999; Rakodi, 1999; Harrison and McVey, 1997).

- Organization in cities can provide greater potential benefits for poor people. This is in large part because of the greater availability and diversity of resources and opportunities in urban areas – for example, jobs, infrastructure, health and education. It is also due in part to the need to organize to secure basic needs – for example, for land and infrastructure. The most documented examples of organization are around land tenure, infrastructure and basic services and housing (Mitlin, 1999). In fact, 'conflictual negotiation' can be an important vehicle for strengthening social capital (Moser, 1996). Access to information is also an important reason for association in urban areas (Meikle, 1999). On the other hand, the greater availability of resources by no means guarantees access for poor people.
- Social relationships – for example, based on gender, ethnicity, caste/class and age – are transformed in cities, providing increased inclusion for some and greater vulnerability and social exclusion for others. This transformation of social relationships affects the relative strength of social capital among and between social groups. For example, women and lower caste groups are often less constrained by traditional values in urban areas. On the other hand, ethnic or religious minorities may be more vulnerable as cities bring together opposing groups in close proximity. Equally, the elderly and children can be left out due to the breakdown of traditional family and community support structures.

Barriers

Although there are opportunities for the formation of social capital in urban areas, the barriers are significant:

- Urban 'communities' are highly differentiated and tend to be more hetero-geneous than rural ones, being made up of individuals and households from different social, economic and geographic backgrounds who come together as strangers. The relative size of cities is also a factor. In reality, of course, while rural communities are often perceived as homogeneous, these too are made up of diverse households and individuals with different interests, positions and access to resources.

- It is often argued that social capital is weaker in urban areas because of the heterogeneity and mobility of the population. This is likely to be particularly true in areas of rental housing and newly established settlements. The break-down of social capital and the 'moral economy' is often manifest in crime and violence, drug and alcohol abuse, threats to personal safety and increased isolation (Moser and Holland, 1997). Increases in crime and violence then lead to a further breakdown in trust and community, leading to a downward spiral of social breakdown and poverty.

- There is evidence that the poorest avoid reciprocal relationships because they cannot meet their obligations and that those people without social connec-tions are the most impoverished of all (Moser, 1996; Gonzales de la Rocha, 1994). Experience in India, for example, is that poorer households are least likely to participate in neighbourhood groups and women casual labourers are unlikely to participate in savings and credit groups (IDD, 1997).

- The poor are often forced to engage in networks and associations which are exploitative in order to access the basic resources that they require for sur-vival. For example, the patronage of politicians, community leaders, gangsters and drug barons may be the only way to secure access to resources such as land, housing and credit. Such patronage relationships are threatened by attempts to create less exploitative forms of social capital.

In summary, what emerges is a picture of dualism, with weakened social capital resulting from the breakdown of traditional relationships and networks on the one hand, and on the other, a rich associational life resulting from the need to form new and varied reciprocal relationships and networks in the complex social milieu of the city (Beall, 1997). Like rural areas, the extent to which people participate in and benefit from this rich associational life depends on their existing economic, social and political resources.

WHAT CAN WE LEARN FROM PAST EXPERIENCE?

While the term 'social capital' is a relatively recent arrival to urban poverty policy discourses, there is a long tradition internationally of policy approaches that promote community-based approaches to urban development. In exploring the usefulness of social capital as an analytical concept in urban policy, we have therefore a wealth of experience on which to draw. The following analysis draws largely on experience from DFID-funded projects in South Asia. It analyses approaches adopted for supporting social capital in government-supported urban programmes and then examines three basic questions:

- Have these projects added to stocks of social capital?
- Do these programmes address those factors which influence the formation of social capital in urban areas?
- Has this helped to reduce vulnerability to shocks, trends and seasonality?

Although this analysis draws heavily, though not uniquely, on Indian projects funded by DFID, this experience is not unique and the models and approaches adopted are mirrored in those of other donors and governments.

Supporting Social Capital Formation in Urban Projects in India

The Slum Improvement Projects (SIPs) analysed here were a series of integrated projects in the five Indian cities of Hyderabad, Visakhapatnam, Vijayawada, Indore and Calcutta.[1] The projects were implemented through municipal corporations or development authorities. They started in the late 1980s and early 1990s, and included settlement upgrading, with infrastructure (water, sanitation, paving, drainage and electricity), and the provision of health, education and community development facilities and services.

Community participation was seen as a necessary part of the SIPs programme. In the early stages of these projects, the objective of participation was to facilitate greater 'community' involvement as a means of ensuring that facilities and services were maintained and continued beyond implementation. Following an earlier UNICEF urban basic services (UBS) model, community participation focused on the formation of Neighbourhood Committees (NHCs) as the interface between government and slum communities, and as an instrument for mobilizing people's inputs into the project (for example, assisting the authorities to plan and implement programmes, monitoring, voluntary action and managing community halls). In some cases, separate women's committees were established in recognition that women would need space to overcome social and cultural norms which discouraged their participation in community decision-making. In practice, these subcommittees became sidelined into health, education and income-generation projects (reproductive and productive roles).

Subsequent DFID-funded urban poverty projects in India and Pakistan, and other government-supported urban projects in India, have continued to use either an externally driven model or a Government of India (GoI) model. Table 8.1 summarizes the community structures used in a variety of urban projects in India and Pakistan. All these projects originated in the mid- to late 1990s. The main difference in the community structures used in the recent projects tends to be the development of more localized institutions (that is, neighbourhood or street level), in addition to slum-level structures. We also see the emergence of city-level networks of local-level groups (such as in Cochin). In the GoI model (the Swarna Jayanti Shahan Rozgar Yojana programme) we also see a shift away from mixed to women's only groups. A significant departure from the basic neighbourhood group model has been the introduction of savings and credit groups, again targeting women. In Faisalabad, management groups were also established around specific activities – for example, schools, health clinics and literacy classes.

Table 8.1 *Examples of approaches to social capital in South Asia*

Project	Main community structures created	Comments
Cochin Urban Poverty Project	• Neighbourhood groups • Area development societies • Community development society (CDS)	• Followed Government of India model to be replicable • Structure based on women's organizations. Men sometimes invited to participate • Increased role for people's participation in project planning, implementation and monitoring. • Community action planning mechanisms developed • Poverty focus places greater emphasis on social inclusion and programmes to address priority needs – for example, financial services, emergency relief fund, safe shelters for women and children • The poor disaggregated into the better-off poor, average poor, poorer and vulnerable • Project designed following urban poverty profile study
Cuttack	• Savings and credit groups	• Infrastructure-focused project • People's participation through community action planning
Chinagadili	• Neighbourhood Committees (NHCs) • Programme Monitoring Committees (PMC) • Project Steering Committee (PSC) • Savings and credit groups	• Recognized the importance of existing associations (*sanghams* and *mahila mandals*), NHCs act as federations of existing groups • NHCs required to consult existing associations • NHCs, PMCs and PSC are forums for project planning, decision-making and monitoring at different levels PMCs and PSC

Table 8.1 *Examples of approaches to social capital in South Asia (contd)*

Project	Main community structures created	Comments
		consist of community, government and NGO representatives
Andhra Pradesh Urban Services for the Poor	• Neighbourhood groups • Area Development Societies • CDS	• Municipal planning process based on participatory poverty assessments (PPAs) • Municipal authorities prepare Municipal Action Plans for poverty reduction (MAPPs) based on PPAs
Faisalabad Area Upgrading Programme	• Multi-purpose community organizations (MPCOs) at lane, neighbourhood and area level • Women's groups formed around savings and credit, literacy • Health, school management and literacy committees	• MPCOs select from menu of inputs • Government staff help MPCOs to prepare projects • MPCOs put projects to government project approval income generation and committee • Cost sharing with MPCOs
Bangalore Urban Poverty Project	• Slum Development Teams (SDTs) • Street and block groups in larger slums • Women's groups and networks based on savings and credit (*Bembala*)	• Strong emphasis on empowerment • Slum Development Plans prepared by SDTs with project staff help • Main aim is to empower slum communities. Projects undertaken to further that objective
Swarna Jayanti Shahari Rozgar Yojana Programme (SJSRY)	• Neighbourhood groups • Area Development Societies • CDS	• Central mechanism for delivery of urban poverty programmes • Focus on women • Neighbourhood to city-level planning based on community-based action plans • Programme driven rather than needs driven

All these projects aim to encourage greater community participation in government programmes than earlier projects. The aim of building social capital is broadly consistent across the projects – that is, to develop the knowledge, skills and organization of poor people in order to increase their access to resources. In all projects this is to be achieved through the establishment of community groups to provide an effective 'interface' between poor people and government. Again, although the stated objective is to empower poor people, the intention remains essentially instrumental.

These projects are also characterized by a more explicit poverty reduction focus. The best have been designed following participatory poverty assessments, highlight the needs of different categories of poor people and aim to promote social inclusion and reduce vulnerability. All these projects are characterized by the use of participatory methodologies and tools to help achieve greater and genuine participation – for example, through community action plans (CAPs) and participatory poverty assessments (PPAs). These projects and programmes therefore represent a significant departure from earlier urban projects in India, both in terms of objectives and approaches, although their impact has yet to be assessed. However, the basic organizational structures intended to facilitate participation remain the same.

Have These Projects Added to Stocks of Social Capital?

One of the traditional ways of assessing the impacts of urban programmes on social capital is to use indicators, such as the number of new groups formed, the size of their membership, the representation of men and women, or the activities undertaken. Unfortunately, these indicators tell us little about whether projects really build on, and have contributed to, existing networks, relationships and associations in urban areas. The following analysis explores the extent to which the models used in India built on existing social capital.

Although it was a major breakthrough at the time, in retrospect the Neighbourhood Committee model can be seen as externally driven and simplistic, simplifying complex social and political reality for administrative and managerial convenience. The model was based on one neighbourhood committee per slum, regardless of settlement size or composition, with a standard formula for membership and representation, and a set of prescribed roles and responsibilities. As such it was a technical solution to facilitating interaction between governments and communities. Without exception, all the models adopted in later programmes (neighbourhood groups, savings and credit groups, and others, such as school management committees in Faisalabad) were also externally imposed forms of organization, following variations of the basic neighbourhood group concept.

With the exception of the Chinagadili project, none of the projects makes any attempt to either identify or build on existing social organizations, networks or relationships. Slum neighbourhoods are highly complex social entities. Individuals and households have extensive networks based on friendship, kin, ethnicity, religion, work, child care, employment, economic and social reciprocity. In effect, all existing formal and informal relationships, networks and associations were overlooked in introducing an organization from outside. This included ignoring any other organizations that had been set up in the past through other government or NGO programmes. Also, there was no recognition that poor people have lives, relationships and networks that go beyond the physical boundaries of a given slum and that a slum is not a bounded unit in social, economic and political terms.

Furthermore, with the exception of the Cochin project, no attempts appear to have been made to analyse existing social capital (what Moser, 1996, refers to as a community institutional analysis). Where participatory poverty assessments have been undertaken, they have not explored issues of networks and relationships in depth or used the information to develop alternative models for strengthening social capital. More in-depth analysis would be required to identify whether the projects had in practice worked with networks and associations beyond those established through the respective projects. However, impact assessments of the SIPs (IDD, 1997), Faisalabad Area Upgrading Project (Phillips with ActionAid, 1997) and Bangalore Urban Poverty Project (Phillips et al, 1997), found these projects to have ignored existing networks and associations (see Box 8.3). It would appear that project designers have assumed uncritically that social capital is weak or non-existent in urban areas and therefore is something that needs to be developed through external assistance.

BOX 8.3 *IGNORING EXISTING SOCIAL CAPITAL IN BANGALORE*

In Bangalore, the study found existing formal community-based organizations in 11 out of the 14 project settlements, based on neighbourhood, gender, age and caste interests. Residents saw the Slum Development Team (SDT) as a temporary, project-related organization and the CBOs as long-term organizations. This finding completely undermines the objective of the SDTs, which was to strengthen rather than duplicate existing CBOs. A simple participatory appraisal Venn diagram exercise identified organizations and their linkages to external organizations. A more in-depth analysis would have been able to identify more informal associations, relationships and networks.

Source: Phillips et al, 1997

The impact assessment undertaken of the India SIPs identified a number of useful but not unexpected findings about the impact of the projects on social capital. On the positive side, NHCs were used by 'communities' as a vehicle to access government resources (at least those that were available through the project). A few NHCs, despite being externally introduced, had taken on a life of their own. In Vijayawada, a city-wide network of NHCs was spawned. The projects had also helped to develop skills among NHC members through their interaction and negotiation with government and had legitimized poor people's right to participate in the management of programmes designed to benefit them. The NHC model (or its variations) has now been institutionalized within government as the mechanism for involving people in poverty programmes.

Unfortunately, the NHCs' appropriateness for institutionalization is questioned by other findings from the study. NHCs were found to be dominated by a limited number of people who were often, but not exclusively, men. Membership was also often along caste or political lines. The majority of the slum population did not participate or feel that they received any benefits from the

NHCs. By the time of the assessment, many of the NHCs were inactive and their sustainability beyond the end of the projects was in serious doubt. Residents involved in the survey were unable to identify any direct poverty reduction impacts of NHCs. Finally, although NHCs were seen as community-based mechanisms for poverty programmes, they were not linked to wider democratic structures such as ward committees and were not mainstreamed, therefore, into governance processes.

From other impact assessments in Faisalabad and Bangalore it is also possible to conclude that there has been some increase in social capital in some areas. This is evident from the new institutional structures that have been created. Again, in some areas neighbourhood groups appear to have brought people together successfully for the first time for collective action. However, the projects had limited impact on poorer and marginalized groups. The most significant impacts have been on women, which is understandable because of the significant attention given to gender in all these projects (see Box 8.4).

Box 8.4 *Women's Inclusion in Faisalabad*

Noticeable changes have occurred for women:

- They have become involved in decision-making and implementation.
- More than half the organizations are female organizations.
- Collective organization has developed among women and given them a stronger voice in articulating their needs.
- Women have begun to be more confident about the role that they can play in their own and their communities' development.

Source: Phillips and ActionAid, 1996

The experience with savings and credit groups appears in some places to have been more positive (see Chapter 7). The review of the Bembala savings and credit programme in Bangalore, for example, found a number of positive impacts resulting from this scheme: increased access to affordable credit when required, increased self-esteem, the nurturing of new leadership, the empowerment of women and networking across the city. Benefits mainly accrued to women. Also, although these schemes have been initiated by outsiders (in this case the Project Management Unit of the Bangalore Urban Poverty Project), they can nurture local ownership very quickly. Equally, they tend to fail where they are seen as government schemes. It would appear that savings and credit groups have more potential to develop social capital than experience to date with neighbourhood groups, suggesting that the former are perceived by users to be valuable.

In conclusion, although social organization has taken on new forms in the cities considered here as a result of these slum improvement projects, it is questionable whether they have really built social capital. It is difficult to draw firm conclusions because a number of questions remain unanswered. Have neighbourhood groups been most effective where social capital is already strong – for example, where 'open democratic models' of social organization already exist (IDD, 1997)? As importantly, has the model tended to perpetuate existing social relationships, just channelling them through a new institutional structure? Have those relationships been strengthened as a result of the project, even though the formal structures established may not continue beyond the life of the project itself? If there has been a strengthening of the social capital of some individuals, households and groups within a 'community', and this has enhanced the reputation and control over resources of elites and better-off groups, have these increased stocks of social capital benefited those with the lowest stocks? Has the formalization and expropriation of social capital by outsiders weakened informal networks and associations? These are questions that need to be answered if we are to improve policy and practice. However, the lack of information on existing levels of social capital and comparative data to assess project impacts is a major constraint.[2]

Do the Projects Address those Factors which Influence the Formation of Social Capital in Urban Areas?

A range of complex social, economic and political processes influence the formation of social capital in urban areas and therefore any attempts to support the development of social capital should seek to understand and build on those processes. It is clear from the above analysis that this is unlikely to have happened in the case study projects.

One of the basic criticisms of the SIPs is that the model failed to consider the processes which might lead to the inclusion or exclusion of individuals, households and social groups in neighbourhood groups. As such, access to resources and services was likely to be inequitable and biased towards those best placed to participate in and control neighbourhood organizations.

To overcome this weakness, the later projects (especially the DFID-supported projects) recognize the diversity of urban populations. Similarly, the economic, social and political processes which lead to the domination of organizations by individuals, households and social groups with better social and political connectedness and those who are more economically secure, are also recognized. Social analysis and participatory learning and planning methodologies are used increasingly to understand the issues that contribute to the poverty and vulnerability of different groups. The Cochin project, in particular, started with an urban poverty analysis and disaggregated the poor into different categories based on relative levels of poverty and deprivation.

Based on such information, these later project designs have attempted to create more inclusive forms of social capital, especially through the promotion of women's groups. In Cochin, for example, following Government of India (GoI) policies, the project works with a network of women's groups. Attempts are made to try to ensure that these groups represent different interests among women by localizing groups to the level of lanes. It remains to be seen, however, to what extent poorer and traditionally excluded women participate in and access benefits through these groups. Are the groups addressing the factors that prevent excluded women from participating? Furthermore, groups that strengthen the social capital of other marginalized groups, such as the elderly, children, ethnic minorities or members of scheduled castes, have rarely been formed.

One aspect of social capital formation in urban areas that does not appear to have been addressed specifically in the projects reviewed is that urban populations are often mobile and transitory, in contrast to the assumption underlying all these projects, that the population is largely stable. The India SIPs Impact Assessment Study did indeed find that turnover was limited to 10–15 per cent of households – that is, 85–90 per cent of the households surveyed had been living in the same location at the beginning of the project. Part of the reason may be that the project targeted formal recognized slums which had been in existence for some time. Newer and more marginal slums (which tend to be more transitory) were excluded. The study did not examine seasonal migration or movement between rural and urban areas of different household members, so we know little about movement patterns even within so-called stable areas. As urban programmes aim to work increasingly with poorer households, who are likely to be the most mobile, it would be advisable for future programmes to consider the issues involved in building social capital among transitory populations.

Another issue that is commonly overlooked or oversimplified is that of power relationships and the 'exploitation' of the poor by those who control access to resources, such as local and national level politicians, money-lenders, 'barons', local leaders, landlords and the police. These individuals tend to have been seen as negative forces that will be neutralized by the development of alternative support networks. In reality, building social capital is about power and any attempts to build alternative support mechanisms among the poor are likely to be contested. In the SIPs, this resistance manifested itself openly in examples of group domination by these leaders, political infiltration and the manipulation of groups, and resistance to the whole concept of neighbourhood groups by local politicians. In Visakhapatnam, this political pressure from local elected representatives extended to a call for the disbandment of NHCs and even of the Urban Community Development Department (UCD). This experience suggests that greater attention needs to be paid to the political implications of social capital formation. This can be approached through analysis of political interests (stakeholder analysis with communities), the development of project activities to address influences perceived as negative, and the greater inclusion of leaders and power brokers in the development process. For example, in a later project in Visakhapatnam (Chinagadili), elected representatives were included in project committees.

Government policies and laws will impact on the more formal types of social organization – that is, associations and institutions. In many contexts there are laws that constrain the conditions under which groups can form and operate. In India, registration is required if community-based groups wish to access government or donor resources. While this brings benefits, it also brings such groups within the orbit and surveillance of government. In other contexts, such registration can be highly restrictive.

Has the Building of Social Capital Helped to Reduce Vulnerability to Shocks, Trends and Seasonality?

It is difficult to assess from the available documentation whether the building of social capital in the SIPs has reduced vulnerability, largely because of the lack of base-line data on pre-existing relationships, networks and associations used by poor people to reduce vulnerability. Box 8.5 lists the poverty perceptions of poor people interviewed in the SIPs Impact Assessment. Lack of support from relatives and friends emerged as the third most important aspect of poverty and vulnerability (after assets and livelihoods) among slum residents questioned about their experiences of poverty. Women, orphans, the elderly and the chronically ill or disabled were the most commonly mentioned vulnerable groups. Vulnerable individuals were seen as unable to support themselves and lacking support from others. People were unable to support themselves either through their inability to gain employment or their physical incapacity to work. Others, such as widows and female-headed households, were socially marginalized because of their cultural ostracism. Poverty was compounded by having too many dependants, particularly those who are unable to contribute to household income, such as the elderly, relatives and the ill.

Box 8.5 *India Impact assessment: Poverty and Vulnerability*

Insecure and unpredictable income
Unskilled labour
Casual labour
Living in rented accommodation
Physical incapacity to work
Lack of support
Social marginalization – for example, widows and female-headed households
Too many dependants
Ill health
Industrial accidents
Alcohol abuse
Domestic violence
Indebtedness
Risk of fire

Source: Based on IDD, 1997

While other components of the SIPs were found to have had a positive impact on some of these aspects of poverty and vulnerability, it was not possible to identify a direct correlation between the strengthening of social capital through neighbourhood groups and reduced vulnerability. Given the overall limited impact of the social institution building components of the projects, this is not surprising. Furthermore, as neighbourhood groups were commonly perceived as a vehicle for accessing government resources, it is not surprising that these groups have not developed to embrace a wider supportive role within their communities. A relationship between groups and external agencies was established in which roles and outcomes were prescribed, not evolved or developed. The Bangalore and Faisalabad impact assessments came to similar conclusions.

Another reason why the links between strengthening social capital and reduced vulnerability are unclear is because the SIPs did not aim directly to tackle many of the issues listed in Box 8.5. However, a greater poverty and vulnerability focus in the later stages of the SIPs did result in the inclusion of new components, such as savings and credit and legal literacy. Subsequent projects, such as the Cochin and Bangalore Urban Poverty Projects, addressed poverty and vulnerability quite explicitly. A greater correlation between social capital formation and the reduction of vulnerability would be expected, therefore, in these projects.

Again, more in-depth research would be required to assess the extent to which social capital developed through these projects helped individuals and households to deal with their poverty and vulnerability, or what other strategies could be adopted to build social capital to tackle critical issues affecting vulnerability. For example, it is not clear whether it would be more effective to focus on supporting or building employment-based associations and networks (such as the SEWA), trade unions and employment collectives, as well as savings and credit groups. In terms of alcohol abuse, the anti-liquor women's movement in Andhra Pradesh demonstrated the power of the mass mobilization of poor women, when they succeeded in obtaining a statewide ban on alcohol consumption. Youth groups, elderly groups and support groups for victims of domestic violence are other examples of a more targeted approach to tackling vulnerability, through building linkages between people who are facing similar difficulties.

WHAT ARE THE POLICY IMPLICATIONS?

The final section outlines some thoughts on the policy implications arising from this analysis.

Supporting Existing Social Capital

The above analysis highlights the need to have a much greater understanding of existing relationships, networks and associations before the development of programmes which are designed to build poor people's social capital. This means:

- The starting point for policy and practice should be to identify, understand and support the strengthening of existing social capital used by the poor to survive and improve their livelihoods (with obvious caveats on the forms of social capital which have negative outcomes). This will mean a less formulaic approach to building interfaces between poor people and external agencies.
- More detailed research into social capital in urban areas is needed, with a view to developing better mechanisms of support. In particular, there is a need to examine whether existing social capital, particularly in its more informal and less visible forms, can provide a basis for dialogue and collaboration between poor people and government or other external agencies.
- At a project or programme level, participatory methodologies should be used to analyse existing social capital and the economic, social and political processes that affect the formation of this asset among different individuals, households and communities of poor people. What exists? What factors constrain the development of relationships, networks and structures for reciprocity? For whom? How can what exists be supported to enhance livelihoods?

- Participatory methodologies and tools need to be better developed and used to empower poor people through analysis of their own social capital, rather than merely to help outsiders develop their own understanding.
- There continues to be a need for developing, testing and disseminating approaches to support the strengthening of social capital among the poorest and socially excluded because, for this group, poverty is in part due to the fact that supportive networks have broken down and they are unable to participate in reciprocal relationships because of their inability to meet the obligations that follow.
- More sophisticated indicators for measuring change need to be developed. Indicators for assessing community development impact remain crude and abstract. Indicators and monitoring mechanisms need to be developed which are both simple and practical and capable of capturing changes (both positive and negative) in social capital.

Alternative Development Strategies

The projects analysed above can be seen as aimed at supporting poor people to improve their claim-making strategies (Mitlin, 1999). The question that this analysis raises is whether SIPs are the most appropriate vehicle for helping the poor to build their social capital. This has a number of implications for policy, research and practice:

1 More in-depth research is needed on the impact of externally imposed forms of social organization. Do they enhance supportive relationships and networks among poor people, or are they primarily an administrative convenience to enable external agencies to interact with poor people? What are the impacts of formalizing social organizations, particularly for the poorest, who are likely to be the most dependent on informal networks?

2 If the aim of building neighbourhood or other community-level groups is to increase the ability of poor people to influence government to redistribute resources in their favour, are project-related community organizations the most effective mechanisms for achieving this end? Would it not be more appropriate to build on existing political arrangements and/or to institutionalize local-level structures as the grassroots level of governance? Such an approach would involve the development of participatory planning and monitoring processes and other mechanisms to increase accountability and representation. As the above analysis demonstrates, suitable methodologies have been developed (certainly in South Asia), and in places they are mainstreamed in government poverty programmes, but they are not used more broadly as mechanisms to improve governance.

3 More emphasis on savings and credit groups as a means of building social capital through addressing a key livelihood constraint may be appropriate. These groups appear to provide an additional bonus by being particularly popular among women. Attention needs to be given to examples of good practice which demonstrate that models can be externally driven but must be designed and operated to be managed and owned by members. More attention should thus be given to supporting indigenous savings and credit

mechanisms. Research on whether these savings and credit groups strengthen and expand existing reciprocal relationships or only provide an alternative institutional structure for existing ones would also be highly informative.

4   The review also questions whether working through government to build social capital is appropriate at all. Would it be more appropriate to concentrate resources on civil society organizations, as has become increasingly popular among donors? Traditionally, community-based groups have been the focus of urban programmes, whereas support to trade unions, employment associations, youth groups and other non-settlement-based organizations might also help to improve livelihoods.

5   This alternative approach does not necessarily mean working solely with NGOs. It is well documented that NGOs often try and impose their own models and approaches and can sometimes stifle local level initiatives (see, for example, Mitlin, 1999). However, some NGOs such as the Asian Coalition of Housing Rights, People's Dialogue in South Africa and SPARC in India, support people-based membership organizations. They attach high importance to advocacy and the mass mobilization for civic action of the members of the grass-roots organizations (GROs) with which they work. Research on the impact of this type of organization on social capital formation would make a valuable contribution to the development of an urban livelihoods policy approach.

6   Direct support to civil society organizations would not necessarily exclude working with government, but would imply a focus on tackling the 'enabling environment' to make it more conducive to civil society action (such as by addressing the legislative and policy context).

NOTES

1   Legislation in India requires all informal settlements to be categorized. Only those in certain categories ('recognized' slums) are considered eligible for regularization and public investment in infrastructure improvements. The term slum is therefore used in the Indian context for all informal settlements and includes a range of land tenure arrangements. In the space available here, it is not possible to do justice to the full complexity and local diversity of practices and outcomes in these projects, or to describe in detail the extent to which there has been learning from experience in successive projects (but see Chapter 14). The views are those of the author and are not necessarily those of the DFID or the Indian public sector agencies involved in the projects

2   DFID has recently commissioned research through its engineering research programme (ENGKARS) which aims to help develop methodologies for identifying, analysing and building up indigenous social capital

REFERENCES

IDD (International Development Department) (1997) *Impact Assessment Study India Slum Improvement Projects*, Draft report (various volumes), School of Public Policy, University of Birmingham, for DFID

Beall, J and Kanji, N (1999) *Households, Livelihoods and Urban Poverty*, Urban Governance, Partnership and Poverty, WP3, International Development Department, School of Public Policy, University of Birmingham

Gonzalez de la Rocha, M (1994) *The Resources of Poverty: Women and Survival in a Mexican City*, Blackwell, Oxford

Harrison, M E and McVey, C E (1997) 'Conflict in the city: street trading in Mexico City', *Third World Planning Review*, vol 19, no 3, pp313–326

Meikle, S (1999) *Sustainable Urban Livelihoods: Concepts and Implications for Policy: A Literature Review*, Development Planning Unit, University College London for DFID, London

Mitlin, D (1999) *Civil Society and Urban Poverty*, Urban Governance, Partnership and Poverty WP 5, International Development Department, School of Public Policy, Birmingham University, Birmingham

Moser, C (1996) *Confronting Crisis: A Comparative Study of Household Responses to Poverty and Vulnerability in Four Urban Communities*, Environmentally Sustainable Development Studies and Monographs Series No 8, World Bank, Washington, DC

Moser, C and Holland, J (1997) *Urban Poverty and Violence in Jamaica*, World Bank, Washington, DC

Phillips, S with ActionAid (1997) *Faisalabad Area Upgrading Project Participatory Impact Assessment*, Department for International Development, London and Faisalabad Development Authority

Phillips, S et al (1997) *Bangalore Urban Poverty Project Review Mission Report*, Royal Netherlands Foreign Ministry, The Hague

Rakodi, C (1999) 'A capital assets framework for analysing household livelihood strategies', *Development Policy Review*, vol 17, no 3, pp315–342

Tacoli, C (1998) 'Rural–urban linkages and sustainable rural livelihoods' in Carney, D (ed) *Sustainable Rural Livelihoods: What Contribution Can We make?* DFID, London, pp67–80

Chapter 9

Tenure and Shelter in Urban Livelihoods

Geoffrey Payne

INTRODUCTION

Access to secure land and shelter in locations which facilitate access to employment opportunities, services and public amenities is a precondition for survival, not just success, in urban areas. Whereas the quality of land is an important consideration in rural areas, its location becomes more important in urban areas, as households seek sites with good access to livelihood opportunities, public services and amenities. The rapid rates of urban growth experienced in many countries during the latter part of the 20th century intensified competition for land, especially in central locations considered to offer the greatest livelihood opportunities. This has created a major dilemma for urban policy-makers, administrators and developers, not to mention the poor majority who are least able to compete on equal terms with more affluent and influential social groups. In rural contexts, as noted in Chapter 1, land is conceptualized, along with environmental resources, as natural capital. However, in urban areas it is more appropriate to see it as a physical asset that enables households to access shelter, has locational attributes that provide access to other livelihood possibilities and has investment potential. A livelihoods approach provides a perspective, from the viewpoint of the poor themselves, regarding the difficulties they face in seeking secure land and shelter, and the challenges they face in taking advantage of the opportunities which these may provide.

LAND AND LIVELIHOODS

Land and shelter issues in urban areas are both complex and dynamic since they are partly determined by cultural traditions and social aspirations as well as resources. This section identifies and considers three aspects of the function of land in livelihoods – namely, access to land, which includes issues of location, cost and credit availability; security of tenure, in terms of de jure and de facto status; and function, in terms of land use and servicing.

Access to Land

Access to land is a key factor since the poor depend for their survival and progress on living in or near locations which maximize livelihood opportunities. Time and money spent in travelling to distant locations is a major constraint on their efforts and many therefore prefer to live on undeveloped land or pavements in central locations. However, these areas are highly visible and therefore attract the attention of the police, making such groups particularly vulnerable to evictions and abuse. Furthermore, central locations attract the most intense competition from all income groups, forcing up prices for formal development to levels which the poor cannot afford without expensive subsidies. It is not uncommon for land to represent more than half of the total shelter costs in inner urban areas.

To compound such problems, experience suggests that subsidies invariably end up benefiting higher income groups, thereby defeating their purpose. For the majority who are unable to obtain subsidies, a common solution is to live in central locations in the oldest and lowest standard accommodation at high densities.

Many such practices operate in defiance or ignorance of official regulations, standards and administrative procedures. This is commonly because such regulatory regimes impose costs which are too high for lower-income households to bear (see Box 9.1) and governments are unable to bridge the gap with subsidies on a long-term basis to all those in need. They also impose too many obstacles to households seeking official documentation (see Box 9.2).

BOX 9.1 *PLANNING STANDARDS IN KENYA*

Discussion of planning and housing standards in Kenya dates from the early 1970s when the World Bank commissioned a review as part of its initial urban loan to Kenya. The review noted that planning standards were too high to be affordable to many households and recommended that they should be relaxed or revised. A later study by Tuts (1996) noted, however, that the planning and building standards established during the colonial period were largely still in place and were 'prohibitively high'. Although some amendments were made in 1995, little has changed on the ground and most land and shelter development continues to ignore official norms.

For households able to bear the time and cost of travel from less central locations, land is more easily available in suburban locations. Plots may be acquired legally or through commercial land subdividers who operate outside the formal development processes. In many cities, the latter option is the single most common form of land supply (Payne, 1989), partly because the official standards raise development costs to levels which are unaffordable by the poor or even many lower middle-income groups. Low and irregular incomes constrain access to formal credit and this in itself may preclude access to legal home ownership.

BOX 9.2 *PLANNING PROCEDURES IN PERU*

An influential study by de Soto (1989) examined why a high proportion of urban development in Peru took place without official approval. The study revealed that, in order to comply fully with relevant legislation and administrative procedures, applicants had to complete 159 bureaucratic steps in order to legalize their settlement, receive titles to their plots and be officially incorporated into the city, a process which took an average of 20 years. It was hardly surprising therefore that most people simply ignored the official requirements and developed new settlements according to their own needs and resources.

Security of Tenure

For the majority of the poor, who are unable to gain access to legal shelter with formal title, the issue of tenure security is vital. However, the lack of titles may not be critical in itself, and tenure security involves perceptions of risk as much as legal status. For example, if a household is alone in living without legal protection, it may feel highly vulnerable, but if a large proportion of an urban population is in the same category, then the perceived and practical risk of eviction may be negligible. In the first case, it is likely that households will concentrate their efforts on reducing their vulnerability to external threats rather than investing in home improvements. In the second case, perceived security may stimulate a positive environment for home improvements and economic activity which can improve living standards and help to lift people out of poverty through individual or collective efforts. An important way to assess the impact of these processes on the poor is to undertake participatory assessments which enable households themselves to express their views and responses to given situations.

As Figure 9.1 shows, in any urban area there may be several forms of legal tenure and rights (such as statutory, customary and religious), together with a range of extra-legal categories (such as squatting, unauthorized land subdivisions, houses constructed or expanded in contravention of official norms, or without official permits). In many cases there are local terms which capture these variations, such as *favela, bidonville, pueblo juvenes, gecekondu, jhuggi jhonpri, bustee* or *kampung*. English or local terms may subsume important submarkets in which land and shelter command different market values and meet the needs of different groups. In some cases, more than one form of tenure may actually exist on a single plot, as in Calcutta where many plots are let to *thika* tenants, who in turn rent out rooms to subtenants, who then rent out beds to sub-sub-tenants, who rent time in the beds to shift workers on a 'hot-bed' system. In these situations, each tenure category fulfils a distinct, if unrecognized, role in land and housing markets, and action in any one has a direct and indirect impact on the others and the relationships between them. In addition, the capability of the land registration system to process applications for land transfer and development also influences the ability of land markets to respond to the changing needs.

While statutory tenure systems are more common in urban areas, especially in countries where towns and cities were established during the colonial period,

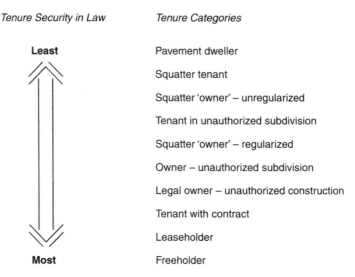

Figure 9.1   *Urban tenure categories by legal status*

urban growth has absorbed large areas of peripheral rural land. Where this is also held under statutory tenure systems, landowners are usually able to obtain attractive prices by subdividing or selling land for conversion to urban use. Urban development agencies may seek to control such processes by acquiring peri-urban land in advance of demand so that it can be released at affordable prices when required. In practice, such approaches have invariably failed because agencies either lack the capability to develop land in ways which reflect effective demand or succumb to the temptation of developing it for more lucrative purposes.

In areas where land is held under customary tenure systems, such as parts of sub-Saharan Africa, government attempts to acquire and develop land may create ambiguity in the relationship between local chiefs who have traditionally allocated land and shelter to their communities and the elected authorities who have officially taken over such responsibilities, but may not be able to match demand through a lack of resources or inefficiency. Where this is the case, people understandably look to the chiefs for support, exacerbating tension between the customary and statutory authorities, especially in peri-urban locations.

The high cost of land resulting from market forces and restrictive regulatory frameworks tends to exclude large numbers of people, especially the poor, from obtaining legal access to land and shelter. As a result, non-formal tenure categories have expanded to fill the gap and are now the largest and most rapidly expanding category, including between 15 and 70 per cent of total urban populations (Durand-Lasserve, 1996). As they have expanded, so they have diversified and various submarkets have evolved to cater for different needs and local conditions. These range from around 250,000 people living on the pavements in

Mumbai, India, to millions living in extra-legal commercial subdivisions or squatting. Each submarket provides different levels of de facto security and access to other livelihood opportunities at a corresponding range of social and economic costs. Some expose households to the threat of forced evictions and others to abuse by landowners or officials. Many are forced to settle in areas which place them at risk from environmental hazards. These include steep slopes in ravines or on river banks, and areas which are vulnerable to landslide or other environmental hazards, such as pollution from nearby industrial plants. The disasters in Bhopal, India, in 1984 and recently in the peri-urban areas of Caracas, Venezuela, are telling reminders of the vulnerability which poor urban households are forced to accept as a price for obtaining access to other livelihood opportunities. Less dramatic, but equally serious, examples can be found throughout the cities of the developing world.

However, evidence also suggests that where the number of households in non-formal tenure categories reaches a critical mass, or when they include government employees, they begin to enjoy de facto security and political protection through the weight of their votes and/or contacts with senior officials (see Box 9.3). This situation varies from one time and place to another, and makes it difficult to assess the ways in which tenure impacts on the well-being and livelihood opportunities of the poor. It is vital therefore to assess perceived tenure security levels. Participatory assessments can reveal the degree of de facto security which households themselves consider they possess in a given political or institutional environment. In Bogota, for example, households in pirate subdivisions do not appear unduly concerned that they lack titles or other formal rights since the constitution guarantees them access to public utilities, provided they pay the connection and consumption charges. In Karachi during the 1980s, about 100,000 households in illegal settlements were offered freehold titles to their plots, but only 10 per cent took up the offer, presumably because the simple fact that the areas were now officially recognized reduced the need for a piece of paper to prove it.

The scale of non-formal tenure developments can be considered largely as a reflection of the extent to which tenure policies have failed to reflect the needs and resources of the urban population within the broader economic environment. Inappropriate policies therefore force households into the very unauthorized settlements that governments seek to prevent. This issue can only be addressed by central governments, as they create the legal, financial, institutional and political framework within which urban development takes place. They also establish the legal procedures (civil and criminal) by which disputes over land are resolved.

Secure tenure is therefore a necessary, but not sufficient, condition for creating sustainable urban livelihoods. Unless the type of tenure available to households provides an adequate level of perceived security, it is likely that they will be forced to allocate scarce resources to increasing their security or finding more secure shelter, rather than meeting other needs. Of course, the type of tenure which households consider appropriate to their needs will vary widely. In some cases, cultural or financial considerations may foster a demand for individual statutory titles, with the long-term benefits these offer. In other cases, households may prefer the flexibility of rental occupancy so that they are free to respond to livelihood opportunities in other locations. In Kenya, the 'owners' of unauthor-

---

Box 9.3 Non-formal settlements in Ankara, Turkey

During the 20th century, the population of Ankara increased from 20,000 to over 3 million. The municipal authorities lacked the financial resources that were required to implement conventional planning and housing programmes, so most of this growth was accommodated within *gecekondus*, or unauthorized settlements. These expanded dramatically from the 1950s when rural–urban migration accelerated. While initial settlements were removed, the settlers became adept at winning protection from local politicians seeking their votes. Every time the municipal boundaries were expanded to reflect the increased population, these areas were granted *mahalle* or ward status, giving them a claim on municipal budgets for public utilities and services. While formal titles were rarely granted, the poor were able to obtain access to land, housing and services. Key factors in this process were the active participation of residents and the collaboration of the authorities.

---

ized housing have exploited the commercial opportunities to provide rental units in the form of rooms or complete buildings and in Nairobi, where land available for informal settlements is limited, multioccupancy has become the norm (Amis, 1984).

Tenure policy is driven increasingly by economic considerations and a desire to impose an arbitrary formal order on urban growth and development. The realities with which the policy has to deal are, however, too complex for such approaches to succeed and they also deny the opportunity for developing more people-centred approaches. However, the evidence suggests that people themselves have taken initiatives to create new forms of tenure which enable them to obtain land in areas where they need to live. Their perceptions of what constitutes secure tenure and their priorities for access to land in different locations can provide the basis for more informed policies and programmes of urban land management.

While land tenure and property rights raise important technical and procedural questions, they are ultimately political and can be considered to reflect benefits and responsibilities in other areas of public life. Societies which place a high priority on communal interests are more likely to advocate customary or co-operative tenure systems, while those which give priority to individual rights are likely to favour private tenure systems. Either way, tenure policy will need to be consistent with other components of urban policy in creating dynamic, efficient and equitable urban areas.

Land-use Policy

Land-use policy also impinges on livelihood opportunities for low-income households. Planning methods which separate residential, commercial and industrial areas through land use zoning reduce the livelihood prospects which can result from the interaction of different activities. Solomon (1999) has demonstrated, in the case of India, that the concentration of mixed land uses, as widely found in older or unauthorized urban areas, can stimulate dramatic increases in both informal and formal economic activity. He concludes that government action is relatively ineffective in creating such conditions, but can inhibit them through inappropriate or restrictive planning methods.

SHELTER AND LIVELIHOODS

The issues affecting urban shelter have much in common with land. Just as a small plot without formal tenure but in a good location may be preferred by many over a larger plot with title in a peripheral location, so similar considerations apply in housing. As Turner (1976) noted, a shack can be more supportive for a poor household and better meet their social and economic needs, because living in a more substantial house increases vulnerability when repayments cannot be met.

Unfortunately, many governments still define their shelter policies in quantitative terms, rather than in terms of the role that shelter plays in livelihood strategies. Data on housing deficits, which indicate a notional number of dwellings required in a country or city, are frequently based on definitions which reflect middle-class perceptions of a desirable house. As such, it is not surprising that projects provide solutions in which the design and location are inappropriate for the needs of poor people. High standards also raise costs to unaffordable levels and depend on the availability of subsidies which are unsustainable.

As with urban land markets, a range of unofficial solutions has emerged to fill this gap. In the early stages of urbanization, many settlements were developed through land invasions or incremental settlement and developed strong community ties. The increasing commercialization of land and housing markets has reduced the scope for these processes and increased the role of commercial developers, so that virtually all urban houses, even shacks on roadsides, now possess a market value. Access to shelter is therefore based on being able to afford what the market offers. As the earthquake in Turkey in 2001 demonstrated, many such shelters are badly constructed and expose households to severe risks, while those constructed by their occupants generally fare far better.

This suggests that people themselves are the best judges of the type of shelter appropriate for their needs. A key consideration for most poor households is the need to enhance livelihood prospects by providing a base for income generation through domestic economic activity, or by subletting rooms to tenants (see Box 9.4). In addition, the location of shelter is vital in facilitating access to essential services and non-residential livelihood opportunities, whether in the formal or informal economic sectors.

For all these reasons, shelter in urban areas is more than just a place to live or the provision of an adequate number of dwelling units, but involves a complex mixture of social, economic and cultural considerations. For many poor households, economic factors outweigh the need for decent accommodation, and housing is seen as a financial asset which can give access to other livelihood opportunities. Consequently, they are prepared, or forced, to accept unhealthy, unsafe or insecure shelter to maximize the potential for enhancing other liveli-

---

Box 9.4 HOUSING AND LIVELIHOODS IN ISMAILIA, EGYPT

As in many cities, a large proportion of Ismailia's population lives in informal settlements. Provided residents pay a ground rent known as a *hekr*, they are free to improve or extend their houses and to use them to increase their incomes and capital assets. Many households construct basic rooms for rent, the income from which provides the cheapest housing for new migrants and valuable incomes for the 'owners'. From this, they can further improve or extend their houses and repeat the process. Over a 30-year period, this incremental development process has provided housing and employment opportunities for most income groups, especially the poor, and has raised incomes and the value of assets on a largely self-financing basis.

---

hood prospects. This may involve occupying sites along roads, railway lines or river banks which are unsuitable for formal development. In some extreme cases, it may even involve occupying parts of the pavement, or demolishing dwellings in the morning and rebuilding them in the evening to prevent the confiscation of materials by public authorities. Simply by living in urban areas, many households are accepting far lower environmental conditions than were available to them in rural areas, a limitation considered acceptable because of the livelihood opportunities which are only available in towns and cities.

Within these limitations, international experience has shown that most poor people are capable of organizing their own shelter construction, maintenance and improvements. In fact, the majority of all urban housing in many cities is developed in this way. What poor households are *not* able to achieve without external assistance is access to secure tenure and services at prices they can afford and in appropriate locations. Given the diversity of needs and resources between households, different strategies are required to satisfy their priorities.

Policies by governments and international agencies have all too often overlooked these aspects and defined shelter simply in terms of the number of units required to accommodate a given number of people. This emphasis on quantitative aspects negates the livelihood considerations which are of primary concern for the poor themselves and produces developments which may actually trap people in poverty rather than help them out of it. For example, dwellings in low-density settlements on the urban fringe isolate people from easy access to places of employment opportunity and the social interactions and spatial clustering in which economic opportunities can flourish.

Regulatory frameworks may also impede households from being able to use shelter for enhancing livelihood possibilities. For example, regulations which prohibit or discourage home-based economic activity or impose high standards, reduce the resources that are available for other investment and force households into accommodation which may expose them to environmental hazards. Since public sector projects are required to conform to official norms, standards and administrative procedures, costs are invariably higher than households can afford, requiring subsidies which in turn reduce the number of units which can be provided. Regulatory frameworks also impose costs which impede the formal private sector from attempting to meet the needs of low-income households. At the same time, the formal private sector is generally unwilling to serve low-income shelter needs, especially when there is ample demand from the middle and higher ends of the market. For these reasons, the main source of shelter for the urban poor is likely to remain the informal commercial sector which bases its forms and standards of provision on market-based costs and levels of affordability. Even this sector is not always able to reconcile disparities between the cost of land, shelter and services and the low and often irregular incomes of the poor.

For those who prefer ownership, empirical evidence suggests that where incomes are low, accessing credit for house purchase, construction or improvements is difficult and most construction is financed from savings. Conventional private-sector financial institutions have rarely been effective in making credit for shelter available to low-income households. In many developing countries, less than a quarter of all new housing is financed through formal credit systems. Information on informal credit systems is limited, but anecdotal evidence suggests that informal commercial lenders charge interest rates which are well above those levied by banks. However, they provide short-term, small-scale credit on flexible repayment terms which matches the needs of households on low and irregular incomes (see Chapter 7). Other households appear to obtain credit through support networks of relatives and friends.

GENDER, LAND AND SHELTER

In many countries, women are not able to obtain access to land and shelter on equal terms with men. Both customary and statutory tenure traditions frequently discriminate against women, despite their generally higher credit-worthiness. Addressing the gender issue is therefore central to the development of equitable and sustainable tenure systems and to enhancing the livelihood opportunities for the urban poor.

Current research being funded by DFID is reviewing the experience of innovative approaches to increasing tenure security for the urban poor. One question being considered in the project is the possibility that various 'intermediate' forms of tenure status, such as 'occupation permits' or 'certificates of use', may help to improve the position of women, since such options do not enjoy the same legal or social status as statutory titles and therefore may be more easily accessible to the poor, especially women.

OPTIONS FOR INTERVENTION IN LAND AND HOUSING MARKETS

A livelihoods framework provides a means of identifying options for transforming policies, structures and processes so that the poor can reduce their vulnerability to environmental risks, build up their assets and improve their well-being. In assessing options for change, it is important to note that the increasing linkage of urban areas into global economic activity is effecting a major change in the options that are available to central and local governments to regulate land and property markets, and to protect the interests of vulnerable groups. Options for intervention are influenced by both global economic developments and short-term political imperatives. Policies to permit or deny the right of property ownership to selected groups (as in Malaysia), or nationals rather than foreigners (as in Lesotho), significantly affect decisions on investment and economic development which may enhance or impede livelihood opportunities for the urban poor. Globalization is tending to favour policy regimes that encourage statutory private land-tenure systems and the repatriation of profits, both of which offer limited benefits for the poor majority of urban households. They also discourage public sector approaches that are dependent on subsidies, among other reasons, because these undermine the ability of the private sector to compete on equal terms.

Another key factor is that central governments may lack a detailed understanding of the intricacies and dynamics of land markets in individual cities, while local governments commonly lack the resources to intervene effectively in their own areas of responsibility. Where local governments act as collection agencies for provincial or central government departments, there is little incentive to collect revenues or accept responsibility for failure to realize policy objectives. This suggests that national governments should establish the legal and regulatory framework applicable to land management and shelter provision, but that urban governments should be empowered to retain a sufficient proportion of property taxes and other revenues to meet stated objectives and be accountable to their constituencies for the outcomes. Providing secure access to land and shelter in ways which meet the needs of the poor, are financially sustainable and minimize distortions to urban land and housing markets, constitutes a major challenge for national and local governments.

Interventions in land tenure need to be within the administrative capacity of the relevant agencies to implement. For example, a policy that entitles residents of all unauthorized settlements to statutory titles will be ineffective if it imposes demands on the land registry which cannot be met. Similarly, interventions that allocate such benefits to a selected few may be within the administrative capacity to implement, but may generate severe distortions in urban land and housing markets (Payne, 2001).

Research on urban land tenure does not yet provide sufficient evidence to be able to predict policy outcomes or their impact on vulnerable social groups. However, it is becoming increasingly clear that donor-assisted policies which emphasize the benefits of private statutory titles have undermined, on occasion, traditional practices such as customary tenure systems (Quan, 1998, p177), further intensified already distorted land and housing markets (Kundu, 1997) and led to the eviction of tenants and subsequent gentrification in regularized settlements. This suggests that, until greater knowledge of policy outcomes is available, emphasis should be placed on approaches that increase de facto rights of residents in extra-legal settlements.

Such approaches may involve the provision of occupancy permits or certificates of use which can enable communities to obtain access to public utility networks and credit through innovative finance institutions. This will reduce exposure to forced evictions, help to stabilize existing situations and also provide a major practical advantage for urban management agencies and land registries. This is because land records in many cities are neither accurate nor up to date and few are presently computerized. As a result, the potentially dramatic increase in land values generated by the allocation of formal titles can be expected to lead to disputes over who has the strongest claim. Such disputes may lead to litigation and social conflict, rather than increased security and social cohesion. While formal tenure systems may be desirable in the long term, the administrative capacity to manage the transition needs to be strengthened and change introduced gradually and at the city scale. Providing intermediate forms of tenure may help to diffuse tension and conflict during the interim.

In terms of shelter provision, it is important to recognize that housing does not exist in isolation from other aspects of urban life. While polluting industries clearly require segregating from other land uses, in many cases a mix of residential, commercial, industrial and recreational uses can stimulate economic activity within neighbourhoods, reducing poverty and improving the quality of urban life. Replacing rigid single-use zoning with mixed uses, based on local action plans which reflect local conditions, can facilitate this process (see also Chapter 12).

Vulnerability to environmental and institutional threats can be reduced by making it easier for households to gain entry to legal shelter. Given the low incomes of many households and the inability of governments to provide large-scale, long-term subsidies, entry costs to legal shelter can only be reduced by revising regulatory frameworks. This will entail:

- Relaxing planning and building regulations to permit commercial uses and small-scale, non-polluting industries within predominantly residential areas and enable residents to provide rooms for rent or to start home-based enterprises which can increase their incomes and capital.
- Reducing the entry costs to new land and shelter developments by relaxing standards for initial plot development so that low-income households can get on to the bottom rung of the legal housing ladder. In practice, this may entail permitting smaller plot sizes, smaller buildings and basic standards of infrastructure provision. Improvements and extensions can then be financed from future incomes, as in most informal settlements.
- Introducing 'one-stop-shops' or other means of streamlining administrative procedures.

Maximizing the options available for a given cost level provides households with more control over their livelihood options and is just as, if not more important, for the poor than for less vulnerable social groups. Developments therefore should include a range of options at each cost level. For example, it may be possible to include different plot sizes and levels of initial infrastructure for a given cost, allowing households to select the option that best meets their needs. Monitoring the take-up of each option can provide a quick and cost-effective basis for planning subsequent developments. Quick surveys or focus group meetings can then assess the reasons for user preferences and identify new options for later inclusion.

Careful consideration should be given to subsidies, since there is ample evidence to suggest that these often distort land and housing markets and benefit higher income groups than those intended. Where subsidies are considered essential, they are likely to be most effective in reducing the cost of access to basic infrastructure, such as clean water and sanitation.

Because of the high cost of shelter in relation to incomes, access to credit is commonly regarded as essential. The lack of collateral in the form of title deeds is often held to be a major constraint on the ability of the poor to access formal credit. Certainly, this is a common requirement among banks and other financial institutions lending for home purchase or improvements. However, it can also be argued that it is the terms and conditions imposed by such institutions, rather than the issue of collateral, which is the main impediment. If formal institutions lend for housing at all they prefer to lend large sums on long-term loans to middle- or high-income groups, as this reduces both transaction costs and perceived risks (Okpala, 1994). For such loans, title deeds represent an obvious form of protection. However, the poor are by definition unable to service large debts, even if they are able to demonstrate creditworthiness; their need is often for small, short-term loans to build an extra room, add a floor or improve the roof, which finance institutions do not consider attractive. The provision of titles will not remove this constraint.

Despite these limitations, a number of innovations have emerged to bridge the gap. In Bolivia, South Africa, Thailand and many other countries, credit unions have made great strides in improving access to credit for households who are unable to provide collateral in the form of formal titles (Mathey, 1995). Since the mid-1980s NGOs have become involved in promoting savings and loan arrangements for low-income communities based on informal group savings schemes and collective or personal guarantees for repayments. Such schemes often provide support with house construction and skills development as well as access to credit, but are limited by the availability of capital. One response is for loans to be provided by a formal institution while the NGO provides a guarantee, although conservative practices by both governments and banks have inhibited the initiation or expansion of such solutions in practice (Mitlin, 1997; see also Datta and Jones (eds), 1998).

One impact of globalization has been to demonstrate that the state on its own cannot meet the diverse and changing needs of increased populations through direct intervention. Similarly, it appears that markets have structural limitations in their ability to meet the needs of all sections of society, while customary management systems find it increasingly difficult to operate efficiently as urban populations become more heterogeneous. Improvements will only be achieved in the long term therefore through the combined efforts of public, private and customary sectors working in positive partnership with civil society. While much attention has concentrated on the potential benefits of public–private partnerships (PPPs), the latter generally exclude the vital contribution of civil society which lends them social credence. This suggests that instead of public–private partnerships, policies should be based on encouraging multi-stakeholder partnerships (MSPs) in the provision of shelter. These can take various forms and, if well managed, may be able to provide shelter for low-income groups as part of commercially viable projects which include a mix of income groups and land uses.

It is important that the methods of formulating policies themselves should be participatory and responsive to the needs of diverse groups. Assessments using qualitative as well as quantitative research methods therefore should be undertaken regularly to ensure that policies respond efficiently to changing needs. These should include a focus on the constraints that impede access to legal, affordable and appropriate shelter for the urban poor. While such assessments may add to the initial time and cost of policy formulation and project design, the benefits will considerably outweigh these costs. They can also offset the lack of detailed and up-to-date information on land and shelter which often constrains the formulation of responsive sectoral policies. Proposals made on this basis are more likely to be accepted and 'owned' than projects with higher standards that may not reflect people's needs or interests. Participatory approaches therefore, may both reduce project costs and also provide a stronger basis for meeting other development policy objectives.

A livelihoods framework has not yet been applied in full as a means of developing or implementing urban land or shelter policies. However, it provides a holistic basis for integrating these policies with other developmental objectives. The capabilities, material and social assets and activities required for a means of living are influenced significantly by the factors which determine access to land and shelter. Livelihoods are held to be sustainable when they can cope with and recover from stresses and shocks, and maintain or enhance their capabilities and assets on a long-term basis. When applied to land and shelter, this has to include social acceptability, financial viability and institutional capability, as well as environmental sustainability. Achieving some without the others will lead invariably to failure.

REFERENCES

Amis, P (1984) 'The commercialisation of unauthorised housing in Nairobi', *World Development*, vol 12, no 1, pp105–114

Datta, K and Jones, G (eds) (1998) *Housing and Finance in Developing Countries*, Routledge, London

de Soto, H (1989) *The Other Path: The Invisible Revolution in the Third World*, IB Taurus, London

Durand-Lasserve, A (1996) '*Gestion Fonciere a l'echelle des regions urbaines: Quelques questions sur les rapports entre le rural et l'urbaines*', in proceedings of the conference on 'Land and rural/urban linkages in the 21st century', Istanbul, June 1996

Mathey, K (1995) 'The poor and the new crisis of housing finance', *Trialog*, no 4

Mitlin, D (1997) 'Building with credit: housing finance for low-income households', *Third World Planning Review*, vol 19, no 1, pp21–50

Okpala, D C I (1994) 'Financing housing in developing countries: a review of the pitfalls and potentials in the development of formal housing finance systems', *Urban Studies*, vol 31, no 9, pp1571–1586

Payne, G (1989) *Informal Housing and Land Subdivisions in Third World Cities: A Review*, Centre for Environment and Development Planning, Oxford Polytechnic, Oxford

Payne, G (2001) 'Urban land tenure policy options: titles or rights?', *Habitat International*, vol 25, pp 415–429

Quan, J (1998) 'Land tenure and sustainable rural livelihoods', in Carney, D (ed) *Sustainable Rural Livelihoods: What Contribution Can we Make?* DFID, London, pp167–180

Solomon, B (1999) 'Productive cities: local governance and land settings', paper presented to the World Bank, Washington, DC

Turner, J F C (1976) *Housing by People,* Marion Boyars, London

Tuts, R (1996) 'Cost modelling for appropriate building and planning standards in Kenya', *Habitat International,* vol 20, no 4, pp607–623

Chapter 10

Health, Health Services and Environmental Health

Trudy Harpham and Emma Grant

INTRODUCTION: A MULTIDIMENSIONAL ANALYTICAL APPROACH FOR A MULTIDIMENSIONAL ISSUE

A livelihoods approach reflects an intersectoral, holistic understanding of people's lives whereby sectors such as health, education, employment and environment are seen as being intrinsically linked. Thus, sectoral analysis of the approach is in some ways paradoxical. However, the value in taking a sectoral perspective here lies in the potential for increasing cross-sectoral understanding of the ways in which the approach can be used. The objective of this chapter is to assess the relevance of a livelihoods approach with regard to current urban and peri-urban health debates and to identify policy implications.

Health (a component of human capital) is both a determinant and outcome of livelihood strategies. Health and livelihood strategies are linked, in that good physical and mental health status are needed for production, reproduction, learning, participation and citizenship, for example. But in turn, livelihood strategies affect health, as expenditure on competing basic needs, living in a poor environment and the non-use of services may lead to poor health. A social and environmental model of health, as opposed to a purely biological or medical approach, is increasingly promulgated by those working in public health research (Harpham and Blue, 1997), which complements a livelihoods approach.

DFID (2000a) presents one framework for analysing livelihoods (see Chapter 1). Before considering how this framework can be used to understand the role of health in livelihoods, it is useful to consider briefly the main themes within urban health.

Issues commonly debated in urban health include the particularly wide range of diseases to which urban populations are exposed, ranging from health problems of poverty, such as malnutrition and infectious diseases, to problems relating to 'industrialization', such as mental ill-health, cancers and heart disease. Linked to this is the wide range of determinants of urban health, from individual factors (the proximate determinants of health) to socio-economic causes (the distal determinants of health). There has been a renewed interest recently in the distal determinants of health, which are closely related to poverty and livelihood strategies, rather than the proximate determinants. These factors were first highlighted in the Victorian public health movement in the UK (Ashton and Seymour, 1988).

While some health patterns are similar in both rural and urban areas, non-communicable diseases are more prevalent in urban areas (Bradley et al, 1991). Even in terms of diseases of poverty such as malnutrition, the urban poor are sometimes more vulnerable than their rural counterparts (Haddad et al, 1999). Urban areas are characterized by a multiplicity of both health and environmental service providers which may diversify health-seeking strategies for the urban poor. Also critical is the need to disaggregate urban health data by income and/or geographical area. Such disaggregation has often not been feasible due to a lack of routinely collected community-based health data, but on the rare occasions where it has been possible, it has demonstrated that the urban poor suffer 'the worst of both worlds' in that they have a higher prevalence of both communicable and non-communicable diseases than their more affluent urban neighbours (Bradley et al, 1991).

VULNERABILITY CONTEXT

There is a tradition of analysing health in vulnerability terms. Vulnerability can be equated with the accumulation of risk factors. The 'upstream' determinants of health have long been recognized as changes in the environment (economic, political, social, physical) which create risk factors for ill health. For this reason, this chapter begins the analysis of urban health and livelihoods by considering the vulnerability context which surrounds and impacts on the everyday livelihood strategies of urban residents. In health terms, there is a difference between vulnerability (societally induced) and susceptibility (genetically induced). This chapter will consider only vulnerability because the focus is on the social model of causation.

The vulnerability context, according to the livelihoods framework, consists of shocks, trends and seasonality. It is difficult to separate shocks from trends, although DFID (2000b) suggests that trends are 'more predictable'. This difficulty is analagous to a debate in the health field regarding the difference between long-term difficulties and life events (both key social determinants of mental ill-health). Harpham (1994) suggests that life events occur due to a change in the external environment which happens sufficiently rapidly to be approximately dated, while long-term difficulties are more ongoing processes. For this chapter, life events will be analagous to shocks and long-term difficulties will be analogous to trends. Trends, seasonality and shocks are considered in turn below, with particular attention to trends since these encompass multilevel economic, political, demographic and social changes.

Trends

Trends can change people's exposure to health risks. They provide a dynamic backdrop to health status and can have both positive and negative health impacts. Within the context of developing country cities, certain key trends can be identified which have particular implications for health.

International Level Trends

SAPs provide an example of an international level trend. It has been argued that, because of their dependence on the cash economy, urban populations are particularly vulnerable to the effects of adjustment policies, including civil service retrenchment, job shedding by the formal sector and saturation of the urban informal sector (Dubresson, 2000). There is much debate regarding SAPs and their effect on health. Generally, research in this area fails to prove an association between structural adjustment and health because of the methodological difficulty of carrying out longitudinal (prospective) studies to demonstrate change in health status over time and attributing such changes to particular policies. However, there are studies which demonstrate that deterioration of health, particularly among children and mothers, is associated with certain outcomes of structural adjustment (for example, changes in child and maternal nutritional status in Brazzaville, Congo, following the 1994 devaluation (Martin-Prével et al, 2000)).

National and Municipal Trends

Health sector reform, encompassing decentralization, privatization and the introduction of health insurance and user fees, has been the dominant trend at the national level for the last decade. This trend has largely been driven by international aid agencies, but is implemented at the national level with implications for the municipal level. This trend, however, has only affected health services that fall under central ministries of health and has largely neglected environmental health services which typically fall under other ministries such as public works or local government. The trend has prompted reliance on a multiplicity of urban health service providers (public, national, district and municipal; private; NGOs; traditional; and retail 'over-the-counter' remedies). The introduction of user fees has sometimes been associated with a reduction in the use of public health services by the urban poor (Gilson, 1997), while health insurance has been difficult to implement, particularly in the urban informal sector (Tangcharoen-sathien, 1990). The decentralization of services to the municipal level has often increased the responsibilities of local government without an accompanying increase in financial resources. This has sometimes resulted in urban district health authorities (which are accountable to central ministries of health) providing care that would normally be the responsibility of the municipality (for example, in Lusaka, Zambia (Atkinson et al, 1999)). Finally, safety nets designed to provide exemption from health service fees for the poorest people have failed in some cases to benefit those intended due to difficulties in raising awareness of such schemes and the inability of the most vulnerable to access the necessary individuals, forms, and so on (as in Lusaka, Atkinson et al, 2000).

The privatization of environmental health services (water supply, sanitation, solid-waste management) is occurring increasingly at the municipal level (see Chapter 11). The health implications for urban residents are linked to the fact that the urban poor are either not covered by such services (particularly peri-urban populations) or have to pay charges that often exceed those paid by their middle- and upper-income counterparts (Hardoy et al, 1992). This leads to a further polarization between the poor and non-poor in terms of access to basic services.

Population Trends

One population trend affecting urban health is the increase in female-headed households, although there is some debate as to whether this phenomenon is urban-specific. The health implications are tied to the need for women household heads to acquire income through employment, often outside the house, in addition to child-rearing and household chores. Although such a triple workload is not confined to women who are household heads, the total burden for the latter and the consequent strain on health are greater. This situation can also mean that children are left at home with inadequate supervision and are thus more exposed to health risks.

Population trends also include changes in lifestyle, such as increased smoking, worsening dietary habits and increased alcohol consumption. These trends are closely tied to societal factors (for example, an association between urban stressors and alcohol consumption). In developing countries, urban areas are leading the health (epidemiological) transition: this means that they are witnessing an increase in chronic as opposed to communicable diseases – for example, cancers, obesity, mental ill-health and heart disease.

In addition to the health transition, urban areas are characterized by an ageing population as a result of age-selective rural–urban migration, reduced fertility, reduced adult mortality and changing patterns of adult morbidity. The health effects of ageing contribute to the health transition and to increased and qualitatively different demands on health services.

The health and demographic transitions, in addition to other trends described above, are by nature outcome trends – that is, they are the downstream, end result of policies and processes. In contrast, SAPs, health sector reform or the privatization of environmental health services are policy trends. In policy terms, it is important to differentiate between outcome trends and policy trends since, in order to address causes rather than symptoms, action needs to be at the policy level. In practice, actors such as NGOs or CBOs may not focus their energies on lobbying macrolevel policy-makers, but choose instead an ameliorative approach, addressing the 'symptoms'. For example, in countries where SAPs are being implemented and national governments are cutting back on health sector expenditure, NGOs typically choose to offer alternative/supplemental healthcare provision, such as an immunization programme.

Seasonality

There is a well-known association between seasonality and health, although little work has been done concerning the particular links between seasonality and urban health. In low-income, overcrowded urban areas, the wet season is strongly associated with exposure to water-borne diseases such as cholera and diarrhoea (Cairncross and Feachem, 1983). In addition, breeding conditions for mosquitoes which transmit malaria and dengue are affected by seasonality. Environmental events may also be seasonally determined – for example, flooding and landslides which may affect living conditions in precarious housing.

Other associations between seasonality and health are seasonal food shortages (including shortages of urban agricultural produce), consequent price rises and resulting increases in malnutrition. Seasonal unemployment among peri-urban residents with agriculture-related jobs and the subsequent decrease in their resources for health-related expenditure has been documented. For example, Scheper-Hughes (1992) discusses the association between child mortality and unemployment, which in turn is related to the post-harvest dry season in peri-urban Brazil. Seasonality also affects urban health through in-migration of rural workers to urban areas during months when rural employment opportunities are low (Bryant and Bailey, 1997). At these times, cities may experience a substantial influx and consequent over-crowding, including saturation of the informal sector, with potential health impacts, such as the spread of communicable diseases, over-burdening of health services and reduction in income for those working in the informal sector (Bocquier and Beauchemin, 2000).

Shocks

From an urban health perspective, shocks represent a sudden exposure to health risk factors. For example, loss of employment, separation from a spouse, migration, illness/incapacitation or death in the family can increase stress and in turn lead to mental ill-health. Such shocks, or 'life events', may also impact on physical health through, for example, the loss of earnings and subsequent lack of finance to spend on medicine, food, shelter and health services. The effect of shocks may be buffered by assets such as social capital, which will be discussed in the next section (see also Chapter 8).

Shocks may also occur at the macrolevel. For example, sudden devaluation of a currency may particularly affect urban populations, with the resulting decline in real incomes leading to cutbacks in household expenditure on health services or health-related expenditure, including food. Box 10.1 summarizes the health effects of the sudden economic crisis in Indonesia at the end of the 1990s.

LIVELIHOOD ASSETS

Assets in the livelihoods framework are human, social, physical, financial and natural capital. Capital is defined as assets whose economic effects must have some persistence over time (Collier, 1998). Health status is included in human capital. However, human capital must not be seen in isolation from other assets

---

Box 10.1 *Economic Crisis and Urban Health: A Case Study of Indonesia*

Indonesia suffered an economic crisis in 1997–1998 which saw output fall by 15 per cent in a year and an annual inflation of 80 per cent. Unusually, a longitudinal study interviewing the same 1934 households in 1997 and 1998 was able to track the health impacts of the crisis. The proportion of households below the poverty line rose by about 25 per cent, with a larger increase in urban than in rural areas. In both urban and rural areas there was a significant increase in the proportion of household budgets spent on food and especially on staples (mainly rice). For men, urban residence appeared to be protective of employment status relative to their rural counterparts. Urban women, however, were more likely to have lost a paying job by 1998 than rural women. The use of health services declined and shifted from public to private and traditional practitioners. There was a significant reduction in the proportion of children receiving vitamin A which protects against various illnesses. The quality of public health services, relative to private providers, declined, but both raised their fees. There was little change in contraceptive use: 'the stability of contraceptive prevalence in the face of economic crisis suggests that for the majority of couples. . . contraception is a more appealing option than the risk of having an additional child in the current economic environment' (p64). In terms of health status, the nutritional status of adults had substantially worsened, but children appeared to have been largely protected from the crisis.

Source: Frankenberg et al, 1999

---

as there are intercapital relationships and a potential for substituting between different forms of capital.

Inter- and Intracapital Relationships

One example of intercapital relationships is the linkages between human and social capital. Seminal research in the United States has demonstrated that components of social capital (trust, reciprocity and membership of voluntary organizations) explain a significant proportion of life expectancy, infant mortality, heart disease, violent crime and self-rated health (Kawachi et al, 1997; Sampson et al, 1997). These associations persist after controlling for income (see Box 10.2). While work in developing countries has demonstrated the link between social capital and general household welfare (expenditure, assets, access to credit, savings and employment) (Narayan and Pritchett, 1997; Grootaert, 1999; Grootaert and Narayan, 1999; and Grootaert et al, 1999), there is little research on the link between social capital and health in the South. This is of particular relevance to urban populations because, as noted in earlier chapters, there is some evidence to suggest that social capital in urban areas is lower than in rural areas (Krishna and Shrader, 1999).

BOX 10. 2 *ASSOCIATION BETWEEN SOCIAL AND HUMAN CAPITAL*

A cross-sectional study of 39 states in the United States measured social capital in terms of the per capita density of membership in voluntary groups and the proportion of residents who believed that people could be trusted. The 1990 age-standardized total and cause-specific mortality rates were also obtained. Income inequality was strongly correlated with group membership and lack of social trust. Both social trust and group membership were associated with total mortality, as well as deaths from heart disease, cancers and infant (under one year of age) mortality. This study supports the notion that income inequality leads to increased mortality via disinvestment in social capital. This research has yet to be replicated in developing countries, but is currently being developed in South Africa and Colombia.

Source: Kawachi et al, 1997

In addition to the linkages outlined between human and social capital, there are links between human capital and other assets. For example, physical capital, such as housing, is an important determinant of health status (Dunn, 2000); financial capital, such as savings, is closely tied to food purchasing; and natural capital, such as air, can affect health through the association between pollution and respiratory problems.

The relationship between different types of capital also involves extensive 'substitution' or 'exchange' activities. For example, in times of extreme financial hardship, households may wish to exchange physical capital – for example, a consumer durable such as a bicycle – for financial capital which may be used to protect human capital – for example, purchasing food or medicine to maintain health.

Education is considered to be another component of human capital. Education affects both health status and access to health services. Female education status is a critical determinant of child mortality in developing countries and a mediating factor is widely believed to be a mother's ability to access health services and other structures (Cleland and van Ginneken, 1988). An interesting and somewhat controversial finding from qualitative research among low-income women in Dar-es-Salaam (Van Eeuwijk, 2000) is that women with higher levels of knowledge regarding the link between environmental conditions and health (in particular, the need to reduce malaria by controlling mosquitoes through window screening, burning mosquito coils and sleeping under impregnated bednets), but without the means to act upon this knowledge in order to protect their children, experienced higher levels of emotional distress as a result. However, women with high levels of knowledge as well as access to financial and social resources stated that knowledge was an enabling factor for them. This suggests that high levels of education (human capital), in the absence of other forms of capital, such as financial or social capital, do not necessarily lead to improved health status. In this instance, mental ill-health resulted from this frustration. The controversy is that one policy response might be to limit environmental health education/promotion to those with the assets to act upon the advice.

Assets and the Vulnerability Context

The vulnerability context has an important effect upon people's assets and the livelihood strategies they employ. A good example of the vulnerability context affecting livelihood assets, particularly health, is the erosion of various types of capital due to violence (see Box 10.3).

BOX 10.3 *THE IMPACT OF VIOLENCE ON LIVELIHOOD ASSETS*

Violence constitutes an important trend (and shock) within the vulnerability context, to which low-income groups face the greatest exposure. Its impact upon the assets bundle is multiple:

- Physical capital – violent attacks on infrastructure, such as vandalism of community facilities.
- Financial capital – losses due to robbery.
- Human capital – night-school drop-out rates increase through fear of street or public transportation crime; increased homicide and injury rates.
- Social capital – destruction of trust and cooperation.
- Natural capital – displaced populations fleeing violence often flow into urban areas, exacerbating environmental problems such as solid waste disposal and water contamination.

Source: Partly drawn from Moser and Shrader, 1999

However, assets may also mediate the effect of the vulnerability context upon health in that stocks of capital may buffer an individual or household's vulnerability to shocks. For example, social capital, by providing emotional, instrumental or informational support, may reduce the threat of mental ill-health.

POLICIES, INSTITUTIONS AND PROCESSES

There is considerable overlap between 'policies/institutions/processes' and the trends discussed above. For example, legislative change, privatization, decentralization and the formation or destruction of safety nets are both trends and policies. In order to maintain a distinction, this section considers organizational arrangements and processes at the microlevel as opposed to the macrolevel which was considered above as part of the vulnerability context. Policies are not considered in this section because it is difficult to identify microlevel policies that are not linked to the macrolevel.

Institutional and Organizational Arrangements

The attributes of institutions may affect livelihood strategies – for example, through the accountability of providers to residents or their geographical location. Residents whose needs are not met by their local health centre or who have to travel long distances to access tertiary care, may seek alternative pathways of care to satisfy their health needs. In addition, the quality of health services may also affect health-seeking behaviour. Poor quality public health centres at both community (primary) and hospital (tertiary) levels may lead urban dwellers to use home-based treatment; to use retail outlets which are known to sell drugs in an unregulated, inappropriate and sometimes dangerous manner; or to consult private and/or traditional practitioners (Harpham and Molyneux, 2001; Atkinson et al, 1999). One example of adaptation to the needs of vulnerable groups is in Cali (Colombia) where health centres in low-income areas have increased their contact with youth groups, started to offer outreach programmes in sexual and reproductive health and violence reduction, and offered their facilities for youth group meetings.

The policy implications are threefold: improving accessibility, increasing the quality of care and the sensitive identification of needs. Health sector reform and decentralization offer increased opportunity for local decision-making by local governments and health centre staff, which can directly affect these three aspects. Mechanisms by which user groups can express their healthcare needs are crucial for improved responses. Neighbourhood health committees that communicate needs to local health centres in Lusaka, Zambia, have had some degree of success in developing such a mechanism (Atkinson et al, 1999).

Processes

The urban environment has characteristics that may be conducive to ill health. In low-income urban communities, long-term difficulties can include living in a poor, overcrowded environment, with high levels of crime and violence and insecure tenure. In addition the change from a subsistence to a cash economy may be accompanied by a need to acculturate migrants. There is evidence that such long-term difficulties, if not buffered by social support, can lead to mental ill-health (Harpham, 1994). In low-income urban areas, mental ill-health is typically twice as high among women as men because of the different level and nature of stressors experienced: in the case of urban women, these result from the demands of combining productive and reproductive roles in a cash economy and poor physical environment (Harpham, 1994). Particular difficulties are associated with specific physical health outcomes – for example, overcrowding is associated with an increase in accidents (Reichenheim and Harpham, 1989).

Risk factors mediate the relationship between livelihood strategies and health. For example, in Colombia, young people (aged 15–24 years) constitute the group most at risk of violence due to their greater exposure to risk factors, such as alcohol consumption and access to arms (Weaver and Madaleno, 1999). At the community level, strategies to reduce both stressors and risk factors might include strengthening social capital by reducing social conflict, increasing social cohesion and providing increased social support, including information, practical and emotional support.

LIVELIHOOD STRATEGIES

Livelihood strategies are the activities that people undertake and the choices they make in order to achieve their livelihood goals. They can be captured largely through verbs. In terms of health, these could be saving for the event of illness; attending a traditional healer; borrowing money to pay for medicine or a health insurance scheme; or migrating for healthcare purposes, such as giving birth. As regards environmental health services, strategies might include sharing tap connections; paying for tanked water; mobilizing to lobby for connections to the city sewerage system; or connecting illegally to a water supply.

The objective of a livelihood strategy is to achieve well-being and security by increasing a household's asset base. Thus, for example, the objective of health-seeking strategies is to increase human capital, but this is not a one-way relationship. HIV/AIDS is an example of bidirectional linkages between livelihood strategies and health status: livelihood strategies can determine health status and health status can affect livelihood strategies. A number of studies in sub-Saharan Africa have reported large HIV prevalence differences between urban areas, roadside settlements and rural areas (Boerma et al, 1999). HIV prevalence has often been observed to be four times as high in urban as in rural areas. This may be associated with the different composition of the population (age, sex, occupation), different sexual lifestyles, or different community characteristics, such as more exposure through greater contact with mobile populations. However, high rates of rural–urban migration, rural-urban circulation, return migration and the considerable disruption in familial and sexual relations that these can involve, suggest that rural–urban links will continue to facilitate the spread of HIV to rural areas in this region. The spread of disease from rural to urban populations can also result from migrants lacking immunity to an endemic disease: serious epidemics can result from their susceptibility. Livelihood strategies influence health status and, in particular, health policy needs to target the most mobile populations.

In turn, HIV/AIDS status affects livelihood strategies. Caring for the ill often imposes constraints on already vulnerable groups. Within the context of increasing HIV/AIDS, Robson (2000) has shown how women and young people are disproportionately burdened by the restructuring of health services and the increase in home-based care in urban Zimbabwe. Young people (especially girls) are becoming carers in the context of increasing health-service fees and decreasing household income resulting from adult incapacity due to HIV/AIDS. Robson argues that these young carers are largely invisible to researchers and policy-makers. The failure of outreach services from urban health centres first, to identify home-based care needs and second, to support carers, needs to be addressed in policy terms. Urban health services by and large remain within the boundaries of health centre walls and past failures in experiments with community health workers, which have mainly relied on voluntary workers rather than on professional outreach workers, make the health sector reluctant to develop outreach services in the context of severe resource constraints. However, limited, targeted support of home-based care is necessary and may be feasible.

The current volume has a particular concern with rural–urban links (see Chapter 4). In terms of health, treatment-seeking strategies and disease transmission illustrate these well. A recent study on the Kenyan coast demonstrated similar treatment-seeking strategies by low-income rural and urban mothers in response to childhood fevers and convulsions (Molyneux et al, 1999). This similarity in rural and urban maternal strategies was unexpected, given differences between the two groups in socio-economic status and physical access to health services. One potential explanation is the exchange of information and ideas about illnesses and appropriate therapy between urban and rural residents; the outcome of strong rural–urban interdependencies established and maintained through migration, mobility and households split between rural and urban areas.

The importance of moving 'beyond the rural–urban divide' in urban health thinking is highlighted by studies exploring referral systems within districts and countries (see, for example, Akin and Hutchinson, 1999; Okello et al, 1998) and by studies revealing return urban–rural migration of sick family members (see, for example, Kitange et al, 1996). The livelihoods framework could be usefully applied in the future to develop a more systematic understanding of the influence of rural ties on livelihood strategies in urban populations.

Conclusions: Policy Implications

Some health policy implications considered below derive directly from the components of a livelihoods framework – for example, livelihood strategies and links between assets – while others relate to changing the 'routine activities' associated with the health sector, such as information collection and evaluation.

Information Collection

It would be difficult to compare results from the application of a livelihoods framework, either between populations or over time. This lack of comparability creates a barrier to applying the framework as a means of identifying the most vulnerable. For example, an urban district health manager seeking to reassess levels of vulnerability on an annual basis in order to allocate resources equitably would need to measure asset distribution at a household and community level each year. The difficulty lies in quantifying and weighting bundles of assets in order to compare households and communities over time. Quantification of the asset bundle as a whole has rarely been carried out and documented. Moreover, the livelihoods framework fails to provide any new answers to the problem of identifying the relative importance of assets. These methodological and practical problems need to be addressed in the development of instruments to measure household assets.

A key policy implication concerns the nature of the information that needs to be collected. In health, information is typically obtained from: routine health-service facility data (which captures only users and neglects non-users); sentinel surveillance systems (which are often limited to pre-disaster situations); and ad hoc community household surveys (which are expensive). These measures usually fail to incorporate household priorities, assets, strategies and the vulnerability context. It is inconceivable that the health sector alone could collect all this information; therefore, a coordinated intersectoral approach to shared data collection and analysis is needed.

Links Between Assets

The livelihoods framework could also be helpful in facilitating policy-makers to identify and act upon links between assets. Health status is part of human capital, and this chapter has emphasized the fact that the links between assets provide various avenues for acting upon urban health – for example, by strengthening social capital. This is already being done by the local government in Cali, Colombia, where the Health Department is investing in projects that strengthen social capital with the objective of reducing violence among low-income urban youths. This type of intervention suggests that the concerns of the health sector must be much broader than provision of health services alone. Indeed, perhaps the most important health policy implication of a livelihoods approach is the need for the health sector to recognize non-health service issues such as employment or housing and their effects on health. Addressing such linked problems implies intersectoral coordination. Experience of attempts to achieve such intersectoral action suggests that a necessary first step is for sectors to plan together, but to implement independently. Initiatives in which joint implementation of activities has been attempted have often failed due to the perceived loss of power and ownership by the individual sectors.

The Synergistic Effects of Macro- and Microcontexts

The way in which a livelihoods approach emphasizes the synergistic influences on health emerging from the vulnerability context reinforces existing trends towards simultaneous consideration of macro- and microlevel factors. For example, household-level long-term difficulties may be offset by decentralization within national health sector reform, allowing and encouraging increased responsiveness to local needs. Thus, attention to both the broader social, economic and political context, and the characteristics and situation of communities or households is critical for developing an understanding of the health needs of a population and devising appropriate interventions.

Livelihood Strategies

A livelihoods approach prompts the need to consider competing livelihood strategies. The health-promotion approach assumes that seeking an increase in human capital is an acceptable prioritized component of a livelihood strategy, but does not take into account the competing uses of assets which might prioritize other outcomes – for example, a low-income family might prioritize saving (for a daughter's wedding, perhaps) rather than spending money on more nutritious food. The policy implication for the health sector relates to the need to understand competing strategies and priorities and adapt programmes, such as health education, accordingly. However, the implications for non-health sector policy-makers and practitioners may be rather different: the livelihoods framework suggests potential intervention paths which might not focus directly on livelihood strategies. Thus, in the above example, a programme to provide food at a reduced cost could be a more effective route to improving nutrition than encouraging families to change their selected livelihood strategies.

To focus on livelihood strategies requires recognition of the importance of informal sector activities among the urban poor. The health risks of such activities tend to be neglected by government health agencies, but emerge from analysing the impact of livelihood strategies on assets.

The Role of Health Services

The main implication of a livelihoods approach for health services is the need to take a comprehensive primary healthcare approach as opposed to a narrow, curative perspective. Although the international declaration on primary health-care in 1978 (at Alma-Ata) advocated a focus on the broader determinants of ill health (such as water supply, housing and work conditions), there is still a reluctance in many countries to move away from a curative emphasis in health services. The current focus of the World Health Organization on specific disease control measures – for example, malaria and tuberculosis – hinders moves towards more comprehensive treatment of health. Achieving such a transition will require that the training of public health professionals incorporate the kinds of analyses and interventions that a livelihoods approach promotes.

Evaluation

A livelihoods framework can be used as a tool to critically assess projects which have multisectoral action as an objective – for example, Healthy City Projects which began in the North but in the last five years have spread to the South. These projects aim to put health on the agenda of all sectors at the municipal level. This objective is replicated in a livelihoods approach through the inter-sectoral manner in which livelihoods are seen to encompass multiple aspects of human development and needs, including health. Practitioners and policy-makers could use a livelihoods framework to identify the roles and activities that impact upon health but are the responsibilities of other sectors.

In conclusion, while many aspects of the livelihoods framework are not new to the health field, the approach provides useful insights into:

- The linkages between assets, which have not been widely considered by the health sector.
- Disaggregation of the vulnerability context into shocks, trends and season-ality which adds greater depth to the analyses of vulnerability that the health sector requires.
- Competing livelihood strategies that impact on health.

The current volume assesses the relevance of a livelihoods framework for urban settings. In health terms, such a framework is applicable to both urban and rural contexts, and can also focus attention on the health issues which are specific to peri-urban areas.

Acknowledgements

Thanks are due to Dr Ilona Blue and Rob Smith for their comments on this chapter.

References

Akin, J S and Hutchinson, P (1999) 'Health-care facility choice and the phenomenon of bypassing', *Health Policy Plan,* vol 14, no 2, pp135–151

Ashton, J and Seymour, H (1988) *The New Public Health,* Open University Press, Milton Keynes

Atkinson, S, Ngwengwe, A, Macwangi, M, Ngulube, T, Harpham, T and O'Connell, A (1999) 'The referral process and urban health care in Sub-Saharan Africa: the case of Lusaka, Zambia', *Social Science and Medicine,* vol 49, pp27–38

Atkinson, S, Harpham, T, O'Connell, A and Owen, M (2000) *The Lusaka Health Project: Final Report*, Department for International Development, London

Bocquier, P and Beauchemin, C (2000) *Migration and Urbanisation in West Afri*ca, paper presented to the Urban Population Dynamics Panel of the National Academy of Sciences, Wood's Hole, USA, September

Boerma, J, Urassa, M et al (1999) 'Spread of HIV infection in a rural area of Tanzania', *AIDS,* vol 13, pp1233–1240

Bradley, D, Cairncross, S, Harpham T and Stephens, C (1991) *A Review of Environmental Health Impacts in Developing Country Cities*, Urban Management Programme Discussion Series no 6, World Bank, Washington, DC

Bryant, R and Bailey, S (1997) *Third World Political Ecology,* Routledge, London

Cairncross, S and Feachem, R (1983) *Environmental Health Engineering in the Tropics: An Introductory Text,* John Wiley & Sons, Chichester

Cleland, J and van Ginneken, J (1988) 'Maternal education and child survival in developing countries: the search for pathways of influence', *Social Science and Medicine*, vol 27, no 12, pp1357–1368

Collier, P (1998) *Social Capital and Poverty,* Social Capital Initiative Working Paper no 4, World Bank, Washington, DC

DFID (2000a) *Sustainable Livelihoods: Building on Strengths*, Department for International Development, London

DFID (2000b) Sustainable livelihoods guidance sheets, Department for International Development, London

Dubresson, A (2000) *Urbanization in Francophone Africa*, paper prepared for the Panel on Urban Population Dynamics, Population Committee, US National Academy of Sciences, Washington, DC

Dunn, J (2000) 'Housing and health inequalities: review and prospects for research', *Housing Studies,* vol 15, no 3, pp341–345

Frankenberg, E, Thomas, D and Beagle, K (1999) *The Real Costs of Indonesia's Economic Crisis,* Rand Working Paper no 99–04, Los Angeles

Gilson, L (1997) 'The lessons of user fee experience in Africa', *Health Policy and Planning,* vol 12, no 4, pp273–285

Grootaert, C (1999) *Social Capital, Household Welfare and Poverty in Indonesia,* Local Level Institutions Study, Study Working Paper No 6, World Bank, Washington, DC

Grootaert, C and Narayan, D (1999) *Local Institutions, Poverty and Household Welfare in Bolivia,* Local Level Institutions Study, World Bank, Washington, DC, mimeo

Grootaert, C, Gi-taik, O and Swamy, A (1999) *Social Capital and Development Outcomes in Burkina Faso, Local Level Institutions Study,* World Bank, Washington, DC, mimeo

Haddad, L, Ruel, M and Garrett, J (1999) 'Are urban poverty and under-nutrition growing? Some newly assembled evidence', *World Development,* vol 27, no 11, pp1891–1904

Hardoy, J, Mitlin, D and Satterthwaite, D (1992) *Environmental Problems in Third World Cities*, Earthscan, London

Harpham, T (1994) 'Urbanization and mental health in developing countries: a research role for social scientists, public health professionals and social psychiatrists', *Social Science and Medicine,* vol 39, no 2, pp233–245

Harpham, T and Blue, I (1997) 'Linking health policy and social policy in urban settings: the new development agenda', *Transactions of the Royal Society of Tropical Medicine and Hygiene,* vol 9, pp497–498

Harpham, T and Molyneux, S (2001) 'Urban health in developing countries: a review', *Progress in Development Studies,* vol 1, no 2, pp113–137

Kawachi, I, Kennedy, B, Lochner, K and Prothrow-Stith, D (1997) 'Social capital, income inequality and mortality', *American Journal of Public Health,* vol 87, pp1491–1498

Kitange, H M, Machibya, H et al (1996) 'Outlook for survivors of childhood in sub-Saharan Africa: adult mortality in Tanzania, Adult Morbidity and Mortality Project [published erratum appears in BMJ 1996 Feb 24; vol 312, no 7029, p483]', *British Medical Journal,* vol 312, no 7025, pp216–20

Krishna, A and Shrader, E (1999) *Social Capital Assessment Tool,* prepared for the conference on Social Capital and Poverty Reduction, World Bank, Washington, DC, 22–24 June

Martin-Prével, Y, Delpeuch, F, Traissac, P, Massamba, J, Adoua-Oyila, G, Coudert, K and Treche, S (2000) 'Deterioration of the nutritional status of young children and their mothers in Brazzaville, Congo, following the 1994 devaluation of the CFA franc', *Bulletin of the World Health Organization,* vol 78, no 1, pp108–118

Molyneux, C S, Mung'Ala-Odera, V et al (1999) 'Maternal responses to childhood fevers: a comparison of rural and urban residents in coastal Kenya', *Tropical Medicine International Health,* vol 4, no 12, pp836–845

Moser, C and Shrader, E (1999) *A Conceptual Framework for Violence Reduction,* Sustainable Development Working Paper no 2, World Bank, Washington, DC

Narayan, D and Pritchett, L (1997) *Cents and Sociability: Household Income and Social Capital in Rural Tanzania,* Policy Research Working Paper No 1796, World Bank, Washington, DC

Okello, D, Lubanga, R et al (1998) 'The challenge to restoring basic health care in Uganda', *Social Science and Medicine,* vol 46, no 1, pp13–21

Reichenheim, M and Harpham, T (1989) 'Child accidents and associated risk factors in a Brazilian squatter settlement', *Health Policy and Planning,* vol 4, no 2, pp162–167

Robson, E (2000) 'Invisible carers: young people in Zimbabwe's home-based health care', *Area,* vol 32, no 1, pp59–70

Sampson, R J, Raudenbush, S W and Earls, F (1997) 'Neighborhoods and violent crime: a multilevel study of collective efficacy', *Science,* vol 277, pp918–924

Scheper-Hughes, N (1992) *Death Without Weeping: The Violence of Everyday Life in Brazil,* University of California Press, Berkeley

Tangcharoensathien, V (1990) *Community Financing: The Urban Health Card in Chiang Mai, Thailand,* unpublished PhD thesis, University of London, London

Van Eeuwijk, B (2000) *Struggling for Health in the City: An Anthropological Enquiry in Dar-es-Salaam, Tanzania,* habilitation thesis, Swiss Tropical Institute, Basel

Weaver, C and Madaleno, M (1999) 'Youth violence in Latin America: Current situation on violence prevention strategies', *Pan American Journal of Public Health,* vol 5, nos 4 and 5, pp338–343

Chapter 11

Infrastructure and Environmental Health Services

Mansoor Ali

INTRODUCTION

Infrastructure and environmental health services (IEHS) directly and indirectly contribute to income and employment. Productive activities are not possible without basic IEHS such as water, sanitation and drainage; and absence of IEHS has adverse impacts on both human health and the environment. There are various types of IEHS and their relative importance varies according to the context in which they are provided and the livelihood goals targeted. For example, irrigation systems, drainage and all-weather roads may be important in a rural setting where the livelihood goal is agricultural production and marketing. In the urban context, the residential and work environment and health may be more important to sustaining a means of living. Consequently, water, sanitation, drainage and solid-waste management become a higher priority. Box 11.1 highlights the importance of these services, each of which is strongly linked with income, employment, health and the local environment of the urban poor.

In the past, IEHS have been seen mainly as a requirement to protect health and the local environment. Environmental factors are responsible for almost a quarter of all disease in low-income countries (DFID, 2001). Wastewater collection and treatment systems, measures to improve the quality of air, the control of noise and proper management of solid-waste disposal sites are an important part of protecting health and the urban environment. As cities and populations grow, open land becomes scarce and expensive. Open areas in the vicinity of living space become important assets and need to be kept clean. As population densities increase, the importance of certain IEHS over others also increases. The importance of IEHS in protecting health and the environment is unchallenged. However, the poor have not been considered seriously as IEHS providers, although a large number are involved in service provision both as formal sector employees and as informal sector entrepreneurs. This chapter considers the conceptualization of IEHS provision as not only environmental and health related but also livelihoods related, in terms of its potential for income and employment generation for the poor.

BOX 11.1 *THE IMPORTANCE OF IEHS IN THE URBAN CONTEXT*

Water supply

Adequate and safe water inside the house or within easy reach is an important part of controlling water-borne and water-washed diseases. Increasing the quantity of water available is important for bringing about health improvements, but leads to the accumulation of wastewater if drainage is inadequate. As water from formal sources is unavailable or inadequate, water vending by local entrepreneurs is common in poor areas.

Solid-waste

Solid-waste management is important because of its impact on both health and other infrastructure. The health risks to residents resulting from poor solid-waste management involve:

- the spread of disease by vectors and other animals;
- the spread of disease by direct contact;
- groundwater contamination;
- contaminated air;
- fire risk; and
- unhygienic overflowing of drains.

Large quantities of urban waste can adversely affect water, sanitation and drainage systems. This may result in poor water quality, stagnant water and floods, which lead to further risks to human lives. Poor solid-waste management also affects people directly involved with the waste – waste workers and waste-pickers, and those who are in direct contact with it through a carrier. Proper solid-waste management is an important IEHS for urban areas. It has strong linkages with the livelihood strategies of the poor because of the presence of a large number of waste-pickers and collectors.

Drainage

Drainage is the systematic removal of rain and wastewater. It is mainly provided to remove surface run-off from rain, but is also frequently used for carrying domestic wastewater and toilet flushes. Poorly maintained drainage systems can lead to flooding and the spread of many diseases. They provide sites for mosquito breeding and can cause damage to roads and properties. The provision and maintenance of urban drainage is important for reducing threats to physical assets and for protecting public health.

Sanitation

Sanitation refers to the proper disposal of excreta and household wastewater. It implies a separate place in houses for excreta disposal which is conveyed either to a soakpit or to a sewer which conveys it to a treatment plant. The provision of sanitation is important for the protection of health, while the treatment and reuse of excreta and wastewater benefits the environment. Sanitation provision through local masons and small-scale contractors is common in poor areas and provides income and employment opportunities.

IEHS AND URBAN LIVELIHOODS

The provision of IEHS has always been considered important for quality of life because of their direct impact on human health and the local environment. These constitute components of human, physical and natural assets. The reliable operation of IEHS reduces the vulnerability to disease of the urban poor, as they live in an environment of congested working and living spaces. Studies have found strong linkages between adequate and safe water, sanitation, drainage and levels of health (see, for example, Cairncross and Feacham, 1993). For formal housing, provision is often, through state structures and processes, regulated by building and services codes. However, for the poor in low-income countries, IEHS do not come automatically with housing.

Many estimates are available which illustrate the scale of the failure of governments in poor countries to provide IEHS to rapidly growing urban populations (Cairncross, 1990). While there was considerable progress during the 1980–1990 water and sanitation decade, in terms of extending services, improvements could not cope with increasing urban populations. To achieve the international development target of halving the population with unimproved water supply by 2015, an additional 1.6 billion people will require access, of whom 64 per cent will be in urban areas (WHO, 2000, Table 2.2).

Urban livelihoods and the provision of IEHS are linked through three pathways:

- Through the protection of human health, which is important for human well-being and reducing vulnerability to shocks (see Chapter 10).
- Through the protection of the local and city environment, which is important for other assets on which residents depend, such as land, water resources and air.
- Through the protection and provision of employment opportunities.

In the past, the provision of IEHS to the poor has been considered a priority to protect health, which in turn is important for pursuing various livelihood goals and reducing vulnerability. Conventional approaches to IEHS provision establish links with residents for cost recovery, operation and maintenance. In some cases communities are also involved in the planning and design processes. However, the role of the poor as IEHS providers has never been considered seriously. Nevertheless, they are significant providers of IEHS in informal and low-income urban areas, and many are able to find employment and earn incomes in doing so. This suggests a number of opportunities for the provision of IEHS to benefit the poor through enhancing income and employment. The principal objectives of the provision of IEHS therefore could fit well into the livelihoods approach by developing a more holistic picture, covering human health, the local and natural environment, and employment. Table 11.1 shows the intended impact and links with livelihood goals of some examples of IEHS.

Table 11.1 *Livelihood goals and infrastructure and environmental health services*

Type of IEHS	Intended impact	Livelihood goals
Water supply	Reduce water-borne disease Reduce water-washed disease Less time on water collection Less payment for good quality water	Reduced vulnerability to poor health More time available for income generation
Sanitation and drainage	Reduce water-borne disease Reduce water-based disease Reduce water-related disease Protect the local environment Protect infrastructure and property	Reduced vulnerability to poor health Productive natural capital: better land, water resources Sustainable physical capital
Solid-waste management	Reduce vector-related disease Improve the appearance of urban areas Protect the local environment Protect infrastructure and properties	Reduced vulnerability to poor health Better living space Productive natural capital Sustainable physical capital

Barriers to Access and Inclusion

Despite all the arguments supporting IEHS, as a result of increased urban populations, emergencies, conflicts and wars, lack of finances and poor political will, there are major shortfalls in the provision of IEHS to the urban poor. There are a few examples of how it has been done well, but generally, past efforts to provide IEHS to the poor have ended up too expensive and residents have had to continue to rely on informal mechanisms. The following are some of the major barriers to access and inclusion at the operational level:

- Urban agencies lack the financial and managerial capacity to provide and manage basic urban services.
- IEHS provision requires substantial initial capital which increasingly is expected to be recovered from beneficiaries, along with the costs of operation and maintenance.
- IEHS are expected to meet certain standards which can help to make them prohibitively expensive.

These three points are elaborated below.

Urban agencies and municipal authorities are generally responsible for IEHS provision, but they generally lack the capacity to provide and manage infrastructure, despite attempts to decentralize government. In addition, they are still largely geared to acting as service providers. Non-conventional approaches designed to enable the urban poor to both acquire conventional IEHS and play more than just a user role have been tried in only a few places. In some cases, politicians do not support such approaches. In a few cases, parallel authorities have developed to fulfil the needs of poor areas and gradually move them to a legitimate status (see the examples in Box 11.2).

BOX 11.2 *EXAMPLES OF INNOVATIVE APPROACHES TO IEHS PROVISION*

Sindh Katchi Abadis Authority (SKAA)

In one of the four provinces of Pakistan, an autonomous body was formed to legalize and upgrade 1293 settlements, with a total population of 3.705 million in 1987. Upgrading and the provision of IEHS to squatter settlements was an important issue from the government's perspective. The creation of a new authority gave freedom to act relatively independently on matters relating to standards, cost recovery and making conventional procedures accessible to the poor (Sohail, 1997). The staff of SKAA worked closely with local NGOs and community groups.

National Housing and Development Authority (NHDA)

The NHDA in Sri Lanka has pioneered a number of innovative approaches to providing IEHS to the urban poor over the last 15 years. The authority promoted local Community Development Councils (CDCs) and provided them with a significant role in community contracts for IEHS. A number of conventional state procedures have been modified to make IEHS accessible to the urban poor.

The provision of IEHS in a conventional manner needs large amounts of capital and implies considerable operational costs. It also needs established state structures and processes, backed up by political stability. To be entitled to IEHS, residents often need to have legal entitlement to the land they occupy. The process of the legalization of informal areas can take many years and some settlements are unsuitable for legalization. As a result, large numbers of poor urban people remain without IEHS, living in illegal settlements and relying on the informal sector. For example, an estimated 20–30 per cent of the urban population in low-income countries are served by water vendors (Briscoe, 1985). Many pilot projects ignore the informal systems in place and develop new systems through the provision of funds for capital costs, but the means of recovering operational costs are not always considered. Ideally, projects should be designed on the basis of what poor people are ready to pay, rather than on a supply-driven approach in which the cost of the project is merely divided by the number of beneficiaries.

IEHS are expected to meet certain standards to minimize the risks to human health and the environment. In many cases the poor cannot afford such protection, but other stakeholders are not ready to use low-cost standards. For example, funders may be unwilling to compromise on what are considered desirable standards of provision. As a result, the poor remain outside the mainstream provision of IEHS. Increasingly, economic reforms include the removal of subsidies and the commercialization of services. While changes to pricing policies and increased cost recovery may be necessary for financial sustainability, they may make IEHS even more expensive for the poor. If reaching the urban poor does not take higher priority on the political agenda, the situation will become worse.

IEHS: An Income for the Poor?

Conventional approaches to IEHS provision do not prioritize income and employment for the poor as an objective. Driven by environmental and health agendas, projects and programmes are often judged on the basis of efficiency, value for money and timeliness. There is a perceived contradiction between these objectives and the informal provision systems developed by poor residents in the absence of official provision, many of which generate work opportunities. If improved IEHS are to be made accessible to the poor and existing livelihoods maintained wherever possible, this means recognizing, integrating and strengthening existing informal IEHS provision.

There are many ways in which the provision of IEHS can be linked with incomes and employment for the poor. Two of these relate to water supply and solid waste management.

The formal water supply systems of house connections and standposts provide water to an average of 85 per cent of the urban population in developing countries (WHO, 1992). Those who are supplied often find that the quantities do not meet their requirements. As a result, a large proportion of the urban population relies on buying water from private and often unregulated providers. Water vending exists because there is a demand for water that the formal system cannot fulfil. It is an important service for the poor, both as consumers and providers. There are, of course, problems with the system. The main issue tends to be the price of water as vendors reportedly charge between 4 and 100 times the official rates charged by the water authorities, depending on the adequacy of the piped supply and the amount of local competition. The other issue is the quality of water which may be poor, although this may also be the case where a formal water supply is in operation (Rakodi, 1998).

The second example of linkage between incomes and IEHS relates to solid-waste management. Municipal authorities in low-income countries employ large numbers of men and women to sweep the streets. Municipal sweepers may enter into informal agreements with households to carry domestic waste to the nearest official dumping point for an agreed monthly or weekly payment. Some households also enter into agreements with private sweepers – persons not in the employment of the municipality – for sweeping their yards and removing household waste. Tips, gifts and food items often supplement payments. The service and payments are generally agreed between sweepers (as service providers) and households (as users of the service). In addition, sweepers may also agree with fellow sweepers 'not to compete', although in some places competition is cut-throat. They may also be forced to make regular payments to municipal supervisors so that the latter do not interfere with this private work – a form of institutionalized corruption. These formal and informal systems within which sweepers operate provide an essential waste collection service to a wide range of income groups and to local commerce (for further details see Ali, 1997; Beall, 1997). According to one estimate, municipal sweepers in Karachi are able to collect informal payments equivalent to the operational budget of the Metropolitan Corporation.

A recent study of waste-pickers in Dhaka showed that provided waste remains available and accessible, waste-picking is an activity that can provide a steady and reliable income for as long as a picker is healthy. However, the livelihoods of waste-pickers can be threatened by improved city conservancy if, for example, they are excluded from dump sites rather than improvements in environmental control being used to reduce the health hazards of their occupation. In addition, the waste pickers consulted felt that they are marginalized from numerous aspects of society. They are not integrated into the formal financial system; they have little access to the legal, health and education systems; and many do not enjoy municipal services such as electricity, clean water and sanitation (Rouse and Ali, 2001).

Poor people are therefore often active in providing IEHS. Nevertheless, they are rarely recognized as legitimate stakeholders in infrastructure systems. They are frequently ignored when improvements are planned and marginalized from the decision-making processes and structures of the formal service provider agencies.

CONCLUSION: THE POOR AS USERS AND PROVIDERS OF IEHS

The provision of IEHS, which supports health, environmental and employment goals, can be a challenging task, particularly in situations when there are contradictions between these goals. A livelihoods approach serves to emphasize two factors: first, the importance of access to IEHS (physical capital) for the poor, for use in productive and reproductive activities and in building human capital in the form of good health; and second, the potential for IEHS provision to provide income-earning opportunities, whether as employees of public sector providers or as part of local informal service provision arrangements. This chapter argues for poor people to be mainstreamed in IEHS, both as users and providers. Moreover, the livelihoods framework recognizes the importance of contextual economic and political factors, and the significance of policies, formal organizational arrangements and official processes of decision-making, operation and maintenance in determining access by poor residents to services.

Future projects must consider the ways in which various groups of poor residents can best be provided with appropriate services and integrated into provision systems as providers. Community contracting and microenterprises are some of the tested options to include the poor in IEHS delivery (see Chapter 7). Residents from poor communities have entered successfully into contracts with funders to provide IEHS. They can be included in the planning, provision and operation of IEHS, with the aim of increasing incomes, promoting entrepreneurship and cooperating with formal institutions (Sohail, 1997). An example is a collaboration between Water Aid, a UK-based charity and a local NGO, Dushta Shasthya Kendra (DSK) in Dhaka, which extended water connections, with the approval of the local water authority, through providing loans to local community groups (Paul, 1999). This has resulted in improved health, a cleaner local environment and increased cost recovery.

The main value of a livelihoods framework is in suggesting potential linkages and interrelationships which may result in improved, more appropriate and sometimes innovative approaches to the provision of IEHS. However, space for examples is limited here and further detailed work will be necessary to identify users and informal providers of specific types of IEHS in order to establish appropriate policies and strategies for meeting their needs, collaborating with formal providers and exploring the potential for achieving income-generation objectives alongside health and environmental improvement goals.

REFERENCES

Ali, M (1997) *Integation of the Official and Private Informal Practices in Solid Waste Management*, unpublished PhD thesis, Department of Civil and Building Engineering, Loughborough University, Loughborough

Beall, J (1997) *Households, Livelihoods and the Urban Environment: Social Development Perspectives on Solid Waste Management in Faisalabad, Pakistan*, unpublished PhD thesis, London School of Economics and Political Science, London

Briscoe, M (1985) *Defining a Role for Water Supply and Sanitation Activities in the Health Sector in the Asia Region: An Issues Paper for the Asia Bureau, USAID*, University of North Carolina, Chapel Hill

Cairncross, S (1990), 'Water supply and the urban poor', in Hardoy, J E et al (eds) *The Poor Die Young: Housing and Health in Third World Cities*, Earthscan, London

Cairncross, S and Feachem, R (1993) *Environmental Health Engineering in the Tropics*, John Wiley & Sons, Chichester

DFID (2001) *Achieving Sustainability: Poverty Elimination and the Environment*, Strategy Paper, DFID, London

Paul, A (1999) *Water Supply Points in the Squatter Settlements of Dhaka – Constraints to Devolution of Management*, unpublished MSc project, Water and Engineering Development Centre, Loughborough University, Loughborough

Rakodi, C (1998) *The Opinions of Health and Water Service Users in India*, The Role of Government in Adjusting Economies Paper 32, International Development Department, School of Public Policy, University of Birmingham, Birmingham

Rouse, J and Ali, M (2001) *Waste Pickers in Dhaka and the Sustainable Livelihoods Approach*, Water and Engineering Development Centre, Loughborough University, Loughborough

Sohail, M (1997) *An Investigation into the Procurement of Urban Infrastructure in Developing Countries*, unpublished PhD thesis, Loughborough University, Loughborough

WHO (1992) *The International Drinking Water Supply and Sanitation Decade: End of Decade Review*, World Health Organization, Geneva

WHO (1996) *Water Supply and Sanitation Sector Monitoring Report*, World Health Organization, Geneva

Chapter 12

Spatial Planning, Access and Infrastructure

Alison Brown and Tony Lloyd-Jones

INTRODUCTION

Complexity is inherent in the spatial distribution of the livelihood activities of the urban poor, with variations between those who live in inner city slums and inhabitants of the urban fringe, between recent migrants to the city and long-term residents, and between people of different life-stages, ethnic groups or gender. The members of any household may adopt a range of livelihood strategies which involve different interactions with urban space at different times. There may also be significant variation between cities, depending on the local economy and municipal approaches to regulation and control (see Chapter 3).

Access is often a problem for poor households because facilities and services are too distant to reach or too expensive. It is not uncommon for poor people living in peripheral locations to spend several hours a day travelling on over-crowded buses or minibuses, and the money and time lost in travel represent an often unrecognized cost for the poor. Many resources available to poor men and women are communal and not individually owned, and access to these can be denied through regulation, cost or social exclusion.

This chapter considers the spatial and access implications of urban liveli-hoods analysis and the implications for urban spatial planning policy. 'Urban spatial planning' is interpreted in a broad sense to include land use and transport planning at different scales, from metropolitan to neighbourhood. Planning is considered in relation to development processes, and both the physical and regulatory dimensions of access are considered. The first part of the chapter looks at the spatial context of urban livelihoods and issues of space and territory. The second part considers how city-wide issues, such as city structure and develop-ment processes, impinge on the livelihood assets and strategies of the urban poor. The next part discusses urban transport both as a means of access and a source of employment. The fourth section considers the role of mixed land use at the neighbourhood level. The final section considers the policy implications of the analysis.

THE SPATIAL CONTEXT OF URBAN LIVELIHOODS

A large proportion of the urban poor derive all or part of their income from small or informal enterprises which may be classified into four main groups: retailing and wholesale; craft, manufacturing and production; services; and transport and construction (excluding marginal or illegal activities such as begging and street crime). Their interaction with urban space is not well documented. Many small businesses draw most of their custom from other poor households, but those which successfully attract a middle- or higher-income clientele make a significant cash contribution to the low-income economy (Islam and Khan, 1988). Location thus tends to be of major importance to small-scale operators.

Some attributes of urban livelihoods which can be gleaned from the literature on urban poverty are discussed briefly below and their implications for space and location are identified.

- *Informal sector* Informal enterprises make a significant contribution to the economy of some low-income cities, accounting for up to 70 per cent of employment (Sethuraman, 1981). In Latin America, 85 per cent of all new jobs in 1998 were in the informal sector (*Latin American Weekly Report*, 24 August 1999). The size of the informal sector has an effect on urban form.
- *Complexity* The urban poor often adopt short-term survival strategies which may be opportunistic rather than planned. They may include mutual help, casual labour, the labour of additional family members, seasonal work, or mortgaging and selling assets. Such strategies are complex, rapidly changing and responsive to shocks and change (Chambers, 1995). Their characteristics, including their spatial distribution, are thus difficult to track and analyse.
- *Size* Informal enterprises tend to be very small. For example, a survey in Colombo found an average of 1.9 people per establishment (Karunanayake and Wanasinghe, 1988). This has implications for their space requirements and means that much informal enterprise can be home-based. However, insecurity of dwelling tenure or insensitive planning regulations can stifle such enterprise (see Chapter 9).
- *Location* This is particularly critical for informal sector activities, partly because informal traders cannot afford high transport costs and partly because they need good access to markets (see Box 12.1). In some locations – for example, in the city centre – high land values and rentals make access to appropriate, well-located accommodation impossible and microenterprises often occupy the interstices between formal and legal activities – pavements, vacant sites or land unsuitable for building.
- *Accessibility* The link between the accessibility of an area and its trading potential is as strong for low-income enterprises as it is for large commercial organizations. The most accessible areas of the city – transport termini and the commercial core – are often those which are most strictly controlled.
- *Mobility* The mobility of the poor is constrained by lack of access to cheap and affordable transport. This may limit the extent to which they can access urban resources. A study in Bangkok found that most of the self-employed poor operate their businesses within 5km of their place of residence (Hongla-

darom and Isarankura, 1988). A recent study of a squatter settlement in Delhi
(see Box 12.1) confirms that residents are often too poor to use public transport.
* *Linkages* The complex trading and economic environment of large cities
  provides the best conditions for informal enterprises to flourish and to find a
  market niche (Clarke, 1995). The network of spatial, financial and social links
  on which the poor depend may be city-wide and may also extend to rural areas.

BOX 12.1 CONTRASTS IN TWO DISTRICTS OF DELHI

Recent studies of two poor urban communities in Delhi (Motia Khan and Peera
Garhi) found that most residents work at home or within 20 minutes' travelling
time of where they live and rely on informal livelihood activities (although a
minority of people in both locations commute for much longer periods).

In Motia Khan, a community of mixed religious backgrounds which is close to
the old city and 2km from the centre of New Delhi (Connaught Place), a large
proportion of people work in the informal sector. Many buy the raw materials
they use to make bamboo baskets, catapults and a variety of other household
products from nearby markets in Old Delhi. As most people in Motia Khan are
very poor and space is a limiting factor (with a density of 804 families per ha) the
finished products that are sold back to wholesale markets in the surrounding
area tend to be basic, small scale and portable. Other notable livelihood activities
include domestic service, singing, monkey training and petty trade.

The relationship between working location and home is significant. The settlement's proximity to working opportunities in surrounding markets such as those
in Old Delhi, the tourist trade in Central New Delhi or adjacent middle-class
residential neighbourhoods is an important reason why 70 per cent of those
interviewed in Motia Khan walk to work. It may also help to explain why people
continue to live in Motia Khan, despite the fact that it is poorly serviced, overcrowded and suffers from crime.

In Peera Garhi, which lies some 13–14 km from Connaught Place, residents
have access to higher-paid employment opportunities and tend to work in service
industries as, for example, self-employed painters – for example, manual workers,
drivers and security guards. Women in Peera Garhi, which is a Sikh community,
tend not to work in domestic service because it is regarded as being culturally
unacceptable.

Although residents from both neighbourhoods rely on established business
networks (social capital) the territory that the residents of Peera Garhi draw on
for their livelihoods is larger. In Motia Khan the physical range of opportunity is
limited by the fact that the majority of people walk to their workplaces. In Peera
Garhi people use a wider range of travel methods to commute to work (public
transport, 34 per cent; bicycle, 17 per cent; walking, 34 per cent) .

The very poor in Motia Khan are able to access a large range of livelihood
opportunities within walking distance and to subsist on incomes that would not
pay for other forms of transport. In Peera Garhi, the density of livelihood opportunities in the surrounding area is lower, which means that the majority of people
need to earn more to pay for transport. This suggests that relative accessibility
and transport costs are an important factor in comparing the conditions of the
poor living in different parts of the city and in the development of spatial planning
policies to support their livelihoods.

Source: Max Lock Centre, 2000

- *Spatial exclusion* Conventional approaches to urban spatial planning and land-use regulation have contributed to the isolation of the poor by creating a dual structure of land tenure and economy, and excluding the livelihood activities of the poor from large parts of the city. For example, much informal activity is street-based and affected by controls on the use of public space. Isolation is a dimension of deprivation, both geographical isolation and exclusion from services, markets and economic support (Chambers, 1995). Men and women's access to space is often unequal, depending on social and cultural norms and the acceptability of different types of work.

Assets and Urban Space

Economic activities in urban areas benefit from the spatial proximity of large markets, economies of scale and the aggregation economies that ensure plentiful supplies of labour, services and finance. In contrast to rural areas, where access to natural capital is key, it is access to the concentration of people and their assets and services that is important for the urban poor. Spatial planners need to recognize the asset base of poor people in cities and how this can be strengthened.

The urban poor have only their labour to sell. Thus, human capital, in terms of their health, capacity and skills, is paramount. Accessing livelihood opportunities in urban areas means being well located in terms of physical proximity to opportunities or access to appropriate public transport. Physical capital, in the form of a place to live (frequently also a place for home-based economic activity), as well as access to appropriate workspace, tools and transport, is also a fundamental livelihood asset. This asset framework sets the basic criteria for urban planners to address the needs of poor communities.

Knowledge of livelihood opportunities is another key factor and, more often than not, this depends on social linkages and is gained by word of mouth. Who you know and trust in cities is critical. This aspect of social capital for the urban poor is crucial in safeguarding against vulnerability (see Chapter 8). Spatial planning policy can be profoundly destructive of social capital as, for example, in slum clearance that results in the wholesale relocation of communities. The consequences are difficult to monitor, but the loss of social capital that may have been years in the making is often incalculable.

Many of the most important vulnerability factors that affect the urban poor are economic in character, but some are also spatial. Poor communities often live in the most precarious conditions – for example, in inaccessible locations, on sites which are vulnerable to floods or landslides, or in makeshift housing which is liable to fire damage or collapse. Better urban planning and infrastructure provision can have an impact on reducing vulnerability by facilitating the supply of secure, serviced land for housing or the relocation of those most at risk to new locations which are sensitive to their livelihood needs.

Space and Territory

Urban space is a key element of physical capital in livelihood strategies for the urban poor. Its use is controlled by a series of physical boundaries, regulations and social conventions, which distinguish between the private and public realm

(Madanipour, 1999). Private space is the internal territory, identified by custom, barriers or signs, where strangers are deterred. Public space is the external territory which is accessible to most people. Between the two extremes there are spaces with less clear functions which can be considered as either semi-public or semi-private such as the *sur* (walled quarters) or *al-fina* (transition spaces) of Arab towns (Nooraddin, 1998).

Public space has social and economic importance as a place for trade and communal activities, or as a channel for movement. It is also politically important, as the control exercised over public space demonstrates state or municipal authority, reflected in restrictions on its use. For the urban poor, public space is a crucial resource as their private space is more restricted and fragmented than that of higher-income groups (Lloyd-Jones, 1993). Dewar (1994) argues that public space is an essential form of social infrastructure for the urban poor but is ignored if there is a narrow policy focus on housing and shelter.

Public space is, however, subject to extensive regulation and control – by municipal authorities, the police or adjoining owners. It may be possible to have physical access to space but not to the activities which take place there, as illustrated by restrictions on informal sector trading. Municipal policy can vary between repression, tolerance or promotion, but control tends to be more rigorous in central business districts or elite residential areas than in informal settlements (Gilbert, 1988).

Several recent development trends serve to exclude the urban poor from public space. The increasing domination of urban streets by traffic has marginalized activities such as pedestrian movement and street trading to residual areas of land. Traffic management and highway improvements may have similar effects. Increasing incidence of crime and violence in some cities is a further deterrent to the use of public space. For example, crime is commonly blamed for the flight of businesses from the centre of Johannesburg, although economic factors may have also played a part (Tomlinson, 1999). Privatization of urban space – for example, in central area shopping malls or in the gated communities of wealthy suburbs, also excludes the poor (Firman, 1998; Woods, 1998).

For many small and informal enterprises, access to public space is critical and they may pay considerable amounts for the privilege. A study in Dhaka found that two-thirds of a hundred producers and entrepreneurs operated from public land or land with unclear ownership (Islam and Khan, 1988). Although they may never pay taxes or licence fees, payments are made to local syndicates who control key trading locations, to the police or to other officials. In Zimbabwe, petty traders sublet space from licensed stallholders at a mark-up of approximately 100 times the municipal licence fee (Brown, 2000).

There is a significant gender divide in the extent to which people have access to public space. Bose (1998), in her study of slum dwellers in Calcutta, describes how the range of settings used by women varies with their stage in the family life cycle, household structure, household size and economic necessity. Young unmarried women and women in their child-bearing years are subject to the greatest spatial confinement. With regards to livelihoods, nearly half the working women reported that they would like to engage in home-based work and over 20 per cent said that this was the only activity which they were allowed to undertake. Selling in the public arena was seen as a last resort. Culture also has an impact, and Chowdhury (1992) vividly illustrates the divisions in the use of space in Islamic settlements in Bangladesh.

CITY-WIDE SPATIAL ISSUES

Urban spatial patterns and the processes of development impinge to a significant extent on the livelihood assets of the poor. The spatial development of a city is the result of historical, cultural, economic and regulatory forces which have shaped the urban form, and this section discusses some of the influences which affect fast-growing, low-income cities of the South.

The spatial segregation of rich and poor neighbourhoods, together with the spatial separation of the poor from areas with income-producing potential, occurs in many developing world cities. The desire of the rich to protect their investment in property has been reinforced by the operation of planning policies and land-use zoning controls. Government approaches to the provision of low-income housing often reinforce the separation by providing large low-income housing projects aimed at a single target group. Even the upgrading of existing informal and unplanned settlements, while addressing the immediate needs of poor communities for shelter and secure tenure, can consolidate social segregation. The polarization in character and appearance between formal and informal trading environments is highlighted by Sinha and Kant (1997) in their study of Lucknow. They compare the thronging market street, Chowk, with the spacious but sterile Hazratganj, the colonial commercial centre, which offers relatively few employment prospects for poor people. The colonization of urban space by large international companies is a by-product of globalization, but its effect in further reinforcing the divided city is highlighted by Benjamin (2000) in his study of Bangalore (see Box 12.2).

Fast-growing cities often contain large areas of unregulated development as shortages in the supply of serviced land, escalating land prices and unregulated land markets force poor households to seek affordable land on the edge of the city (Khan and Lanarch, 1995). Typically, 70 per cent or more of all new urban development is concentrated on the peri-urban fringe, spreading into agricultural land and creating low-density settlements that are prohibitively expensive to service. In such cities, the poorest people have to travel furthest to reach employment opportunities in the city core. The trend is intensified by high land values in the centre and the planned relocation of slum neighbourhoods which exclude the poor from central areas. In cities with relatively strong development authorities, such as Delhi, poor residents from inner city communities (together with newcomers to the city) are typically relocated in huge public housing estates or sites and services projects on the urban fringe (Max Lock Centre, 2000). Such new developments are often relatively devoid of livelihood opportunities and displaced residents may move back into the city to survive.

Furthermore, fast-growing cities often create pressures for growth well beyond their urban boundaries (UNCHS, 1996; Aguilar, 1999), which can impact negatively on poor households. Regional planners in global mega-cities such as Delhi and Cairo have promoted new growth 'centres' far enough away

---

Box 12.2 Land-use Planning in Bangalore

Benjamin (2000) has shown the adverse effects of the economic and spatial strategy adopted in Bangalore. Bangalore is one of India's fastest growing cities, with a current population of around 6 million. Dubbed India's 'Silicon Valley', the plan to make Bangalore globally competitive through IT-led growth became a political slogan. The Bangalore Development Authority drew up a comprehensive spatial development plan and national funds were channelled via a new financial corporation to relocate the traditional iron and steel markets and fund the construction of a modern infrastructure, including ring roads, flyovers and satellite towns. Yet Bangalore is a divided city – some 25–40 per cent of the urban population lives in slums and almost a third has no access to piped water. For the poor, master planning had the effect of reducing employment opportunities by restricting mixed land use and making it more difficult for poor families to establish their claims to land, with the result that many have had their plots taken over. Furthermore, the construction of infrastructure and new markets has reduced trading opportunities. Land-use restrictions promote enclaves from which the poor are excluded, and attempts to decongest the city have resulted in the relocation of many informal sector businesses and reduced takings for others. The master planning process has thus had the effect of increasing poverty.

Source: Benjamin, 2000

---

from the central city to become partially autonomous. The result can be a system of interconnecting urban centres, creating urban sprawl on a massive scale – for example, the Pearl River Delta region on the eastern seaboard of China and the urban regions of South Korea and Taiwan. As regional economic systems, such urban agglomerations are thriving, but their dispersion has environmental consequences (Lloyd-Jones, 2000) and means that, for low-income households, affordable housing locations may be very far from the economic hub.

Development Processes and Spatial Planning

The development process is a significant contextual factor within the broader setting of urban governance and management which impacts on the livelihood assets of the urban poor. It is influenced by different actors and institutions working within markets organized on the basis of supply and demand (Madanipour, 1996). The property development system is usually regulated by municipal authorities, based on a legal code that establishes land ownership and use rights, and defines criteria for state intervention. It is also influenced by the availability of development finance and by the investment decisions of government agencies, private sector institutions and individuals.

   Urban spatial planning contributes to the development process through the regulation of land use and development. The aim of urban planning should be to provide a context in which people can access services and shelter, which promotes economic development and environmental protection, and which improves the quality of life, particularly for poor people. Yet traditional approaches to land-use control and regulation, including master planning, single-use zoning and decentralization, have often exacerbated urban sprawl and disadvantaged the urban poor (see Box 12.2). The disbenefits include unrealistic development standards which force people to invest outside the formal land economy, the clearance of unauthorized development and increased segregation of poor communities.

The failure of traditional 'end-state' plans to create a useful framework for fast-growing cities has led to experiments with a planning framework which is more flexible, action-oriented and participatory, and seeks to achieve greater integration between agencies which are involved in urban development, both public and private (Clarke, 1992; Davidson, 1996). In such an approach, strategic planning becomes broad brush, and local or action-oriented plans provide a focus for tackling specific problems within an established spatial framework. Despite this new emphasis, administrators and planners often fail to recognize the economic contribution and locational needs of the urban poor who pursue activities at variance with the planners' concept of a modern city (Yeung, 1988). Zoning, plot development regulations, traffic control and public health regulations combine to restrict the activities of small and informal enterprises, which are often seen as causes of street congestion, environmental problems or street crime, and may be subject to regular harassment by the police and municipal officials (Brown, 2000).

The poor are marginalized from the physical environment, have no access to development agencies or resources, are hindered in their livelihood strategies by development regulation and control, and are forced to rely on the social environment to survive. The aim of livelihood strategies should be to broaden their access to other assets through the development process. One way in which this can be done is by improving their access to and security within the public domain by decreasing the risks which small and informal enterprises face. A second is a more flexible approach to regulation and control.

TRANSPORT, LIVELIHOODS AND SPACE

Urban transport is a means of access, a method for transporting materials and goods, and a source of employment and investment for the urban economy. Transport is inherent in the way a city functions and can have a profound effect on its spatial development and investment patterns. Several concepts are relevant to a livelihoods analysis and will be explored briefly here.

The accessibility of a location is the ease with which it can be accessed by a variety of means of transport. There is a strong link between accessibility and the economy (see Figure 12.1) as areas with good accessibility, which attract large numbers of people, are also those which are most attractive for commerce. This link has been widely explored in studies of major investment in, for example, light rapid transport, expressways and major new office locations. The link is equally important for the informal economy, but is much less widely recognized, and for informal traders, the best sites are those which are highly accessible – for example, bus stations.

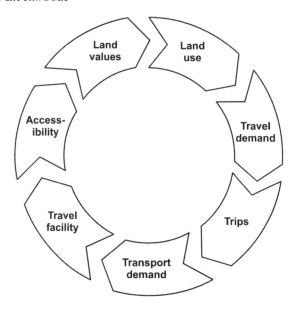

Figure 12.1 *The link between transport and land use*

People's mobility is affected by various factors, including income, health, life-stage, gender, availability of means of transport and its affordability, and there are usually very significant differences between the rich and poor. Those who own and have use of private transport (cars, motorcycles and, to a lesser extent, bicycles) have the greatest mobility. In major cities, car ownership per head of the population is closely related to GDP, but the availability of transport used by the lower-income population varies considerably. For example the availability of buses varies from 0.33 per 1000 people in Calcutta to 5.3 in Manila (Dimitriou, 1990).

The efficiency of use of transport infrastructure is greatly influenced by its management, capacity and the geographical character of the city. In many cities of the South, traffic congestion, pollution and traffic accidents are major hazards (although car ownership may be quite low), which leads to major problems in the use of the limited infrastructure. The predominance of a single, high-density central area encourages congestion by attracting large numbers of trips to the central core and promoting long journeys from outlying areas, creating a demand for low-cost public transport from those least able to afford it (Hilling, 1996).

Despite many variations, several key characteristics can be identified in the transport systems of cities of the South:

Road networks tend to be poorly developed and managed, with a limited extent of tarred roads and chronic central area congestion. Even where the tarred roads are provided throughout the city, maintenance may be poor, with limited facilities for pedestrians. Management of the existing system, where it exists, is usually intended to maximize the vehicular capacity of roads without considering pedestrians or other users.

Public transport systems usually depend on a combination of conventional large buses and paratransit (informal transport). Paratransit systems range from collective taxis or minibuses which run on set routes with variable stops, such as the *jitneys* of the Philippines or *dolmus* of Turkey, to the motorcycle transport and cycle rickshaws of south Asian cities. There are considerable variations in the level of informality of paratransit operations in terms of their regulation and licensing, and in the availability of public transport suited to the needs of women (see Figure 12.2). Paratransit is often a major contributor to urban road traffic congestion because it is poorly organized (Poernomosidhi, 1992).

Walking is a key means of transport in low-income cities, but its importance is rarely recognized. For example, around 40 per cent of all journeys were made on foot in Harare in the early 1990s (Mbara and Maunder, 1994). Long journeys to work (of over an hour) reduce people's productive capacity and their effective working day, and those reliant on walking waste productive time on travel. Walking may make people, especially women, more vulnerable to crime and violence. In cities where more than half of all journeys are made on foot, the lack of recognition of the needs of pedestrians is scandalous.

Transport is normally considered in terms of its physical aspects, including routes (streets, paths, public transport routes and tracks), infrastructure (vehicles, stops, termini and depots) and organization. This takes in transport operations, including the operators, policing and management systems, licensing, routing and

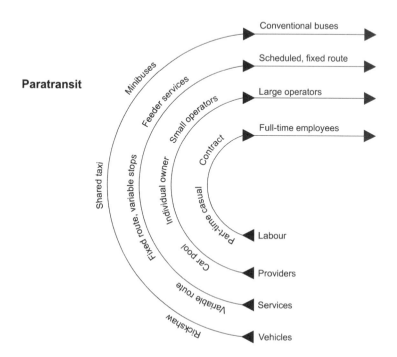

Figure 12.2 *Operating contrasts between paratransit and conventional transit*

Source: Based on Britton, 1980

pricing. Less commonly considered are the effects of transport strategies on livelihoods for the urban poor, which include:

Exclusion The transport poor are those who have limited access to transport to support their livelihoods, either because there is no appropriate facility or because it is not affordable. Transport poverty is linked to life-stage and gender, as the old, the young and women with children have more limited mobility.

Employment opportunities The informal transport sector is a major source of employment, with relatively low entry costs for unskilled jobs such as fare collectors. Taxi or rickshaw drivers may hire a vehicle on a day-rate basis, while owners of bicycles or handcarts may rent these out.

Movement of goods Limited access to transport is a major constraint on small and informal enterprises. Loads are limited to those which can be carried on foot or crowded public transport, or wheeled on a handcart.

Transport regulation The effectiveness of informal transport is often limited by inappropriate regulation and control (see Box 12.3). Informal transport is seen as a cause of urban congestion, instead of a vital support for the low-income economy.

Trading opportunities Public transport stops and roadsides provide some of the best opportunities for informal trading because of their accessibility and the numbers of people who pass them. Yet informal trading is often restricted, with a view to reducing traffic and pedestrian congestion.

Box 12.3 *Public Transport in Faisalabad*

In Pakistan bus services are subject to extensive regulation, but generally provide inefficient, unreliable and poor quality services. Faisalabad is one of the fastest growing cities in Pakistan, with an estimated population of 1.63 million in 1994. Public buses were introduced in 1983 but were gradually replaced by minibus services. A visit by the prime minister provided a spur to improve public transport, and in 1994 the divisional commissioner created an NGO, the Faisalabad Urban Transport Society (FUTS), to manage public transport in collaboration with local operators. FUTS membership is dominated by private transport operators and is administered by a governing body drawn from government officials, the police and members (of whom 25 per cent are elected on to the board).

The object of FUTS is to improve urban transport, traffic management, road safety and the environment. Operators enter into a contract with FUTS to provide a service, and the society makes a monthly charge which is used for supervision and administration. This allows FUTS to operate outside the official, but inefficient and corrupt regulatory system. Fares are set at levels which allow operators to make a profit. A rapid improvement in public transport services and an increased number of minibuses on the roads resulted, although there are still capacity problems at peak times.

Source: Anjum, 1997

MIXED-USE NEIGHBOURHOODS

At the neighbourhood level, land uses and the organization of space can have a significant effect on livelihood opportunities for the poor. Areas with mixed use and mixed tenure provide a rich environment in which a variety of livelihood activities can flourish, particularly areas nearest to the city centre. These are precisely the activities that may be condemned by authorities for exacerbating traffic congestion or street crime and hindering the modern development of a city. Mixed-income development, which maintains high population densities while avoiding overcrowding, can support economic growth and development within existing urban areas, reinforcing the existing livelihood systems of the poor. It may provide a particularly conducive environment for women's income-earning activities. In contrast, single-use areas, such as low-income housing or employment areas, provide more limited opportunities for income generation. However, where the planning regime is sufficiently flexible, single-use neighbourhoods can change over time to accommodate the informal economy. Buraglia (1998) describes this effect in Bogota (see Box 12.4).

Mixed-use areas also support spatial linkages, thus supplementing the physical capital of poor households. There may be links between home-based operations and those which take place outside the home, such as the preparation and selling of cooked food. Family members and children may help the main worker, or there may be a degree of casual and part-time working. There may also be links to the formal sector – for example, for outworking or the purchase of materials. Other enterprises, such as plastic recycling or waste sorting, make use of waste products (see Chapter 11).

Within mixed use areas there are also key locations with particular potential. Some, such as street intersections, have significant opportunities for trading and commerce. Others have opportunity because of their proximity to a market – for example, a government office or a hospital.

BOX 12.4 *URBAN EVOLUTION UNDER A FLEXIBLE PLANNING REGIMEN*

Bogota had become spatially polarized, with poorer groups living on the outskirts. New housing schemes were mostly single-use complexes, with single-storey dwellings or low-rise apartments. Jobs were concentrated in the central area and the outlying settlements were effectively dormitory suburbs. A weak system of planning control permitted individual adaptations, with houses transformed into shops, offices, schools or industrial units. It allowed some houses to be amalgamated into collective family dwellings and others to be subdivided into smaller apartments. Even apartment blocks have been converted to commercial use on the ground floor. This has dramatically changed the character of new areas by creating an environment which is reminiscent of the traditional *barrio* – a mixed-use neighbourhood with a strong cultural identity.

Source: Buraglia, 1998

As Chapter 4 stresses, it is also important to consider a specific and widespread livelihood activity, that of urban agriculture. Smit and Nasr (1992) argue that urban agriculture occurs on a wide scale, quoting the examples of Kenya and Tanzania where two out of three urban families are engaged in farming, and Taiwan where over half of all urban families are members of farming associations. Designing new areas with large garden plots may be unrealistic because of the land take required, but there are other ways in which urban agriculture can be accommodated. Areas which are too steep or wet for intensive building may be cultivated using appropriate methods, and there is significant potential for temporary use of idle or under-used land, but a major shift in attitudes or regulations may be required to release this. Community land – for example, in schools – has been successfully cultivated in some cities, while the potential use of rooftops and balconies are numerous. The authors cite examples of medicinal herbs in Santiago, silkworms in Delhi, rabbits in Mexico and orchids in Bangkok.

POLICY IMPLICATIONS

The final section looks at the policy implications of this analysis of spatial planning and access within a livelihoods framework. The arguments tend to favour urban areas which maximize interaction between communities and reduce isolation so that people can benefit fully from the opportunities that cities provide. These arguments mirror the debate on sustainable development which promotes mixed-use areas and a compact urban form (Haughton and Hunter, 1994). They also point to the need for a radical reappraisal of conventional planning approaches which result in spatial segregation, and regulations that inhibit the economic activities of poor households. The policy implications are grouped under four broad headings – city-wide initiatives; transport and access initiatives; local action; and approaches to regulation – but many are cross-cutting and cannot be confined to the specific context identified.

City-wide Initiatives

The focus of economic and commercial activities in the city centre, typical of many fast-growing cities, tends to restrict the access of poor households to employment opportunities in both the formal and informal sectors because of the time and cost that are needed to reach the city centre from outlying low-income areas. The growth of a polycentric city and decentralization of commercial activities can provide a more even distribution of opportunities, but this needs to be supported carefully by appropriate transport and infrastructure links. Such an approach must be balanced against the adverse effects of urban sprawl which can result in the isolation of poor families in peri-urban areas and the loss of agricultural land.

    Planning policies and development processes which lead to the spatial segregation of high- and low-income households, or to the relegation of poor communities to the urban fringe, mitigate against the ability of the poor to pursue effective livelihood strategies. These can include policies such as slum relocation, master planning and single-use land-use zoning. Areas which allow mixed land uses, a variety of plot sizes and mixed tenure have a much greater potential to support a variety of livelihoods than single-use, homogenous areas. Mixed-income areas permit a trickle-down effect of cross-subsidy from richer to poorer households. They allow small and informal traders good access to a wealthier clientele, and often provide a variety of short-term and inexpensive tenures for employment activities. However, policies that allow poor households to live close to areas with a choice of employment opportunities must be supported by appropriate regulation to enable them to access opportunities – for example, by allowing street trading in key locations.

Globalization and foreign direct investment by major companies is usually seen as a positive force in improving the wealth of an urban economy. However, such investment can have an immediate and adverse effect for the urban poor by excluding them from areas such as new office locations and segregating them from potential wealthy markets. The extent to which the informal sector itself contributes to the urban economy may not be fully recognized. This sector has spatial requirements and depends on linkages which need to be better understood. These include production and consumption linkages for activities which take place at both fixed and variable locations. Policies intended to support livelihoods for the poor should recognize the interconnected nature of enterprises and avoid disrupting established linkages.

Transport and Accessibility

Access to affordable and appropriate transport is of critical importance in widening the employment opportunities of the urban poor who need cheap access to centres of economic and commercial activity. In low-income cities, paratransit has a key role in meeting this need and serves both as a means of transport for poor households and as a source of employment in its own right. The management of paratransit should reflect this dual function and improve ease of entry for potential operators and other workers. Innovative forms of regulation which involve operators can improve access to transport services for poor people, and also increase the efficiency and profitability of the services. The transport system should accommodate the needs of small entrepreneurs to transport goods and materials, and should pay particular attention to the needs of women.

For the very poor, walking is the only possible means of travel. The needs of pedestrians should be understood so that road improvements, traffic management or other development do not make pedestrian journeys more difficult or prohibit pedestrians from using large parts of the street network. Low-density development limits the employment potential of those who cannot afford transport. Within a city centre, pedestrian links to and from bus termini are particularly important. Bus termini and other transport nodes have considerable potential as trading locations, and locations for informal sector trading on the main pedestrian routes should be allowed. These should be managed so that the very poor are not excluded from these trading locations by inappropriate levies or local syndicates.

Local Initiatives

The function of the home as a place for both shelter and income-generating activities is not fully recognized. Building types that accommodate both residential and livelihood functions, such as the 'shop-house' that is typical of parts of Southeast Asia, are to be preferred over single-use types, and regulations which restrict homeworking and other income-generating activities should be reviewed. Homeworking is particularly important for women because of its potential to combine earning with child care. A lenient planning regimen which allows easy conversion to new uses, amalgamation or subdivision of units, and increasing density, can enable new employment opportunities to emerge.

Access to public space for trading is vital for small and informal sector enterprises because their private space is so circumscribed. This includes space within the city centre, and other underused land. Access may include space for trading, the temporary use of open land or shared activities at certain times of the day (such as a car park used as a night market). The provision of well-maintained amenities and infrastructure near markets and other trading locations is important, including water taps, toilets, shade and lock-up facilities. Women traders are particularly vulnerable and may need special support – for example, through cooperative enterprises. Children living or working on the street are also vulnerable, needing both social support programmes and protection from crime and harassment.

Regulation for an Enabling Approach

The livelihoods framework points to the need for policy approaches which enable poor households to supplement their social and human capital with better access to physical capital, so that they can be more resilient to shocks and change. This entails a review of all regulations and other restrictions which affect informal entrepreneurs in order to increase their income security, and to reduce both their anxiety and humiliation, and the petty rents they pay to officials (Chambers, 1995). This may involve a review of regulations on zoning, plot development, traffic control and public health, and of bylaws controlling markets, food sale, vendors, services and licensing.

The security of livelihoods is an essential component of family security. Security of tenure at the place of trading for informal enterprises is important in order to promote the local economy and limit illicit payments to informal regulators. For example, the potential for flexible licensing or cooperative management of space could be explored, and municipal authorities should work with the police to reduce the harassment of informal traders. Small entrepreneurs are particularly vulnerable to petty crime, but innovative methods of community protection may help to reduce this as part of wider initiatives to reduce crime in housing areas and on the streets.

An enabling approach to the support of urban livelihoods will necessitate new means of conflict resolution. At neighbourhood level, conflicts may occur when enterprises adversely impinge on residents – for example, through noise or air pollution, or for social reasons. A neighbourhood council or committee could manage the process, so long as this is not controlled by a profiteering syndicate. At the city level, the problems of congestion and competing demands on the common resource of urban space are more difficult to resolve, as the views of major property interests usually prevail. This indicates that a fundamental reappraisal is needed of some of the tenets which underlie current spatial planning philosophy and the mechanisms through which it is achieved.

REFERENCES

Aguilar, A (1999) 'Mexico City growth and regional dispersal: the expansion of largest cities and new spatial forms', *Habitat International,* vol 23, no 3, pp335–343

Anjum, G (1997) 'Government wearing an NGO hat: improving public transport regulation in Pakistan', *Proceedings of the International Schools Conference,* Edinburgh College of Art, Edinburgh

Benjamin, S (2000) 'Governance, economic settings and poverty in Bangalore', *Environment and Urbanization,* vol 12, no 1, pp35–56

Bose, M (1998) 'Surveillance, circumscriber of women's spatial experience: the case of slum dwellers in Calcutta', in Dandekar, H (ed) *City Space and Globalization: An International Perspective,* College of Architecture and Urban Planning, University of Michigan, Ann Arbor

Britton, F E K (1980) 'Transport issues, priorities and options in the 1980s', in *Paratransit: Changing Perceptions of Public Transport,* Canberra

Brown, A (2000) 'Urban space in the context of sustainability: a case study of Harare', *Proceedings: Interschools Conference,* Oxford Brookes University, Oxford

Buraglia, P (1998) 'The Bogotanian Bario: return to the traditional?' *Urban Design International* vol 3, no 3, pp101–113

Chambers, R (1995) 'Poverty and livelihoods: whose reality counts?' *Environment and Urbanization,* vol 7, no 1, pp173–204

Chowdhury, T (1992) 'Segregation of women in Islamic cultures and its reflection in housing: A study of spaces for women in a Bangladesh village' in Dandekar, H (ed) *Shelter, Women and Development: First and Third World Perspectives,* George Wahr Publishing, Ann Arbor

Clarke, G (1992) 'Towards appropriate forms of urban spatial planning', *Habitat International,* vol 16, pp149–165

Clarke, G (1995) 'Megacity management: trends and issues' in Stubbs, J and Clarke, G (eds), *Megacity Management in the Asian and Pacific Region,* Asian Development Bank and United Nations/World Bank Urban Management Programme for Asia and the Pacific Countries, Manila

Davidson, F (1996) 'Planning for performance: requirements for sustainable development', *Habitat International,* vol 20, no 3, pp445–463

Dewar, D (1994) 'Urban housing in Southern Africa: the need for a paradigm shift' in *2nd Symposium – Housing for the Urban Poor – Housing, Poverty and Developing Countries,* Birmingham, UK, April

Dimitriou, H (1990) 'Transport problems of Third World Cities' in Dimitriou, H and Banjo, G (eds) *Transport Planning for Third World Cities,* Routledge, London and New York

Firman, T (1998) 'Towards an Indonesian urban land development policy' in Dandekar, H (ed) *City Space and Globalization: An International Perspective,* Proceedings of an International Symposium, College of Architecture and Urban Planning, University of Michigan, Ann Arbor

Gilbert, A. (1988) 'Home enterprises in poor urban settlements', *Regional Development Dialogue,* vol 9, no 4, pp21–37

Haughton, G and Hunter, C (1994) *Sustainable Cities,* Jessica Kingsley Publishers, London

Hilling, D (1996) *Transport and Developing Countries,* Routledge, New York, London

Hongladarom, C and Isarankura W (1988) 'Increasing the absorptive capacity of the urban economy: the case of Bangkok', *Regional Development Dialogue,* vol 9, no 4, pp134–159

Islam, N and Khan, A (1988) 'Increasing the absorptive capacity of metropolitan economies of Asia: a case study of Dhaka', *Regional Development Dialogue,* vol 9, no 4, pp107–131

Karunanayake, M and Wanasinghe, Y (1988) 'Generating urban livelihoods: a study of the poor in Colombo', *Regional Development Dialogue,* vol 9, no 4, pp80–104

Khan, A and Lanarch, A (1995) 'Land management: key concerns and future options' in Stubbs, J and Clarke, G (eds), *Megacity Management in the Asian and Pacific Region,* Asian Development Bank and United Nations/World Bank Urban Management Programme for Asia and the Pacific Countries, Manila

Lloyd-Jones, T (1993) *Social Space and Urban Design in Informal Settlements: Perspectives on the Informal City in Latin America,* unpublished MA dissertation, University of Westminster, London

Lloyd-Jones, T (2000) 'Compact city policies for megacities', in Jenks, M and Burgess, R (eds) *The Compact City in Developing Countries,* E & F N Spon, London, pp37–53

Madanipour, A (1996) *Design of Urban Space: An Inquiry into a Socio-spatial Process,* John Wiley & Sons, Chichester

Madanipour, A (1999) 'Why are the design and development of public spaces significant for cities?', *Environment and Planning B: Planning and Design,* vol 26, pp879–891

Max Lock Centre (2000) *Guide to Good Practice in Core Area Development – Livelihood Survey,* University of Westminster, London

Mbara, T and Maunder, D (1994) 'The effect of regular fare increases on stage bus patronage in Harare, Zimbabwe', *Indian Journal of Transport Management,* March 1995 (Overseas Centre, Transport Research Laboratory reprints, Crowthorne, Berks)

Mukhtar, N (1997) *Housing Policy in Libya,* unpublished PhD thesis, Cardiff University

Nooraddin, H (1998) '*Al-Fina,* in between spaces as an urban design concept: making public and private places along streets in Islamic cities of the Middle East', *Urban Design International,* vol 3, no 1

Poernomosidhi, I (1992) *The Impact of Paratransit on Urban Road Performance in the Third World,* unpublished PhD thesis, Cardiff University, Cardiff

Sethuraman, S (1981) *The Urban Informal Sector in Developing Countries: Employment, Poverty and Environment,* International Labour Office, Geneva

Sinha, A and Kant, R (1997) 'Urban evolution and transformation in Lucknow, India – A comparative study of its streets', *Open House International,* vol 22, no 1, pp34–42

Smit J and Nasr, J (1992) 'Urban agriculture for sustainable cities: using wastes and idle land and water bodies as resources', *Environment and Urbanisation,* vol 4, no 2, pp141–152

Sringagan, K (2000) *Public Land, Property Development and Cross Subsidisation for Low Income Housing,* Max Lock Centre Working Paper, University of Westminster, London

Tomlinson, R (1999) 'From exclusion to inclusion: rethinking Johannesburg's central city', *Environment and Planning A,* vol 31, pp1655–1678

Woods, L (1998) 'Expatriate global investment and squatter displacement in Manila', in Dandekar, H (ed) *City Space and Globalization: An International Perspective,* College of Architecture and Urban Planning, University of Michigan, Ann Arbor

UNCHS (1996) *An Urbanizing World: Global Report on Human Settlements,* Oxford University Press, New York

Yeung, Y (1988) 'Livelihoods for the urban poor: a case for a greater role by Metropolitan Governments', *Regional Development Dialogue,* vol 9, no 4, pp40–54

Chapter 13

Urban Livelihoods – Issues for Urban Governance and Management

Nick Devas

INTRODUCTION

Urban livelihoods analysis is concerned with how the urban poor, given their capabilities and assets, can maintain and enhance their means of living in a secure and sustainable way. This chapter considers how the structures and processes of urban governance and urban management impinge on the ability of the urban poor to achieve secure livelihoods, and what patterns of urban governance and urban management might facilitate, or hinder, urban livelihoods.

Limitations of the Livelihoods Framework

The principles of the livelihoods framework, as outlined in Chapter 1, are wide-ranging and all-embracing. This raises questions about whether such a framework can be applied at all rigorously, especially when the principles encounter conflicts and trade-offs. In particular, the model so far developed does not seem to address adequately two key contextual issues: economics and politics. The first concerns the constraints of operating within a local and global market economy which is highly unequal. This can be illustrated by a typical dilemma faced by city governments all around the world: a version of the classic growth versus equity dilemma. On the one hand, a city government may recognize the pressing needs of the urban poor and may wish to use its resources to enhance the livelihood opportunities of the poor. On the other hand, it perceives that economic growth and prosperity provide both the opportunities for the poor to improve their position and the resources for the city to address the needs of the poor. Thus, in order to encourage investment, the city government diverts its limited resources from the immediate needs of the poor to provide facilities to serve commerce and industry. Worse, the shortage of prime land for industry means that the poor are forced off land that they have occupied informally, while regulations designed to

promote an attractive environment for investors and tourists destroy the livelihoods of informal sector traders. But the alternative of ignoring the needs of
formal sector commerce and industry, investors and tourists, risks economic
stagnation and decline, which would not be in the interests of anyone, least of all
the poor. Thus, city governance faces economic and political choices which are
not simply pro- or anti-poor, and the choices about what does or does not
support secure urban livelihoods are not clear-cut.

The second issue is the nature of political power. The principles and objectives of the livelihoods approach are highly laudable, but how they can be
achieved within highly unequal political power structures is not addressed. Even
within an open, democratic society, political power is highly unequal – all the
more so in countries where institutions are weak and political power is often
exercised in arbitrary ways without adequate democratic safeguards. In such
circumstances, the poor are at a huge disadvantage. Given the unequal nature of
political power, it requires more than statements about the desirability of secure
livelihoods to change what actually happens. Moreover, political conflicts and
conflicts of interest are not merely about rich versus poor, but arise within and
between groups of the poor. For example, pollution from informal industrial
processes from which some poor people may derive their incomes contaminates
the air and water for nearby poor residents. Regulations to protect children from
exploitation may also prevent them from earning a living. How does a livelihoods
analysis help us to resolve such dilemmas? The real world situation of the
poor presents us with political and economic conflicts and dilemmas which a
livelihoods approach as it stands may not enable us to resolve. Thus, further
development of the approach is needed to take more account of the institutional,
economic and political context within which poor people have to try to maintain
their livelihoods.

Having said all that, there are ways in which we can use a livelihoods framework to analyse issues of urban governance and urban management. One way
is to apply the assets and vulnerability analysis (Moser, 1998) to identify how
urban governance and management impact on the various forms of capital on
which the poor depend.

Urban Governance and Management

The livelihoods of the urban poor are primarily determined by how individuals
and households respond to the circumstances in which they find themselves and
the economic opportunities available to them. City (and national) governments
may be perceived as largely irrelevant to the livelihoods and survival of the urban
poor, offering them few, if any, benefits. Nevertheless, the actions of the institutions of city governance can significantly affect the circumstances and opportunities which confront poor urban people, whether positively or negatively. It is
important, therefore, to consider the particular ways in which the structures,
processes, policies and activities of the institutions of city governance influence
the livelihoods of the urban poor.

Urban governance is concerned with the whole range of structures, processes
and relationships between civil society and the local state which determine how
a city functions and what takes place within it. It is much broader than just city

government, although the city government, as an organization, may be the most obvious player. Thus, urban governance includes a range of organizations that between them control or influence what happens within the civic–public realm at city level: national (and state level) government, local agencies of national (and state) government, special purpose public agencies operating locally, private-sector businesses, NGOs and a host of civil society organizations (see Figure 13.1). Nor is urban governance concerned simply with the formal organizations and processes, but with a mass of informal relationships and processes that may often be more significant than the formal processes in determining what actually happens.

The distinction between urban governance and urban management is not precise. Urban governance tends to refer to both the formal and informal political processes which determine, or at least influence, what happens in a city. Urban management generally refers to the more formal, technical-bureaucratic structures and processes of implementation which operate within the wider political-governance framework. In practice, though, the boundaries are unclear. Urban management and implementation often involve de facto political choices, whether they are subject to any structure of accountability or not, and often involve informal as well as formal arrangements. Meanwhile, the political processes of urban governance are often concerned with the minutiae of management and implementation, not just with policy choices. Conventional analyses of urban management (and urban government) tend to view things from a top-down point of view, whereas the perspective of livelihoods analysis is bottom-up – from the microlevel of the poor household to the macrolevel.

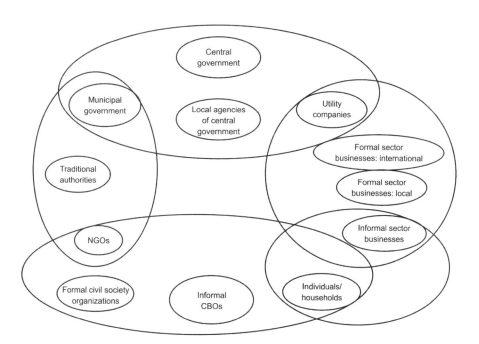

Figure 13.1 *Actors in urban governance*

Applying a Livelihoods Framework to Urban Governance and Management

In this section, we analyse the impact of urban governance and management on the livelihoods of the poor, using an assets-vulnerability framework (Moser, 1998). Table 13.1 summarizes the ways in which governance action may enhance the assets of the poor or increase their vulnerability. These are analysed according to the various forms of 'capital' which are important for the livelihoods of the poor – natural, human, financial, physical, social and political.

Political capital is treated separately from social capital because, in the context of a discussion of governance issues, it has distinct characteristics (see also Chapter 1). Political capital is essentially the scope which individuals and/ or groups have to exert influence on decision-making which affects them, decision-making being defined widely to include both formal and informal processes of de facto as well as de jure decision-making.

In the following sections, we look at a number of aspects of urban governance and management in terms of how they impact on the livelihoods of the urban poor. Not all the items listed in Table 13.1 will be considered in detail since earlier chapters have already covered a number of these aspects. These include, in particular, decisions about the use and development of land, the development, operation and pricing of infrastructure and services, and the regulation of the local economy and trading activities (see discussions in Chapters 6, 9, 11 and 12).

First, though, it is important to recognize that those in positions of power, whether they are politicians, administrators or activists, may have a very limited understanding of urban poverty, particularly of the differentiated nature of poverty and of the livelihood systems of the poor. Information about poverty at city level is often seriously inadequate and rarely goes beyond broad, quantitative indicators. Despite the official rhetoric, many involved in city governance may have little real commitment to reducing poverty. But even where they have, communication with the poor and understanding of their livelihood situations may be so limited that policies adopted and actions taken may be quite inappropriate. Worse, many actions of city governance institutions can be seriously damaging to the livelihoods of the poor.

Formal Political Systems

Representative democracy is, in principle at least, one of the main ways in which the urban poor can bring their influence to bear on decisions affecting their well-being. Direct, competitive elections for mayors and councillors give citizens an opportunity to express their views. Since poor people constitute a large proportion of the urban population, this should provide in principle a mechanism for them to influence the agenda of city government. In practice, the electoral process is often firmly in the hands of elite groups. Electoral arrangements may exclude poor people through such factors as illiteracy, failure to register voters, the exclusion of migrants who do not qualify to vote locally and intimidation. Urban poor people may also exclude themselves because they feel that the process is irrelevant to their needs or offers no real political choice. Minority groups and those who oppose the current order may fear to make themselves visible, particularly if voting secrecy is not secure.

But the political system can also work for the poor. The fact that their votes count gives them some leverage, especially at election time. In India, 'vote banks' in poor communities can be and are used to their advantage to achieve real improvements in services. The use of their votes helps to account for the fact that electoral turnout in poor communities is significantly higher than it is in middle-class neighbourhoods. Of course, such arrangements reinforce patron–client relationships between elected politicians and poor communities, but clientelism can deliver tangible benefits for the poor. In Cebu, in the Philippines, like many other cities, the poor have become skilled at informal negotiations with the Mayor and other politicians which enable them to obtain improvements in their conditions and protection from harassment (Etemadi and Satterthwaite, 1999).

Box 13.1 Ward Councillors in Bangalore

'An active councillor means more to a slum than a lot of broad-based policy objectives . . . A slum which does not meet the criteria to be part of an improvement programme, but has an active councillor, can be better provided in terms of infrastructure than an adjacent constituency that does meet the criteria but has no one to endorse them . . . The authority, be it a political one like a councillor, or a non-political one like an NGO, is regarded as a source of goods . . . a source to be treated with respect, do not bite the hand that feeds you . . . Only the political source is accountable, needs something from the dwellers as well, and can be voted out of office, whereas the NGO remains aloof, untouchable.'

Source: Dewit, M 'Slum perceptions and cognitions', in Schenk, H (ed), 1996, pp109–110, quoted in Benjamin and Bhuvaneswari, 1999, p106

In recent research on poverty and urban governance we have observed that:[1]

- In those systems with executive mayors direct election does bring a degree of accountability to the urban poor since they represent a large proportion of the city's population. By contrast, appointed mayors (or equivalents) are answerable to no one locally.
- In systems based on decision-making by elected councillors, ward-based councillors can provide an accessible avenue of influence for poor communities (see Box 13.1). In contrast, electing councillors by proportional representation from a city-wide party-list system gives more power to the party machinery. In Colombo, Sri Lanka, the shift from a ward-basis to a party-list system is perceived to have made elected members more remote from their constituents, thereby reducing the voice of poor communities (Fernando et al, 1999, p59). The 74th Constitutional Amendment in India required the replacement of multicouncillor divisions with single councillor wards in order to make representation at ward level more effective (Benjamin and Bhuvaneswari, 1999, p13)

Table 13.1 *Applying an assets/vulnerability framework to urban governance and management*

Capital	Governance actions which may enhance assets of the poor	Governance actions which may increase vulnerability of the poor
Natural	Ensuring access to land which is affordable by the poor and with sufficiently secure tenure, both for residential use and for economic activities	Zoning regulations and development standards which prevent access by the poor
		Minimum plot size regulations and construction standards which are unattainable by the poor
		Forced relocation and clearance of informal housing areas
		Upgrading projects which raise service levels and security to the point where the area becomes attractive to higher-income groups.
	Environmental controls on water and air pollution and effective waste management	Failing to control pollution and waste disposal 'upstream' of where the poor live
		'Rent seeking' by enforcement agencies on activities in poor areas such as waste sorting, pollution from economic and domestic activities
		Restrictions on urban agriculture
Human	Universal, quality (primary) education, as an initial goal	Imposing fees (official and unofficial) for primary education
	Ensuring equal provision for girls	
	Involving parents in the management of schools	
	Skills training related to real skills needs of the poor	
	Accessible healthcare	Imposing fees (official and unofficial) for primary health care
	Food/nutrition support programmes	
	Public works programmes that absorb surplus labour (and increase skills)	
Financial	Providing access to suitable housing finance (eg, community mortgages)	Refusing to recognize informal housing areas or to resolve tenure insecurities
	Providing access to financial services for the poor, including microcredit for informal businesses	Regulatory controls on informal sector trading
		Costly and cumbersome licensing requirements for traders
		Harassment of informal sector traders
	Provision of market facilities in suitable locations, with provision for small, informal sector businesses	Local taxes which impinge negatively on the poor
		Charges for services which are not related to the ability to pay
		Unofficial charges and demands for bribes

Physical	Providing access to safe, reliable water supplies, including community provision (eg, communal taps)	Unsafe water which requires boiling, and unreliable supplies which require storage, queuing, collection at night; Enforcement action against illegal connections
	Providing access to safe sanitation (including community provision)	Inadequate sanitation that creates environmental hazards and increases the vulnerability of women
	Providing proper systems of waste management (collection, transport, reuse and disposal), including those that involve communities	Irregular collection that may not serve informal residential areas; Inadequate waste disposal which creates environmental hazards; Privatization which results in poor areas being excluded; Regulation of waste collection/sorting/recycling which reduces income-earning opportunities for the poor and results in 'rent-seeking' by enforcers
	Providing all-weather pedestrian access; Providing vehicle access to within reach of areas where the poor live	Provision of too high levels of vehicle access which make areas attractive to higher-income groups
	Providing drainage systems to prevent flooding; Provision of public space for economic and social activities in informal housing areas; Ensuring safe and reliable public transport	Displacement of poor households as a result of upgrading
	Ensuring the availability of electricity supplies	'Rent-seeking' by traffic police that increases the costs of public transport without improving safety; Regulations that discriminate against paratransit; Enforcement action against illegal connections
Social	Helping to build community organizations among the poor; Ensuring safety/security/freedom from fear of crime in poor areas	Creating dependence on external agents; Forced relocation (or relocation caused by pressure from higher-income groups) which destroys informal networks
Political	Accessible, ward-based councillors who have influence; Mechanisms to make decision-making and resource allocation more accountable and transparent; Mechanisms for participation; Responsive systems	Dependent relations with local politicians; Service/resource providers not subject to democratic accountability
		Exclusion of certain groups
	Supporting collective action by the poor and enabling them to make demands	Cooption of leadership of community organizations

- However, the ward-based councillor system tends to disadvantage women and minority groups. Thus, some countries – for example, South Africa – adopt a mixture of the two systems, while others (notably India) reserve seats for women and minority groups. While the reservation of seats has its weaknesses (weak accountability to the groups notionally being represented, and risks of capture by political parties and business interests (Blair, 2000, p24)), it does provide an opportunity for at least some disadvantaged groups to have a voice at the centre of city government.
- Unfortunately, elected councillors often perform poorly, particularly in Africa, as they are interested in maximizing personal gains before they are thrown out of office. As a result, they may not be regarded by the urban poor as effective avenues of influence and support.
- Multiparty competition can help to clarify issues – for example, whether the agenda is pro-poor or not. Contesting local elections on individual merit rather than on a party basis, as in Ghana, might sound good, but prevents the development of any coherent platform for action. However, in many cases party agendas are unclear and parties may simply reinforce ethnic or other divisions.
- Electoral turnout does indicate, to a certain extent, the degree of confidence in local elections. In our case studies, turnout ranged from 65–84 per cent in recent local elections in Cebu to 27 per cent in Kumasi, Ghana, where the city government is totally dominated by the centrally appointed mayor and elections are contested (officially, at least) on non-party lines.

Decision-making and Accountability

How representatives are elected is one thing; how decisions are made, in principle and in practice, is another. In some systems, mayors, whether elected or appointed, have all the power, and councillors have only a marginal role in challenging executive decisions. In other systems councillors are part of the executive and so have a greater role. What matters is the extent to which those making the decisions are accessible and accountable to the urban poor. This partly relates to the electoral arrangements mentioned above (elected rather than appointed mayors, ward-based rather than party-list councillors), but it also relates to the degree of transparency of decision-making. All too often, decision-making is done behind closed doors, through lobbying and deal-making behind the scenes, through the exercise of political power and patronage, and through informal negotiation.

Nor is decision-making limited to elected representatives: many of the decisions which most affect the poor are taken by officials as part of the implementation process. Where administrative discretion is large, there is scope for rent-seeking abuse, usually with little or no scope for complaint or redress.

There is often a serious lack of accountability to citizens for the decisions made. Basic information is not available – for example, the budgets and accounts of the local government are either not available, out of date or in a form which is incomprehensible to most people. Indicators of performance on local service delivery (such as the proportion of the population served, the quality and reliability of the service, and unit costs) are not available – indeed, performance may not even be considered. Even basic data on who is being served with what services may be unavailable.

In this context, the media can play a significant role in raising and investigating issues, if allowed to and if the capacity to do so exists. However, the press often limits its coverage to national and capital city issues, leaving local issues unreported. The media are generally owned by businesses whose interests are likely to be very different from those of the poor. In a number of places local radio has developed as an adjunct to traditional print media, and perhaps one which is more locally accessible. Civil society organizations and NGOs also play a crucial role in holding elected representatives and decision-makers to account. This will be discussed further in the next section.

One key area of decision-making – perhaps *the* key area – is the local government's budget. Whatever plans and policies are adopted, it is the choices made in the budget which really determine who gets what local services. Yet this process is often tightly controlled by the finance professionals together with key politicians, such as the mayor. Other elected representatives may have little or no say in how resources are used. In practice, the position may be even worse since the formal budget process, in which elected representatives have some say, may actually be replaced by a 'shadow budget' in which the real use of resources is determined by a very small group. This typically occurs where, as in many local governments in Africa, revenue projections are not achieved so that ad hoc decisions have to be made about how the more limited resources will be used. But it also reflects the political realities in many places where ad hoc decisions are made in response to lobbying and political pressure, and to facilitate political patronage, regardless of the formal budgeting process. The absence of information and transparency ensures that no one can be held to account.

There have been interesting attempts in Brazil to open up the municipal budgeting processes to ordinary citizens through 'participatory budgeting'. In a number of cities this has radically altered the way in which budget priorities are assessed and has greatly increased the transparency of the process, reducing the scope for clientelistic relationships. But the system is far from perfect, with questions about the extent to which the poor really participate, the small proportion of the budget subject to the participatory process, the discretion left to the executive to manipulate the approved budget, and conflicts between this process and the role of elected representatives (Souza, 2001; Melo, 2001). The practice of participatory budgeting is gaining momentum, but has still been adopted in only a few municipalities and is vulnerable to changes in political control.

At the heart of the budgetary process are fundamental choices about how resources are to be used. In this, there are issues which go beyond simply whether expenditures are pro-poor or anti-poor. For example, investing in improved road infrastructure to a city's port or industrial area might not be perceived immediately as being pro-poor, but if, as a result of failure to invest, the city's economic base is constrained and employment shrinks, the poor will suffer along with everyone else. Another sort of choice is whether to use the limited resources available to extend the city's water distribution network into low-income housing areas or to upgrade the capacity of the bulk water-treatment facility. Responding to pressure from poor communities may result in the former rather than the latter, with the consequence that the poor have taps but no water comes forth because there is insufficient bulk supply.

Another critical issue in relation to decision-making and accountability is the fact that many of the services on which the poor depend are not the responsibility of the elected municipal government but of various special purpose agencies which lack any direct democratic accountability. For example, of the 23 members of the board of the Bangalore Development Authority, only two are elected members of the Municipal Corporation. Even where services are provided by state or national government, lines of accountability are very tenuous. The study of Bangalore indicated how the middle and upper classes are able to use their networks to influence state government and semi-autonomous agencies, while the urban poor have a greater chance of influence through their ward councillor. Therefore, the tendency over recent years to shift responsibilities from municipal government to special purpose agencies and to state government has further eroded the limited influence which the poor might have over vital services (Benjamin and Bhuvanewhari, 1999).

Relationships Between Civil Society and City Governance

Civil society organizations (CSOs), including CBOs and NGOs, can play a vital role in city governance, whether in representing the interests of sections of society or in lobbying city government on behalf of the poor. Most towns and cities have a range of CSOs and NGOs, but from our case studies we found great differences between cities in terms of the capacity of these organizations to engage with city governments on behalf of the poor. On the whole, CSOs were strongest and most dynamic during and after 'struggle' situations (apartheid in South Africa, the Philippines under Marcos and Chile under Pinochet). Once the struggle has been won, CSOs may become less active (a retreat from solidarity into private space (Rodriguez et al, 1999, p2)), and many activists move from NGOs to the government. Nevertheless, civil society may remain more dynamic than elsewhere. Thus, in Cebu, a forum of local NGOs scrutinizes the electoral platforms of mayoral candidates in terms of their agenda for the urban poor and seeks to hold to account those elected during their term in office (Etemadi and Satterthwaite, 1999).

Of course, not all CSOs are pro-poor. The most powerful community organization in Johannesburg is the Sandton Ratepayers Association (SRA), representing the interests of the affluent white suburbs. In order to protest against a substantial rise in property tax, SRA organized a highly effective tax boycott which virtually crippled the Greater Johannesburg Metropolitan Council (Beall et al, 1999).

Where the poor organize themselves, whether on an area or occupational basis, they may be able to exert influence on the decision-making process through, for example, lobbying, demonstrations and the organization of voters. But almost by definition, they have limited capacity to do so on their own. The fact that they are poor means that they have few resources of either time or money to devote to organizing and sustaining collective action. In addition, they have to deal with internal differences and conflicts which undermine solidarity and sap the energy of the leadership. One way to increase the influence of the poor is through the networking of community organizations in pursuit of a common cause (see also Chapter 8). This has been a successful technique adopted by street vendors in Cebu to defend themselves against forced removal (Etemadi and Satterthwaite, 1999).

Relationships between community organizations and elected representatives can be difficult. Elected representatives may view community organizations as a threat to their position as the voice of the local people (for example, Colombo (Fernando et al, 1999, p112)), while community organizations may be highly critical of elected representatives. In other cases, elected representatives or their political parties may seek to capture community organizations and community leaders may be bought off with rewards or offers of jobs (Rodriguez et al, 1999, p61). Political divisions, like ethnic or religious divisions, can undermine solidarity within community organizations. In the end, the avenues of influence for community organizations of the poor, whether direct or through their elected representatives, can only bear fruit if the municipal government has something to offer in terms of responsibilities for services, resources and the capacity to deliver. This will be addressed in the next section.

Another branch of civil society which traditionally in Western democracies has been a key player in bringing about social reform in the interests of the poor is the trade union movement. In South Africa, trade unions were deeply involved in the struggle against apartheid, but in many developing countries today trade unions appear to be comparatively weak. Where they are significant, their concern is primarily for their members who are generally formal sector employees, rather than with the poor. Trade union action – for example, by municipal workers unions in India and South Africa – may even inhibit the reforms which are necessary to make resources available for the urban poor.

Trade associations can be quite effective in protecting their members' interests – for example, associations of traders, taxi operators and vehicle repairers in Kumasi (Korboe et al, 1999, p156), but may not represent the interests of the really poor. Indeed, there may be conflicts of interest with the poor – for example, over the level of taxi fares. One of the most positive examples of a trade association is SEWA in Ahmedabad which has had a huge impact on the livelihoods of poor urban women (Dutta and Batley, 1999, p115).

Churches and other religious organizations have often been associated with the struggles of the poor, notably in Latin America and South Africa, but there seem to be few current examples from our case study cities. Such organizations can have an independence and authority which, if allied with the interests of the poor, can be influential, both at national and local level.

Constraints Within which Municipal Governments Operate

The ability of municipal governments to respond to the livelihood needs of the urban poor is constrained, often severely, by a number of factors:

1   Municipal boundaries which do not reflect the pattern of urban growth (see also Chapter 2). As a result, a large proportion of the urban poor may live on the periphery, beyond the municipal boundary, in jurisdictions which are even less capable of addressing their needs for services and infrastructure than the

city government. Larger urban areas may be fragmented between a number of jurisdictions, making it difficult to address infrastructure and service needs properly across the city.

2 The limited range of their responsibilities, often excluding those services which most affect the urban poor, such as water supply, education and health services, policing and security. Even such key matters as land and housing may be the responsibility of separate agencies, such as development authorities in many Indian cities. This fragmentation of responsibilities between agencies not only makes for problems of coordination and accountability, but also (as already noted) limits the influence which the poor might have through the democratic process.

3 Municipal governments are often severely constrained by their lack of skilled and capable staff. Low rates of remuneration and low job status make it difficult to attract and retain staff, and contribute to rent-seeking by employees. As a result, municipal governments often have very limited capacity to deliver services to anyone, let alone the poor. The secondment of senior staff from central government can bring needed expertise, but can also create serious tensions with elected representatives and undermine local accountability.

4 Internal organizational structures and procedures may also constrain municipal governments in responding to the needs of the poor. Departmental boundaries and rivalries, and attempts to maximize departmental budgets, may prevent the efficient use of resources and service delivery. Professional priorities may inhibit responsiveness to the poor. In Ahmedabad, engineers were reluctant to divert water-supply lines into low-income areas for fear of reducing supplies to regularly serviced areas (Dutta and Batley, 1999, p76). In Johannesburg, the city government's ability to redirect resources to meet the needs of the urban poor has been constrained by the culture of high standards carried over from the apartheid era.

5 A related issue is that of the different time horizons to which city governments have to work. Longer-term strategic planning is constrained by the annual budget cycle, and undermined by short-term political expediency and uncertainty over financial resources. Politicians have their sights fixed on the next election and are concerned with those activities that will bring short-term gains. Thus, there is a reluctance to put effort and resources into longer-term investment in economic development, bulk infrastructure and poverty reduction, which are essential to the well-being of the poor.

6 In a number of systems, there are legal constraints on providing infrastructure and services to informal housing areas. Until the mayor obtained a dispensation, Colombo Municipal Corporation was legally prevented from spending money in underserved settlements which were not included in the property tax system (Fernando et al, 1999, p67). In India, the various state Slum Acts establish an elaborate system for classifying slums, and the ability of the municipal government to intervene depends on the classification.

7 Intergovernmental conflicts can be another constraint on responsiveness to the poor. State–municipal conflicts are common in India and are usually party political in origin. In Bangalore, the municipal government is effectively prevented from regularizing land tenure because land is a state matter. In Colombo, the Western Provincial Council (which is dominated by the national

governing party) has persistently obstructed attempts by the Municipal Corporation (which is opposition controlled) to invest in poor communities and has impeded the flow of central funds to the city (Fernando et al, 1999).

8   One of the greatest constraints for most municipal governments is the paucity of financial resources. Local revenue sources are often unsatisfactory, difficult to collect and impinge negatively on the poor. Resources transferred from national or state governments are often inadequate and erratic. The resources which are available are badly managed. Some of these issues will be discussed further in the next section.

Financial Resources and Their Use

Municipal finance impinges on the livelihoods of the poor in a number of ways:

• the inadequacy of resources available to improve the infrastructure and services for poor residents and microenterprises;
• the impact of local taxes and charges on the poor;
• the way that decisions about budgetary choices are made; and
• accountability, or the lack of it, for the use of resources.

Municipal governments are often heavily dependent on fiscal transfers from the centre, whether in the form of grants or shares of national taxes. However, transfers are often allocated in non-transparent ways and without proper consideration of relative expenditure needs or local revenue capacities between municipalities. Transfer amounts may vary unpredictably from one year to the next and be provided in ways which do not encourage effective or efficient use of resources (such as grants which just pay for the costs of staff and grants to cover deficits). In addition, agreed transfers are often not actually paid, or are paid late, thereby undermining the budgetary process and preventing municipal governments from delivering agreed services. In Uganda, attempts have been made to increase the local governments' accountability for transferred resources by publicizing locally the amounts involved.

Municipal governments generally have a range of local revenue sources: taxes on property, taxes on economic activities, taxes on individual consumption or assets, charges for services, and fees for permits and licences, as well as transfers from central or state government. The boundaries between the categories are not always precise.

In most countries, the largest revenue sources, and the ones which have the least negative impact on equity, are assigned to central government. Local governments are generally left with a number of small and problematic local taxes. The most common tax for urban local government is on property (whether on land or buildings or both). This has the advantage of an immovable tax object which can be clearly assigned to the right local government. However, if revenues are to keep pace with inflation, properties have to be revalued regularly, which requires skilled valuers. The high visibility of the tax makes it relatively unpopular and it can be difficult to collect. Revenue collection performance is often quite poor, with as much as half of the potential revenue going uncollected. Inasmuch as the tax is based on property values, and property values tend to reflect the ability to pay, the tax can be said to be crudely equitable. However, the relationship with ability to pay is only approximate, and if the poor pay a larger share of their income on housing than the rich, then the tax can be regressive. Some systems give an exemption to low value properties (for example, in Indonesia), or do not include informal housing areas in their tax registers. Overall, the impact of property tax on the poor is probably less a result of the direct burden of the tax than the indirect effect on municipal resources of the problems of collecting the tax from those who can afford to pay.

Other local taxes may impinge rather more on the poor – for example, taxes on bicycles and non-motorized vehicles, business licences (effectively a tax) on informal sector traders, market fees (also effectively a tax in most cases since the fee greatly exceeds the cost of the service provided), road tolls, taxes on agricultural produce and poll taxes (even if graduated according to income). In Uganda, the graduated personal tax, the main local revenue source, has a basic minimum amount which all have to pay so that its impact is clearly regressive. Attempts to collect the tax involve draconian punishments, and people have been known to spend days in the bush trying to avoid tax collectors. All this can have a serious impact on the livelihoods of poor households.

In most countries, business licence fees vary only modestly according to the type of business so that the burden on small and informal sector businesses is relatively much greater than on large businesses. Other local taxes, such as those on electricity consumption, entertainments and fuel (passed on to the consumers of public transport), may affect the poor. But they generally impinge much more on higher income groups and so can be used to generate resources to benefit the poor.

Charging for services raises some difficult issues. Economists normally advocate full cost recovery for those services with private benefits, such as water and electricity, as being both efficient and equitable (in the sense that those who benefit should pay). But this raises problems of affordability for the poor. The solution is not a general subsidy which would benefit only those connected to the system – usually the rich. All too often, the poor pay much more dearly for water than the rich by having to buy from a private vendor or use distant and/or polluted water sources (see also Chapter 11). They would benefit more from an expansion to the public system which enabled them to connect to it, even at full economic cost, than from a subsidized public system from which they are effectively excluded.

Subsidies for a small, basic needs volume of water (or electricity) may be a way to help the poor without upsetting the overall viability of a water-supply system. Another approach is to cross-subsidize between high-income and low-income consumers, where it is possible to identify income groups clearly, which is rarely the case. However, adopting progressive tariffs by volume on the assumption that the rich consume more than the poor, can penalize those poor who share a tap between a large number of people – a common situation in many urban areas (such as Kumasi (Korboe et al, 1999, p74)). One of the main obstacles to accessing to the public water system is the high initial cost of connection. Subsidizing this cost or spreading it over a period of time, can be a better way to ensure access to the system by the poor than a general subsidy. Free or subsidized public standpipes are another common solution. While public taps have their disadvantages (such as queues, having to carry the water, contamination of containers, breakage of taps and waste of water), public standpipes do serve large numbers of the urban poor who would otherwise not be served in India and elsewhere.

In the case of services with substantial public benefits, such as sanitation, waste disposal, health and education, subsidies can be justified on efficiency as well as on equity grounds. But that still leaves the problem that there may be inadequate funds to finance the service unless there is a direct charge. In Mombasa, privatization of the waste-collection service resulted in a large increase in the charge; since the poor were unable or unwilling to pay this, the private contractor simply abandoned collections in poor areas, leaving the municipality with the problem (Gatabaki-Kamau et al, 1999, p44).

Charges for public or shared toilets can be a real burden to poor households, and the resulting indiscriminate defecation poses a serious health hazard (for example, Korboe et al, 1999, p80). On the other hand, the absence of any charging mechanism means that resources are not available to maintain and extend facilities. The Sulabh privately-provided toilets in India are an example of charging which enables the service to be maintained to everyone's benefit. There may also be potential for CBOs, such as women's groups, to manage communal toilets at the local level.

In the case of health services, there is a long-standing debate over charging. There is a wide consensus that the cost sharing (that is, charging) systems introduced in many countries for health services create a serious burden for the poor and discourage use, and that attempts at exemptions for the poor do not work (see also Chapter 10). Yet even the poor would prefer to pay for a service that they actually receive (as exemplified by their use of private dispensaries), rather than being offered a service which is nominally free but turns out to be non-existent because there is no money to pay the staff or replenish the medicine supply.

In practice, official charges are often not the main problem. Where services are in short supply, those allocating them are often in a position to extract an informal charge or bribe to access the service. For example, the real cost of a clinic visit in Kumasi is said to be around ten times the official charge (Devas and Korboe, 2000). Thus, subsidies are effectively creamed off by the gate-keepers. Rules – for example, that schools may not charge fees – may be unenforceable where parents are willing to pay under the table to register their child. Such payments clearly impinge on the poor without any commensurate increase in the resources available for the service.

One way in which the poor may be able to gain access to free services such as water and electricity is through illegal connections. Such methods are extremely unsatisfactory: mortal risks from illegal electricity connections; contamination of water through illegal pipe connections; uncertainty of provision; and the bribes which have to be paid to those making the connections or to officials not to disconnect. In practice, illegal connections are not free, and the damage caused to the overall system increases the costs to everyone else, including those who pay to use the service. Yet for many, illegal connections may be the only way to obtain access.

Another important financial issue is the poor revenue collection performance in many municipal governments. A large proportion of money due is not collected, and a further proportion is not accounted for after being collected. Collection costs absorb yet more of what is collected. All this reduces the resources which could be used to provide essential services for the poor. A similar issue relates to poor management of expenditures, with large amounts being siphoned off by politicians and officials, and more being wasted or not accounted for. Financial procedures are not followed, financial controls are not effective and the misuse of public money is widely accepted. Again, all this reduces the resources available to address urban poverty.

Conclusions

The livelihoods of the urban poor are deeply affected by how cities are governed and managed. There are many actions which city governments can take to improve the well-being and livelihood opportunities of the poor, but frequently they are heavily constrained by limited financial and human resources, and other institutional constraints. All too often, the actions of city governments, whether through ignorance or deliberate choice, undermine rather than support the livelihood strategies of poor households.

Poor people face a vicious circle: they are poor because they lack the resources, the influence and the power to change their circumstances. The institutions of city governance should be responsive to their needs. But decision-making is (almost by definition) dominated by elites and the powerful whose interests are likely to be very different from those of the poor. That need not always be the case. For one thing, in a democratic system, those seeking election need the votes of the poor. This gives them some leverage, especially if they manage to organize themselves. Informal networks and negotiations through elected mayors or local councillors can bring results, albeit often on a clientelistic basis. By persistence and by solidarity, the poor can achieve certain results. The more accountable, transparent and participatory the decision-making processes, the greater the chances of success.

If that influence is to yield real results, city governments also need to have sufficient powers, resources and staff to be able to deliver services. If city governments are not responsible for the services on which the poor depend, if they have no financial resources to extend those services, and if they lack skilled staff and management capacity, then no amount of influence is likely to produce results.

Making the institutions of city governance more supportive of the livelihoods of the poor requires a combination of factors: a better understanding by those in power of the livelihoods of the poor, political commitment from the leadership, resources to do something about the situation and a dynamic civil society which brings pressure to bear on the decision-making process. Democratization at the local level, together with greater accountability and transparency, can produce results which benefit the urban poor, but it takes time and a great deal of effort.

NOTE

1 DFID funded research on Urban Governance, Partnership and Poverty, conducted by an international team from the University of Birmingham, International Institute for Environment and Development, London, London School of Economics and Cardiff University, together with local researchers, on ten cities in Asia, Africa and Latin America, 1998–2000

REFERENCES

Beall J, Crankshaw, O and Parnell, S (1999) *Johannesburg*, Urban Governance, Partnership and Poverty WP 12, International Development Department, School of Public Policy, University of Birmingham, Birmingham

Benjamin S and Bhuvanaswari, R (1999) *Bangalore,* Urban Governance, Partnership and Poverty WP 15, International Development Department, School of Public Policy, University of Birmingham, Birmingham

Blair, H (2000) 'Participation and accountability at the periphery: democratic local government in six countries', *World Development,* vol 28, no 1, pp21–39

Devas, N and Korboe, D (2000) 'City governance and poverty: the case of Kumasi', *Environment and Urbanization*, vol 12, no 1, pp123–136

Dutta, S and Batley, R (1999) *Ahmedabad,* Urban Governance, Partnership and Poverty WP 16, International Development Department, School of Public Policy, University of Birmingham, Birmingham

Etemadi, F and Satterthwaite, D (1999) *Cebu,* Urban Governance, Partnership and Poverty WP 13, International Development Department, School of Public Policy, University of Birmingham, Birmingham

Fernando, A, Russell, S, Wilson, A and Vidler, E (1999) *Colombo,* Urban Governance, Partnership and Poverty WP 9, International Development Department, School of Public Policy, University of Birmingham, Birmingham

Gatabaki-Kamau, R and Rakodi, C with Devas, N (1999) *Mombasa*, Urban Governance, Partnership and Poverty WP 11, International Development Department, School of Public Policy, University of Birmingham, Birmingham

Korboe, D, Diaw, K and Devas, N (1999) *Kumasi,* Urban Governance, Partnership and Poverty WP 10, International Development Department, School of Public Policy, University of Birmingham, Birmingham

Melo, M (2001) *Urban Governance, Accountability and Poverty: The Politics of Participatory Budgeting in Recife, Brazil*, Urban Governance, Partnership and Poverty WP 27, International Development Department, School of Public Policy, University of Birmingham, Birmingham

Moser, C O N (1998) 'The asset vulnerability framework: reassessing urban poverty reduction strategies', *World Development*, vol 26, no 1, pp1–19

Rodriguez, A, Winchester, L and Richards, B (1999) *Santiago*, Urban Governance, Partnership and Poverty, WP 14, International Development Department, School of Public Policy, University of Birmingham, Birmingham

Souza, C (2001) *Participatory Budgeting in Brazilian Cities: Limits and Possibilities in Building Democratic Institutions*, Urban Governance, Partnership and Poverty, WP 28, International Development Department, School of Public Policy, University of Birmingham, Birmingham

Part 4

Urban Poverty Reduction: Lessons from Experience

In this part of the book, practical experiences with attempts to reduce urban poverty are reviewed. The first three of these are drawn from projects supported by DFID and the fourth from a recent research project which compared a number of projects in which NGOs have had a significant role. These illustrate a variety of roles played by central and local governments, CBOs, indigenous NGOs, and external donors and NGOs. They reflect long-standing and more recent experience, and they represent different scales and levels of intervention.

Chapter 14

Reducing Urban Poverty in India – Lessons from Projects Supported by DFID

Susan Loughhead[1] and Carole Rakodi

Introduction

DFID has been supporting urban poverty reduction efforts in India since the mid-1980s. During the late 1980s and early 1990s, DFID was the largest single bilateral donor in the urban sector, spending £120 million in Hyderabad, Indore, Vijayawada, Visakhapatnam and Calcutta, which affected 1 million people. The lessons learnt from these projects (see also Chapter 8) have been built into the design of DFID's current urban portfolio in India – in Cochin, Cuttack and, more recently, 32 towns in Andhra Pradesh. A new project currently in the planning stages in Calcutta will take this process one stage further. The scale and diversity of the programme precludes any detailed discussion here. Instead, some of the key lessons learned are summarized below in two sections. The first demonstrates how DFID India and its partners in local, state and central government have deepened their understanding of the causes and symptoms of urban poverty over the last 15 years, and have begun to change their policy and programme response accordingly. This has involved an increasing engagement with social protection measures, as well as more traditional development work. The second demonstrates the importance of getting the policy and institutional context right before sustained reductions in urban poverty can take place.

Urban Poverty and Vulnerability

The first DFID-supported urban poverty projects were consistent with the Government of India's approach to urban poverty at the time. The Environmental Improvement of Urban Slums scheme which began in 1974 was paralleled by state programmes focusing on a standard package of environmental infrastructure improvements, the granting of *patta* (tenure rights) and shelter upgrading.[2]

The DFID-supported SIPs in Hyderabad, Indore, Vijayawada, Visakhapatnam and Calcutta concentrated on infrastructure improvements in registered slums: roads, drains, latrines, street lighting, water supply and community halls. The projects were engineering-led and the design of infrastructure improvements was heavily influenced by the package and standards specified in existing public sector programmes. Over time, a number of community development activities were included in these area-based programmes. These ranged from supporting CBOs, promoting financial services and providing vocational training, to supporting pre-school non-formal education, primary, mainly preventive, healthcare, legal literacy and gender awareness training.

A series of impact assessment studies of the projects in Visakhapatnam, Indore and Vijayawada (IDD, 1999) and Calcutta (PIAS, 1997) commissioned by DFID in 1996 and 1997, revealed the extent to which these projects had improved the quality of life of the urban poor and suggested where improvements could be made in future programmes.

Lessons from Earlier Slum Improvement Projects

The assessments were unequivocal in their view that infrastructural improvements (roads, drains, street lighting and water) within slums had made a significant impact on poor people's lives. They had reduced environmental hazards and reduced the drudgery in many women's lives. Road improvements were appreciated for improving access for both pedestrian and vehicular traffic, changing the image of a slum, increasing social integration with surrounding areas, stimulating investment in housing, increasing land and property values and rents (apparently without significant displacement effects) and enabling increased economic activity. Improved access was of key importance to the latter, but the increased availability of well-drained outside space and the longer day enabled by the provision of electric lighting were also important. The improvements in water supply, drainage, access and lighting particularly benefited women. They appreciated the overall improvement in cleanliness, especially private bathing areas and latrines, as well as reductions in flooding, the increased availability and versatility of public space, and the provision of street lighting which increased their security at night.

The impact of other activities on poor people's lives was variable. One of the reasons why infrastructure improvements were so successful was because the benefits were non-divisible, benefiting a whole slum, not particular areas or groups of people within it. The projects were much less successful in meeting the needs of particularly vulnerable groups, or in strengthening the capacity of slum-based organizations to address the variable needs of all slum members. In effect, many existing power relations were simply reproduced. Slum-based community organizations remained heavily influenced by the wider context within which they were developed or strengthened – for example, the presence of local political leaders or other elites. Benefits which were targeted at individuals, such as vocational training, did not necessarily reach those most in need.

As far as health changes were concerned, it was hoped that a combination of basic infrastructure provision, environmental improvement and improved health care would result in improvements in the health status of slum populations. Although it was not possible to measure health outcomes in the 1996–1997 studies, let alone to attribute them solely to initiatives undertaken as part of the DFID-funded projects, studies demonstrated increased health awareness and immunization rates, as well as increased use of Oral Rehydration Solution for diarrhoea, family planning and antenatal care. However, the programmes did not reach many residents, did not tackle some important health issues – such as curative care and tuberculosis (TB) – and nor did they address ill health–poverty–indebtedness linkages.

In order to assess impacts, the IDD study had sought to understand poor people's priorities and then to link these to actual project interventions. They found that poor urban people highlight employment, income, assets and savings as the key determinants of their well-being. This is heavily related to the security and predictability of income, as well as to the security of assets, such as land and tenure – that is, secure tenure rather than ownership per se. The studies also found that support and dependency are critical factors. These relate to instances where people cannot look after themselves or obtain support from others, and/ or those having an excessive number of dependants, which compounded their problems. Women, the elderly, the chronically ill and the disabled were commonly described as the most vulnerable.

Directly related to these vulnerability factors, the poor highlighted the link between ill health and the cost of treatment, indebtedness and the loss of work. Ill health was associated with chronic illness, such as TB, industrial accidents, or alcohol and drug abuse. In addition, alcoholism and drug abuse was often related to domestic violence, and the diversion of household income to drug and alcohol purchases. The poorest households experienced a combination of many of the above factors: erratic employment, consumption constraints, domestic violence, alcoholism and drug abuse, and insecurity of tenure.

It is useful to summarize the impact assessors' poverty framework here. They concluded that poor urban people's needs can be categorized broadly under three headings: survival, security and quality of life. These conditions are not mutually exclusive; rather, they each have relevance for poor people at different stages in their lives.

- *Survival* The bottom line for all poor people is a fear of destitution and homelessness, and a desire to survive. In times of crisis, they need access to ready cash to purchase the items required for survival – food and shelter – and access to support systems.
- *Security* The next key objective for poor people is a search for security. This is associated with reliable income streams, access to consumption and investment savings and loans, educational opportunities which are an investment for the future, and strong social networks to support families in times of crisis. For women, improved security includes income as well as protection against violence and discrimination.
- *Quality of life* Once these needs are met, but also alongside them, poor people are interested in improving their quality of life. They may want to participate in local politics and in decisions about their local area. They are interested in participating in skill training programmes which may offer them the chance of better employment prospects in the future. They may also want to invest

time and resources in lobbying for, and maintaining, basic environmental infrastructure, and in attending courses to improve basic hygiene and healthcare.

Many of these lessons were already apparent to DFID's urban team in India. The studies were useful, however, because, for the first time, they documented and provided substantive conclusions about the strengths and weaknesses of the SIPs supported by DFID. Before these studies were completed, DFID had already begun to develop a new phase of urban projects, drawing on the lessons from the past and making specific reference to the experiences of poor people's lives.

Recent Urban Poverty Reduction Projects

The Cochin Urban Poverty Reduction Project, approved in 1997, focuses on the needs of the poor and the vulnerable, irrespective of their location in the city. It recognizes that poor people do not necessarily live in officially recognized slums. An effective poverty-reduction programme must also embrace the needs of those who live on illegal sites, often located in the most precarious and untenable conditions (such as along canal banks and railway lines) where there is constant fear of eviction and natural disasters, as well as those who live on pavements, in brothels and in scattered dwellings alongside richer houses. The Cochin project aims to improve and sustain access to, and the usage of, a broad range of services that poor and vulnerable people need and want, ranging from in-slum environmental improvements to de-addiction programmes, homes for abandoned women, support to the mentally ill, TB care, and eye camps. As part of a programme to reach women, it works through a federal CDS which links neighbourhood groups representing vulnerable women and their households to Area Development Societies at ward level and the CDS at city level. In this context, women's empowerment is seen as an end in itself, as well as a means to an end. One experimental part of the project involves building on the lessons learnt from earlier projects' support to vocational training as a way to improve poor people's opportunities in competitive labour markets. It includes a specific economic development component aimed at developing business opportunities and linking the development of poor and vulnerable people's skills more specifically to market needs.

More recently, the statewide Andhra Pradesh Urban Services for the Poor Project, which began in 1999, includes a component to address the specific needs of poor and vulnerable people in 32 towns. Towards this end, the project has supported a PPA aimed at identifying the needs and interests of poor people, which has involved local partners in the process. It includes a fund to support initiatives from NGOs, CBOs and municipalities, aimed at addressing these identified needs.

A new project being planned in Calcutta is likely to build on this type of initiative. It is also likely to take the economic development component of the Cochin project one stage further, by identifying opportunities to work within the macroeconomic and regulatory framework that affects the context within which poor people obtain access to, and security within, the labour market.

Disaggregating Poverty, Developing Policies and Projects

Alongside the development of new projects, the urban team in Delhi found that the International Development Department's (IDD's) classification of poor urban people's needs and priorities provided a useful starting point in developing its own framework for understanding urban poverty (IDD, 1999). Project experience has shown that many households encounter a number of interlinked shocks and stresses at any one time, and that they spend the majority, if not all of their lives, in a highly precarious state, balancing potentially difficult situations so that they can survive. This means that urban poverty is a dynamic condition. Both its characteristics and external influences change over time, and together these determine a household's capacity to cope, to improve its well-being, or its vulnerability to entrapment in chronic poverty or further impoverishment.

In 2000, therefore, DFID's urban team in India developed its own framework to understand poverty and vulnerability (Loughhead et al, 2001). It is intended, where possible, to incorporate this thinking in both future programme planning and support to on-going projects. DFID also links this understanding to discussions with the GoI whose own policies and Five Year Plan (Planning Commission 1999) recognize the need to incorporate different aspects of vulnerability in planning frameworks and anti-poverty programmes.

The framework builds on poor people's own priorities, described above, and captures the dynamic nature of their experiences. It demonstrates that households, and the individuals within them, move between three dynamic categories at different points in time. These categories can be described as follows:

- *Improving* households have a range of assets, including tenure security, more sons than daughters in a dowry culture, links to local leaders and saleable skills; they are in a position to increase their well-being and to take positive actions (such as investment in education) to do so.
- *Coping* households have some assets and are able to meet their basic needs, but they have no resources to deal with shocks and stresses, so are vulnerable. They are unlikely to increase their security and well-being without help.
- *Declining* households lack assets, suffer from multiple deprivation and are extremely vulnerable to shocks such as loss of earning, illness, eviction or a breakdown of support. These people include the elderly without families, the dying, the destitute, abandoned women, and victims of disability and severe illnesses, such as TB.

Table 14.1 demonstrates how these dynamic categories can be matched against poor people's priorities. It illustrates how all three categories of poor people – the declining, coping and improving – want their varied needs to be met, but that the way in which these needs should be interpreted and responded to differs according to their current conditions.

This analysis demonstrates that poor people require a wide range of interventions in order to support their varied needs. Traditional SIPs are clearly neither essential nor sufficient for meeting survival and security needs. Basic infrastructure and environmental services need to be part of a wider range of activities. In

Table 14.1 *Poor people's priorities*

	Declining poor	Coping poor	Improving poor
Survival	Free and accessible healthcare	Free or affordable healthcare	Affordable healthcare
	Cash, pensions, unemployment and disability benefits	Food subsidies and public works programmes	State and employer insurance schemes
	Food subsidies, legal aid	Financial services	Regulations against discrimination, etc enforced
	Housing/shelter	Community-based support	Financial services – loans
Security	Income stream	Income stream	Income stream
	Tenure rights	Secure housing tenure/ownership	Home ownership
	Basic education, plus some skills training	Skills up-gradation opportunities	Enterprise development schemes
	Savings schemes	Education, legal support	Loans for enterprises
	Community support systems	Savings and credit	Legal support
Quality of life	Participate in decision-making about matters of immediate concern	Participate in community-based decision-making	Health and safety at work
	Environmental improvements	Environmental improvements	Environmental improvements
			Political role

addition, those activities need to be differentiated to meet the needs of diverse households in very different situations, distinguishing particularly between households which can translate development opportunities into positive outcomes and those which are unable to take advantage of these opportunities or need special support to do so.

DFID's current programme in India is designed to take account of these diverse needs. The agency and its project partners have begun to take a more proactive and innovative approach towards urban poverty and vulnerability. Activities on the ground are increasingly combining a range of development and social protection measures. The former are targeted at those who are able to translate development opportunities into productive outcomes (such as to turn a training opportunity into a better job or a participation opportunity into a decision-making role). The latter are designed to:

- insure the improving poor against a reversal of fortunes;
- protect the coping poor against risk and to ensure some graduation prospects; and
- provide safety nets for declining households and individuals in order to support those who are unable (and may never be able) to look after themselves, and to create the possibility for graduation into the coping and improving categories.

A suggested list of activities, which many of the projects are beginning to unpack, is shown in Table 14.2. Activities to improve the capacity of poor people to take advantage of development opportunities include a range of educational and skills enhancement schemes, as well as improvements in the broad regulatory environment within which transactions are made, better access to loans for enterprise development, and the promotion of real opportunities to participate in political decision-making at council, ward and community level.

The long list of social protection measures on the right-hand side of the table demonstrates the diversity and importance of these interventions for *all* poor urban people. These create the enabling environment within which investments in social action programmes can produce social, economic and political returns.

This analysis of poverty and vulnerability, identifying the type and range of services that poor people need, has been complemented by a parallel examination of the wider institutional context which determines whether and how these services can be provided. Changes in how projects have been conceptualized as a result of this analysis are discussed in the next section.

POVERTY REDUCTION AND GOVERNANCE

As stated above, DFID India's earlier urban projects concentrated on the micro-level, namely the provision of environmental services to officially recognized slum communities in particular cities. The SIPs demonstrated that municipal services could be extended to slums on a large scale and permanent basis. This has contributed to an on-going programme of in-situ upgrading and regularization, preventing the disruption to livelihoods caused by relocation and contributing to the social integration of slum populations into cities. However, this site-specific approach often gave rise to serious problems when the infrastructure provided in slums was either not connected to city-wide networks (such as drainage), when city-wide systems lacked the capacity to serve extended areas (such as water supply, waste collection and disposal), or when the agencies responsible for operation and maintenance (such as drain cleaning and repairs to standpipes) had not been involved in implementation. The latter resulted in some systems breaking down soon after a project ended.[3]

As a result, there was increased recognition that the way that different service providers in a city are organized and financed affects the quality and efficiency

Table 14.2 *Examples of developmental and social protection activities to reduce urban poverty*

	Social action	Social protection
Improving poor	Appropriate education and skills training, matched to the job market	Essential social services: basic education, healthcare, water, sanitation, drainage, solid waste collection
	Improvements in the regulatory environment to assist job creation and economic growth	State and employer (or employee) insurance schemes (unemployment benefit, pension)
	Opportunities to participate in decision-making about distribution and usage of resources (within community and at municipal level)	Laws outlawing discrimination and exploitation (for example, core labour standards) enacted and enforced
	Financial services, such as loans for enterprise development	Financial services – savings and loans
Coping poor	Strong community-based social capital	Food subsidies and public works programmes
	Opportunity for secure tenure rights	Free and accessible healthcare
	Skill upgrading programmes	Community-based support systems – for example, financial services (savings plus small loans for consumption purposes)
	Community-based financial services – for example, loans for enterprise development	
Declining poor	Improve asset base (tenure, equipment and so on)	Free and accessible healthcare services
	Participate in decision-making about how to improve quality of life	Income (pensions, loans, insurance, disability benefit, and so on) to address immediate consumption needs (such as rent)
		Food subsidies
		Legal aid
		Housing/shelter for the abandoned elderly, women, the disabled, children

Source: Loughhead et al, 2001

of the service provided, and their capacity to maintain and replicate improvements. From the mid-1990s onwards, this led to an increasing focus on a more holistic approach to service provision, involving greater attention to an appropriate allocation of responsibilities, activities to support financial management reform and efforts to promote increased coordination between potential service providers. This city-wide approach to improvements in particular services has been adopted, for example, in the Cuttack Urban Services Improvement Project, which was approved in 1997. Emphasis has been placed on developing mechanisms to improve the linkages between environmental services provided within slums and city-wide systems – drainage, water, waste collection – accompanied by support to operation and maintenance systems.

In Cochin, the analysis has been taken one stage further. Here, emphasis is placed on developing the capacity of urban bodies to plan and manage their resources on a city-wide basis, and to link work with poor people to a broader city-wide poverty-reduction strategy. In this project, this capacity is being developed through the Urban Poverty Alleviation Department of Cochin Corporation which is tasked with delivering direct services to poor people, as well as acting as a nodal point for information for other service providers whose work impacts on the poor. These include other departments in the Corporation, other agencies in the city and NGOs.

Alongside these experiences in Cuttack and Cochin, DFID has also learnt that improvements in urban management at city level alone are necessary but not sufficient to reduce poverty on a sustainable basis. Changes in one city will not necessarily impact on state or national policy, or be replicated in other cities. More importantly, a city government's room for manoeuvre is constrained by the wider policy, institutional and economic context within which it exists. This means that sustainable reforms require an engagement with the broader policy and institutional environment at state and national levels, where policies are framed that determine the capacity of city-level players (local government, the private sector and civil society) to effect systemic change. DFID in its newer programmes has therefore increasingly sought to build on the opportunities afforded by India's constitutional reforms which promote decentralized government and some local autonomy.

These changes in the urban programme parallel recent thinking within DFID India as a whole. All new programme development is framed within the context of state strategies and state partnerships, guided internationally by DFID's commitment to work with other donors and national governments to achieve a set of International Development Targets.

The Andhra Pradesh Urban Services for the Poor Project, which began in 2000, is therefore based on a state-level partnership with the Government of Andhra Pradesh and covers 32 towns with populations in excess of 100,000. It aims to support the government's efforts to improve performance by bridging the gap between the responsibilities of municipalities and their ability to deliver services. In order to do this, it focuses on municipal reforms (improved financial, planning and implementation capacity), as well as financing direct support to the poor, including measures to strengthen civil society. Finance for slum improvements will be directed, on a challenge basis, through municipalities that achieve performance improvements in respect of revenue generation, financial management and development of an urban poverty strategy, and also demonstrate capacity and commitment to operate and maintain the infrastructure provided. A separate civil society fund should ultimately improve the capacity of poor people to make demands on the system.

Similarly, a new project currently being designed in Calcutta will work with the State Government of West Bengal and more than 40 municipalities in the Calcutta Metropolitan Area. It will also aim similarly to support institutional and financial management reforms to ensure the sustainability and replicability of interventions designed to benefit the poor directly and indirectly. The new Calcutta Urban Services Project is also likely to take some account of the economic and regulatory framework which affects the urban economy and hence the capacity of city governments to raise revenue, the role of the private sector, and the interrelationship between poverty and access to labour markets. Present discussions are focusing on local economic development efforts by municipalities in partnership with the private sector. In addition, this project is being framed in the context of a new partnership with the Asian Development Bank which is aimed at achieving environmental improvements in Calcutta.

DFID India's new Urban Poverty Reduction Strategy illustrates this progression (Table 14.3). The framework demonstrates increasing levels of complexity from the bottom to the top of the table, by showing the progression of DFID's projects over the last 20 years or so. The programme has built on the lessons learnt in earlier years and incorporated these in new project designs. Slum upgrading, for instance, is still an integral part of the current project portfolio, but is now packaged within a much more complex reform agenda.

CONCLUSION

The above sections have summarized the increasing complexity of DFID's urban projects in India. These projects have built on lessons learnt from past slum-level interventions and have become increasingly sophisticated not only in their analysis of poverty and vulnerability, but also in their understanding of the need to work at policy level. To meet their survival, security and quality of life needs, poor people need sustained access to appropriate services, as well as to labour markets. The necessity of engaging with the economic and institutional contexts which affect their access is now acknowledged.

The key lessons learnt during a 20-year period have been a recognition that:

- Poverty and deprivation is multidimensional and far from static. Responses therefore need to be wide-ranging and flexible.
- While some households are able to attain secure livelihoods and improve their well-being, many are unable to do this without assistance to increase their asset base and enable them to take advantage of development opportunities. Programmes therefore should directly engage in social protection measures for the most vulnerable.
- All households, whether improving, coping or declining, are vulnerable. They are vulnerable to shocks and stress, resulting from natural disasters, ill health,

Table 14.3 *DFID India's evolving urban poverty reduction strategy*

Intervention	Emphasis	Poverty angle	DFID projects

Urbanization	□ Rural/urban links
	□ District/state-level
	  planning
		□ Considers *all* poor
		□ Addresses poverty
		  at source	

Urban development	□ Investment
	□ Employment
	□ Economic growth
		□ Good labour markets
		□ Well-regulated
		  employment
		  opportunities
			Calcutta 2

Urban governance	□ Municipal reform
	□ Pro-poor policies
	□ Decentralization
		□ Responsible and
		  accountable elected
		  representatives
		□ From patronage to
		  civic rights
			Andhra Pradesh Urban Services for the Poor

Urban management	□ City planning
	□ Municipal finance
	□ Capacity building
		□ Poor 'planned' into
		  city
		□ Sustainability of
		  services
		□ Formal/informal
		  sector partnerships
			Cochin, Calcutta 1c

Urban services	□ City systems
	□ Stakeholder
	  participation
	□ Vulnerable groups
		□ Poor included in the
		  city
		□ Stakeholder choice
		□ Non-slum poor
		  included
			Cuttack

Slum improvement	□ Physical
	  improvements
	□ Area specific
	□ Community
	  initiatives
		□ Improved
		  environmental
		  conditions within
		  recognized slums
		□ Improved 'quality of
		  life' for the better-off
		  poor
		□ Skills upgrading
			Hyderabad, Vizag, Vijaywada, Calcutta 1a/b, Indore

Source: DFID India, 2001

violence, unemployment, a surplus of daughters, and so on. Appropriate social protection measures are necessary to protect all from risk and to ensure that reductions in poverty are sustained.
- Slum upgrading is a necessary but not sufficient condition for improving services to poor people. Infrastructure installation in slums needs to be linked to improvements in city-wide provision systems.
- City government management systems need to be improved to ensure that services are planned, financed and managed effectively, and meet the various needs of city populations.
- Reforms at city level need to be integrated with changes to state- and national-level policy frameworks. In an Indian context, this implies active engagement

with the decentralization agenda and government moves to increase local autonomy and democracy.

NOTES

1 Susan Loughhead was Social Development Adviser with the DFID Urban Poverty Group in Delhi from 1998–2000. This chapter has been prepared in consultation with a former member of the Urban Poverty Group, Dr Onkar Mittal, Health Adviser
2 In accordance with that policy, informal settlements (termed slums) had to be categorized into those eligible for regularization and upgrading, and those which, because of the ownership of the land on which they were situated or their unsuitability for residential use, were not considered suitable. Recognition as a 'slum' was desired, therefore, in order to qualify for infrastructure installation
3 In 2000, DFID was planning a second impact assessment in the same locations four years on from the original studies, in order to learn further lessons on the long-term sustainability of the improvements

REFERENCES

DFID India (2001) *Urban Poverty Reduction Strategy,* DFID, New Delhi
IDD (International Development Department) (1999) *Impact Assessment Study: Slum Improvement Project, Final Report*, School of Public Policy, University of Birmingham, Birmingham, for DFID
Loughhead, S, Mittal, O and Wood, G (2001) *Urban Poverty and Vulnerability in India: DFID's Experience from a Social Policy Perspective*, DFID, New Delhi
PIAS (Participatory Impact Assessment Study) (1997) *Calcutta Slum Improvement Project Main Findings Report,* Calcutta Metropolitan Development Authority and Urban Poverty Group of DFID, New Delhi
Planning Commission (1999) *Ninth Five Year Plan 1997–2002*, Government of India, New Delhi
Verma, G D (2000) 'Indore's Habitat Improvement Project: success or failure?', *Habitat International*, vol 24, no 1, pp91–118

Chapter 15

The Jamaica Urban Poverty Project

Sue Jones and Kingston Restoration Company

INTRODUCTION AND BACKGROUND

Starting with a pilot in one area, action is now being taken in 11 of the 17 or so inner city areas in Kingston, Jamaica. The Jamaica Urban Poverty Project (JUPP) illustrates what an NGO funded by donor agency money and working with communities can do to promote community action in poor and violent inner city areas. This case study focuses on how an urban poverty project, based on participatory planning and a people-centred approach, is developing and refining an implementation strategy as part of the process. The analysis first considers the way in which the project evolved. It then reviews what has been achieved. Finally, it assesses the contribution that this experience can make to the debate on urban livelihoods.

The political upheavals and feuding of the 1970s in Jamaica meant significant social and physical as well as economic changes in downtown Kingston. People fled from areas that were in turmoil and where buildings were being destroyed by fire and riots. The middle classes fled the country. People squatted where they could find space. Residents defended their areas, at times escalating into periodic gun battles between opposing groups over territory. Areas increasingly developed alternative systems of protection.

By the 1980s downtown Kingston was a series of blighted and dilapidated areas that presented a grim picture:

- An estimated 21 per cent of residents were below the poverty line.
- Practically all the children of poor families left secondary school (if they attended at all) without a certificate and ended up in the ranks of the unemployed.
- Poor or non-existent social amenities.
- Poor access to water, sanitary facilities, electricity, health provision and good quality education.
- Extremely high densities, as people squatted and built dwellings of temporary materials in what used to be middle-income housing compounds (yards) where basic facilities were inadequate for such large numbers.

- High rates of crime and violence.
- Abandonment of the areas by government services because of the disruptive violence.
- Disillusioned young people (61 per cent of poor residents are below 25 years of age), with little prospect of employment, given the high rates of unemployment (42 per cent of the labour force) and the stigma of an inner city address.

By the 1990s, gunfights had become the main way of resolving differences and territorial disputes. Police enforced a zero tolerance policy. Everyone was affected by the insecurity in these areas – children as well as adults and women as well as men. Gunmen would run into schools as protection. They knew the police would not risk a shoot-out in a schoolyard. During times of hostility, people could not leave their areas or cut across other communities to reach shops or services or to go downtown. When any trouble erupted, the few municipal services that were still being provided were immediately suspended. Taxis would not go into these areas.

So residential areas in the inner city were marginalized communities with little chance of changing their circumstances within the existing municipal management system. But there was also within these areas a strong sense of community and a determination on the part of residents to take action themselves. In the early 1990s, the Government of Jamaica (GoJ) had committed itself to a National Poverty Reduction Policy and to the use of a community-based approach. With a resurgence of violence in 1992, the National Inner City Committee asked Kingston Restoration Company (KRC), a non-profit public purpose organization, to undertake a pilot revitalization project. KRC had already built up a reputation and expertise through its regeneration work in downtown Kingston, rehabilitating productive space, improving the public environment and promoting community action.

KRC's new work began in 1995 in the pilot area of Jones Town. Planning students had made a physical and quantitative assessment of conditions in the area. With DFID support, KRC began to explore the possibility of developing this into a community-based, participatory approach to the problems of the area, promoting GoJ's poverty policy approach.

STAGES IN PROJECT EVOLUTION

The Early Pilot Work

A DFID-funded project, JUPP, began in 1997 with a series of participatory planning exercises with residents in Jones Town, using Participatory Rapid Appraisal (PRA) and Planning for Real techniques. At that stage there were very few local organizations to work through. An Area Council was in operation, but it had very limited membership and representation. Working with the Area Council and the local councillor, KRC worked directly with as many people in the community as it could. Based in the area, KRC field staff encouraged local people to become involved in developing community maps for their localities on street corners, by local bars and in local halls. The aim was for as many residents as possible to be involved in the process of identifying problems and possible action.

What emerged from this planning exercise was the priority given by the community to action in four key areas:

- *Education for change* To support children to keep them in school, to guide youths away from the drug gangs and to focus on the younger generation to help them to expect a different life.
- *Supporting enterprise* Identification of a range of business and employment opportunities for men and women.
- *Safer communities* To address the wide range of violent circumstances that people faced.
- *Security, shelter, services and the environment* Adequate and safe living conditions.

Residents, with help from KRC, identified initial entry points related to each. This became the basis of an implementation strategy for work in Jones Town. Starting with these four entry points, KRC helped residents, in participatory sessions, to identify small-scale actions that they could take themselves. The aim was to respond to what people saw as their needs, give the community the confidence that it could make a difference and show the government that something positive could happen (fairly easily) in these difficult areas. Residents who suggested small-scale action were encouraged to involve people in their locality, put together a proposal and organize and arrange action in a participatory way, with support from KRC. In this way local groups of people, many of whom had not previously been involved in any action, undertook a number of initial activities – a community newsletter, youths building a fence around an empty lot that they made into their own park, a mobile stage that could be rented out for musical events and improvement of an empty lot for a football pitch.

Consolidation in the Pilot Area

With this experience, people in the community began to gain confidence and to suggest new activities to KRC. The Jones Town Area Council had also benefited from its involvement in the initial community actions. It began to expand its membership significantly, especially of the more marginalized women and men within the community, to identify representatives for each locality and to play a larger part in project activities. The success of some of this community action, in spite of periodic local violence, meant greater confidence and some action in the area by government and utility agencies.

All of this was a gradual process, but by 1998 more substantive improvements, proposed by residents, were being undertaken by different 'committees' of local people in Jones Town. These eventually included the provision of signs for the area, made by local craftsmen; urban farms on vacant lots run by committees of local 'farmers'; a refuse amnesty to remove rubbish that had accumulated over the previous 10–15 years, creating a health hazard as well as providing cover for gunmen; a programme of support for the elderly; and supervised school homeworking and computer training in the office that KRC had constructed.

Community contracts were introduced whereby the local group undertaking action – for example, in the provision and management of sanitation in the yards – agreed to make contributions and take over the management of the facility concerned.

Expansion of the Project into Other Areas

No one had known what was possible at the beginning. By November 1998, KRC was helping four adjoining communities at their request, after they had seen the action in Jones Town. Based on the pilot area work, KRC had developed an overall framework for action with a community. By July 1999 this had expanded to an outreach programme in nine communities, with an established KRC team.

KRC's work (and role) was beginning to expand in several directions:

Upwards: KRC was more able to advise and become involved in strategic discussions with the National Poverty Eradication Unit and the GoJ.

Outwards: as other areas saw the changes that were taking place, they too began to approach KRC for support.

In depth: as KRC saw the possibilities, it began to consider how to consolidate the initial actions into more strategic support for the communities concerned and to build up income generation and shelter strategies.

Inwards: bringing in other partners (local groups and NGOs) to work with KRC and to help the communities themselves to develop as partners through strengthened Area Councils.

Through its work, KRC had also now identified the different types of communities that can be found in Kingston and the level of support/self-help needed in each:

- Type A *A (relatively) inactive CBO,* with few or no current developmental activities but a community in need, often with particularly difficult circumstances (such as violence). Such a community needs intensive support to generate any action.
- Type B *A weak CBO,* but in operation and wanting to take action. Such a CBO has some community support but limited capacity to undertake action without assistance. The community faces considerable problems. Comprehensive support is needed to generate community action.
- Type C *One group within the community* is promoting a specific development activity (such as youth actions), which might form the basis for wider community action, but at present has little community-wide support. In such a situation, the first focus is on generating some specialist action.
- Type D *The community has already come together to take action* and has undertaken some community action itself ('now' style action). Sometimes the community has been promoted/supported by an outsider (for example, an MP or donor agency), but residents have shown the capacity to organize

themselves, have a programme of action and are aware of possible sources of funding or agencies that might give help. Such a community is looking for support and/or sources of funding for bigger problems that it wants to tackle.

- **Type E** *The community is taking action but this is generally generated or organized from above* or by an outside agency or a wider group (maybe with political support). Any initiative has to go through these 'gatekeepers' and the possibility for generating 'bottom-up' action is affected.

This understanding was important because it indicated the different levels of support needed to help different types of communities to help themselves. With this understanding and experience of what action worked, KRC developed a more substantive and flexible model for inner city action (see Figure 15.1).

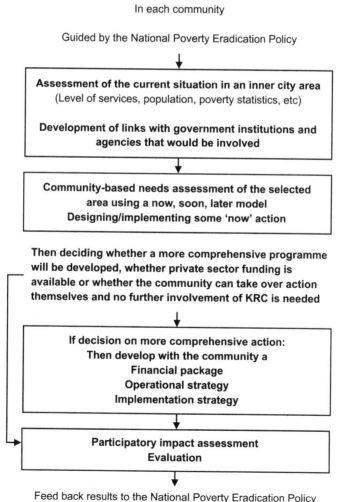

In each community

Guided by the National Poverty Eradication Policy

Assessment of the current situation in an inner city area
(Level of services, population, poverty statistics, etc)

Development of links with government institutions and agencies that would be involved

Community-based needs assessment of the selected area using a now, soon, later model
Designing/implementing some 'now' action

Then deciding whether a more comprehensive programme will be developed, whether private sector funding is available or whether the community can take over action themselves and no further involvement of KRC is needed

If decision on more comprehensive action:
Then develop with the community a
Financial package
Operational strategy
Implementation strategy

Participatory impact assessment
Evaluation

Feed back results to the National Poverty Eradication Policy

Figure 15.1 *The revised (July 1999) urban poverty-reduction approach of the Kingston Restoration Company*

Current Actions of JUPP

By 2000 the project had expanded to tackle inner city issues more broadly. KRC now:

- Has consolidated its work in 11 inner city areas with a modest team of five staff, a team leader and a secretary.
- Understands the dynamics for providing effective support in a range of communities and responding to different types of needs.
- Is currently handling or helping Area Councils/CBOs to undertake 74 community-based projects.
- Has established procedures and systems for a manageable outreach programme.
- Has established community contract arrangements that are accepted and adhered to.
- Is working with 27 private, public and NGO partners.
- Has helped to ensure that at least seven service providers have now returned and provide services in these areas.
- Is increasingly handing over local control and management to Area Councils and CBOs.

Most importantly, KRC has gained significant credibility with other key players. Both the Social Development Commission and the Jamaica Social Investment Fund, the other agencies concerned with social development and poverty reduction, are interested to develop joint work with the NGO.

KRC has also learnt some important lessons about approaches that do and do not work that will help others to develop poverty-reduction responses. The JUPP process has indicated just how long it can take to set up this type of participatory, demand-led work. A three-year cycle is clearly too short a period of time for pro-poor projects that aim to have a direct impact. Only now has KRC developed sufficient action and evidence of how GoJ's poverty policy can be operationalized to begin to influence policy. Just as significant, it has taken three years to reach and maintain the spend profile that was forecast for the project. Substantive community action/poverty responses require great patience to unlock action through a whole series of negotiations.

But it is not just the actual achievements of JUPP that are important. It is also what the project has done in terms of increasing the access of residents to decision-making, helping to open up a channel so that communities can say what they want, take action and show others the way forward. Increasingly, the Area Council in the pilot area has become a more democratic group with broader membership and local election hustings. Very gradually, it has taken over the management of local action. This process will be encouraged in other areas. JUPP has helped to strengthen social capital not only for residents, but especially for poorer and more marginalized groups within these areas who it has positively tried to involve in decision-making, through encouragement of their involvement either in the Area Council or in the residents' committees. All this had to be developed over time and in response to residents' needs.

Table 15.1 *Quantifiable achievements of JUPP*

Action in terms of	Identified numbers that have benefited
Environmental management	15,000 beneficiaries
Water and sanitation	846 beneficiaries, 30 housing compounds (yards) with improved water/toilet facilities, built and managed by the yard residents
Security and emergency services	500 beneficiaries
Health services	48 elderly people in Drugs for the Elderly programme
Transport	On average, one route taxi/minibus every 40 seconds where before there were none

MEASURING THE PROJECT'S ACHIEVEMENT

Table 15.1 provides some quantifiable measurements of what JUPP has achieved. But an assessment of impact and a more qualitative understanding of achievements from the communities' perspective has been an integral part of the project. An impact assessment has been undertaken as a participatory process with the communities. When residents decided on the indicators that were of most concern to them, safety and security were high on the list. The baseline and subsequent assessment of indicators, developed by and with the communities, confirmed the importance of improved safety and security for residents. But it is the actual words of a resident, Craig Town, that illustrate the changes in security:

> *For the past year and a half violence is low low. You can stand up at your gate until 2, 3 o'clock at night and nothing happen. You can sleep with the windows dem open and not a soul bother you. First time you could not go on certain streets. You just have to hold your corner. Or, you would hear someone shout 'Dem a come!' – who fi run, run gone lock up and who fi defend, tek up position. All dem tings de done now.*

The participatory monitoring of the indicators, in June 2000, showed how residents saw the impact of the project:

- The rate of violent crime had been falling dramatically.
- People's mobility between inner city areas was high, whereas at one time it was not possible to cross into another area without being in danger.
- The general provision of private transport services was good.
- There had been a significant growth of CBOs.
- Many examples were apparent of community-led problem solving.

However, since then there have been some interruptions in progress and occasional outbreaks of violence, so one cannot expect to measure success or impact in a straight line within such urban contexts. Rather, measurement needs to be made of the contribution of project activities to people's sense of security at different stages. An urban poverty project has to recognize its limitations: it can support people's attempts to improve their circumstances and livelihoods, but it cannot necessarily affect the underlying structural issues that make areas and households poor.

So while much progress has been made, the project cannot be seen in terms of clear before-and-after conditions. It has been a much more iterative process, responding to community needs; taking action as the community, groups of residents, vulnerable people and the Area Council identify and prioritize needs and request action; and also coping with the periodic violence that has disrupted action and has to be accommodated within the project. In such potentially difficult circumstances, the project was a learning process in a number of ways:

- *In terms of implementation* In the early days the focus was on entry point 'now' action that the community could take by itself. But increasingly it was clear that small-scale action was not enough and additional or related activities were organized – for example, an income generation strategy.
- *In terms of the approach* The pilot approach was an all-inclusive community development package, but it became clear that this was very resource intensive and not necessarily appropriate for all types of communities and the different circumstances of different poor groups.
- *In terms of the geographical spread of the project* KRC now operates in a wide range of community contexts where communities have different capacities to help themselves.
- *In terms of the community partnership arrangements that were built up* The initial proposal for a community development partnership was replaced by more local partnership arrangements owned by local people – strengthened Area Councils and community contracts.

JUPP AND A LIVELIHOODS APPROACH

It is interesting to consider an urban poverty project like the Jamaica project alongside the livelihoods approach now promoted by DFID and other agencies, such as CARE and UNDP.

JUPP provides a particular illustration of one type of urban poverty response. It did not begin as a large, national urban poverty-reduction programme. It started from a microlevel (a pilot in one neighbourhood) and has expanded from there into a further 11 inner urban areas, based on what did and did not work. Other agencies have adopted similar approaches in other inner city areas in Kingston, so the approach is now used more widely in the city. The project was in 2000 trying to engage policy-makers at the macrolevel. It is very much an illustration of an urban poverty implementation approach, addressing the problem from a bottom-up, participatory planning starting point. This is perhaps its most significant contribution to the current urban livelihoods debate.

Looking at JUPP in relation to a livelihoods approach, there are two questions to ask. If the livelihoods guidance and framework had been available from DFID at the time of project development for JUPP, would it have been designed differently? Conversely, what does the experience of JUPP contribute to the livelihoods debate?

The JUPP is based on participation. It is concerned with identifying different groups of vulnerable people in poor localities (such as youths, the elderly, children and women) and addressing their needs. The project began with an assessment of people's coping strategies. People themselves undertook a local skills survey. Action was based on their assessment of needs. Entry points identified by the community were used to start the process of addressing poverty issues. The project has been concerned to make macro–micro links and especially to begin to feed the experience back into policy considerations.

With hindsight, perhaps the most significant contribution the livelihoods guidance could have made, if it had been available at the time JUPP was being developed, would have been to give the design process greater legitimacy. A livelihoods approach would have provided an agreed approach within which to work, that was acceptable to the various stakeholders. At the time of the design of JUPP, no agreed framework or strategy for analysis and no approach for DFID urban projects was available. As with Stakeholder Analysis, the livelihoods analysis framework could have provided a useful categorization of interventions recognized by the donor agency. Especially with urban poverty projects, it can be difficult to convince a donor agency that projects can have an impact in such high-risk, poor circumstances. Urban poverty contexts are often so complex, so linked to difficult urban circumstances of insecurity and violence and so beset by political complications that donor agencies need to be convinced that a substantive output can be achieved. The way around this in the JUPP was to include, as an integral part of the project, a participatory impact assessment. An accepted livelihoods approach could have helped to establish indicators (with the community) that would have had immediate legitimacy with the donor agency. The participatory impact assessment indicators developed during the project have done this effectively.

In turn, the experience of JUPP indicates how a number of additional factors need to be taken into account in developing an effective livelihoods approach to tackle urban poverty: disaggregated analysis of poor households and their livelihood strategies; more guidance on the type of implementation process to adopt; and a more realistic (and pragmatic) assessment of potential achievements, given the political and community tensions and conflict that can affect the project process. These are elaborated below.

Analysis

The Jamaican experience demonstrates that, in an urban context, a livelihoods approach needs to make an explicit, disaggregated analysis of poverty:

- It needs to identify the different groups of poor people with different needs that typify urban poverty.
- It needs to take into account not only assets but constraints on the access of poor groups to resources and services.

- The framework for analysis needs to be able to reflect a very complicated social capital context. For example, in urban Jamaica, people do not just see themselves in household units or as individuals concerned with their own livelihoods. They are dependent on and concerned for each other, closely interlinked as they try to make ends meet. For example, youths meet together on street corners each day and often share their cash resources to organize food for themselves. This local social capital is critical.
- An understanding of how informal sector activities operate and intertwine with other aspects of individual and household strategies is essential.
- A livelihoods approach needs to assess the multilayered nature of urban poverty in a particular locality in order to be realistic about any improvements in livelihoods that can be expected. The problems are too intertwined and complicated for the full range to be tackled.

Implementation Guidance

As it stands, DFID's livelihoods framework would not have been able to provide guidance on an implementation strategy for JUPP. It needs to provide more guidance on the mechanisms or processes involved in addressing the needs of the poor in ways that they see as effective. In the JUPP, after the initial implementation period, it became clear that the small-scale actions being undertaken needed to be consolidated into more strategic activities covering each community more generally, as well as incorporating actions to address the special needs of vulnerable groups, such as the elderly or unemployed youths.

A More Realistic (and Pragmatic) Assessment of Achievement

Livelihood improvements in urban contexts are likely to result from negotiation, to be affected by outside circumstances and therefore to fluctuate. Attention needs to be given to the range of political and local circumstances that can disrupt livelihoods, treated only schematically in the summary diagram (see Chapter 1).

The implementation of support to the livelihoods of different groups of poor people in an urban context has to be capable of small-scale actions, providing scope for evolution and allowing for setbacks. The JUPP experience illustrates clearly that such flexibility and responsiveness, based on participation, community ownership and action, is the key to an urban poverty-reduction project.

Chapter 16

Strengthening Urban Livelihoods in Zambia – PUSH II and PROSPECT

David Sanderson and Darren Hedley

INTRODUCTION

In peri-urban settlements in developing countries, securing a livelihood can be complex and confusing. Peri-urban residents live in uncertain environments, with urban growth which outstrips economic opportunities, government services which are often reducing and deteriorating, rapid cultural change and increasing crime. People employ varied strategies, often living on credit and networks of support, undertaking seasonal work, earning incomes in the informal economy, shifting from one temporary household arrangement to another (see Chapter 1). Strategy outcomes often do not meet even the most basic of households' needs, increasing the vulnerability of those already marginalized.

Within this muddle, livelihoods-based approaches provide a map for analysing the problems of the urban poor and developing appropriate interventions. The starting point is vulnerable households and their livelihood strategies – how they secure the means of living, what assets they build up, the resources they need and use, and importantly, who controls these resources and how they do it. Since the mid-1990s CARE International has been implementing and refining its own livelihoods approach, household livelihood security (HLS). Born from rural methodologies concerning food security, livelihoods approaches find remarkable resonance in helping to interpret the complexities of urban living. Key aspects of the approach include:

- Vulnerable women, men and children are the starting point.
- The building and enhancement of household-level assets (both tangible and intangible) is at the heart of programming activities.
- A holistic analysis of programming problems and opportunities is followed by the implementation of focused intervention strategies that may be single or multisectoral.
- Interventions address different levels, from household-level asset building to municipal-level control of resources.

- Programming tools that are participatory and aimed at empowering those involved at all stages are used.
- Programmes require coherent information and learning systems. This implies not only good monitoring and evaluation, but also reflective and self-critical practice, feedback among participants and a knowledge base for the programme which is consciously evolving.

The following case study from Zambia seeks to illustrate these points. The study describes CARE's experiences of implementing urban livelihoods-based programming in two projects: PUSH and its successor, PROSPECT.

TRANSITIONS FROM PUSH TO PUSH II AND PROSPECT

One of the first projects that CARE Zambia implemented was PUSH (Peri-Urban Self-Help), funded by the Canadian International Development Agency and the World Food Programme. The two-year project involved 2000 poorer residents – mainly women – in rehabilitating roads and drains and solid-waste removal, in return for which they received food rations. In response to initiatives of the project participants and requests by the municipal councils concerned, CARE began a second phase in 1994, PUSH II, with funding from DFID, to elicit a more sustainable community development focus. PUSH II took place in three settlements or 'compounds' in Lusaka and one in Livingstone.

The aim of PUSH II was to reduce poverty by strengthening people's capabilities to initiate and maintain their own development. Key to this was 'ownership' of the prioritization of needs and the means of achieving improvements, as well as a shared understanding of the situation and nature of the challenge. To these ends PUSH II was designed as a process project, wherein specific outputs and activities were defined in consultation with residents. Hence the project began with an extensive Participatory Appraisal and Needs Assessment (PANA), which involved training residents and co-conducting exercises to prioritize and characterize critical issues affecting their livelihoods. Activities included semi-structured interviews, institutional inventories, listening surveys, role play to stimulate discussion and group analysis of the key issues.

In 1998, after extensive evaluation and consultation, PUSH II was superseded by PROSPECT (Programme of Support for Poverty Elimination and Community Transformation). PROSPECT maintains the PUSH II focus, but is considerably scaled up to 14 settlements with a population of 600,000, emphasizes institutional and policy strengthening and the role of the urban council, and includes a new element of environmental health. The following case study refers to PUSH II, as well as some innovations within PROSPECT.

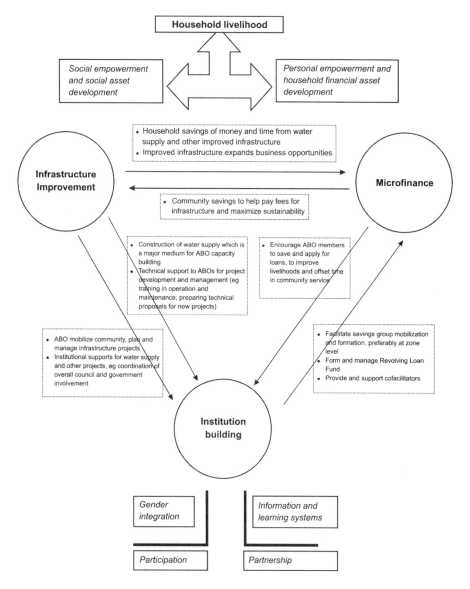

Figure 16.1 *PROSPECT conception of household livelihood security*

COMPONENTS OF PUSH II AND PROSPECT – HOLISTIC ANALYSIS, STRATEGIC FOCUS

Based on the conclusions of the 1994 PANA, PUSH II was structured into three components: personal empowerment (now renamed microfinance to convey the actual strategic focus), social empowerment (or institution building) and infrastructure improvement. This is represented in Figure 16.1, a diagram used currently by PROSPECT staff and the project's partners to show the interrelated nature of these programming components in support of livelihood security.

The programme interventions are founded on a base of participation and partnership, gender equity, and information and learning systems (including monitoring and evaluation), and ideally lead to a virtuous cycle of livelihood improvement through personal and social empowerment.

Personal Empowerment/Microfinance

Personal empowerment focused initially on the training of the 2000 food-for-work participants. A savings and loan system was designed specifically for income-generation needs, emphasizing group solidarity and opening a savings account as a guarantee for the loan. In PUSH II, 900 people formed savings groups and saved US$18,000, while loans were issued to 73 groups for a total value of US$10,000. These were 92 per cent repaid without recourse to drawing on the savings that were used as a guarantee. Monitoring is done through the composite indicator of 'livelihood categories', comprising elements such as number and content of meals and being able to send children to school. Over 70 per cent of residents reported having stable or improved livelihoods, in contrast to only 11 per cent in control groups. Since the prevailing view was that microfinance may be unsustainable for the very poorest, these achievements were encouraging.

In PROSPECT, this component has been revised to give greater emphasis to savings and institutional sustainability, and early pilot results show surprisingly strong capabilities in this regard. While repayments on the PROSPECT loans of US$15,000 are as expected, more notable is the fact that all the financial services societies – with some 1000 members – have been issuing loans from their own savings, worth approximately US$8000. PROSPECT's focus remains on the lower two of the four livelihood categories, as other microfinance providers (including CARE's PULSE) target the more economically active and advanced entrepreneurs, although as yet few of the very poorest are participating.

Particular concerns for the PUSH II empowerment training were women and their ability to retain control over resources. Prior to the training, many women stated that they did not participate in decision-making on household issues such as family planning or the use of income. Half of these women found a significant improvement following the training. An outgrowth of this activity was the training of groups of voluntary gender facilitators for educating the community. These facilitators also serve as referral agents in cases of property grabbing, a serious problem which frequently occurs following a man's death, in which his relatives seize all the family assets. This leaves the widow destitute and unable to support the children. In 2000, groups were at work in five areas and in some cases had evolved into universally recognized institutions of conflict resolution.

Social Empowerment/Institution Building

The aim of social empowerment has implied working concurrently at two levels: at neighbourhood level through the formation of representative area-based organizations (ABOs); and at City Council level through supporting policy reform and improved provision of services. Both activities aim to improve the supply of resources by mobilizing and managing at one end primarily internal resources, and at the other end accessing government resources.

Within neighbourhoods, given the weakness of existing organizations, a democratic process was initiated leading to the election of Zone Development Committees (ZDCs). A federal structure combines ZDCs into an area-wide structure (a Forum of Zone Representatives from which a development committee is elected). The structure and mode of formation are shown in Figure 16.2 and Box 16.1. Approximately 2000 members of ABOs have received training in leadership of community development, with topics such as participation and self-help, consultation and conflict resolution, planning and evaluation. People are encouraged to participate in ways they find familiar and culturally appropriate, such as with local proverbs, to help people find a deeper resonance with some of the ideas discussed. For example, *Uwawa, taimina* (Bemba) – 'He who falls does not rise on his own'; *Kupa nkwaanzika* (Tonga) – 'To give is to store', implying that giving is a form of savings, since the people you give things to will come to your aid in time of need.

Residents' Development Committee (RDC)

- *Elected by members of the Forum of Zone Representatives*
- *To provide compound-wide coordination*

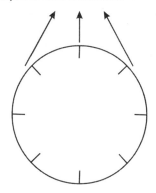

Forum of Zone Representatives

- *One man and one woman from each zone*
- *Coordination and decision-making on policy issues*

Zone Development Committees (ZDCs)

- *Several meetings and exercises to discuss and plan projects*
- *Grassroots accountability of ABO and project implementation*

Figure 16.2 *The structure of area-based organizations in project areas*

The ABOs play several roles. The most obvious is the organization of services, in particular water supply. However, their impact has been far greater. The process of neighbourhood organization has produced a platform on which residents can engage with Lusaka and Livingstone City Councils. Project activities have focused on improving the City Councils' ability to work with ABOs. These efforts include direct training of Council staff and their collaboration in project work in each settlement, regular meetings of ABOs and councillors, as well as the formation of a steering committee which oversees a number of issues, such as the ABO legal framework.

The Lusaka City Council (LCC) has been responsive to this approach, and has requested CARE to continue this support and also to assist in strengthening relations between Council staff and existing neighbourhood organizations (known as Residents' Development Committees) in all of Lusaka's informal settlements. Interest has also been shown by national government. Several ministers have visited neighbourhood initiatives, while the vice-president officially opened one of the water projects.

Water Supply and Infrastructure Improvement

The third major area of PUSH II was the implementation of projects to provide services, ranging from supporting pre-schools and gender educators to building bridges. The major priority of residents, however, was to have a piped water supply. To this end, CARE collaborated on a Japanese-funded project in George, Lusaka, a large informal settlement regularized and improved in the late 1970s, and from 1996 to 1997 implemented a water project in Chipata, an informal settlement on the northern periphery of the city.

The water scheme in Chipata is managed and owned by the RDC in the name of the residents of the area, with support from CARE and Lusaka City Council. The project involved extensive involvement of ABOs, which organized and educated residents. ABOs were key in the planning of the scheme, deciding the location and design of communal water points, the level of service required, and the residents' monthly fees and capital contributions. Community participation was such that an estimated 70 per cent of the families each contributed five days' labour in laying pipes (see Box 16.2).

Fees for using the water supply are paid to trained local residents who are employed by the scheme. By mid-1999 over 4000 families had subscribed. All operating costs are paid from these fees and the scheme already has US$13,000 banked towards capital replacements. In addition to CARE's support services, financial management support has been provided by the Council, and operational assistance from the Lusaka Water and Sewerage Company (LWSC).

After the Chipata scheme had been operational for two years, a major review was conducted, comprising extensive consultations and a survey, recommendations for improvement of the scheme, and a discussion among all stakeholders about the optimum future management system. The scheme assets will be handed over to the Lusaka City Council, and leased for a long term to a Trust with members from the ABO, other community members, LCC, LWSC and CARE.

Box 16.1 Overview of Area-based Organization Formation within an Appraisal Process

The model for moving into a new area and starting work is to operate in very close partnership with the Council in a combined PANA and ABO formation process. The following are the steps taken, although in reality, the various parts of the process often do not follow a straight line.

Surveillance (intelligence gathering)

CARE and Council officials begin to discuss what is known about the community, consulting with other agencies that may have worked in it. The Council officer then calls together some CBOs and other leaders to introduce PROSPECT. They discuss the major needs felt by the community, the number of CBOs and their relationships, the history of the compound and types of activities done in the past, as well as their willingness to work with CARE and to plan the next steps, including the eventual formation of a full ABO. Mapping, Venn diagramming, and historical time lines are some of the participatory tools used. At this stage, the concern is to understand some of the issues which will be faced in the process, but to avoid raising expectations too early, thereby running the risk of setting in motion distortions and biases.

Area-wide rapid appraisal

The existing RDC (or other CBOs) mobilize a group of residents to meet at a central point. The purpose of the meeting is explained to them, after which they are divided (disaggregated) into three groups – men, women and a mixed group – to confirm the issues discussed at the surveillance stage, expand the analysis and obtain more information. A number of participatory tools are used, such as causality analysis, problem ranking, an activity profile, a seasonality calendar and a historical time line. Residents are also asked about their knowledge of the existing RDC to get their perspectives on its representativeness.

Area-wide appraisal

At a certain stage, when CARE is sure that it is in a position to begin operations soon in an area, the process moves into a more intensive PANA phase. The area is divided into two or more sub-areas, depending on its size, and meetings are held in each area, facilitated by Council and PROSPECT staff and some community leaders. In addition to the procedure of the compound-wide meetings, residents arrive at a consensus on zone demarcations. From this meeting, a group of people volunteer to assist with the ABO formation process.

Zone-level meetings and elections

Zoning volunteers undergo a week-long training in non-partisan community participation, the role of an ABO and its structure, and how to facilitate discussions on the qualities of people to be elected to the ABO. After trial-run meetings to build the confidence of the volunteers, a series of three meetings are held in each zone, with a specific agenda for each, including election of the ZDC in the third meeting. Council officials facilitate the elections and generally residents nominate about 15 people who are qualified to be in the ZDC. Out of these, each person secretly writes ten names on a ballot sheet, each of which is counted in full view of everyone. Issues which come forward from the meeting are recorded for future reference.

BOX 16.2 *PARTICIPATION IN COMMUNITY DEVELOPMENT WORK*

Noah and his family members said that they were very active in the implementation of the water project in Chipata. He had come to appreciate the need for the project, in large part due to the education that was provided by the project staff on the need for clean and safe water. The rest of the family members said that they were motivated to work because the water they drank previously was from shallow wells and was not clean, the source was very far and they paid a lot of money for it. They also said that some people died in search of water, while others spent sleepless nights in long queues. All family members had to get involved, as water had to be fetched from a distance, but this is no longer so. Everyone felt the impact and was motivated to work. Noah was very involved in mobilizing people to work and would wake up his family early, leave them working on site and go to mobilize other people. His children participated in digging trenches, laying concrete and plastering. His wife Agnes dug trenches and poured water on the concrete. They said that they volunteered their services because they were convinced the project was going to bring them a lot of good.

Source: Excerpt from 'life story' of Noah and Agnes Musanshiko and Family, Chipata, Lusaka

---

KEY COMPONENTS OF LIVELIHOOD PROGRAMMING

The livelihoods approach provides a framework with which to map out factors that affect people's lives. These range from everyday relationships to achieve a common goal, to the influences which governments and other organizations have on those lives. The tools of livelihoods programming therefore seek to build household assets, improve resource access and control, reduce vulnerability and improve shared control over resources by making structures and processes more equitable.

Within PUSH II, components for implementing livelihoods programming were experimented with and refined. These components – participation, developing capabilities, building links between sectors – are already within the mainstream of development practice and are by no means unique to livelihoods thinking. This illustrates an important point: that a livelihoods approach as yet does not necessarily offer new tools for implementation; rather it provides a fresh perspective on existing problems.

PUSH has been noted in evaluations for the high degree of *participation* by residents. Key lessons learned in refining this process include:

- Guided participation, not 'participationism'. Participation fundamentally involves 'handing over the stick', letting residents take an increasing leadership role. It is, however, easy to fall into the trap of 'participationism', seeing development as a simplistic process of asking the community to 'identify the project they want to implement', or taking the opinion of a small group as being that of 'the community'. The key to meaningful participation is to establish respectful but honest relationships and equitable consultation.

- Taking time to avoid a disempowering charity approach. The fundamental question is always: how can residents be assisted to do this themselves in the long term, when outside agencies are not around? If a community avoids taking responsibility for what it can and should do, asking the project to pay members to participate, that must be challenged in a way that leads residents to realize that it would be in no one's long-term interest. Poor urban dwellers are sitting on a huge renewable resource – their own human and social capital. Development projects must tap that resource and use limited project resources strategically.

Capabilities can be thought of as the ability to do something – for example, the capability to work in teams, to consult equitably or to exercise leadership. Part of the project approach is analysing that capability in terms of what concepts, skills, attitudes and qualities are needed. In training to develop these capabilities, respect and support is needed for the way that residents understand them – for example, in Zambia love and prayer are commonly included among the ingredients of leadership or conflict resolution. Traditional proverbs and stories, powerful images and metaphors, songs and dances need to be drawn on to help people develop capabilities.

CARE sees its role partly as working to strengthen the three sectors of society – public, private and civil. PUSH focused more on the third sector, developing grass-roots capabilities and institutions. PROSPECT is expanding that focus by building links to achieve more effective coordination and policy impact with councils and the government, as evidenced by the work on community management of water supplies.

The livelihood aspects of PUSH II may be summarized as follows:

Building household level assets The project seeks to build assets in several ways:

- Through the promotion of income-generating activities and the development of savings and loans services to improve financial status (financial assets).
- Through personal empowerment and livelihood improvement training to increase knowledge and skills (human assets).
- Through involvement in ABOs and gender groups which builds community relationships for better group-based activities (social assets).
- Through the provision of local services, especially improved water supply (physical assets).

The building of assets is intended to lead to more secure livelihoods (such as through the increased ability to access resources, more available income to eat better or pay for education) and better resilience to shocks and stresses (such as increased quality and quantity of water, leading to fewer water-related diseases). For the long term, the building of household assets and community-owned structures and processes strengthens both households and communities for longer-term efforts to address other problems without outside intervention.

Using social capital CARE has seen the presence of many capable, enthusiastic residents who are willing to participate for the benefit of themselves and their communities. They have shown that they can construct and manage, relatively independently, complicated water-supply systems and bridges, intervene in cases of gender abuse, save money and manage loans. Women and the poor are among the best participators, which makes it even more important to ensure that they reap the benefits and are not subsequently marginalized from a newly established service.

Challenging structures and processes Council staff have enthusiastically taken on ABO formation and support as a legitimate role for themselves, and are beginning to gain credibility and the trust of residents. They have spearheaded the formation of 12 area-wide ABOs in Lusaka, have a task force which can assist in resolving conflicts, and are providing invaluable financial management training and auditing services. Some mayors and councillors have been very cooperative and played strategic roles in facilitating projects, while other politicians continue to make moves to control community participation for their own benefit. In addition to the established agreement with stakeholders on community management of water supplies, PROSPECT is now working to stimulate greater recognition among political leaders of the benefit of autonomous community-based development organizations.

Infrastructure development as the vehicle to promoting livelihoods Water-supply development is seen in the eyes of household members – and in particular, women and children – as providing a service that directly increases their livelihood security. The poorest save up to one-third of their incomes, previously spent on water from makeshift and inadequate sources, and improved health means reduced stress and medical expenses, and increased time available for productive work. It is also crucial that the process of infrastructure development and its subsequent management, combined with training and access to income-generating activities, strengthen capabilities for increasing the security of livelihoods.

Chapter 17

Lessons from the Experience of Some Urban Poverty-reduction Programmes

David Satterthwaite

INTRODUCTION

This paper discusses the experiences of a number of urban poverty-reduction programmes in Africa, Asia and Latin America and relates them to the livelihoods framework described in Chapter 1. These programmes highlight the importance for poverty reduction of changing the 'policies, institutions and processes' identified in Figure 1.1, both to improve the relationships between urban poor groups and government institutions, and to ensure responses from these government institutions that better serve poorer groups' needs and priorities. These programmes also demonstrate how tightly related the different components of the livelihoods framework are, and how challenging it can be to discuss any one of these outside the context of their mutually reinforcing relationships.

THE URBAN POVERTY-REDUCTION PROGRAMMES

This chapter draws mainly on a series of case studies of urban poverty-reduction initiatives that were prepared during 1999–2000 (see Box 17.1) as part of an International Institute for Environment and Development (IIED) project funded by DFID and the Swiss Agency for Development and Cooperation (SDC). In most instances, the authors of the case studies were involved in the formulation and implementation of the programmes they describe and they were asked to reflect on these programmes' strengths and weaknesses. This chapter also draws on a series of workshops on urban poverty-reduction held between 1995 and 1997 and the documents prepared for them with support from the Swedish International Development Cooperation Agency (Sida) and the Dutch Government (see Anzorena et al, 1998, for a summary of the findings).

Box 17.1 THE CASE STUDIES

Participation and sustainability in social projects: the experience of the Local Development Programme (PRODEL) in Nicaragua – Alfredo Stein

The age of cities and organizations of the urban poor: The South African Homeless People's Federation and People's Dialogue on Land and Shelter – Ted Baumann, Joel Bolnick and Diana Mitlin

Urban poverty reduction experiences in Cali, Colombia: Lessons from the work of local non-profit organizations – Julio D Dávila

Poverty reduction in action: Participatory planning in Barrio San Jorge, San Fernando, Buenos Aires – Ricardo Schusterman, Florencia Almansi, Ana Hardoy, Cecilia Monti and Gastón Urquiza

Community-driven water and sanitation: The work of the Anjuman Samaji Behbood and the larger Faisalabad context – Salim Alimuddin, Arif Hasan and Asiya Sadiq

El Mezquital, Guatemala City – A community's struggle for development – Andrés Cabanas Díaz, Emma Grant, Paula Irene del Cid Vargas and Verónica Sajbin Velásquez

SPARC (Society for the Promotion of Area Resource Centres) and its work with the National Slum Dwellers Federation and Mahila Milan women's groups in India – Sheela Patel and Diana Mitlin

Each of the above is published by IIED as a working paper within a series on poverty reduction in urban areas.

All the poverty-reduction programmes studied are a combination of direct action by low-income residents working to develop their homes and neighbourhoods and represented by CBOs, with some support negotiated from one or more external agencies (local government, national agency, national or international donor). Most work on different fronts, in response to the multiple deprivations that low-income groups face. All have the improvement of housing and living conditions and/or the provision or improvement of infrastructure and services as important components, both in recognition of the key role that these play in supporting household livelihoods, and because they also directly reduce such aspects of deprivation as ill health, injury and premature death, and heavy physical workloads. Most of the case studies also had, as a central goal, improving relations between urban poor groups and government (and improved performance by a range of government agencies). Most included support for employment generation, but the scale and scope of such support was limited by what was possible.

The experience of these programmes is discussed in terms of their contribution both to increasing low-income households' asset base and income-earning opportunities, and addressing other factors that create or maintain poverty.

INCREASING ASSET BASES

This section describes how the different programmes sought to increase the assets that form the basis of household livelihood strategies and some of the difficulties that some of them have encountered. The goals (and achievements) of these programmes, in terms of increasing asset bases, are not described easily in terms of the five kinds of capital assets highlighted in the livelihoods framework (see Chapter 1). For example, as described in more detail below, community-based learning blurs the line between social and physical capital, and community-based savings schemes create both social and financial capital. In addition, increasing poorer groups' access to natural capital, which is so central to most rural livelihood strategies, is generally inappropriate and does not capture the urban environmental problems that contribute most to urban deprivation.

Social and Political Capital

Social and political capital can be considered as the social resources on which people draw in pursuit of livelihoods (see Chapters 1 and 8). An important distinction can be made between social capital built on informal local networks and social capital derived from participating in formal market arrangements, the wider political system and civil society organizations (Moser and McIlwaine, 1999). Two of the most important aspects of social capital for groups of the urban poor are their capacity to form organizations which can undertake joint tasks, making best use of individual and community resources, and the potential of these organizations to negotiate resources and support from external agencies, especially the agencies that control access to land (or the right to occupy it), infrastructure and services. The relative importance of these two different aspects varies considerably between the different programmes, in large part as a result of what external government agencies are able and/or prepared to do. There are also obvious links between the two since the extent to which relations with external agencies prove useful in acquiring land and obtaining infrastructure and services influences the extent to which people organize to negotiate for these.

In regard to the first aspect, all the programmes emphasize the central importance of community participation, although there are also differences in the extent of ownership by low-income groups. At one extreme are programmes where community ownership is very strong (for example, in South Africa and India, with community leadership supported by the local NGOs, People's Dialogue and SPARC); at the other extreme are the programmes of private non-profit organizations in Cali which are designed and directed by professionals, although they are also changing to reflect community needs and priorities. All the initiatives saw the need for continuity over time and aimed to support processes, not one-off short-term projects. However, the scope for such long-term support was often limited because, for instance, an external agency may consider that once it has supported one project in an area, it is inappropriate to support another.

One inevitable constraint on the development of informal (and formal) social capital within low-income communities is the negative influence of authoritarian or paternalistic external agencies. This also results in a lack of experience with any form of democratic process, limited resident involvement and scepticism about the prospects for positive outcomes. For instance, the Argentine NGO supporting community-based development found that there was little community reciprocity, representation, accountability or participation in Barrio San Jorge, the informal settlement in which it began work, and that the most frequent reactions to any community initiative among most of the inhabitants were passivity, scepticism and mistrust. Attitudes such as these are probably not unusual in places where the inhabitants are suffering extreme poverty and where there is a history of little or no positive support from external agencies. While many of the inhabitants in Barrio San Jorge now show a change in attitude, contribute to water and sanitation costs, show solidarity with families in the worst situations and are actively involved in negotiations with local government and private companies on the provision of services, this has taken a long time (certainly longer than any project cycle) and there are no obvious shortcuts to accelerate this process (Schusterman and Hardoy, 1997).

Another important feature of several of the initiatives is an explicit attempt to create conditions in which women can take lead roles. For instance, the South African Homeless People's Federation creates conditions for women to take lead roles in community processes, including being at the forefront of community negotiations with external agencies (a role usually reserved for men). Men are never excluded, but new leadership opportunities are for collective rather than individual actions, and in many low-income communities, a collective approach appeals more to women than to men. The experience of the programmes reviewed shows that initiatives which strive to increase gender equality are often met with suspicion and may give rise to tensions, as established patriarchal organizations, accustomed to controlling resource flows and dominating development in informal settlements, perceive these new groups as a threat. This generally changes over time when the material benefits of an initiative for the whole settlement become clear.

Nearly all the initiatives consciously sought to strengthen the capacity of community organizations to negotiate for resources and support from external agencies – usually local government agencies since it is only through these that land, infrastructure and services can be obtained. In the long term, much poverty reduction in urban areas depends on the quality of the relationship between the inhabitants of low-income settlements and all the public agencies that influence their pursuit of livelihoods and access to infrastructure, services, land, justice, and so on. It is difficult for international agencies to play a role in improving such relationships if their institutional and financial structure is set up to fund 'projects'. For instance, in Bombay/Mumbai, it is the capacity of the women pavement dwellers to negotiate access to land on which they can develop their own housing that has such importance for improving their asset base. The same is true in South Africa, where improved well-being depends, among other things, on the capacity of each group within the South African Homeless People's Federation to negotiate access to land and (where possible) government housing subsidies, to support the self-help solutions they develop themselves, rather than contractor-built housing developed 'for' them. In Barrio San Jorge in Argentina, it was the residents' capacity to negotiate for land tenure and access to a nearby site, to decongest the existing settlement and allow families most at risk of flooding to obtain new plots, that did most to increase their asset base.

Two of the main roles of support NGOs in most of the programmes were to increase the capacity of low-income communities to develop their own projects for presentation to external agencies and to enhance residents' negotiating skills and collective leadership capabilities. These are key elements of human capital, but also of social and political capital.

Sometimes, the most effective international support will be that which supports low-income groups working autonomously because there is little or no possibility of support from local authorities. In Faisalabad (Pakistan), the Anjuman Samaji Behbood sought to develop improved water and sanitation provision for which low-income households could afford to pay full costs, since there was little possibility of getting the local water and sanitation agency to do so. It drew on the early work of the Pakistan NGO Orangi Pilot Project which supported community-directed sewer construction in Karachi. As in Karachi, 'sustainability' and 'going to scale' were only possible if significant improvements could be made in the absence of government support, at a cost that low-income households were able and willing to pay. In the case of El Mezquital, the support of international agencies for improved infrastructure and services was critical because municipal agencies were weak and disinterested. It was only when the achievements of the community-led initiatives became evident that the possibility of support from government (in this instance a national agency, not the local authority) increased. This was also the case for the Barrio San Jorge programme: municipal agencies had little interest at the outset, but later came to draw heavily on this experience in supporting new poverty-reduction initiatives that sought to greatly increase the number of households reached.

The approach developed by the Indian NGO SPARC has particular relevance and is one that has been followed (with local adaptations) by many other NGOs. It involves two critical components. The first is the development of pilot projects with low-income groups and their community organizations to show alternative ways of doing things (for example, building or improving homes, running savings and credit schemes, or setting up and running public toilets). The second is engaging local and national officials in a dialogue with communities about these pilot projects and about how they can be scaled up (or the number of such initiatives multiplied) without removing community management. The negotiation with government agencies can be done with constant reference to what has already been achieved, an important part of which is bringing government officials and politicians to visit the pilot projects and talk to those who implemented them. This approach includes demands made on government agencies, but by being able to demonstrate solutions, engagement with these agencies (or with politicians) is more productive. The pilot projects stimulate other groups to initiate comparable actions and, as described in more detail later, there is a constant interchange between those involved in different community initiatives. This then leads to work to change local institutional constraints on community initiatives – for instance, changing building regulations to enable housing developments to better suit the needs of low-income groups; participating in the design and realization of a new state policy for legalizing and improving housing for the poor in Mumbai; and proposing and implementing schemes for the resettlement of urban communities in which the resettled people have a key role in determining the location, timing and form of their relocation.

Although the Local Development Programme (PRODEL) in Nicaragua has many concrete achievements, between 1994 and 1998, the 260 community infrastructure projects it supported in eight different cities were always seen as a means of developing more effective relationships between municipal authorities and community organizations formed by the urban poor, and this may prove to have made a more important contribution to poverty reduction than the specific items that were funded. The importance of many of the programmes funded by local foundations in Cali is as much in demonstrating to government how to provide schools and healthcare, support self-build and microenterprise development and develop recreational facilities in informal settlements where government agencies would not enter, as in what they actually funded.

Physical Capital: Housing and Basic Infrastructure

Although most initiatives have several components, the improvement of housing and living conditions (including secure tenure) and/or the provision or improvement of infrastructure and services is an important component in all of them. For the poverty-reduction initiatives reviewed here, housing was recognized as having benefits that included this, but they went far beyond it. There was a recognition that better quality and more secure housing with good quality infrastructure and services is highly significant in household well-being. For many of the poorest households – for instance, households who live in very rudimentary shelters on sites from which they are constantly at risk of eviction, such as the pavement dwellers in Bombay/Mumbai – obtaining a secure home of their own in a settlement they helped to create and continue to help to manage is a transformation. For most poor women and men, acquiring and developing their own homes through self-help or mutual aid not only provides them with their single most valuable asset, but it also means that they no longer have to pay rent or to squat at a constant risk of eviction. It allows households to convert daily expenditures on housing into assets - for instance, SPARC found that over 20 years many Indian pavement dwellers spend the equivalent of the cost of a small apartment in repairing their pavement dwellings, but in the end are left with no assets. In many cities or areas within cities, a house is an asset, the value of which rises in real terms over time. Obtaining a secure house also means that households can negotiate for access to infrastructure and services. In addition, obtaining a legal house may be essential for obtaining key state entitlements – for instance, enrolling children in school or obtaining healthcare or access to subsidized food. The range and diversity of benefits that better quality, more secure housing can provide for low-income households in urban areas is often not appreciated by external agencies. Nor is the fact that supporting community-driven house-construction programmes can reduce unit costs (so many more households can be reached with limited resources) and can be funded in part by loans. These points were particularly evident in the studies in India and South Africa.

In addition, there are important links between enhancing physical capital and improving access to other assets. Improving housing and basic services can greatly reduce the health burden associated with poor living conditions (see

Chapter 10). Aside from the benefits of good health for people's ability to work (part of their human capital) and for avoiding expenditures on healthcare and medicines, good health is also central to a satisfactory quality of life and therefore an end in itself. Small enterprises based in people's houses are important for many households' livelihoods (see Chapters 7 and 12), as confirmed by the demand for microenterprise loans in several of the programmes studied. Such economic activities are often particularly important for women, perhaps because they allow income-earning to be combined with looking after children or because of social controls that restrict women's ability to work outside the home. The quality of housing also has a very large impact on children's physical, social and intellectual development. Any improvements are likely to have a positive impact, not only by providing safe, more stimulating and more varied environments, but also by easing parental anxieties linked to insufficient space and poor facilities (Bartlett et al, 1999).

Access to Credit and Financial Capital

In most of the initiatives reviewed here, savings and credit schemes had an important role in enabling low-income people to afford better quality housing or basic services; in some, they also had an important role in helping households cope with crises (see Chapter 7). Credit can provide the means by which low-income households can spread the cost of more expensive capital investments and can make previously unaffordable capital costs affordable (see Chapters 7 and 13). In many cases, savings schemes are linked to housing improvement activities. However, inevitably, the capacity of low-income groups to save is limited. In most urban settings, they cannot save enough to allow them to afford adequate quality housing within legal private land or housing markets. Nevertheless, many low-income households have shown themselves able to afford loans for improving existing housing, installing infrastructure or building a house once a plot is acquired.

In several of the initiatives, especially in South Africa and India, savings and credit has another, perhaps more important role as a means of mobilizing poor people. One slogan of the South African Homeless People's Federation is that their savings schemes collect people, not money. As the members of each savings scheme develop their own savings account from the very limited funds, they develop a material stake in their organization and its decision-making. Saving encourages regular interaction and enables strong bonds to be created. Such savings schemes also create a space for the central participation of women who are usually more interested than men in saving for credit and housing. Finally, savings and credit schemes enable community organizations to develop the capacity to manage and control finance and to demonstrate this ability to the outside world. Cost recovery and loan repayment rates are generally higher in these community-controlled schemes than in the ones managed by external agencies.

Natural Capital

There is considerable confusion in the literature as to what is meant by natural capital and its role within sustainable livelihoods. Most discussions of natural capital fail to distinguish between environmental hazards and environmental degradation, or they classify environmental hazards as part of natural capital. A very large part of the health burden suffered by most low-income groups (in both rural and urban areas) arises from environmental hazards, including biological pathogens (and their vectors) chemical pollutants in the air, water, food or soil, and physical hazards. Within most urban settlements with poor quality housing and a lack of provision for basic infrastructure and services, there are many environmental hazards (and high levels of environmental risk) but little evidence of the depletion of natural capital (that is, damage or destruction of natural resources such as soils, forests or fisheries; ecosystem malfunctioning; the overuse of fresh water or scarce mineral resources; or high levels of waste generation and greenhouse gas emissions).[1] All the poverty-reduction case studies included major components that seek to reduce environmental hazards or their health impact. Some also seek to improve the quality of the environment through, for instance, setting aside and managing public spaces or providing facilities for sport and recreation.

The links between households' access to natural capital and their livelihoods is clearly important in most rural areas and may be important in urban areas for those households who rely on access to land for urban agriculture (see Chapter 5). But a discussion of the links between natural capital and poverty has to avoid equating environmental risk with environmental degradation. In addition, any discussion of poverty has to give adequate attention to the extent to which environmental risks underpin high levels of ill health, injury and premature death.

Human capital

Chapter 1 notes that human capital includes the quantity of labour resources available to households, levels of education and skills, and the health status of household members. The distinction between informal social capital and human capital becomes blurred in many of the case studies in which the initiatives under review support collective skill and knowledge development among households.

The alliance formed between SPARC, *Mahila Milan* and the National Slum Dwellers Federation in India places a high priority on training, in part because this prevents the consolidation of power in the hands of a small number of dominant leaders, in part because it also increases people's confidence and reduces the need for full-time professional staff. The training operates through community exchanges in which people from one low-income settlement visit other low-income communities. The learning is achieved as one group observes how another is approaching a common problem and then works alongside it. The exchange process takes place at three levels: between settlements in the same city, between settlements in different cities in India and internationally (in particular with the South African Homeless People's Federation). These exchanges are not primarily for NGO staff, but are for community members who are active in organizing savings and credit schemes or developing projects. They increase each local organization's ability to learn from others' experience and to negotiate with government and local authorities.

The South African Homeless People's Federation also ensures a constant interchange of experience between its 2000 or so member groups. Newly formed savings groups have the opportunity to visit savings groups that have succeeded in negotiating land for housing (including some that have succeeded in obtaining modest government housing subsidies) and building their own (good quality) homes in neighbourhoods with infrastructure and services negotiated from other government agencies. Members can see the quality of the (typically four-room) homes constructed by people like themselves, discuss the appropriateness of the design and find a full costing of all aspects of house construction.

The Homeless People's Federation recognizes that, without pressure from communities, state agencies rarely produce alternatives that serve low-income households' needs. The challenge is to ensure that communities contribute practically and cohesively to the planning and implementation of improvements, without being disheartened by the uncertain and usually lengthy process. Drawing on the Indian experience, the Federation has introduced a community-based training and house enumeration exercise that produces a detailed map of a settlement. This is undertaken by members of other settlements' housing saving schemes who have mastered the process, members of the local settlement's savings scheme and members from other settlements who are interested in learning the process. The enumeration exercise is a participatory mapping conducted by several teams and allows the local organization to gather a fairly accurate picture of the settlement and its inhabitants, and of the different needs and priorities expressed by individual households and groups. People then begin to discuss what kinds of houses they want to build – for instance, through building models using different kinds of materials, from cardboard boxes to tins. It is also common in both India and South Africa for full-scale house models to be built collectively. These allow a more detailed discussion of the most appropriate design and use of space. In many of the case studies, technical improvements have been most effective when developed by the communities themselves, and then spread and adapted through horizontal exchanges of information and experiences with other settlements.

The international exchange programmes have been expanding to support initiatives in other countries, including Zimbabwe, Namibia and a number of Asian countries (where the Asian Coalition for Housing Rights has also supported such exchanges). An international umbrella organization made up of representatives from these different groups, Shack Dwellers International, also seeks to support such exchanges.[2]

Human and social capital can easily be damaged by external agencies. One of the most damaging aspects of many externally supported poverty-reduction programmes is the extent to which the professionals that manage them assume that they know best regarding the most appropriate use of resources, technologies and forms of intervention. One of the keys to building human (and social) capital is supporting processes which allow low-income households to develop their own solutions, such as houses, water and sanitation systems, healthcare programmes, savings and credit schemes, and day-care centres. This does not necessarily imply self-help construction, although circumstances dictate that there is often no alternative. The financial management of savings and credit schemes has been developed successfully by many local groups and the acquisition of financial management skills is particularly important for successful housing improvement. This is because, while securing land is crucial, there is little point in negotiating for it if the households and communities involved do not have the resources that are necessary to develop the land. There is a need for communities to be ready with strategies for residential development as soon as land or tenure of the land they already occupy is obtained. However, in the programmes of the South African Homeless People's Federation and of the SPARC–*Mahila Milan*–National Slum Dwellers Federation alliance, one major difficulty has been finding professionals – for instance, architects and engineers – who can listen and respond to low-income households' priorities and who do not try to impose their own 'solutions'.

Raising Incomes/increasing Employment

Raising incomes and supporting new employment opportunities should be the most direct form of poverty reduction in most urban areas since higher incomes should allow low-income households to meet their consumption needs, increase their assets and afford better quality housing and basic services. But these often present the most difficulties, both to low-income households themselves and to external agencies (from local authorities and local NGOs to national agencies and international donors), because they lack the means to increase the prosperity of a city and/or improve employment opportunities or income levels for low-income groups (see Chapters 6, 7 12 and 13). This is not to say that there is no scope for employment generation or microenterprise development, only that initiatives must be rooted in an understanding of the real potential and constraints.

Interventions that centre on improving housing, infrastructure and services do create some additional jobs, especially when they are designed in ways that maximize employment opportunities for the settlements in which they are implemented, rather than relying primarily on external contractors. But interventions to improve conditions and services are unlikely to increase incomes for more than a small proportion of the population. In El Mezquital (Guatemala City), despite the success of the externally supported, community-driven development which has improved housing conditions, infrastructure and services (and health), the fundamental problem of inadequate incomes was not addressed, apart from the short-term jobs generated for around 1000 people by the public works. Similarly, in Barrio San Jorge in Buenos Aires, housing conditions and basic services have improved greatly and some additional employment opportunities have been created. However, for most households, income levels have not increased and for many they have declined in real terms, largely as a result of the poor economic performance of the Argentine economy.

Improved infrastructure will generally support more productive enterprises within a settlement – for instance, through the availability of electricity, improved water and waste removal, and paved access ways. It can also increase real incomes by reducing costs – that is, by being expenditure reducing rather than income-generating. Examples include a piped water supply that not only improves provision but also cuts expenditure on water purchase from vendors, or a primary healthcare centre that reduces ill health (and its economic costs) and reduces the cost of treatment for those who fall sick or are injured.

Any poverty-reduction intervention in which low-income households can influence the design will seek, where possible, to support increased incomes. The PRODEL programme in Nicaragua, along with its support for infrastructure and community works and loans for housing improvement, included microfinance loans of between US$300 and US$1500 which supported 2400 enterprises. The South African Homeless People's Federation has concentrated on obtaining land and supporting housing development for the 80,000 households that form its member groups, but it has also developed funds to support income-generating activities and is seeking to integrate support for microenterprises and facilities to encourage new businesses in its new housing developments. In Cali, one of the focuses of the main local non-profit foundations was support for micro-enterprises (including training, advice on business development and access to credit) and small shopkeeper programmes (which included training and access to the wholesale stores). Between 1977 and 1996, 24,500 small-scale entrepreneurs received training.

These experiences illustrate that, despite local organizations' lack of influence over wider economic trends, there may be scope for generating new jobs, increasing incomes, supporting new enterprises and maximizing local multipliers. They also demonstrate the need to locate these efforts within broader community development programmes and to ensure that they are based on a realistic appraisal of local and wider constraints.

CHANGING RELATIONSHIPS THAT PREVIOUSLY CREATED OR MAINTAINED POVERTY

Most of the case studies highlight how changing the relationships between poor groups and local government agencies and political structures is a central part of poverty reduction. In the programmes in Nicaragua, South Africa, Pakistan, Argentina and India, alliances with local NGOs proved to be important in supporting poor groups' capacities to deal with local authorities and the agencies of higher levels of government. The programmes in South Africa and India were unusual in their emphasis on supporting not only the development of inclusive community-based groups among the urban poor, but also city-wide, regional and national federations of such groups which increase the potential for negotiating with higher levels of government. The scope for successful negotiation depends on the responsiveness of government structures and the presence of political and legal frameworks that provide some protection for organized urban poor groups. To state the obvious, perhaps the South African Homeless People's Federation could not have worked as it does within the former apartheid government structure.

SOME TENTATIVE CONCLUSIONS

For most low-income urban households, a real reduction in poverty is a long and complex process since it requires reducing many different aspects of deprivation

– for instance, insecure and badly paid employment, lack of basic services, illegal land occupation, poor quality housing, low educational attainment, high levels of permanent disablement within the population, dangerous residential locations, peripheral locations in relation to income-earning opportunities, high levels of violence, and a distrust of external agencies generated by years of repression and/ or broken promises. Ironically, the new stress on livelihoods comes at a time when the possibilities for the urban poor to find safe, adequately paid employment and secure sources of income have diminished in many instances, and when governments and international agencies have never been so powerless to address the problems. Governments and international agencies are promoting more open economies, which in turn increase competition in the labour markets in which poor people with few assets and skills must survive.

The other aspects of deprivation described cannot be eliminated through one-off, single-sector projects, but require coordinated action by many different agencies, on many fronts and in many settlements. In each settlement, action needs to be developed in a form and at a pace that responds to the specific needs of the inhabitants, keeps down costs and ensures that there is a local capacity (within the community or local government agency) to maintain the new or improved buildings and infrastructure and fund the operation of new or improved services. Supporting the multiplicity of local processes and institutions that may help to reduce different aspects of deprivation is never easy for any external agency, whether a local NGO or local government agency or an international aid agency.

What the case studies highlight is the importance for poor urban groups of 'good governance'. Government institutions are particularly important for poorer urban groups in that only these can ensure the rule of law and the presence of democratic and accountable political and bureaucratic structures (see also Chapter 13). The way that government institutions function has tremendous implications for the scale and nature of poverty; indeed, their actions often exacerbate deprivation. As Amis has demonstrated (Chapter 6), governments have large capacities to destroy or curtail livelihood opportunities for poorer groups. They also have large capacities to limit the possibilities of urban poor groups finding or building housing and getting access to basic services. However, public agencies neither can nor should attempt to provide all assets, services and work opportunities directly themselves. Given the complexity and diversity of urban poverty and household strategies, responses must also be diverse.

The poverty-reduction programmes emphasize the key role of local organizations which are capable of providing services or access to resources, as well as the need for controls on 'bad' governance. Most of these local organizations should be government agencies fulfilling their roles and responsibilities in regard to ensuring infrastructure and service provision, the protection of civil and political rights and law enforcement, including protecting poorer groups from discrimination, exploitation, violence and other crimes. Private organizations such as CBOs, NGOs and occasionally private enterprises therefore also have important roles in poverty reduction and for external agencies may be the only means of supporting poor groups if public sector organizations are ineffective, uncommitted to increasing the well-being of the poor or corrupt.

Better governance may be given too little attention if a livelihoods approach concentrates on increasing the assets and capabilities of 'poor' individuals and households rather than on addressing deprivation that is more linked to the failures or limitations of both the political and administrative/bureaucratic aspects of government. Many of the 'poverty-reducing' actions in the case studies reviewed here relate on the one hand to secure, healthy housing, basic infrastructure and services, and on the other to more inclusive political and legal structures and improved working relationships between urban poor groups and government agencies.

NOTES

1   The lack of any association between urban poverty and environmental degradation and the strong association between urban poverty and environmental risk is discussed in more detail in Hardoy, Mitlin and Satterthwaite, 2001
2   The work of Shack Dwellers International and the national federations of urban poor groups that it represents is described in vol 13, no 2 of *Environment and Urbanization* (October 2001)

REFERENCES

Anzorena, J, Bolnick, J, Boonyabancha, S, Cabannes, Y, Hardoy, A, Hasan, A, Levy, C, Mitlin, D et al (1998) 'Reducing urban poverty: some lessons from experience', *Environment and Urbanization*, vol 10, no 1, pp167–186

Bartlett, S, Hart, R, Satterthwaite, D, de la Barra, X and Missair, A (1999) *Cities for Children: Children's Rights, Poverty and Urban Management*, Earthscan, London

Hardoy, J E, Mitlin D and Satterthwaite D (2001) *Environmental Problems in an Urbanizing World*, Earthscan, London

Moser, C O N and McIlwaine, C (1999) 'Participatory urban appraisal and its application for research on violence', *Environment and Urbanization*, vol 11, no 2, pp203–226

Schusterman, R and Hardoy, A (1997) 'Reconstructing social capital in a poor urban settlement: the Integrated Improvement Programme in Barrio San Jorge, Argentina', *Environment and Urbanization*, vol 9, no 1, pp91–119

Part 5
Conclusions

*The first chapter in this concluding section considers whether a liveli-
hoods approach and framework provides an effective mechanism for
the design and implementation of new projects and programmes. Sue
Jones assesses the potential contributions of a livelihoods approach
and identifies a range of issues that would need to be resolved during
project and programme design and implementation. The final chapter
provides an overall conclusion to the book by identifying key issues
and themes, and reviewing the potential contribution of a livelihoods
approach to understanding and reducing urban poverty.*

Chapter 18

Issues in Designing New Projects and Programmes

Sue Jones

INTRODUCTION

An assessment of the lessons learnt from early experience of a sustainable liveli-hoods approach in a rural context clearly sees it as having a practical value: 'SL approaches can enhance the effectiveness of development activity . . . Practical application of SL approaches . . . represent[s] a positive way forward' (Ashley and Carney, 1999, p3).

The concern in this chapter is to consider whether a livelihoods approach/ framework might provide an effective mechanism for the design and implementa-tion of new projects and programmes in the urban context, identifying both the potential contribution of the approach to more effective poverty reduction and issues which will need to be resolved during the process of programme and project design and implementation.

A consideration of the practical implications of urban livelihoods analysis is complicated because of the range of debates about poverty responses and their effectiveness. In the context of high levels of uncertainty, a number of questions need to be posed. First, no clear poverty policy guidance is available:

> *As yet, the literature provides little guidance on which policies are most effective in poverty reduction, sequencing (which assets should be strengthened first and for whom) . . . or sustainability (non-reversibility of improved well-being and environmental sustainability)* (Rakodi, 1999, p25).

Does a livelihoods approach provide guidance in selecting the most effective interventions, or is it only a broad tool for holistic analysis – a useful exercise but not able to provide a badly needed lead on effective urban poverty action? Is it realistic to expect a livelihoods approach to provide answers or should it be seen as a contribution to help professionals agree on some of the difficult development trade-offs that have to be faced when deciding on urban poverty action?

Second, developing policies and frameworks is one thing, but finding ways to design the most appropriate responses in a particular context and then implementing them effectively can be quite another. For example, the poverty-reduction policy in a country can include a clear and strong commitment to community-based, demand-led poverty action; there can be a commitment to greater partnership with poor communities and a whole variety of actions may be undertaken, but these may still not tackle poverty effectively. The livelihoods framework itself provides little guidance after potential entry points have been identified, which is the point at which the design and implementation processes begin. How far can the adoption of a livelihoods approach assist in the process of moving from analysis to action?

Third, the livelihoods debate is an evolving one – DFID is only one of the organizations (with Oxfam, CARE and UNDP) considering and refining a livelihoods approach to guide its work so that it is more people-centred. This is a healthy debate, but it means that livelihoods is used to refer, often inter-changeably, to a tool, an operational objective, a set of principles, an attitude, an approach and a framework for analysis and action. Does this provide a flexible and dynamic conceptual framework or a confusing array of terms?

Fourth, a number of agencies have already decided that a livelihoods approach is the way forward, based on their experience so far, mainly in reducing rural poverty. Action based on a livelihoods approach is beginning in urban areas – for example, by CARE in Zambia, Ethiopia, and Togo (Carney et al, 1999, p5) but there is not yet a significant amount of experience on which to reflect. This discussion has to be mainly exploratory, as it may be too early to draw firm conclusions about the practical value of urban livelihoods analysis.

It is useful to begin with a review of what a livelihoods approach *does* contribute to a debate about programme and project design and implementation.

A CRITICAL REVIEW OF A LIVELIHOODS APPROACH IN THE URBAN CONTEXT

The livelihoods framework makes no claim to being something entirely new. It is concerned to build on existing knowledge and action and to give it greater coherence; it builds on existing research on the livelihood strategies of urban households and accepted practical participatory approaches which are intended to provide people-centred responses in poor urban areas. However, the liveli-hoods approach does add to the debate in two ways – how to focus on the poor in a positive way and how to ensure that everyone involved in a project has a common purpose. It has several contributions to make:

- It allows for flexibility of design which is appropriate to different country contexts.
- It gives due emphasis to the coping strategies that make poor people's lives work.
- It demands a detailed consideration of the assets of poor households.
- It tries to provide an analysis of needs from poor people's points of view.

- It puts the initial focus on demand rather than on supply.
- It shows the need and scope for multidimensional action and tries to ensure that everyone involved in a project agrees on the diagnosis and approach to be adopted.
- It focuses on enhancing household assets, but acknowledges that access to resources may be constrained and so actions related to the wider economic, physical and social contexts may be needed.
- It identifies a way in which impact assessment can be included in projects more systematically by focusing on livelihood outcomes.

These characteristics are not necessarily addressed in previous urban poverty responses.

The idea of developing a shared understanding of the nature and experience of poverty and deprivation, starting with poor people's assets and identifying ways of building on them, and agreeing on what to expect from a poverty project, are clearly positive attributes of a livelihoods framework when applied to a project design. However, various contributions in this book have shown some limitations in analysis and the identification of sectoral responses. Clearly, a range of issues have to be considered in the design of any new projects or programmes. A key concern is that the conceptual framework itself is distributionally neutral (Ashley and Carney, 1999, p2) and therefore its use needs to be accompanied by an explicit commitment to prioritizing the needs of the poor. In addition, disaggregation of categories of the poor is crucial for effective implementation. The framework places household assets and livelihood strategies at the centre of analysis and the assessment of outcomes. However, it acknowledges that interventions to change the context that provides opportunities or exacerbates vulnerability may be as, if not more important than actions designed to build up household assets directly. Nevertheless, it is not clear whether it provides sufficient guidance on the relative importance of macro- and microlevels of intervention. The framework acknowledges the importance of the economic and political context, but in itself does not provide a means of dealing with anti-poor political priorities. It stresses the multidimensional nature of deprivation and household strategies and places people at the centre of analysis and action. If this implies multisectoral projects at the local level, issues about feasibility for both agencies and residents are raised: what are the implications for external agencies of the management requirements of multisectoral local projects and do such projects place an undue burden on residents?

So how might a livelihoods approach be of greater value in providing practical urban responses?

ISSUES IN DESIGNING NEW URBAN PROJECTS AND PROGRAMMES

Building on the principles of a livelihoods approach to poverty reduction (see Chapter 1) and the broader implications of many of the discussions in the chapters in Part 3, it is possible to identify a set of ideals with respect to the design of interventions to improve the well-being and livelihoods of poor urban house-holds. These are listed in Box 18.1. The subsequent discussion explores issues raised by such aims, with respect to first, the content of programmes, and second, the process of design, implementation and monitoring and evaluation.

Box 18.1 WHAT NEEDS TO BE ACHIEVED WHEN DEVELOPING
AN URBAN POVERTY RESPONSE

- Ensure coverage in urban areas at an appropriate level for which continuous funding is possible as part of national and/or local government activities.
- Ensure that there is ownership and support in key organizations and at relevant decision-making levels so that action is sustainable.
- Tackle the causes of poverty (such as the lack of access and rights) and not just the symptoms (such as inadequate water and sanitation).
- Ensure an effective and strategic poverty response at the policy level with sufficient direct or targeted interventions for the needs of the most vulnerable and excluded groups.
- Ensure that the approach is multisectoral to respond to the multidimensional nature of poverty, but at the same time that it is realistic in the aims and complexity of individual projects.
- Provide support in those marginal and excluded poor areas that general urban management fails to service, but also address city-wide issues such as income generation, more employment opportunities and service delivery.
- Recognize that poverty initiatives focused on the capacity building of government agencies may mean that no action takes place that the poor can see.
- Work at a sufficiently local level that communities (men, women and children) are effectively involved in decision-making so that activities are more sustainable in the long term, but also work at the mesolevel with service deliverers to ensure that the institutional, management and attitudinal changes which are necessary to increase responsiveness to city dwellers, especially the poor, are made.
- Design responses based on strengthening existing structures at both city and neighbourhood levels rather than introducing new and externally imposed arrangements, even where existing arrangements are currently inadequate or mismanaged.
- Ensure that community-based responses also focus on the links between community and outside agencies, especially government and political structures, with the aim of strengthening those links to increase residents' access to and control with respect to local resources and services.
- Involve a range of agencies in decision-making, including the private sector and NGOs, in an effort to build consensus and appropriately allocate roles in programmes or projects.
- Ensure that interventions demonstrably increase the livelihood security of target groups and give the urban poor more control over their lives.

Content of Programmes and Projects

Looking at the content of programmes and projects, there are a range of issues to consider.

Action Needs to be Based on a Disaggregated Understanding of Poverty

It is clear from earlier chapters in this book that:

- In the urban context, poverty is a very complex issue because of the numbers and types of circumstances that poor people face.
- There are different groups of poor and vulnerable people with different problems and different needs, and also a range of coping and livelihood strategies.
- Any action has to take account of the range of coping strategies that poor people have developed and that work, if they are not to undermine existing solutions.
- Unless support is specifically identified for the poorest, it is likely that they will not benefit from general poverty action.
- Poverty is dynamic. People and households may move in and out of poverty or be chronically poor. The causes and characteristics of these changes may relate to economic trends, stages in the life-cycle, seasonality or the impact of shocks and stresses.

With this analysis and understanding, how can action be designed that does not have unintended consequences for poor people?

Given the diversity among poor people and the multidimensionality of both poverty and deprivation and household livelihood strategies, practical action requires a disaggregated approach. The mistake often made by officials and decision-makers is their failure to see that 'the "urban poor" are not one "lumpen" mass' (Nelson, 1999, pxiii). Recent analyses and project design processes adopt different categorizations in their quest to recognize that the needs and priorities of different groups of poor people may vary. For example, Jones and Nelson (eds, 1999) distinguish between the 'rich' poor, middle poor and very poor; Loughhead and Mittal (2000) between the improving, coping and declining poor; and CARE between those who are unable to provide for their basic daily needs without outside assistance, those potentially able to provide for their basic needs but currently unable to meet all of them, and those who are able to provide for their basic needs but not sustainably (Drinkwater and Rusinow, 1999, p4). Local poverty assessments will identify categorizations that are meaningful to residents of particular cities, enabling exploration of the needs and priorities of different groups. The emphasis of the livelihoods approach on assets may lead to the identification of actions which assist better-off poor households to develop their asset bases and protect themselves against shocks and stresses. The poorest and most vulnerable households, however, may not be able to take advantage of such opportunities and are likely to need specific safety nets and ongoing external support.

'Urban poverty is a series of interlinked difficulties . . . [a] reinforcing cycle of problems that the poor face' (Jones, 1999, p12). Poor people, as noted in earlier chapters, define their problems more in terms of security, safety, well-being and access than in terms of poverty (Moser and Holland, 1997; World Bank, 2000). Access is a key factor in an urban context: proximity to resources and facilities means very little when access to them is denied. Without understanding these issues and the multidimensionality of livelihood strategies, action in one sector may not have the intended impact or may affect people adversely in other ways, forcing them into trade-offs that increase their insecurity.

A mechanism (or forum) is needed where issues of access and the prioritization and likely impact of different sectoral poverty responses and interventions can be considered. Some urban poverty responses have used the process of developing a poverty strategy as the way to do this (see below), based on a shared understanding of the assets on which poor households depend.

Consideration Needs to be Given to Different Levels of Intervention – Macro, Meso and Micro

Practical poverty interventions have tended to be focused on a specific level – for example, NGOs working at the community level, institutional strengthening at the meso- or city level, and pro-poor growth strategies or poverty policy formulation at the macro- or national level. Very often sectoral responses focus attention at two of the three levels.

Since the large-scale, blueprint World Bank urban development projects of the 1970s and 1980s – site and service and slum upgrading schemes (see Thomas, 1994) – urban poverty responses have been a mixed bag of sectoral, institutional and community-based action, with a national, city or local ('community') focus. Each has merits and demerits (see Table 18.1).

The use of a livelihoods framework to identify entry points is important, but this needs to be developed further, with guidance on entry points at the different intervention levels and how to make macro–micro links.

Most needs-based approaches defined practical responses for specific areas: slum and squatter areas were identified, localities were agreed, and local communities or local political entities were defined. While this provides a context for multidisciplinary action, it means that only some areas are covered. Not only are there cost issues (that is, available resources are concentrated in some areas), but area-based action does not necessarily tackle crucial city-level problems such as employment generation or effective service delivery. City-wide interventions, on the other hand, allow a more equitable spread of resources to a greater number of people.

The meso- or city level is often not given due consideration in urban poverty response but, unless there are changes at the level of service delivery/urban management, action to improve livelihoods at community or household level may not be effective. Municipal-level capacity to deliver and the attitudes of public sector agencies to poor people (a client-focused approach) are key concerns. However, there are constraints on the resources available to local government and decisions that affect poor people's lives may be outside its control. Capacity building and change management to develop people-centred attitudes in the processes of service delivery and support programmes have to be an integral part of action, if urban poverty reduction is to be effective.

Focusing on one sector, such as health or education, can ensure that attention and whatever resources are available can be more strongly targeted towards poorer people. One recent approach has been the development of Sector Wide Approaches to resource allocation (SWAPs). This has the benefit of working

Table 18.1 *Pros and cons of different intervention levels*

City-level support can:	Microlevel support can:
• Ensure a wider response (at least city-wide) • In principle mean more transparent and equitable distribution of resources between areas • Provide broader coverage • Link into policy development	• More clearly identify and earmark support for poor people/communities through field-level action • Be more likely to ensure that action happens on the ground • Be more responsive to communities' identified needs and solutions
But • It may not link to or specifically benefit poorer communities • It does not necessarily deal with the particular livelihood problems faced by the very poor	*But* • Increasingly, as agencies have recognized how interlinked the problems are, microlevel projects can become very complex, causing management problems • The focus is on a small area and is not necessarily replicable • Such projects generally do not address the macroissues – strengthening and changing the institutional and organizational context in which services are provided • Projects do not necessarily link to policy level • The issue of how actions can be integrated into the existing administrative systems at a later date is neglected

within existing structures, strengthening the existing system and delivery of the service. Guidance can be given, as in the Jamaica Education support project, to focus action on poorer areas. But this does not necessarily reach poor residents since current services do not generally cover informal areas and are neither affordable nor accessible. Apart from accessibility, as noted above, the difficulty of focusing on one sector is that the problems and choices facing the urban poor are multidimensional.

The livelihoods framework recognizes that the content of national economic and social policies that are specifically concerned with neither poverty and livelihoods nor urban areas and also the policy and legislative framework for city-level action are important. However, the evidence on the distributional impacts of national policies and actions is mixed and the framework provides little guidance is available on relative priorities for attention.

The debate about micro- or macrolevel interventions is linked to considerable concern about the cost and efficiency of local action. A vast array of urban poverty action has been taken in the past, but it is often in small and isolated projects, there is no effective mechanism for sharing the lessons learnt from these practical experiences and the costs per beneficiary may be too great if such action is to be scaled up or replicated. There have been some examples where action has been successfully scaled up, such as the activities of savings and credit NGOs in Bangladesh, generally where there is a pivotal person acting as an entrepreneur. However, scaling up does not always happen since practitioners in field projects tend to be more focused on immediate action and practical results. Some projects have broadened their activities – for example, from infrastructure installation to include community development issues, from water and sanitation to include health components, or from a women's development project to income generation and self-help housing. This has tended to happen where a project has been refocused into using more participatory approaches and responding to demand. So projects can change internally, especially if there are the individuals who have the foresight and the capacity to guide this change management. They can also be scaled up. In general, such reshaping of an existing project occurs without a shared starting concept, causing difficulties that may detract from a project's achievements. Any project framework therefore needs to be sufficiently flexible to allow for such changes to occur.

From an external agency's point of view, a project focus may be valid only if it has policy implications, can be replicated cost effectively or is a pilot for broader activities.

Ensuring a More Responsive, Dynamic and Iterative Process

Arrangements for Design

Discussion so far has focused on content and actions, but the process of how an intervention/project is designed can have a fundamental effect on its outcome and impact. Traditionally, agencies have focused on one or a few related sectors when developing urban poverty responses – for example, infrastructure, community development, health, education, income generation or legal literacy. Recognition of the multidimensional nature of deprivation and livelihoods implies that projects may need more components, requiring multidisciplinary teams and interagency collaboration. The design of such projects may reflect the relative influence of the departments or individuals involved, rather than the needs of intended beneficiaries. In a donor agency, for example, a range of advisers is likely to work together on the design of a project. How far they decide that each of their technical specialisms is incorporated into the design can be a matter of negotiation or even a result of having the loudest voice. The livelihoods framework can provide a basis for more appropriate prioritization.

Not all donor agency project design is undertaken in-house because of issues of time and competing work demands. However, currently consultants may be faced with agency staff pushing for their own sphere of work, rather than for what is most appropriate for intended beneficiaries. An appropriate project design can be difficult to negotiate in such circumstances, especially for a consultant who is an outsider. Recognizing this, DFID has now produced sustainable livelihoods guidance sheets with advice about the need for a team leader who is familiar with a livelihoods approach and able to coordinate.

Another shift in project design has been the increasing involvement of a range of stakeholders. These may be identified using stakeholder analysis carried out either in a resource and time intensive exercise – for example, three-day workshops in India – or simply by one person negotiating with each of the various parties. There is much discussion about ownership and partnership in projects, but unless there is effective involvement (with scope to change the shape of action fundamentally) at the design stage, then this discussion may be meaningless.

With the growth in participatory analysis and planning, communities are more likely to be involved at the design stage. It is increasingly recognized that ownership by a community does not begin when an agency wants it to take over the management or funding of action. Residents have to be involved in the process from the design stage. A range of participatory planning techniques is available – PPAs feeding into the planning process, CAPs, Planning for Real, community mapping. Some specifically focus on the process of prioritizing action. For example, Planning for Real identifies 'now, soon and later' actions that communities can undertake themselves or with some help, or that others need to undertake. Increasingly, participatory techniques are being developed to be used at an institutional level as well as in residential areas (see Leurs, 1998; Thompson, 1998). CARE, for example, has been very concerned to increase ownership by negotiating at local level, which makes design a much more itera-tive process than in traditional blueprint projects (see Chapter 16). An NGO like CARE or Oxfam can undertake project design with local communities on behalf of an agency/government. Its approach is likely to be based on the participation of the communities concerned, but it is possible that proposed actions will neglect the wider issues. NGOs also face the difficulty of how to relate to municipal government or a donor agency that is sectorally organized when they are not (Kar and Phillips, 1998).

Translating analysis into interventions involves a number of stages. Once there is an analysis of the problems, a second stage of assessment is needed in order to prepare a strategy and identify the most effective actions. At this stage, entry points also have to be agreed. The idea of entry points seems to be the project design and implementation mechanism introduced by a livelihoods approach that has been most helpful. They have been employed mainly by those taking action at microlevel, working with communities. CARE uses entry points to make its work manageable. The JUPP case study indicates how entry points, based on the most immediate community needs, were the starting point for action (Chapter 15). But entry points also need to be considered for action at the macro-level. Unless there are massive amounts of money, action has to be targeted, limited in scope and time, to test what does and does not work in an institutional context.

Consideration also needs to be given to entry points as part of a process. They may be identified in different ways – in a series of workshops, as part of stakeholder analysis or in sessions with different interest groups that would need to be involved in this process (see Figure 13.1). Entry points are possibly the most immediate points of support, but what happens once these initial aims are achieved? How can initial limited actions be developed into more substantive measures that have a wider impact? Initial entry points need to be agreed, based on access/asset assessments. This action then has to be delivered. As action takes place, attention should be focused on how this could be scaled up, broadened, or more strategic interventions be made. Then there has to be space for consideration, with stakeholders, of what more substantive responses could be made, followed by review and modifications where necessary. This suggests a more complicated implementation process than in traditional blueprint project design.

Implementation Arrangements

In implementation, as in design, an urban initiative can have a very different approach, depending on how the project/programme action is set up. There is no one solution and appropriate arrangements depend on the strengths and weakness of different stakeholders, as well as their varying power and influence, and other local factors. The common strengths and weaknesses of NGOs, communities, municipalities and national governments are summarized in Table 18.2.

Sustainability and Impact Assessment

As funding agencies focus more on project outcomes than inputs, greater attention is given to impact assessments of what the project has achieved. Especially in field-level poverty projects, there are initiatives for self-evaluation and participatory assessments of the impact of projects – for example, in Calcutta (Kar et al, 1997), Faisalabad (Phillips with ActionAid, 1997) and Jamaica (Holland, 1998; Thomas, 1998). However, these are often added after a project has begun, so that there are problems of base-line information. The use of a livelihoods framework could provide a more consistent basis for ensuring that impact assessment is an integral part of new projects.

Alongside a consideration of scaling-up activity to ensure greater replicability and therefore value for money, there is also the question of sustainability of any of the initiatives promoted in a project. This is especially true of microlevel action, if it is initiated outside existing institutional structures and uses resources which are not available through governmental channels.

How far any activities are sustainable after a project finishes generates significant debate within donor agencies and failure is continuously raised as an indicator of weakness in the design of a project. As part of any poverty strategy, agreement should be reached as to what can be achieved in terms of sustainability. If an agency is promoting change management, wanting to see action that is not currently provided or needs to be more effective, is working with agencies, especially local government, that are weak and understaffed, then what sort of sustainability should it be expecting? Perhaps it is necessary to stop seeing sustainability as the purpose of poverty action and recognize it as a goal that is rarely fully achieved.

The possible role of the private sector also needs to be considered. It is not included in Box 18.1 because so far, private sector actors have played a limited role in urban poverty responses. In the past, there have been specific examples in some countries of local businesses funding individual activities – for example, in India where they have funded community halls and so on. The main area where there has been some engagement is in relation to private–public partnerships (PPPs) for utility provision. UNDP is particularly concerned to identify more pro-poor PSPs.

The Implementation Process as a Means – Developing Ownership/Building Social Capital/Targeting Pro-poor Growth

It is clear from the discussion above that communities are being asked to take on new roles if they own or manage aspects of implementation. It would be unfair to expect them to have the capacity to do this from the start. Rather, action focused on poor people can include processes for increasing their capacity and strengthening social capital. In Chapter 8 Phillips discusses this issue in detail, based on a recognition of the importance of social capital in enabling poor people to increase their security and improve their livelihoods. The issue is discussed here, as part of implementation arrangements, in order to stress that implementation has to take account of and build on existing social capital networks. Any implementation arrangements need to identify existing networks specifically and how they will be built on.

SO WHERE COULD WE GO FROM HERE?

A number of questions about a livelihoods approach and what it can and cannot do were asked at the beginning of this chapter. If the debate about livelihoods approaches teaches us only one thing, it is that solutions cannot be imposed from outside but must be decided and negotiated through partnerships in a particular locality. As it stands, the area where a livelihoods approach seems to have the most practical benefit is in terms of providing a framework within which to identify and agree on entry points, beginning the process of moving the debate from analysis to action. But much clearer guidance on a range of poverty/livelihood trade-offs and implementation issues is needed if the framework is to be a useful tool (if only one of several) in the development of practical action.

Customizing a livelihoods framework in a particular context is necessary to open up discussion and reconciliation of various competing and undermining factors, as well as identifying the positive assets on which to build. Such a process needs to take into account a wide range of competing and constraining, as well as promotional, aspects of livelihoods issues in order to provide the dynamic needed for practical solutions.

To do this it is suggested that the following components need to be included in the design of programmes and projects designed to enable poor urban residents to improve their livelihoods:

- In terms of analysis, ensure a disaggregated assessment of poverty as well as a livelihoods analysis, identifying different categories of poor and vulnerable men and women and their specific needs.
- On the basis of this analysis, develop a poverty/livelihoods strategy as part of each project assessment/design that all stakeholders buy into and which indicates, realistically, what changes it is anticipated that the proposed actions will achieve, together with the entry or starting points for action.
- On the basis of the poverty/livelihoods strategy and entry points, identify different levels of intervention at the macro-, meso- and microlevels that will be mutually supportive in helping to achieve the identified goals. In addition,

Table 18.2 *The possible implementation role of different stakeholders*

NGOs	Communities	Municipalities	National Government
They can:	*They can:*	*They can:*	*It can:*
• Tackle poverty in the field and implement • Be more responsive to people-centred action – for example, the rights of the child, micro-credit for women • Be likely to promote innovative responses • Have greater flexibility because of the way they operate	• Take action themselves • Be motivated to improve their lives/circumstances • Undertake action with limited resources • Be partners in implementation • Make community agreements work, as a way of achieving greater ownership and management of the process • Strengthen particular vulnerable or marginalized groups	• Have local responsibility • Provide some services • Have staff available • Have some capacity to deliver • Have local knowledge • Have local councillors with existing links in poor areas	• Have more strategic understanding of problems • Have resources and staff • Initiate larger-scale interventions • Provide state/national-level services • Have an understanding of urban poverty via policy-making
But:	*But:*	*But:*	*But:*
• Their focus is more field/community level than policy • They are not alternative service deliverers to government arrangements, except on a small scale	• Community-based projects are very time intensive • A longer lead-in time is needed for mobilization suited to the time and other commitments of residents	• They may not have the resources to provide support or take action • Increasingly, with privatization of government services, they may not be responsible for	• It may be focused on policy rather than action • Sectoral ministries may be reluctant to work together • It may be necessary to change the attitudes of central agencies

- They may not have the capacity for larger-scale implementation
- They may not want/do not have the mandate to act as a proxy local government agency
- They are not homogenous; there are great differences in their aims and objectives
- They do not all have a focus on poverty
- They are not seen as having equal status by government officials
- Many experience difficulties of engaging sufficiently with service deliverers
- They may have limited policy-making capacity and if they try to influence policy may come into conflict with government agencies which see this as their role

- Their focus is likely to be local
- They are unlikely to be able to manage larger-scale implementation
- Projects are based on presumptions about the nature of a 'community', which may contain competing rather than homogeneous interests
- How a partnership can be set up and how equitable and successful it will be depends on the characteristics of the community
- Outcomes depend on how residents perceive the initiative and their capacity to organize themselves
- A clear idea of who is powerful/will benefit/is self-interested is needed to ensure successful implementation
- Capacity of leaders and residents to take on roles and tasks may be lacking

- services that are/should be provided for poor urban people
- Central or state government may impose constraints on the action they may want to take
- They are likely to be more technical than people-centred in their approach
- They are likely to be organized in sectoral departments with ineffective coordinating mechanisms and professional rivalries
- Possible lack of under-standing and attitude problems with respect to poverty and participation/partnerships
- Limited capacity/skills because of resource shortages
- Focused on resource allocations
- Field/community involvement may be seen as a responsibility of junior staff
- May not focus on policy/strategic issues
- Officials and councillors may not work together

- about the poor and how to deal with them
- It is unlikely to have a participatory, people-centred approach
- Its perspective on appropriate poverty-focused policies may not be linked to circumstances on the ground/ground-level action it can be a constraining influence on innovative action

indicate what specific mechanisms will be used or introduced and what actions will be undertaken to link micro- and macroactions.
• Based on the poverty/livelihoods strategy and the identified initial interventions, develop an implementation strategy that allows for an iterative process for broadening or scaling up planned interventions and their implementation.
• Ensure that impact assessments are designed as an integral part of any action and are part of the implementation process.

REFERENCES

Ashley, C and Carney, D (1999) *Sustainable Livelihooods: Lessons from Early Experience,* DFID, London

Carney, D, Drinkwater, M, Rusinow, T, Neefjes, K, Wanmali, S and Singh, N (1999) *Livelihoods Approaches Compared,* DFID, London

DFID (1999) Sustainable Livelihoods Guidance Sheets, <www.livelihoods.org>

Drinkwater, M and Rusinow, T (1999) *Application of Care's Livelihoods Approach,* presentation for DFID Natural Resource Advisers Conference

Holland, J (1998) *Visit Report to set up a Participatory Baseline in Jones Town,* JUPP, Kingston and DFID, London

Jones, S (1999) 'Defining urban poverty: an overview' in Jones, S and Nelson, N (eds) *Urban Poverty in Africa: From Understanding to Alleviation,* IT Publications, London, pp9–15

Jones, S and Nelson, N (eds) (1999) *Urban Poverty in Africa: From Understanding to Alleviation,* IT Publications, London

Kar, K et al (1997) *Participatory Impact Assesment: Calcutta Slum Improvement Project, Main Findings Report,* Calcutta Metropolitan Development Authority and Urban Poverty Office, DFID, New Delhi

Kar, K and Phillips, S (1998) 'Scaling-up or scaling-down? The experience of institutionalizing PRA in the slum improvement projects in India' in Blackburn, J with Holland, J (eds) *Who Changes? Institutionalizing Participation in Development,* IT Publications, London pp57–64

Leurs, R (1998) 'Current challenges facing Participatory Rural Appraisal', in Blackburn, J with Holland, J (eds) *Who Changes? Institutionalizing Participation in Development,* IT Publications, London, pp124–34

Loughhead, S and Mittal, O (2000) *Urban Poverty and Vulnerability in India: A Social Development Perspective,* discussion paper prepared for South Asia Urban and City Management Course, Goa, India, 9-21 January 2000

Moser, C and Holland, J (1997) *Urban Poverty and Violence in Jamaica,* World Bank, Washington, DC

Nelson, N (1999) 'Introduction', in Jones, S and Nelson, N (eds) *Urban Poverty in Africa: From Understanding to Alleviation,* IT Publications, London, ppxi–xiii

Phillips, S and ActionAid (1997) *Faisalabad Area Upgrading Project Participatory Impact Assessment,* DFID, London and Faisalabad Development Authority

Rakodi, C (1999) 'A capital assets framework for analysing household livelihood strategies', *Development Policy Review,* vol 17, no 3, pp315–342

Thomas, L (1994) *Urban Poverty and Development Interventions,* INTRAC Occasional Papers Series No 4, INTRAC, Oxford

Thomas, L (1998) *Jones Town Community Participatory Baseline Study,* JUPP, Kingston and DFID, London

Thompson, J (1998) 'Participatory approaches in government bureaucracies: facilitating institutional change', in Blackburn, J with Holland, J (eds) *Who Changes? Institutionalizing Participation in Development*, IT Publications, London, pp108–19

World Bank (2000) *Voices of the Poor – Can Anyone Hear Us?* Oxford University Press, New York

Chapter 19

Conclusions

Carole Rakodi

The intention of this book was to address the question of whether a livelihoods approach to analysing development problems and informing the design of policies and programmes for poverty reduction is appropriate for the urban context and can provide an effective framework for addressing urban poverty reduction. It was noted at the outset that the livelihoods approach is first, a way of thinking about objectives – the scope and priorities for development policy and action; second, it is a set of principles and a framework for analysis and policy or project preparation; and third, it is a basis for evaluating interventions with respect to their effectiveness in achieving policy reduction. It is, in other words, potentially both a conceptual framework for analysis and a guide to development policy and practice. Some of the practical and operational implications of adopting a livelihoods approach have been discussed in the previous chapter, so this conclusion will identify initially some of the key issues and themes which have emerged from the book in relation to the reduction of urban poverty. It will then review the livelihoods approach and framework itself, with respect to its utility as an analytical framework, some of the important distinctions and relationships between the use of a livelihoods approach in urban and rural areas, and a range of broader issues which are related to its operationalization in policy and practice. At each stage in the discussion, attention will be paid to issues on which further research is required.[1]

REDUCING URBAN POVERTY

A number of points of agreement between the contributors to this volume can be identified, with respect to the characteristics of urban poverty and ways in which it can be tackled. Many of these are not new, but their centrality to understanding the nature of poverty and deprivation in towns and cities, and the importance of devising relevant and appropriate policy approaches emerges clearly.

First, the relationship between the livelihoods of the poor and the urban economy is stressed. There are three aspects to this relationship. The state of the urban economy determines the economic opportunities available to its residents, including poor people. Growth in employment in manufacturing or services benefits poor people both directly, if they have the education, skills and contacts to obtain access to wage jobs, and indirectly, if demand for the products of microenterprises is generated by formal sector expansion. However, most research on the drivers of economic restructuring has concentrated on the national level or particular sectors, and there has been relatively little research on the restructuring of urban economies, especially in poorer countries. Globalization, national economic trends, the inherited urban economic structure and the presence or absence of the conditions for economic growth – available land, infrastructure, appropriately skilled labour and a sensible regulatory framework – may all have an impact on the characteristics of and trends in the economy of an urban area. With the exception of recent analyses of the impact of the Asian financial crisis at the end of the 1990s, little seems to be known about the characteristics of urban economies that can deliver the most opportunities for the poor and why, or their corollary, those characteristics which are the most constraining, increasing poverty or insecurity of livelihoods. The 2001 Global Report on Human Settlements discusses the influence of globalization in general terms (UNCHS, 2001), but the detailed research to underpin its arguments is lacking, as is evaluation of the outcomes and impacts of alternative local economic development policies and strategies, and recent research on the relationships between formal and informal sector economic activities.

A second issue is the extent to which the economic activities of the poor contribute to the urban economy, which is not discussed by the contributors, in part because data is not available to quantify the size of the economy in most towns and cities. The focus of the livelihoods approach is on strengthening the income-earning capacity of poor people in order to improve their well-being, and not how that could in turn contribute to the urban economy and to the large-scale/formal sector. Recognition of the contribution of poor workers' labour could provide a justification for revisions to regulatory frameworks affecting both the formal and informal sectors. The attention of most contributors is on the harmful effect of inappropriate regulations, particularly on the informal sector, although it is not denied that there are difficult trade-offs – for example, between employment generation and minimum wages and health and environmental regulations affecting workplace conditions, or between the interests of street traders and consumers with respect to environmental health regulations. It is commonly recognized that planning policies and other regulations affecting the location of informal sector activities and the residential location decisions of poor residents are often restrictive, and that the effects of disruption due to relocation are potentially devastating for the livelihoods of the people affected. However, in-depth research on the spatial requirements of different informal sector activities and various groups of residents and the interlinkages between them is limited.

Urban economic growth or decline is transmitted to residents directly through labour markets and indirectly through the generation of revenue that in turn may or may not be spent on services which are beneficial to the poor. Earlier research has demonstrated the importance of both the structure of labour markets and the conditions that influence access to good quality economic opportunities, including labour availability at household level; levels of education, skills and health; and access to physical and financial assets. The importance of social characteristics, such as gender, in determining labour market access is emphasized. These are all reinforced by contributors to this book, but the dearth of recent research on urban labour markets is also noted.

Closely related to this first theme is the reiteration by all contributors of the importance of access to infrastructure and services. This reflects wider debates over the aim of development and the relative importance of private incomes and public services in attaining basic capabilities. Broadly, if the reduction of income poverty is seen as the main objective of development, and there is a strong link between increased incomes and improved capabilities, then a concentration on achieving economic growth is valid. However, if well-being is seen as the ability to live a long and healthy life and there is a weak link between reducing income poverty and improving capabilities, then there is a much stronger argument for the public provision of services being the leading instrument for human development, implying less emphasis on maximizing economic growth. The evidence has been reviewed by Anand and Ravallion (1993) who stress that the importance of economic growth lies in the way its benefits are distributed and used to fund appropriate public services, especially those related to health. Ranis et al (2000) reinforce this conclusion, noting that all those countries which had achieved a lasting virtuous circle of economic growth and improved human development had invested first in human development, especially education and health. Improvements in these are both the result of increased national prosperity and in turn increase growth as a result of the improved quality of the labour force. The benefits of access to infrastructure and services by poor residents in urban areas are direct, in terms of improved health, increased knowledge, easier working and living conditions, and access to income-generating opportunities through transport infrastructure and services. They are also indirect in that access to a range of basic services releases income and other resources, such as time, for other purposes. It is stressed that the proximity to infrastructure and services which many commentators believe advantages the urban poor over their rural counterparts does not mean that they have access since services are often not extended to the areas in which poor people live or are unaffordable. In addition, people may be ineligible because they lack proof of residency or citizenship or live in illegal areas. Recognition of the importance of infrastructure and service provision to improving well-being and livelihoods raises the issues of provision and delivery arrangements. Although not considered in detail in this volume, questions relate to:

1   What type of provision arrangements are most likely to deliver appropriate and affordable services to poor residents? Critical comments on the inadequate services delivered by large-scale providers, both public and private, are common. However, condemnations of privatization per se may not be appropriate, as demonstrated, for example, by Malcolm Harper and Mansoor Ali's advocacy of microprivatization.

2   Can some arrangements generate more livelihood opportunities for the poor than others? Publicly provided services have been criticized for overstaffing arising from the political imperative to generate benefits for supporters and the political difficulty of shedding jobs. However, they are, at least, under political control and so may be more accountable to residents than private

providers. The costs and benefits of the role of public utilities or large-scale public works programmes in generating employment for poor residents needs careful consideration alongside the issues of efficiency and financial sustainability. The scope for interorganizational arrangements involving existing or new microenterprises, CBOs or NGOs and large-scale providers needs further investigation, paying particular attention to their potential implications for the livelihoods of poor people.

The importance of accountability on the part of infrastructure and service providers has been mentioned above, and is illustrative of the broader significance of good governance in supporting the livelihoods of the urban poor. Despite the weaknesses of local government in many parts of the world, its potential role in addressing the problems faced by poor residents in constructing their livelihoods is agreed by all the contributors. Although governments do not necessarily have to provide all services directly themselves, they have a critical role in ensuring provision that is equitable, affordable and accessible to the poor as well as efficient. Where municipal government has the resources (financial, human and political) to fulfil this role, it is best placed to understand and respond to varying local needs. However, it needs sufficient autonomy from central government, as well as the capacity to formulate policy, plan urban expansion and allocate resources.

In responding to different groups of residents with different needs and in resolving conflicts between their legitimate aims and the many demands on their resources, the political mechanisms for allowing residents a say and ensuring accountability are important. Local government is more likely to provide the necessary channels than either central government, which is more remote, or public or private agencies which are not locally accountable. However, it is not possible to identify which political arrangements are always either responsive or inimical to the interests of the poor – both the design of representational arrangements at city and local levels and the processes of decision-making and budgeting are important.

The importance of security to poor people emerges clearly – the three main aspects of this (regular income flows, secure tenure and personal safety) are interrelated. Crime and violence is identified as a priority concern of many poor urban people, affecting their living environments and their economic activities. Maintaining the rule of law, to ensure security and the absence of intimidation is, therefore, a key government function. Although secure tenure (not necessarily title to land) is recognized as an important aspect of overall security, as well as a potential base for economic activities, detailed evidence on the multiple roles of housing in livelihoods and the implications of alternative forms of tenure is lacking.

Both secure tenure and personal safety reflect the importance of place and location that is identified by several contributors. However, not all poor people live in low-income areas, and even where they do, their work activities and social networks are not confined to those areas. While undoubtedly practical improvements to the homes and neighbourhoods where poor people live can be beneficial, especially for those who spend most of their time within a local area such as women, elderly people and young children, these neither reach all those in need nor deliver improvements to city-wide service delivery systems. Clearly, the area in which people live affects their livelihood opportunities and choices, by its location, connections to the rest of the city and internal characteristics. Despite the examples given in the book, however, our understanding of the relationships between place, space and livelihoods is limited.

THE VALUE OF THE LIVELIHOODS FRAMEWORK FOR ANALYSING URBAN POVERTY

The livelihoods framework, as captured in Figure 1.1, is said to provide an analytical starting point for understanding urban poverty and deprivation, by identifying the main factors which affect livelihoods and the relationships between them. Researchers on urban household strategies and the contributors to this volume generally agree that the framework has already proved itself as an analytical tool, although there is always a danger that such a framework and the concepts on which it is based will become a rigid straitjacket rather than an aid to understanding. Livelihoods analysis has contributed to the development of a bottom-up understanding of the nature of urban poverty and deprivation that does not impose preconceived concepts, although quantitative analysis of the incidence and characteristics of poverty should complement the more qualitative approach that is typically adopted in studying livelihood strategies. This book brings new perspectives that can contribute to the further evolution of understanding. However, as well as its considerable strengths, the discussion has revealed some difficulties with its constituent concepts and components.

The framework places poor households at the centre. Analysis of livelihood strategies is important in understanding their situation, how they manage their lives, how they cope or improve their well-being and their vulnerability to changes, whether policy induced or not. However, there is a danger that a livelihoods focus will downplay other aspects of deprivation that are potentially more amenable to action. In addition, although for many the household is the basic social unit, it is not an unproblematic concept and should not be emphasized to the exclusion of the characteristics of social relationships between individuals within households and in wider networks. It is clear that households are vulnerable to changes in the economic, environmental, social and political context, but such changes may also provide opportunities. The impact of macro-economic trends and policies is often to increase poverty and even where economic changes generate opportunities, they may be insecure, raising a question about what trade-offs people would make faced with a choice between increased security and fewer opportunities. To complicate the analysis further, many changes (such as privatization of state-owned enterprises or decentralization) may either improve livelihood opportunities or exacerbate vulnerability, depending on the form they take. The vulnerability context, in other words, both influences and is influenced by structures, policies and processes, in complex ways that cannot be captured by a diagram.

The conceptual framework for analysis of livelihoods rests on the idea of different forms of capital or assets. Contributors to this volume stress that the categories of capital suggested are often not distinct and point to the inter-relationships between them and the substitutability of one for another. Perhaps, it is suggested, the categories lead to false distinctions and a misleading sense of clarity. While the pentagon is useful to illustrate the idea of trade-offs between assets, it is of little use in analysing actual trade-offs and the impact of policy decisions on these. Methods for measuring both vulnerability and household asset bundles in order to understand how households view different assets, prioritize between them and act to increase or change them, are lacking. Unless such methods are developed, Harpham and Grant (Chapter 10) suggest that it will not be possible to assess the impact of alternative policies or to understand and explain chronic poverty, impoverishment or sustained improvements in well-being.

The livelihoods framework can be useful for organizing understanding that is emerging from detailed social analysis and for enabling the identification of linkages between assets, structures and processes. However, these linkages are not specified, so there is considerable leeway in the application of the analytical framework to specific urban centres, resulting in more or less accurate and convincing diagnoses of the nature and implications of the linkages identified. Moreover, although the framework recognizes both tangible and intangible assets, some – for example, Beall – are wary of a tendency to view different types of capital as goods or commodities, pointing out that they rely on relational systems, which may be very unequal, for access and distribution. Access itself may be the most important resource since proximity and availability mean little if access is denied. Policies that enable poor households to build on their assets may merely reinforce unequal access to and control over resources unless they are accompanied by redistributive policies. Yet the framework itself is distribu-tionally neutral and there is also, it is suggested, a danger that the household focus will downplay the importance of policy, governance and macro or struc-tural factors.

Households live within systems of economic, social and political relations, investment in which results in the accumulation of stocks of assets, including social and political capital, which yield flows that can be drawn on in construct-ing livelihoods. Social capital, however, is a problematic concept. In the urban context, it is generally thought to be weak because people are often mobile and residential areas heterogeneous. However, there is little research on which to base a judgement about whether there is less social capital in urban than in rural areas, or whether it is merely different, and in what circumstances. Nor is there much evidence on the extent of cooperative or reciprocal behaviour, or the relative prevalence of social capital that has positive or perverse effects on the poor. For example, research in the North quoted by Harpham and Grant shows that social capital explains a significant proportion of variations in several health indicators, but there has been little comparable research in the South.

The livelihoods approach adds another dimension to traditional approaches to urban development which have tended to be technocratic and to see the provision of infrastructure and services as a technical issue dependent on the selection of appropriate design and standards, rather than an issue of rights and political power. In Box 1.1 social capital is extended to incorporate political capital. It is arguable, however, that the critical importance of the latter justifies its separate consideration (see also Moser and Norton, 2001). Political relationships are, however, neither just capital nor necessarily beneficial for the poor. In part, political capital is the product of past investment in political relationships. However, political systems are also an important aspect of institutions and processes, and can be clientelist and inequitable. In general, therefore, the framework is criticized for paying insufficient attention to the unequal distribution of power within households, between poor groups and at the city level, and for failing to specify methodological approaches that will enable the contents of its boxes, especially policies, institutions and processes, to be unpacked. In addition, the approach, it is asserted, does not address how its norms and policy objectives can be achieved, given the prevalence of unequal power structures within which the poor are at a disadvantage. Therefore, it does not help those concerned to improve livelihoods to resolve distributional issues or political and economic dilemmas. It is this concern that leads contributors to assert that accountable political systems at the national and urban levels are essential for the needs of the poor to be addressed and their rights to be fulfilled.

Increasingly, thinking about the fulfilment of rights is focusing on different forms of state obligation: obligations to respect, protect and fulfil, with the latter in turn leading to obligations to facilitate, provide and promote. These are underlaid by normative values of equity, transparency, inclusion and participation, and expressed as rights to secure livelihoods and the forms of capital that make these possible. In order that claims can be made and processed into outcomes, a better understanding is needed on the part of both governance actors and poor people themselves. Analysis is needed of the structures of authority and control at different levels, the social and political processes that affect the likelihood of claims being reflected in policy and resource allocation, and the social characteristics that empower or disempower people in such negotiations. Thus, understanding of the legal structure and systems of law in which rights are embodied is needed (the rights regime); diagnosis of the institutional structures that define, interpret and implement rights, and the scope that they provide for negotiation and participation; and the channels through which claims can be contested ((Moser and Norton, 2001). For poor urban people to claim their rights, they require access to information and knowledge about what those rights are, implying a need to be literate and a role for government and civil society organizations. Legal frameworks and political relationships, structures and processes at both town or city and national levels are critical in this respect.

Rural–Urban Comparisons and Connections

Underlying this book is a question about whether the adoption of a livelihoods framework and approach in both rural and urban areas is appropriate and helpful. Despite a number of issues raised by its use in urban areas, the general view put forward is that it is appropriate, with certain caveats and limitations. A brief comparison of our findings with the debate on rural livelihoods is instructive.

In urban areas, the emphases within a livelihoods framework differ from those typical of rural analyses. The livelihoods approach in rural areas originated in a concern for the well-being of poor peasant farm households. However, if a peasant household has access to various types of capital, it is capable of considerable self-provisioning with respect to food, water, sanitation, fuel and shelter, by which it can achieve a basic level of well-being. Although urban households do provide themselves with food from urban agriculture, well water and pit latrine sanitation, the scope to do so, particularly in large cities, is limited and the quality poor. The potential for basic self-sufficiency is limited in urban areas and households are more universally dependent on markets (and the cash economy) for labour, land and housing and on organized services (for water, sanitation and energy). The interaction of poor urban households with governance structures is thus more immediate and everyday than for most rural households, the level of income needed to avoid poverty is higher because of the high cost of non-food items, and the way in which markets and services operate is crucial.

Clearly, the mix of assets typically assembled by urban households differs from that available to most rural households. In addition, the links between different forms of capital seem to be stressed more by many contributors to this volume. This arises partly out of the fact that conceptualizing land as natural capital is less appropriate in urban areas, partly because of the dependence of urban households on externally provided infrastructure and partly because contributors have been able to stand back from sectoral points of view.

A further difference in emphasis is the attention given to space and location, largely because of the tendency for poor urban people to live in informal settlements with insecure tenure and inadequate infrastructure and services. Poverty arising from low incomes is thus exacerbated by these other forms of deprivation. Although the remoteness often associated with rural poverty does not apply in urban areas, it cannot be assumed that propinquity equals access. The conditions in which poor urban people live and work expose them to considerable risks and hazards, increasing their vulnerability. Increased security emerges as a top priority for poor households, yet with few exceptions (including Harpham and Grant, Rutherford and Harper) less attention is paid by contributors to this volume to reducing risk and ensuring lasting improvements to livelihoods (that is, to sustainability in its broadest sense) than is typical in considerations of rural livelihoods.

However, we must be wary of exaggerating the differences between rural and urban and rural livelihoods since, as stressed particularly by Satterthaite and Tacoli, links with rural areas are as important for urban households as with urban areas for rural households.

APPLICATION OF A LIVELIHOODS APPROACH TO POLICY AND ACTION

In Chapter 1 it was suggested that the livelihoods approach provides a shared point of reference for all those concerned with supporting the livelihoods of poor people and enables the complementarity of and trade-offs between interventions to be identified, leading to joined-up policy and action. It also provides a basis for identifying appropriate policy objectives and interventions. It would be fair to say that among the contributors to this volume, views differ from the relatively sceptical to the very positive. Most consider the approach useful but either insufficient by itself or not sufficiently developed to replace other approaches to policy and action. While it is possible from the discussions in this book to identify a number of key issues related to its operationalization in policy and practice, drawing on relevant experience, there has been limited experience with implementation and little evaluation of urban projects developed within a livelihoods frame.

The livelihoods approach is seen as a way of getting more joined-up policy and action. The approach, and the diagram specifically, can be useful in both the policy debate and selection of interventions, despite its shortcomings. In particular:

1   It roots interventions in an understanding of household coping strategies and recognition of the important role played in livelihoods by social capital. Interventions should be developed by means of a participatory approach to programme and project planning. However, Phillips warns of the danger of imposing a local organizational structure that fails to recognize existing social networks and CBOs, and questions whether externally imposed community organizational structures and/or NGOs are the best mechanisms for building social capital.

2   It stresses the importance of complementary actions at macro-, meso- (including city) and micro- (community, household) levels, and recognizes that poverty is not a static state and that poor households are vulnerable to external trends and shocks. It emphasizes the need, therefore, to pay attention to ways of reducing vulnerability by avoiding economic policy changes that have adverse impacts on the poor, mitigating such shocks when they are unavoidable, ensuring access to financial services, providing safety nets both for the working poor and those unable to work, maintaining law and order, ensuring that households can obtain access to land and shelter, and reducing environmental hazards and their effects through infrastructure and environmental health services and appropriate healthcare. However, what constitutes a pro-poor intervention is not always clear, as there are often trade-offs between different policy objectives and between different groups of intended beneficiaries. In addition, the methods and data for understanding trends in the incidence of poverty and the trajectories of poor households are not well developed.

3   It stresses the need to understand diversity and disaggregate poverty, although the framework itself does not provide guidance on how this should be done or how to prioritize between poor groups – for example, those just below the poverty line compared with the chronically poor. There is a danger that if policies are based on building up assets, they will favour the former, reinforcing inequality among the poor.

4   It stresses the importance of secure access to both public and private space for individuals and households and for the enterprises of the poor. Transport that facilitates links between locations, activities and people is also critical to livelihoods. These have implications for urban planning principles, standards and practices.

5 It emphasizes the role of good governance, including political decision-making based on a good understanding of the situation and needs of the poor, commitment from leaders and a dynamic civil society that brings pressure to bear by and on behalf of poor people. In the urban context, the potential contribution of local government is stressed. For this potential to be realized, municipalities need appropriate powers, financial resources and staff, backed by well-designed systems for the generation and use of revenue. Municipal governments can exacerbate or mitigate urban poverty by preventing or facilitating access to land and services, and by the design and operation of regulatory frameworks related to land, construction and economic activity. It is suggested, especially by Philip Amis, that not destroying livelihoods is more important than facilitating them, given the limited understanding of how best to do the latter, but also that there is still a role for the public sector in ensuring infrastructure provision and maintaining law and order. His recommendation is, in part, based on the limited experience and evaluation of policies to support local economic development.

6 It recognizes the great variety of economic activities which poor households undertake in order to diversify their livelihoods and increase their security. Grierson emphasizes the need to improve the capacity of residents to access economic opportunities in wage or self-employment, by improved access to education, which enhances assets, and training, which imparts skills for particular tasks that are relevant to fast-changing labour markets. Both should develop capacities appropriate for varied kinds of work, but evaluation of attempts to 'vocationalize' primary education and reform vocational education is needed. Small-scale enterprises are important to many, but may be particularly risky. Support programmes should pay particular attention, Harper suggests, to reducing artificial risks, such as harassment by municipal officials, and providing safety nets in case of business failure. Access to flexible general-purpose financial services is needed for household management, enterprise development and risk reduction. However, according to Rutherford, detailed research on the financial mechanisms used by poor urban households in the course of their livelihood strategies is currently limited.

7 It recognizes the importance of infrastructure and services in building assets and supporting livelihoods, and the dependence of poor households in urban areas on city-wide systems. Issues include the choice of provision arrangements, how to reach both poor settlements and poor people living elsewhere in the city, and ways of securing livelihood objectives alongside health and environmental improvements. The advantages of comprehensive approaches to infrastructure and environmental health services over narrowly sectoral and curative approaches are stressed.

A livelihoods approach provides a useful framework for understanding and identifying action to reduce urban poverty. It does not deny the importance of increased incomes. It recognizes the need for structural economic change, including redistribution, to achieve this. However, because it starts from a people-centred analysis and adopts people-centred methods to identifying interventions, it places more emphasis on addressing non-income aspects of deprivation and increasing security. A secure livelihood is one that provides economic security, personal safety, and healthy living and working conditions. Many of the policy interventions that can help to secure these outcomes depend less on economic growth and increased wealth than on political commitment to addressing the concerns of the poor. Such a commitment will only be secured if poor people can exercise their right to make claims on those who wield power at local, national and international levels.

NOTE

1   I am indebted to Tony Lloyd-Jones, Anne Thomson and Alison Brown for inputs to this chapter

REFERENCES

Anand, S and Ravallion, M (1993) 'Human development in poor countries: on the role of private incomes and public services', *Journal of Economic Perspectives*, vol 7, no 1, pp133–150

Moser, C and Norton, A (2001) *To Claim Our Rights: Livelihood Security, Human Rights and Sustainable Development*, Background Concept Paper for the Workshop on Human Rights, Assets and Livelihood Security, and Sustainable Development, Overseas Development Institute, London

Ranis, G, Stewart, F and Ramirez, A (2000) Economic growth and human development, *World Development*, vol 28, no 2, pp197–219

UNCHS (2001) *Cities in a Globalizing World*, Earthscan, London

Index

Page references in *italics* refer to tables, figures and boxes